BROKEN NARRATIVE

Before you start to read this book, take this moment to think about making a donation to punctum books, an independent non-profit press,

@ https://punctumbooks.com/support/

If you're reading the e-book, you can click on the image below to go directly to our donations site. Any amount, no matter the size, is appreciated and will help us to keep our ship of fools afloat. Contributions from dedicated readers will also help us to keep our commons open and to cultivate new work that can't find a welcoming port elsewhere. Our adventure is not possible without your support.

Vive la Open Access.

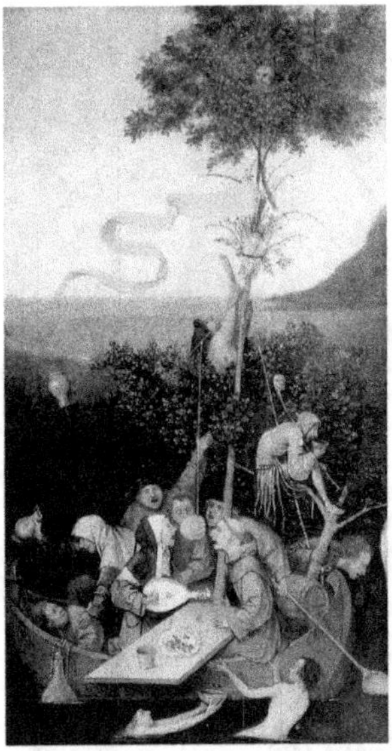

Fig. 1. Hieronymus Bosch, *Ship of Fools* (1490–1500)

First published in 2022 by The Department of Eagles, an imprint of punctum books, Earth, Milky Way.
https://punctumbooks.com

ISBN-13: 978-1-68571-058-3 (print)
ISBN-13: 978-1-68571-059-0 (ePDF)

DOI: 10.53288/0341.1.00

LCCN: 2022930407
Library of Congress Cataloging Data is available from the Library of Congress

Book design: Vincent W.J. van Gerven Oei
Front cover image: *Cave Painting (Towers)* by Armando Lulaj, 2019. Installation. American flag, Gold paint, ca. 150×100cm. Production photo by Ergys Zhabjaku.
Back cover image: *Cave Painting (enlightening torch)* by David Kampi, 2019. Installation. American flag, Gold paint, ca. 150×100cm. Production photo by Ergys Zhabjaku.

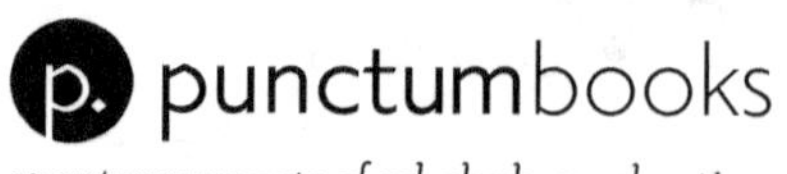

spontaneous acts of scholarly combustion

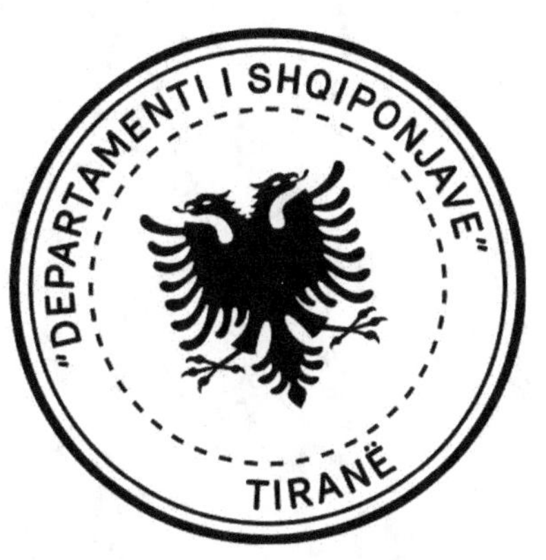

"DEPARTAMENTI I SHQIPONJAVE"
TIRANË

Armando Lulaj & Marco Mazzi

Broken Narrative
The Politics of Contemporary Art in Albania

with a preface by Jonida Gashi

アルマンド・ルラーイとマルコ・マッツィ

ブロークン・ナラティヴ
アルバニアにおける現代美術のポリティクス

金村修による序文付き

p.

Contents
目次

Preface

Jonida Gashi

No escape route inside the narrative…

There is more than one broken narrative to be found in Armando Lulaj and Marco Mazzi's *Broken Narrative: The Politics of Contemporary Art in Albania*. Indeed, the book is full of them, from the interrupted utopian future(s) of the communist past, to the borrowed dystopian future(s) of the neoliberal present, to the radically reduced, almost elemental actions impregnated with political possibility that are inherently "broken," since their only *raison d'être* seems to be being performed again and again, as if on a loop. There is only one narrative, however, that the book specifically sets out to break. That would be the official, or perhaps semi-official, narrative about the relationship between art and politics in contemporary Albania as embodied in the figure of Edi Rama, Albania's artist-turned-prime minister. Denouncing the reduction of the project for the fusion of art and politics to the figure of the artist–politician, Lulaj also points his finger at the rarefied art circles in which this politically dubious if not downright reactionary idea was not only accepted but also thrived. The latter come across as vulture-type creatures roaming the globe in hot pursuit of the next experimental utopia (the more exotic the better!), a process not unlike the fervent pursuit of regime change by the United States in equally exotic, faraway lands in the aftermath of the September 11, 2001 terrorist attacks, and with about the same amount of grace and thoughtfulness. The comparison is especially fitting because when the utopian experiment inevitably fails — which in Albania failed long ago — these vulture-type creatures simply pick up and leave, moving on to the next experimental utopia without facing any repercussions, if only of an ethical nature.

… the gallows of contemporary art.

This is easy enough to understand. The challenge for the reader is following the links in the chain connecting the politics of contemporary art in Albania to the crisis of contemporary art more broadly. One could describe the relationship between the two as one of inverse mirroring. In the case of Albania, reality has, as Lulaj puts it, "overreached the intended experimental utopia." The second project for the union of art and politics (in Albania) — the first one being socialist realism under communism — has metamorphosed into a "contemporary art–organized crime" complex. The problem with contemporary art on the other hand, contemporary art being by definition postconceptual in Lulaj's appraisal, is that postconceptual art has reached a sort of historical impass. Its tools have exhausted their potential and are no longer adequate in coming to grips with the current state of the world. Ultimately, however, what unites the politics of contemporary art in Albania to the crisis of contemporary art on a broad scale is the neoliberal matrix that underpins both of them. At its most extreme, this neoliberal matrix manifests itself in the reliance of world governments on cycles of crises that they themselves manufacture and perpetuate. The art system is also dependent on these crises, since they determine where the world's (read: the economy's) reflectors will be pointed at next. This is especially true of the art market, but artists too, argues Lulaj, are always waiting for "a war, a natural cataclysm, an earthquake." In hindsight, Lulaj's words come across as eerily prophetic. Less than a year after this interview was completed in May 2019, we would have the opportunity to witness the mightily unsightly spectacle of the international art world trying to chew on the new global reality and repackage it for artistic consumption with the kind of zeal and speed that can only be described as exploitative.

... an alarm from the past is ringing.

Most interestingly, this book represents an attempt by the artist to map the themes and topics that have always inhabited his work, especially the body of works that relate to his country's postwar history. Lulaj's obsession with the tropes of both repetition/return and rupture as a means of understanding said history comes across quite strongly. Thus, the new love for the United States echoes the old love for the People's Republic of China and the USSR before it. Something(s) are or have been inevitably lost in the (ex)change however. In particular, Lulaj laments the ease with which the just causes of the past, such as Palestine and Vietnam, have been abandoned in favor of the unjust wars of the present, such as Afghanistan and Iraq. The events of the year 1997 are another example. Lulaj argues persuasively that the combined economic, political, and social collapse of the year 1997 ought to be seen as a repetition of the symbolic rupture that the events of 1991 initiated, culminating in the collapse of the Albanian communist regime, but in a different register, namely that of the real. It is a shift brilliantly captured by an anecdote the artist recounts halfway through the first chapter — or the first "track" — of the book, describing how in his neighborhood the collective mania for color TV monitors and deep-dish antennas that marked the early 1990s was replaced by that for bullets, rifles, and machine gun parts in 1997. More often than not, however, (personal) memory and recollection complicate attempts to historicize the contemporary era. (Indeed, personal memory often manifests itself as blocked memory. A case in point is the artist's admission that his memories of the events of 1991 far outnumber those of the events of 1997, leading him to compare the latter to a "black hole.") This is a condition of the present itself — *our* present *now,* that is — rather than a subjective condition, which is also reflected in the radically different strategies employed by the artist when approaching the communist past versus those employed in his approach toward the post-communist period. The material from the communist period, archival or otherwise, must be reused, reworked, and rewritten so as to mobilize the political (but not only) knowledge inherited from the past in order to make sense of the present. By contrast, the present condition itself is something to escape, or, to be more precise, the present condition must first be diagnosed and then deserted in anticipation of a radically different future. So difficult has it become to imagine such a future, or, indeed, the ways of getting there, that the artist's strategies of escape resemble (doomed) attempts to pierce wormholes in/ through the fabric of space-time.

The violence that is in the air...

In the process of mapping the themes and topics that animate his work, what emerges — and it is unclear whether Lulaj did this intentionally or whether it was unconscious, initially at least — is a sense of his artistic practice as an idiosyncratic type of mapmaking. Just as he rummages through the garbage heap of history in order to find seemingly absurd, uncertain, and unreliable "incidents" bordering between fact and fiction with the aim of reactivating fragments of the communist past in the present, Lulaj indicates again and again that he sees his own interventions in the present as traces to be uncovered in the future. It should be said, however, that the traces of the present that the artist is accumulating and painstakingly collecting for this future map are not entirely of his own making. Indeed, the scope of the artist's endeavor here can be described as almost encyclopedic, albeit a rather morbid encyclopedia populated with madmen and serial killers, whose "perfect" acts the artist clearly admires vis-à-vis the aborted, impotent, stillborn gestures that populate the middle ground between these two extremes. The figure of crime seems to be central to this endeavor. Firstly, because the criminal mind's agility is appealing to the artist, and the outlaw in general remains a liminal figure, just as the artist ought to be according to Lulaj, especially at a time when crime, or, to be more precise, organized crime and the state in Albania have virtually merged into a single entity. It follows that if today's artist must behave like a criminal, then the artist of tomorrow, whom this book is implicitly dedicated to, must behave like a homicide detective; they must be able to correctly interpret the signs and traces from the past inscribed onto the body of the work. Secondly, and more importantly perhaps, the trope of crime also raises the specter of violence, two types of violence to be precise. On the one hand, there is the pervasive violence meted out by the power structure which insinuates itself into every corner of both public and private life and, indeed, into the very fabric of reality. On the other hand, there is the (potential) violence simmering under the surface, which must be carefully studied in order to detect all the signs pointing to its transformation over the past thirty years from a symptom of the catastrophic breakdown in social relations precipitated by the collapse of communism to a symptom of the social dissensus to come. The artist's interventions in the present are thus conceived as being part of an enormous arsenal of tools and, indeed, weapons, to be used during this future uprising, which is still impossible to anticipate when it will occur. Lulaj is adamant, however, that when the time comes today's artist must stand back and not interfere. Another line is thus firmly drawn: the revolution can only be trusted to the artist of tomorrow. It is herein that the political dimension of Lulaj's strategies of desertion and escape is revealed. The present must not be rejected in order to "save" the figure of the artist. On the contrary, it is the figure of the artist that — at the limit — ought to be used as a kamikaze (by the artist themself) in order to deliver a fatal blow to the present on the way out.

序文

金村修

持っている石を路上に叩きつけながら夜の街を徘徊し続ける男。叩きつけた石を拾い上げては、また何度も何度も叩きつける。『Breaking Stones』は、一人の男が路上で石を叩きつけながら歩いている映像だ。何故路上に石を叩きつけているのか、叩きつけながらどこに行こうとしているのか、その理由は分からない。石を叩きつけながら歩いている男の姿は何かに抗議しているようにも見えるし、どうにもならない怒りを路上にぶつけている酔っ払いの無意味な行為のようにも見える。「《Breaking Stones》のパフォーマンスは、ある序曲、将来の抗議の準備と理解することができる」/（Armando Lulaj 本書より）。「《Breaking Stones》は不測の事態に基づいている。通り過ぎる車、「生じる」世界、「存在する」都市。また、《Breaking Stones》はことさらに「宗教的な」作品だと私は思う。実際、石の連打は投石のテーマを鮮烈に連想させる。だが、投石される殉教者の躯体を打つ代わりに、石は道路の舗装を強硬に絶望的なまでに打ち付ける。さらに、ビデオの行程、開始・進行・終了は、十字架の経路、カルヴァリオの丘への歩みを思わせる。電柱など、ビデオ内の(多数の)垂直構造は、十字架、磔刑を思い起こさせる」、「《Breaking Stones》と不能のコンセプト。石を激烈に砕くというアイデアは、怒りと性の抑圧をも思い出させる」/(Marco Mazzi 本書より)。

　石を叩きつけながら歩く男の姿は、自分のテリトリーを拡大、延長させていく動物のマーキングのように思える。自己のテリトリーの拡大がマーキングであるのなら、マーキングとは動物が自分の身体を空間的に拡大させていく行為であり、男の行動はそのような動物の身体的な測量行為に類似している。国家を形作り、領土化するために土地を測量する行政機関に対して、石を叩きつけながら歩くという動物的な測量を演じることで、測量によって数値化された国家の空間を破壊しようとしているのではないだろうか。国家のテリトリーの中に人間の身体を封じ込め、支配するために土地が測量される。測量とは、国家による土地の可視化、数値化、領土化であり、本来なら誰のものでもない土地を、測量によって数値化することで国家という形が形成される。無名であるはずだった土地が測量され、国家の名前がそこに烙印されることで空間が現れる。わたし達は無拓な自然の中で生きているのではなく、測量され、数値化されたことで生まれた国家という虚構の空間の中で生きている。一木一草に天皇制があると竹内好によって批判された日本の自然の風景が、無拓で美しい自然などではなく、天皇制によって作られた虚構の風景のように、わたし達の生きているこの空間は、既に支配階級のイデオロギーによって作られた虚構の世界でしかないのだ。

　石を持った男の行為は、支配階級の作った境界線を破壊するための行為であり、測量によって作られた国家の虚構の領土から土地を奪回するために、石は路上に叩きつけられるのだ。支配階級が作った線に対して、もう一度その線を引き直すこと。それは測量によって数値化され、作られた空間に対して、「うつしよは夢、よるの夢こそまこと」といった日本の推理小説家、江戸川乱歩のように、「うつしよ」という昼の数値化された空間に対して、「よるの夢」というもう一つのオルタナティブな空間を構築することだ。男が夜に石を投げることを選択したのは、昼という可視化された空間に対して、夜という暗闇の不可視な空間を導入するためなのではないだろうか。数値化されない不可視の空間を歩く石の男の姿は、カミュの『シーシュポスの神話』のように石を頂上に運んでは落とされるという徒労に満ちた奴隷の歩き方ではなく、アルトーのいうように、「わたしの内部の夜の身体を拡張すること」（アルトー「神の裁きと訣別するため」）のためであり、より不可視な世界を覗き込むために歩いているように見える。

　昼の空間が、世界を可視化することで生まれた秩序ある空間なら、夜の空間は先の見通せない、何が起きるのかも分からない不可視な闇の空間だ。夜の空間は遊撃戦や武装蜂起を目指す者達の空間であり、距離が生まれたことで成立した三次元的な昼の空間の秩序を、先の見えない夜の暗闇がその距離を廃棄することで昼の空間を壊乱させるだろう。遊撃戦とは可視化された空間を迷路に変質させることであり、明晰な昼の光が支配するブルジョア達の空間に対して、不可視な夜の空間で石を叩き続けながら歩くという不明瞭な妖怪の蠢きのような歩行を対峙させるだろう。共産主義者という妖怪がヨーロッパを歩いているとマルクスがいったように、ブルジョアジーはプロレタリアートを妖怪のようにしか見ることができない。彼らには、その男の行動は何か不明瞭なものが蠢いている妖怪の動きにしか見えないのだ。

　夜の街を石を叩きつけながら歩くその姿は、「敵が進めば我は退き、敵が占領すれば我は乱し、敵が疲れれば我は打ち、敵が退けば我は追う」/（中国人民解放軍:「習近平軍事改革」の実像と限界/茅原郁生）という毛沢東の遊撃戦を思い出させる。敵と同じ空間で戦わない、敵に対して姿を現さない。けれどそこで何かがそこで蠢いているような雰囲気を常に醸し出し、敵を不安にさせ続けるという毛沢東の遊撃戦は、正体を現さず、自己の存在を不透明な存在に変容させ、気配だけは敵に対して表象し続けることであり、それは自分の存在を幽霊のような存在に変容させることではないだろうか。はっきりと輪郭を現すことがない幽霊は、測量不可能な非数値的な存在だ。それは遠くのものと近くのものが闇に紛れて境界がなくなり、あらゆるものの輪郭が消えていく夜的な存在だ。遠近法の消失点が消えて、三次元的な秩序を曖昧な空間に変質させていく夜に自己を同期させること。ヨーロッパのアナキストが黒いパーカーを着てデモに参加し、かつての日本の学生運動のデモがヘルメットにタオルで顔を隠したのは、自己の存在をデモ隊という群衆の中に溶解させるためであり、それは個の領域を決定する輪郭を消滅させることで、個の領域から外に出ていくことだ。個を個として自己を形成するのが昼の人々であるのなら、夜の人々は自分の輪郭を溶解させ、不可視の幽霊に個を変容させ、自己をさらに夜へと同期させていく。黒い服に帽子という石の男の格好も、それは夜の中に自分の存在を溶解させるためであり、「将来の抗議の準備」/（Armando Lulaj 本書より）としての石を叩きつける男の行動は、武装蜂起を準備する幽霊のように見える。

　秩序を表現する昼は、資本主義の時間に支配されている。そのような時間を夜の闇の中に溶解させてしまうこと。資本主義社会における時間とは世界を分節化することであり、それは分節して断片化した世界を国家、秩序、市民という言葉で再度束ねるために分節化されるのだ。フォードの生産システムが効率という名の労働の分断化であり、それは人間の身体を徹底的に切り刻み、資本の論理によって人間の身体を再構築しようと目論んでいるのと同じように、明晰な光と遠近法のもとで成り立つ昼の時間は、国家、秩序、市民という言葉で人間を再編成するだろう。

　資本の時間が目的という前方を設定することで成り立つのなら、石の男が目的もなく歩き続けるのは、そのような目的に向かって直線的に進む時間を廃棄するために歩き続けているのではないだろうか。直線的に流れる時間とは、目標という前方に向かって効率的に流れる資本の時間であり、そのような直線的な時間の流れに対して、投げる、拾う、投げるという円環的な時間の運動を石の男が対峙させる。時間を分割することはできない。時間を分割することが、時間の数値化であり、それが最終的にはフォードシステム的な時間の流れを成立させるのなら、石の男の行為は目標に向かって直線的に流れるフォード的な時間の中に、ひたすら蛇行しながら歩くという円環のような持続の時間を侵入させるだろう。

　夜、路上で石を投げつけながら歩くのは、そのような資本の時間への抗議であり、この男が無言なのは、言葉はすでに自分のものではないからだ。彼には行為しか残されていない。日本赤軍が「プロパガンダの最高形態は武装闘争である」（『赤軍－PFLP世界戦争宣言』/監督若松孝二、足立正生）といったように、言葉もまた世界を分節化して、支配するための昼の世界のものであり、言葉はすでに権力のツールでしかないのだから、彼は無言で石を路上に叩きつける以外に抵抗の道がない。

Broken Narrative

Armando Lulaj
interviewed by Marco Mazzi

This interview/conversation was conducted in an open form. The questions were sent to the artist, and the answers were recorded and later transcribed at different times inside our contemporary penitentiaries.

TRACK 01

1997: why did you choose to begin this testimonial starting from that year? What happened in those months, what was 1997? And why did this year leave such a deep mark on contemporary Albanian history? What really happened in Albania? And what do you remember personally? Many historians would probably place the start of contemporary Albanian history in the early nineties, at the time of the fall of the communist regime. Why have you chosen a later date?

I was born in 1980 and obviously the main episodes of the nineties that left a mark in my memory are connected with the fall of the communist regime.[1] These memories come to mind in the form of images linked to facts that occurred in parallel with the historical events you refer to. For instance, I have a very clear

---

1   To give the reader a brief frame of reference regarding the political events that took place in Albania starting with the death of Enver Hoxha (1985): after the fall of the communist regime in 1991, under his successor Ramiz Alia the country transitioned to a presidential republic. He was succeeded by Bashkim Fino. The government collapsed in 1997 due to the crisis of the pyramid financial schemes that threw the country into anarchy. In the following elections, when Albania had become a parliamentary republic, the Socialist Party prevailed, with Fatos Nano as Prime Minister. In 1998, he was replaced by Pandeli Majko. The decline of the socialists was accompanied by the birth of other political formations until Sali Berisha regained power in 2005. The 2013 elections were won by the Socialist Party in coalition with the LSI (Socialist Movement for Integration) in the Alliance for a European Albania. The Socialist Party leader Edi Rama was appointed as Prime Minister, a position he still holds.

memory of the moment when the magnificent gilded statue of Enver Hoxha in Skanderbeg Square in Tirana was torn down by demonstrators. I remember it well because at the same time on one of the city's main streets, as my mother and I were trying to find a safe way to get back to our house in the city's outskirts, there was a tank blocking the street. The soldier on top of the tank had a machine gun in his hand; the turret turned around slowly until at a certain point it stopped, and the barrel was pointing right at the two of us. We stood there petrified while people were running down the street and we could hear them screaming that Enver Hoxha's statue had been torn down.

I remember clearly the images on television that showed the intense, dramatic excitement of the people who were scrambling up the high walls of the foreign embassies to escape from the country. I remember my parents' discussions about that — should we, too, leave the country, or not? My father was in the army, so he said he couldn't violate his oath. For this reason we didn't leave. The same question was raised again at home when masses of people fleeing the country covered iron ships with their naked skin.

If I were to throw a sounding line down into the depths of recent history, I'd stop right away at the most memorable sight to have been left in my pre-adolescent memory. It happened in 1992 — the public hanging of two brothers in Fier, in the southern part of the country. I remember it well because it took place on June 25, the day after my twelfth birthday. The interesting thing about this execution is that it was carried out just after the change and so in a certain sense it was the "last" death penalty imposed by the former regime, understood as a state judiciary apparatus that hadn't yet been reformed. But the most important thing was that it was the first death sentence in the new (ostensibly) democratic system. I think this was (and still is) a highly significant sign for the future, this future, for the progress of the country and the development of the democratic system that reached its acme precisely in 1997.

There is an anecdote about Jean Genet connected to an image relating to the exodus of my countrymen, included in the Desertion Archive, an integral part of the DebatikCenter of Contemporary Art.[2] On July 13, 1990, the first ship to leave the port of Durrës, carrying more than four thousand Albanians who had taken refuge in the German and Italian Embassies, arrived in Brindisi. A significant moment was documented that day, not by the media that was present, but by an immigrant who was on that ship and who had brought along a Russian-made camera, property of Kinostudio "Shqipëria e Re" (New Albania Film Studio). That photo is very different from the ones circulated by the mainstream media. It is a picture that attempts to develop and at the same time, in a certain sense, to distance itself from the usual narrative about the Albanians, which was (is) mainly based on media clichés.

In this reverse shot we see this ship, which had just touched foreign soil, from the other point of view. The moment immortalized by the media came just before he himself, the photographer, touched the other shore and came into focus. The half-naked body walking between the lenses of the foreign photographers and cameramen documents an important moment of our recent history. That body is crossing the lens of history and was captured at this precise moment. It seems as though it is a body entering history and escaping from it at the same time. In this picture what magnifies the factor of flight, an essential part of the contemporary condition of my country, is the ship at anchor. The ship is a mirror image, a presence that reflects the past while at the same time anticipating the future,

---

2   DebatikCenter of Contemporary Art (DCCA) was founded in 2003 by a group of young Albanian contemporary artists and launched the same year with a performance on the occasion of the second edition of the Tirana Biennial. Among its goals is investigating the mechanisms of inclusion exclusion practiced by contemporary art institutions. In its current incarnation, the DebatikCenter of Contemporary Art is a collective of academics, activists, architects, artists, imaginary and real collectives, critics, curators, journalists, translators, etc., who are trying to shed light on these practices, but also to offer the tools necessary to imagine alternative futures and strategies of resistance to the status quo.

underscoring the perennial condition of flight, which is also an important presence in my work.

My country has a singular creative power and has always been a sort of harvester of strange narratives that drill holes in time, creating ellipses and parallel events — a *collector* country, in possession of strange archives still to be discovered, with the capacity to create stories parallel to and at the same time very far from the official narrative.

It is said, for example, that certain unsuspected figures of contemporary history — scientists, revolutionaries, and important heads of state — have visited Albania for a very short time in obscure circumstances. About some of them there are only stories circulating. There is no proof of their presence on Albanian soil, not a single document or photo, like the undocumented visit of Ernesto Che Guevara, but only the accounts of witnesses. In other cases documents exist, as in the case of the young Yasser Arafat, who spent some time in the country, obviously when it was under communism. These visits, whether documented or not, are rooted in the construction of our still-evolving identity. The same holds for the case of Jean Genet, whom I mentioned before.

The criminal beginnings of a future genius are symptomatic traces but not ones significantly tied to the country's development. For me, the image of a semi-naked body sailing from Durrës to land in Brindisi has a strangely tangential link to the journey to Albania undertaken by Jean Genet in July of 1936. Three years before the fascists invaded the country another ship, this time going in the opposite direction, left Brindisi to cross the Adriatic and cast anchor in Durrës. On board that ship was the still very young Genet. He had just deserted the army and was traveling with a passport under a false name. His intention was to use Albania as a stop-over on the way to other places where he would have far more exciting adventures. After touching Albanian soil he spent a few days in Durrës, where it is said he even stole some livestock. In Durrës, he managed to find a car and reached the capital, Tirana. In the main square, Skanderbeg

Square, his suspicious appearance attracted the attention of a gendarme, who examined his passport and figured out that it was false. Mr. Gejietti (the name written on the passport) was therefore escorted to the police station for further checks, after which he was granted twenty-four hours to leave the country if he wanted to avoid being put under arrest. Heading south, he tried unsuccessfully to reach Corfu, after which he turned north toward Yugoslavia. There he was arrested and imprisoned as a suspected spy. And so his story continues… I am and always will be fascinated by tangential connections, by these images, by these (sought after) metaphors that create an alternative landscape for the identity of this country.

The main difference between 1990 and 1997 is that in 1990 we underwent a sort of symbolic separation from the past, while on the contrary the events of 1997, which marked the historical peak of change, forever cemented the road to neoliberalism. To all this we should add that there was a sort of refusal, a resistance on everyone's part. In some ways, in 1997 we were trying to vomit the future before swallowing it. Historically speaking, the year 1997 remains problematic because of the challenges posed by the events themselves, which are multifaceted and multilayered, and also because of the difficulties faced by those involved in investigating these events to glean their true significance, whether separately or as a totality.

That year had and still has a uniqueness, a peculiar capacity to stop time, contrasting and cancelling it. There have been many definitions of that year, including *annus horribilis*, "The year of total destruction," "The cursed year," "The year of the pyramids," "The year of deception," "The unforgettable year," or else "The year to forget," "The year of the shock," exaggeratedly and stupidly even "Hiroshima minus the atomic bomb," but also simply *Nineteen Ninety Seven*. These formulas were spread mainly by the media, by local and foreign politicians, by NGOs, by religious activists infiltrated into the country, and by the emanations of powerful world structures operating in the shadows. I believe that the chaos and shock of that year, just like the conditions that preceded it as well as the situations that followed the events of that year, were the effects of a carefully orchestrated plan,, just like the economic shock therapy was first tested in other countries.

In the 1970s, Jeffrey Sachs and David Lipton devised in the space of one night Milton Friedman's plan for Chile, which aimed at transforming the country's socialist economy into a market economy. I believe that in the case of Albania there was not that much urgency: there was plenty of time available to orchestrate a geostrategic plan conceived on various levels, not only for our country, but for the entire Balkan area, especially the part that had been involved in war since the early nineties. Today it is a generally accepted conviction that the plan was the work of the Americans, and that it started to develop with the introduction of the pyramid schemes[3] that began to operate in the country in early 1992, exploding in 1996–1997, and then continued in 1999 with the war in Kosovo.

In those years the majority of Albanians had lost their jobs. The main productive activities had shut down as industry collapsed: factories closed, machinery was sold as scrap, and state companies went into private hands for peanuts. The majority of the population lived on the returns from the investments in the pyramid schemes and/or on the remittances sent by Albanian immigrants working and living abroad. In the years leading up to 1997, people had started selling their homes so as to "invest" the proceeds in the Ponzi schemes. They had repeatedly been encouraged by the government to put their "clean" money into this great money laundering machine, which one fine day simply imploded. The economy was, as they said, "taken to the emergency room" on the verge of collapse. The fatal day arrived, and the savings of the Albanian people disappeared forever.

---

3   The expression "pyramid scheme" is used to describe a model of
marketing or investment in which the gains of each investor are linked to
the recruitment of others, not unlike the way so-called chain letters work.
The "Ponzi schemes" alluded to further down are in reality the fraudulent
version of this model, according to which income derives exclusively from
the amounts paid by new investors and not from earnings in productive or
financial activities.

Parliament barred the activity of the pyramid companies with a special law and some of their collaborators were arrested, but their assets were not frozen. People began to protest, demanding to get their money back. Despite the endless promises made by all the political parties, the money was never returned. What followed looks like a well-known script, from the eruption of protests to the raids on ammunition depots, and finally the arrival of so-called anarchy and rebellion against the state. The corrupt Democratic Party government, which had taken part in the pyramid fraud, collapsed while trying to put down the protests. The country was in the hands of criminal groups supported by the opposition, which in a very short time rose to power. To this day there are no accurate statistics, but it is thought that as a result of the events of 1997 more than three thousand civilians and 360 policemen were killed; five thousand civilians were wounded, and USD 1.2 billion (one billion and two hundred million) were devoured by the pyramid schemes.

In those years we were experiencing the CNN effect — we mainly watched foreign TV channels and listened to foreign radio stations, because they seemed to us more credible than our local broadcasters, which were mostly controlled by the government. Contrary to the early nineties, which I remember far more clearly, I remember only a few unfocused episodes from 1997. For me it is still like a sort of deep black hole, and in answer to your question this is the other reason why I am so interested in the events of that year. I have some images impressed in my mind, but they are few compared to what was almost a year of violent events. My experiences during that period are in some way frozen, hidden, and they pass through my mind as a frame of disorderly photograms, accompanied by a clear sound that is repeated continually. It is like finding oneself inside a space where a distinct sound is perpetually accompanied by an image from that period. Strangely enough though, it's not necessarily an image from 1997 Albania, but instead other images that are reflections of parallel stories. In my opinion, the "Year of electroshock," as I call it, even if it produced many contradictory images and documentation of all sorts, which we nourished ourselves on, has more to do with sound than with image.

This reminds me of something we did when we were boys. Before 1990 and for a short time afterward, like many other people of my generation I used a cassette player. Since we couldn't make copies of the tapes, when we ran out of cassettes we would play the one cassette we had repeatedly, running it backwards and forwards to hear the piece we liked best over and over, or to try and understand the lyrics of the song or the chorus. At times the tape got caught in the recorder and we had to get it free. Then we would try to fix it, spool the tape back into the cassette so as to restore it, but when we pushed the play button at times we heard pauses of silence or distorted passages of music. Somehow these gaps created in the middle of the pieces, between the sounds that came before and after, strengthened the memory of the *original* piece, by now lost, and the distorted melody and words became clearer and more well-defined. This gap, which could reinforce the original sound but could also cancel it to produce something different, is what I am still trying to identify about 1997.

During the year 1997, for many months almost all of us heard the same sound in every town and village of the country. The same sound went around and came out of the television and the radio. I think the sound is the right key to remember and to use against our desire to forget. What is really frightening, but at the same time encouraging, is that there is in people's minds a common understanding in a certain sense, like a *silent harmony,* of what happened. But this is not (as yet) clear collective comprehension, in the sense of historical knowledge about the recent past. This *silence* has become a space to violate, a space where memories tend to be fragmentary, as it were, and are replaced by the official narrative of the International Monetary Fund, by the propagandistic images and documents of the corrupt media, by the interests of the United States, our guardian angels and God's right hand, by the propaganda of our neoliberal governments, by the nationalistic ideas of certain parties, by the specific agendas of other countries, the apparatuses of recent political history. Memories are also manipulated by time, but what I find disastrous is that the great majority of people, encouraged by politics, are sliding into oblivion. This is how the political apparatus manages to transform the people into a bunch of puppets in the hands of a great ventriloquist who interprets the script dictated by the great orchestra conductor. Against this backdrop, the voices of the artist, the socially committed film director and the investigative reporter are completely absent.

Today and 1997. The Italian and western media have spoken relatively little of the real causes that led to the situation of anarchy that the Albanian nation was plunged into in 1997. They have spoken only of illegal immigration, criminality, etc. Many people, even today in Italy, believe that the crisis of 1997 was caused by the bad administration of the communist regime, whereas we know that responsibility for the emergency and the disorders were not connected as much to the communist past as to the crash of economic models of a "democratic" nature. Can you talk to us about the transition from a communist-type economy to the current one? How would you define this passage? What has changed economically? What has happened?

The global media gave wide coverage to the events of 1997. They gave their version: in general, their conclusions went back to the poor previous administration and always put the blame on the dictatorial regime. They almost never produced different narratives, which remain in the shadows even today and still have to be unveiled. As I said before, the model proposed, or better imposed and still in fashion, is neoliberalism, but it has never been adequately analyzed. The media try to treat 1997 as a symbolic situation, rather like 1990, but in my opinion it is not. They also try to demonize the past regime in order to glorify our current one. This is a naive approach that needs reconsideration. Only now, in the light of recent economic and political developments, is the curtain being lifted, allowing us to make connections and to carry out detailed analyses. Performed chiefly by serious young scholars, both local and foreign, these analyses link the economic models set up in Albania in those days to the economic and political developments of the present day.

Edward Said writes in *Culture and Imperialism,* "The threat to independence in the late twentieth century from the new electronics could be greater than was colonialism itself. [...] The new media have the power to penetrate more deeply into a 'receiving' culture than any previous manifestation of western technology."[4]

In the 1990s we became great "receptors" of novelty. Everything began with the explosion of household appliances that came from Bulgaria, South Korea, Germany, Italy, and Turkey. New color monitors were present in every household, and deep-dish antennas adorned balconies and windows on every building. This thirst for the televisual image, for its perpetual, incessant realism, together with the desire for the new electronics, continues to this day more than ever.

I got my first computer in 1997. It was a Power Macintosh 8500. At the time I had no idea what to do with it. Our parents encouraged us, my sister and me, to work on it, to use it, but I didn't know what to do with it. In my first videos in those years, the computer, sometimes turned on, at other times off, is almost always in the background of the shot, like an extra in the short études I made in those days.

At the time I lived near one of the largest ammunition and weapons depots, Shkolla e Bashkuar (The United School). This was the most important army training center in the country, which Arafat had visited and also where he had trained. We knew that place well since we often gathered there to exercise and watch the soldiers train. When the depot was dismantled, most of my neighbors and friends rushed there to grab weapons. I didn't go. I wasn't interested in having a weapon. My father

---

4   Edward W. Said, *Culture and Imperialism* (New York: Alfred A. Knopf, 1993), 291–92.

owned a pistol and so I was familiar with firearms. From my balcony I saw my friends walking down the street carrying large quantities of ammunitions/weapons. Some of them had only pillaged boxes of the famous Russian 12.7×108 mm bullets. Others, from other neighborhoods, took only rifles and machine gun parts. To get those weapons to work various people had to collaborate, at first swapping ammunitions for weapons, and then buying and selling them. In a short time everyone was armed. Almost overnight firearms had become more common and important than household appliances.

I think that deep down the rebellion, anger, and excitement that were produced at that time were actually aimed at something very different. In the fragments of memory I still hold, as in the thousands of images I witnessed, there is a *genuine,* authentic element that the standard narrative misses, an element more pertinent to the idea of a very different and far more interesting revolution. I often ask myself who or what this enemy that everyone kept shooting at really was, and the most accurate answer is that it was capitalism itself, the reality and the future that have now been unveiled.

There are various narratives concerning 1997, but the most widespread one is that conceived by the International Monetary Fund. The report made by Christopher Jarvis reconstructs the main economic events from immediately after the fall of the communist regime to 1997.[5] According to this report, but also others published after 1997, the main thing to take into account is that the economic crisis had in fact begun long before 1997 and was caused by a scarce familiarity with the financial market. Jarvis goes on to cite the country's inaccessibility to the market, which was due to its purely formal financial system and an economy that excluded almost every form of private property. The report holds that after the collapse of the communist regime the three banks operating in the country were not able

---

5   Christopher Jarvis, "The Rise and Fall of Albania's Pyramid Schemes," *Finance and Development* 37, no. 1 (2000), https://www.imf.org/external/pubs/ft/fandd/2000/03/jarvis.htm.

to sustain the private sector that was successfully developing, and this favored the growth of informal loan companies. From 1992 onward all these loan companies started to change into pyramid schemes. With the government's full support, they also "sponsored" political parties, as well as numerous Members of Parliament, or, as has been proven, high government officials who benefitted personally from the pyramid schemes. According to the IMF, during the rise — but also during the collapse — of these pyramid schemes, the government remained a passive spectator of the crisis. The escalation of that bubble was catastrophic in economic terms, but — again according to the IMF — it was short-lived and, we might say, controlled. By contrast, the civil disorders that followed had a long-term impact on society, and it can be said that they still do.

Those years were very fruitful for local criminal organizations as well as for foreign mafias, which laundered dirty money through the pyramid schemes, controlled illegal immigration, and later came to control weapons and drug trafficking as well. The alarm that signaled the imminent collapse came when the interest paid by the pyramid schemes began to soar as high as thirty per cent a month. The implosion of the schemes in 1996 is colorfully described by Jarvis, "Albanians sold their houses to invest in the schemes, farmers sold their livestock. The mood is vividly captured by a resident who said that, in the fall of 1996, Tirana smelled and sounded like a slaughterhouse as farmers drove their animals to market to invest the proceeds in the pyramid schemes."

As I've already said, it is my impression that something has been deliberately left out of this report, something that concerns the geopolitical aspect… Albania has always been considered a factor of stability in a turbulent region, one often darkened by tragic events such as repression, genocide, and religious hatred. Keeping in mind the various geopolitical agendas of the time, still alive in the Balkans today in order to control the region, preserve the calm and continue expanding, we cannot fail to see the events of 1997 as an essential piece in a bigger puzzle, a piece that can be blown up by remote control from one moment to the next.

The social impact that the events of '97 could have on the future was the main thread of some extraordinary never-completed filmed material, called *Kronikë '97* (*Chronicle '97*). This raw material was produced by a group of people who worked for the former Kinostudio during the communist regime, including a cameraman who had shot numerous films for this regime, and a director who had made many Kinostudio productions in the past and had also worked on Gianni Amelio's 1994 feature film *Lamerica*. There are 8,500 meters of 35mm film, preserved in the National Film Archive, which capture something very different from what the media version showed, and that includes both local and foreign reporters. The group took several months long trip in search of a matrix that was both different and at the same time profoundly connected to the strategies of economic "shock therapy." Part of this rather naïf footage was shot, among other places, in a psychiatric hospital where the group interviewed doctors and filmed patients in an attempt to explore the depths of the shock they had suffered and the impact that the events that had taken place might have on the future of society. Then they went to the zoo to film the caged animals, a lion, a tiger, and a wolf, trying to understand the levels of stress the animals had suffered. They also went to the police-dog school, asking the trainers the same questions. They continued their research in institutes for the deaf-mute and the blind, in archaeological parks and destroyed museums, in penitentiaries, in local cemeteries and the foreign cemeteries of the First and Second World Wars. The film, which is divided in 31 acts and has never been edited and nor should it be, is still an open work. In my view this material from 1997 constitutes the first readymade film to be signed in our country. It may be the only material which attempts to carry out a complex research project in search of alternative testimonies that allow us to get beyond the distorted representations we find in media images.

Le fond de l'air est noir.
I left Albania in October 1998 and I lived in Italy for over ten years. I always considered Italy as a port of passage that could give me the possibility to move elsewhere through obtaining the necessary paperwork I would need. We were students, but we were also treated violently as immigrants with limited rights, or as foreign workers with no dignity. You could smell this violence in the air; it materialized above all in the behavior of the police, who were xenophobic and quick to teach certain so-called European rules, consisting in the use of force and violence.

It is unforgivable, though understandable, that so many of my countrymen have camouflaged themselves and tried to hide themselves in that society. I can remember a very troubling episode concerning one of the most tragic events of 1997. Just one month after my arrival in Florence, I went to see the uncle of a close friend of mine, who had lived there for years in spite of which him and his wife as well as their son where still undocumented. We were talking about the ship *Katër i Radës,* which had been rammed by the Italian navy corvette *Sibilla* and had gone down in the Channel of Otranto on March 28, 1997, resulting in 81 victims and dozens of others who were classified as missing, among them women and children. His wife said the Italians had sunk the Albanian ship. The owner of the apartment was also there, an Italian. Then the husband snapped and ordered her to correct what she'd said and never to repeat those lies to anyone, not even to herself. On the contrary, she should repeat the Italian media version, according to which the incident had been a tragedy, and was therefore "justified." This was the same version given by the owner of the apartment. I tried to state my opinion, because I agreed with the woman. That is how I understood I was no longer welcome in their apartment. This is the general attitude that has been perpetuated — it has never been contested as it should be, not even by contemporary Albanian artists living in Italy, and to this day it represents a great tragedy for our people.

"In Italy, Albanians are first of all future immigrants," wrote Susan Sontag in an article in the *New York Times* while she was living in Bari to write about the 1999 war in Kosovo.[6] I find this to be pretty much the truth. Sontag stayed in southern Italy for a long time, and one of her favorite movies in this decade was Amelio's *Lamerica*. In the spring of 1998 she visited Albania, which had just surfaced from the disaster of 1997. When the director of the Albanian Soros Foundation, who accompanied her and had organized her visit, asked her what she thought after observing the Albanian landscape and the people, she answered, frankly, "I'm thinking about what this place will be like in twenty years…" And then she added, "I think it will be hard to change it."[7] It is now exactly twenty years after that visit, and we still have the same political class. There is still this absurd desire on the part of the politicians to begin from square one, changing their skin, erasing the hard disk, and inscribing a new chapter.

As I said a little while ago, the expansion of neoliberalism that started in the nineties had its peak, the greatest force of impact, in 1997. This political orientation — and I'm referring here mainly to what is happening today — is devouring the country completely, thanks to privatization of all public goods and services, lack of competition, special laws that violate the constitution being passed to accommodate the oligarchs, widespread corruption, and, above all, growth of public debt as a consequence of the borrowing/spending of the current government, which drowns itself in luxury. Organized crime and gangs control power hand in hand with the government and the country has become an important actor in the international drug trade. There has always existed a tie between mafia organizations and the Albanian government, even prior to this government, but it was never so bald-faced. Today the criminal gangs use the Balkans as a bridge between East and West. Albania has become a place to bury European trash, a halfway stop for the cocaine that comes from Afghanistan or Latin

---

6 Susan Sontag, "Why Are We In Kosovo?" *New York Times Magazine*, May 2, 1999, https://www.nytimes.com/1999/05/02/magazine/why-are-we-in-kosovo.html.

7 Piro Misha, *Arratisja nga burgjet e historisë* (Tirana: Toena, 2008), 16.

America, directed toward the heart of Europe. The country itself has become a large-scale producer of marijuana; in fact, the suspicion exists that some of these plantations have become sources of financing for fundamentalist organizations like ISIS.

Before coming to power in 2013 the socialists, forming the most right-wing government this country has seen since the fall of communism, took *Rebirth* as their emblem. They stole the idea and the program from Tony Blair's New Labour, which won the British elections in 1997. The emblem fits Blair's and New Labour's scams better than the historical movement it is meant to be associated with which is known as *Rilindja Kombëtare,* or The National Renaissance, the historical period between the end of the 19th century and the declaration of independence in 1912. In a very short time, the reborn socialists have proved to be the greatest con-men in our contemporary history. Transforming their leader, Edi Rama, into a sort of international brand, like Adidas or Coca-Cola, they've shown themselves to be a huge machine for corruption and crime, and consequently people's desire to escape from the country has sharply increased. In fact, almost half a million people have left the country during this legislature in hopes of finding a better life elsewhere in Europe.

NEVER.[8] *Ideology and the economy: are these perhaps two different types of "narrative"? How would you define ideology and how would you define the economy? How do you explore and how do you treat ideology from an artistic point of view? And the economy? On the whole your work seems to aim at exploring both the ideological superstructure of the contemporary political narrative and the economic structure. I'm thinking above all of your video* NEVER. *Can you talk to us about it in detail? I'd like you to speak about* NEVER *from*

---

8   The video NEVER (2012, 22', b/w and color), along with *It Wears as It Grows* (2011) and *Recapitulation* (2011), is part of the *Albanian Trilogy: A Series of Devious Stratagems* project presented by Lulaj at the 2015 Venice Biennale. See Armando Lulaj, *Albanian Trilogy: A Series of Devious Stratagems,* ed. Marco Scotini (Berlin: Sternberg Press, 2015).

the "formal" point of view as well. You used the word, an instrument that has a long tradition in contemporary art. Can video art be considered a great example of concrete poetry and conceptual writing?

Fakt (Albanian) — *Fact* (English) / *Fucked* (English) — *I shkërdhyer* (Albanian).

The pronunciation of the English word *fucked* is /fʌkt/. The sound of *fucked* is very like that of the Albanian word *fakt* ("fact, that is, something real, true"). So when we say *fucked*, Albanians understand *fakt*, and this leads me to say that *in fact* we are *fucked*.

As I've said more than once, the contemporary perception of a country like mine has largely come out of images produced by the photo-reporting of photographers who arrived in the country at certain historical moments and *invented* a stereotyped way to represent the contemporary history of Albania and its people. This way of operating took hold in the early nineties and spread to the mainstream. The Benetton advertising campaign represents an important example of appropriation, genius, and configuration. The photo used by Benetton was shot by an Albanian photographer. The original is in black and white, but in the campaign it was retouched and so was seen by the whole world in color. The passage from black and white to color, from reality to perception, was a conceptual operation that structured a mentality through the language of advertising. Photography has greater force, an extreme power that has been used in the past by large companies and powerful media actors, as well as by political parties. Never, however, like now, because nowadays photography has assumed a new role in the representation of politics.

Every artistic movement, however rebellious it may be, is linked to a social movement or political ideology. It should be said that global interest in contemporary Albanian art began precisely in 1997 and was "consecrated" only a few years later with its presence at the Venice Biennale. Political forces and certain private foreign foundations that operated in the country, and still do, have played a very important supporting role. What I continue to disagree with in this strategy is the narrative produced, which presents absurd falsities. This small country should not have limited itself to a single narrative, the one proposed by people who have the power to be the most visible and well connected. Many personalities in the Albanian art world have taken part in the construction of this narrative, according to which art and politics closely agree in proclaiming a sort of utopian success. My thinking is the exact opposite. Only to very few others, who are part of the Albanian art system but haven't contributed to the creation of the official narrative, is it clear that in this country art and politics are farther apart than ever, I'd even say poles apart.

In the construction of the official falsehood there's a very interesting aspect that involves something that came to the fore in the sixties in other countries and is useful now for politics but not for artists. To allow artists to fight against a terrible political and social situation, the production and intersection of surrealist type "scandals" is needed in order to spark off a movement of rebirth and innovation. Here in Albania the opposite happens: nourished by today's art and architecture, it is the corrupt state that produces the "scandal" (surrealistic) in the form of stratospheric corruption, filtering everything through the public relations machine which the "contemporary Renaissance" is in reality. The younger artists, and older ones as well (a couple of them who continue to be successful have a shadowy past), have become disciples or ambassadors of governmental art and produce nothing of interest, since they are the products of this corrupt state. This is a country where there is no art system able to organize, filter, and promote… And today an extremely important factor for development is still missing: namely, independent strategies.

To make NEVER I had to meet many people connected to politicians as well as the politicians themselves. At the time, the village where the mountain is located, the township, and the government, were the property of three different entities controlled by three different political parties, the most important in the country. It seemed very unlikely that they could collaborate to give me the permits required. Later on I realized that the idea obviously interested them more as a business transaction rather than as art: in return for the permits, one party tried to get me to use its youth wing — obviously as a PR gimmick, another tried to get me to buy vast amounts fuel from a company associated with it, yet another tried to get me to hire the acquaintances of its local party leadership, and, last but not least, they all tried to exploit my project to improve their public image. In the end I tried to remove the various pressures, which at times were even threatening, by choosing not to collaborate with any of them and to organize everything myself independently, without any permits: to do without them, changing my strategy totally and working "underground," as it were. It was a very hard thing to carry out.

My operation envisioned a gigantic written message that occupied a space of 36,000 square meters, visible from every point of the city of Berat. The symbolic act of transforming the gigantic message on Mount Shpirag, made with large stones by the communists in the sixties, has a long story. It wasn't my own idea originally, nor an idea of the democrats, who tried to destroy and eliminate it forever in 1994. Instead, it was the bright idea of an American diplomat who, on seeing the letters that spelled the name of the communist dictator Enver Hoxha, proposed to the mayor of Berat to add another letter. Since the diplomat came from Denver (Colorado), thinking he was being original and funny (in the way of foreign colonizers, like all diplomats in my country), he suggested adding the letter D in front of the name. Obviously this never happened, also because in 1994 the democrats, that is the right-wing party, used explosives to blow up the inscription, in the process destroying the homes of farmers as the stones rolled down the mountain. But since they still didn't manage to completely erase the dictator's name, they then proceeded to use napalm and set fire to the mountain. Two soldiers were seriously burnt during this operation.

I climbed the mountain in 2011 to see what was left, since it was impossible to see anything from a distance or to understand anything from close up. I inspected the area. The access road had just been built. Shell was drilling nearby because the area had good oil sources. They'd just opened a well and were preparing to drill the second. The first idea was to replicate the fire of 1994 in a controlled way, using fuel to outline the letters on the steep slope. We performed a small tryout — it was a disaster. That was a typical military operation and I lacked the necessary equipment. The other problem was that the mountain was a dense mat of weeds crawling with snakes. We couldn't do anything like what we'd wanted to do without the risk of damaging the environment, given that under those conditions the unpredictability of the wind made it impossible to control the fire. A few months later I went up the mountain again to meet the farmers. It took months of negotiations and explanations to finally convince them to help me. One of them, who can be seen in the film, was a boy in 1968 when the inscription was made and had taken part in its production. It had been an enormous challenge, a colossal job that began with the army carrying the stones up the mountain on mules and was eventually completed by the communist youth — our witness was one of them — who painted the rocks placed by the army with lime to make them white. The old man knew the position of the missing letters perfectly, since in 1997 the Albanian Communist Party had commissioned him and others to redraw them in their original position by cutting back the vegetation and then drawing them on the ground in lime.

I explained to the farmers that I didn't want to rewrite the name as it had been, but rather to introduce a substantial change both to the diplomat's D and the communists' idea. I wanted to invert the order of the first two letters, so that ENVER became NEVER. A gesture. Yet another gesture. An imitation of facts anchored to reality, but which nevertheless should not be seen only in this sense. Associations and similarity are inevitable in all cases, whether in the gesture of adding or in that of subtracting/ burying, rewriting the name as it was or completely changing its sense. The new word held a negation within itself, but not the negation of an idea or an ideology, as has often erroneously been written. That word conceals an undesirable message from a past that is not allowed to show itself in our future, this stolen future.

Back in 2012, when I first created this image in black and white, I told everyone who helped me that this work, though so emphatically visible, would only start being perceived after ten years or so, or perhaps will only really be perceived when it begins to disappear, when it will once again be covered by time. In the past I'm interested in exploring there are clear signs of refusal, but there are also signs of a future different from the one we are living in.

I found very little material about the stone message in the public archives. It all seemed to have vanished, but I didn't believe that at all. It's all hidden in the personal archives of the people who worked for these institutions, or who had access to the documents or to photos which they appropriated. In the National Film Archive there are only a few seconds of colored footage where the writing appears, and very few photos, also in color, of the dictator's name.

These news clips and documentaries date back to the late sixties and early seventies and, for the most part, are about the air force. Other accounts and reports from those years found in the archive folders concern the building of a nation under communist ideology, worldwide communist resistance, mutual aid, the training of militants in Albania, the war in Vietnam, the Palestinian question, and the perennial destruction of Africa, always accompanied by the disastrous political, economic, and military presence of the United States in conflict zones. All these sequences were repeated by the propaganda apparatus as if on a loop that seems (not) to have influenced this future. They seem to belong to a [not] not very distant past of a collective memory that must (not) be analyzed.

Man produces himself through thought, and only another kind of loop can replace this past. This new loop to which we are subjected is a kind of torture that produces a lobotomy, just like the one described and analyzed in the early sixties in the Kubark manual.[9] Obviously, everything is far more complicated today, because the means used to manipulate truth and reality are very different and more sophisticated. Marx wrote, "The means is as much part of the truth as the result. The quest for truth must itself be true, the true quest is the unfurling of a truth whose different parts combine in the result."[10]

In Albania in those days there was no Godard, no Marker, but only the state cinema apparatus that edited film materials as absolute truth in order to produce its own narrative. We need to reactivate the fuse to make it catch fire, we need to reuse this political material, rework it, rewrite it, associate it with the political knowledge that we have today of the Israeli–Palestinian conflict, of Iran, and of the American presence in Afghanistan and Iraq. Our participation in these wars in defense of a diabolic lie that mouths the words liberty and democracy is an episode that needs to be analyzed. We have to put together information in ways as yet unimaginable and rewrite the collective political memory of the nation. The past defended these just causes while the present denies them. The present reveals itself as the murderer of truth and creator of a lethal image.

There is yet another aspect of NEVER that has to do with the idea of landscape, which started to change and transform itself radically beginning in the nineties. It concerns both the economy and surveillance. Just like the devious actions of a serial killer who deliberately leaves traces behind only for the pleasure of the game he plays with the spectator he's created, but who is never captured because he is always two steps ahead and so he goes on committing more and more complicated murders. Here I'm not talking only about the disastrous ecological impact that private business has had on the environment and the damage it continues to inflict on nature. I'm not talking about

---

9   The Kubark Counterintelligence Interrogation is a detailed manual for conducting interrogations, even using extreme techniques like torture, created in 1963 for CIA agents and made public in 1997. Available online at https://archive.org/details/kubark.

10 Georges Perec, *Things: A Story of the Sixties / A Man Asleep*, trans. David Bellos (London: Vintage, 2011).

the cancer of the concessionary contracts that have transformed big cities like Tirana, Durrës, Fier, and Vlorë, nor about the laws passed especially to favor the plans of the construction industry mafia. Rather, I'm talking about the fixed stare, the panoptic stare of the surveillance that surrounds each one of us nowadays and turns us into conscious prisoners and a homogeneous part of the landscape. As Masao Adachi[11] rightly says, "even the human existence as substance has been turned into landscape. Because of global homogenization, and because everything now is subjected to the purpose of industries and market economy, our way of thinking is seeking to adjust to the changes. So, as a sequel to landscape theory, film should begin with patiently recording real human beings."[12] Essentially, it is not only us that look at and observe it, the landscape itself observes us and thereby creates, through consciousness, a conflict that makes us into an immobile, frozen society.

Unable to Perform because *Unfree to Perform.*

I believe that to change the situation we have to rewrite the rules. We mustn't film or record the event any more, but instead do our part there, inside the fray, create a new collectivity, in order to change the filmed document. Throw away the camera, not film the event, do something else to produce a new film. Produce another event that goes beyond the image that the camera can perceive. We need to produce a new type of evidence, a new image that we have to shape in a completely different way. To do this, we need to work, again, underground.

In these years I've produced a map and have documented the concrete changes the name on the mountain has undergone. The landscape, from the ENVER of 1968, changed toward FEVER (in

---

11   Masao Adachi (Fukuoka, 1939) is a Japanese director and set designer known for his sympathies with the Palestinian Popular Liberation Front. Member of the Nihon Sekigun, or Japanese Red Army, he was imprisoned in Lebanon and Japan and subsequently deprived of the right of expatriation.

12   "Empire and Revolution: Conversation Between Masao Adachi and Takashi Sakai," *Nihon Cine Art,* March 17, 2009, http://eigageijutsu.blogspot.com/2009/03/empire-and-revolution-conversation.html.

economic terms, I suppose) in 2013, when an artist expressed the idea of wanting to modify NEVER. He didn't succeed physically but only conceptually. In 2018 others simulated the burning of the letter N to leave only the adverb EVER on the mountain.

ENVER	1968
DENVER	1993
	1994
ENVER	1997
NEVER	2012
FEVER	2013
EVER	2018
NEVER	2021

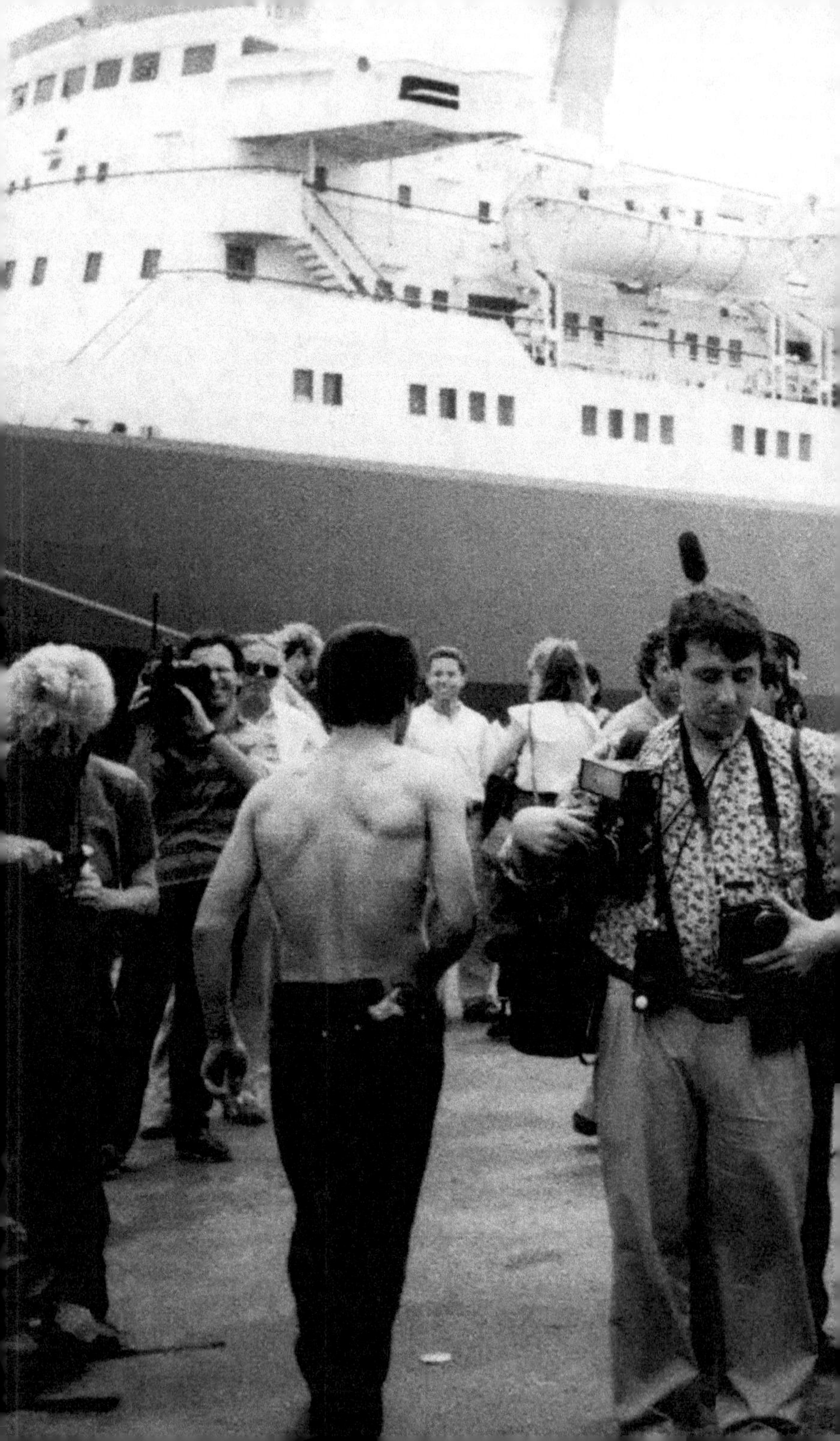

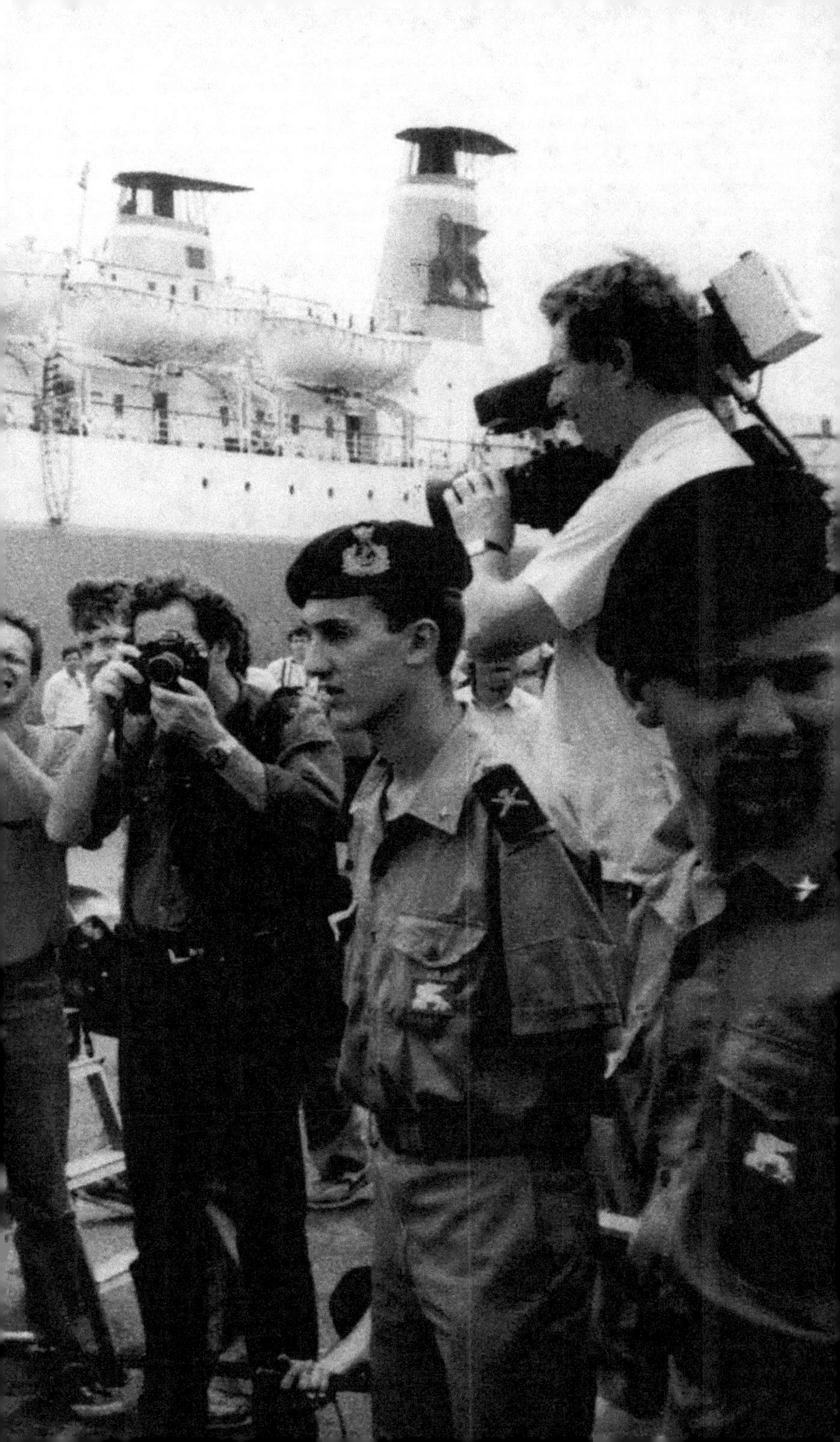

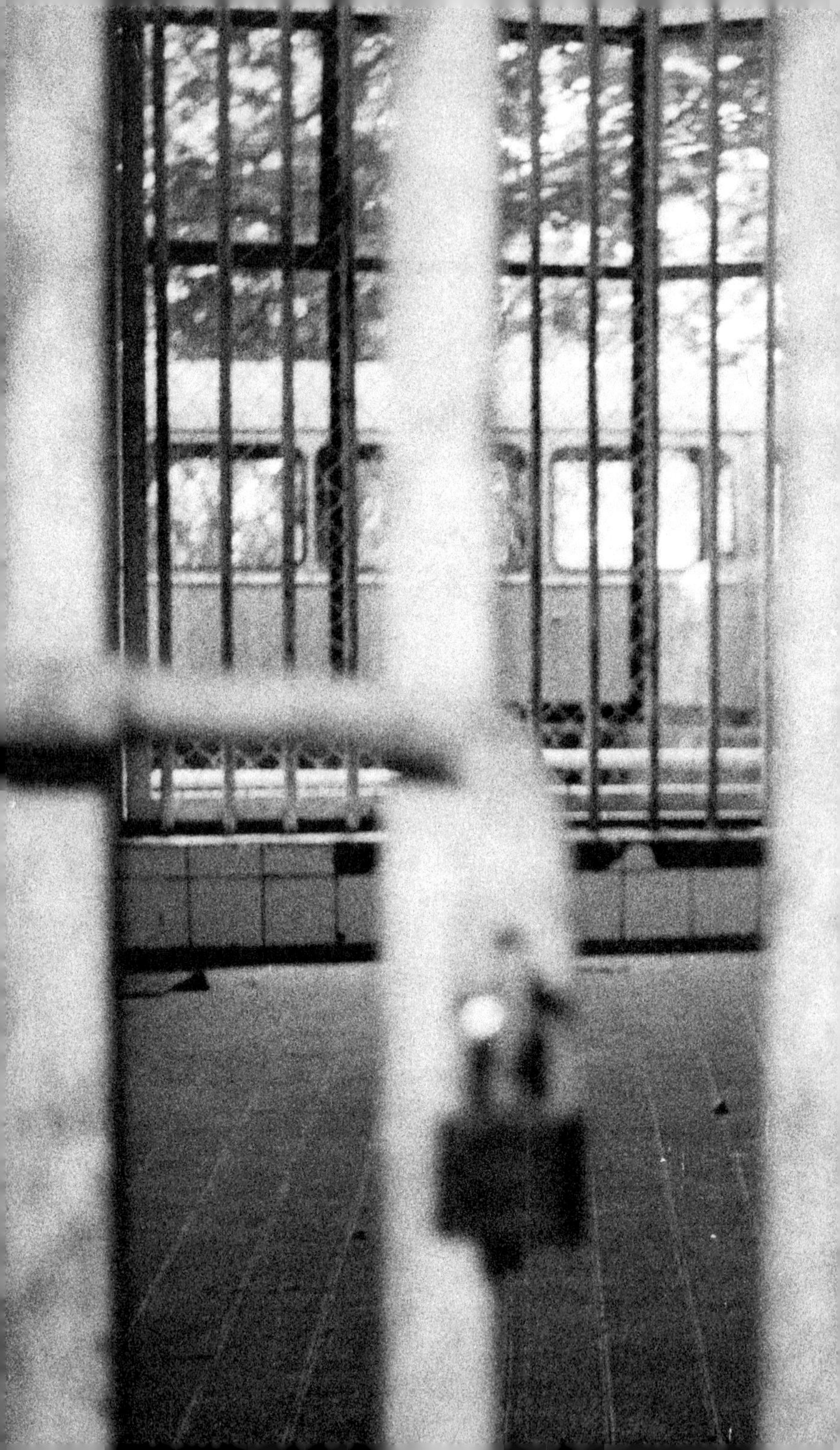

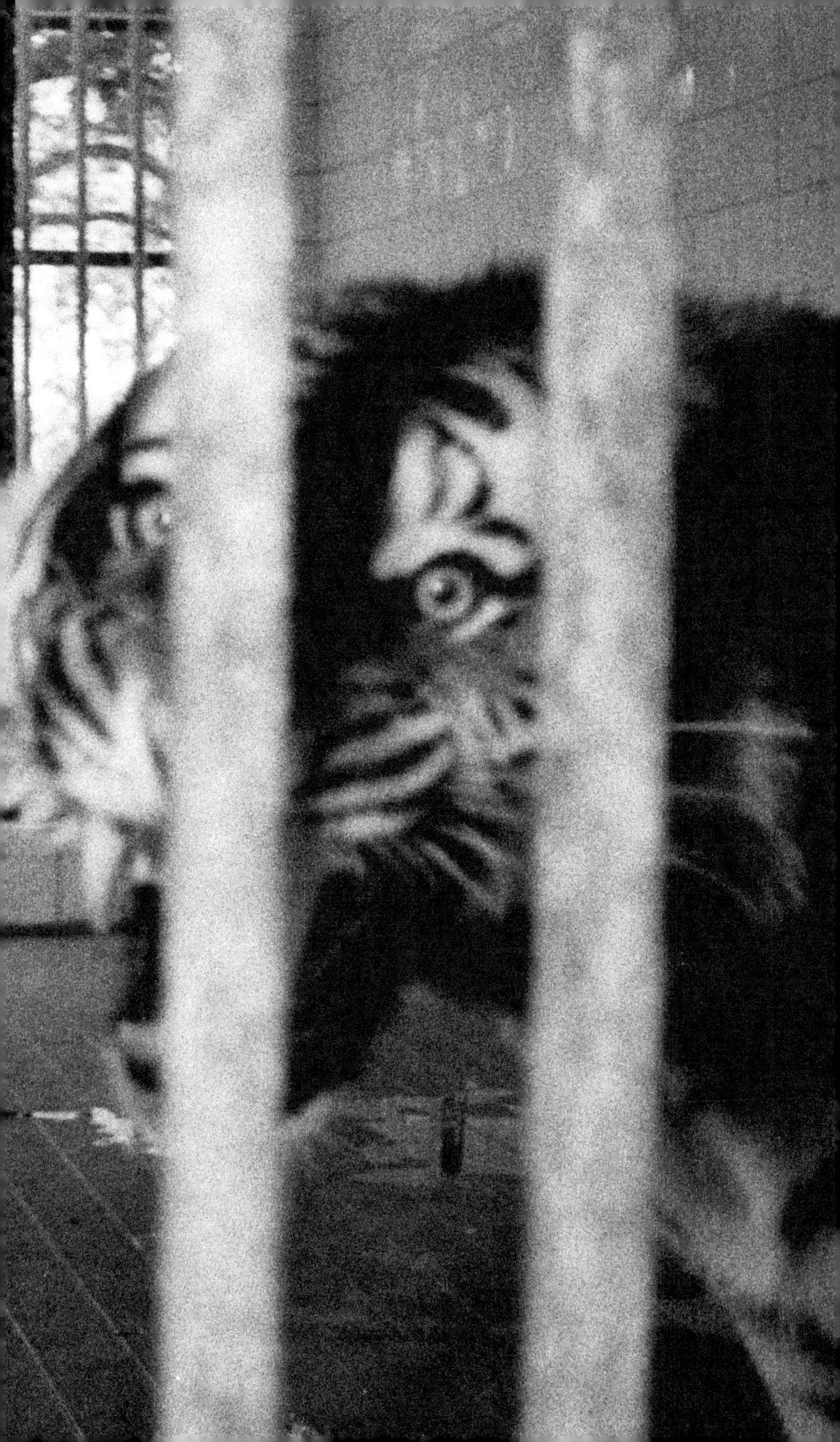

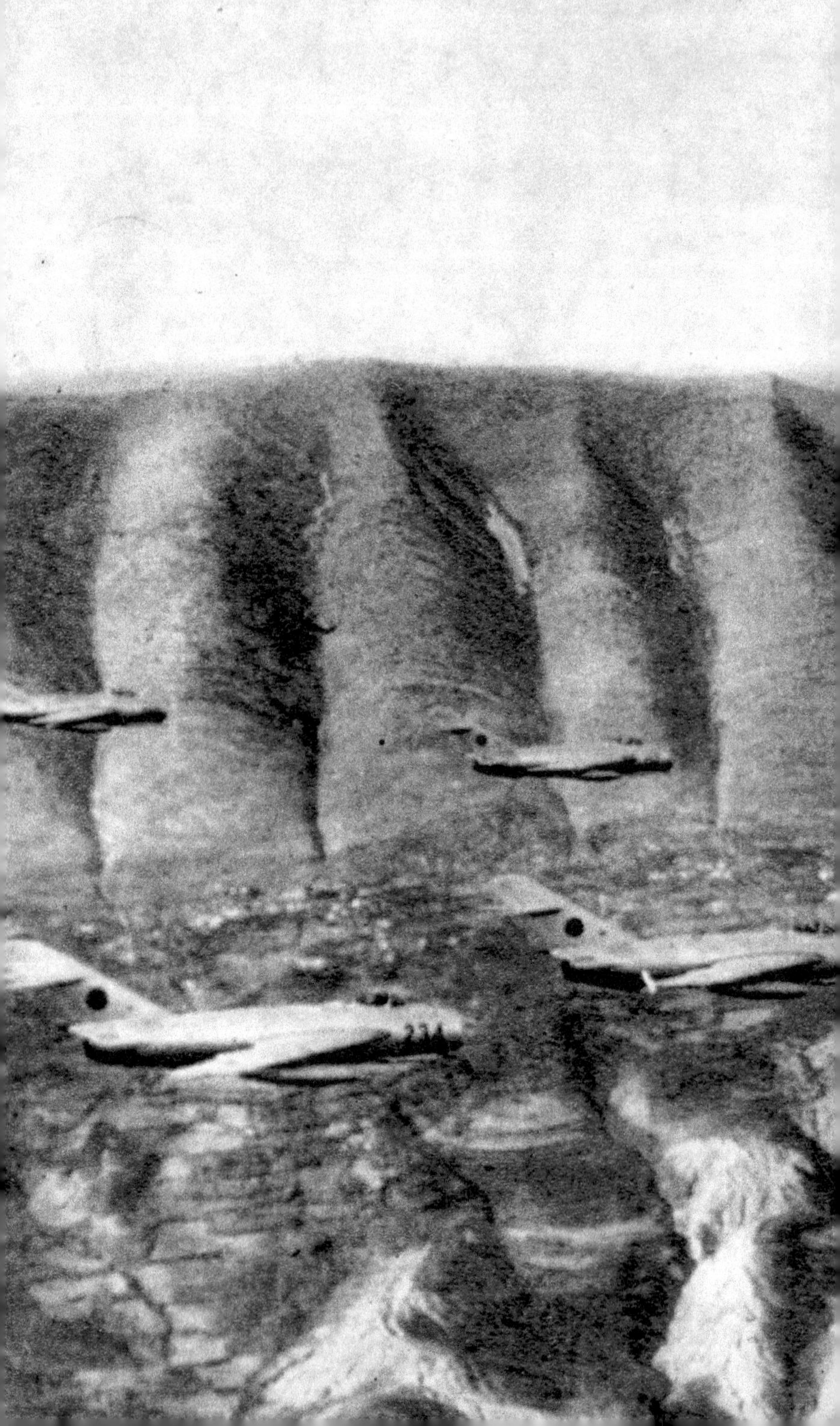

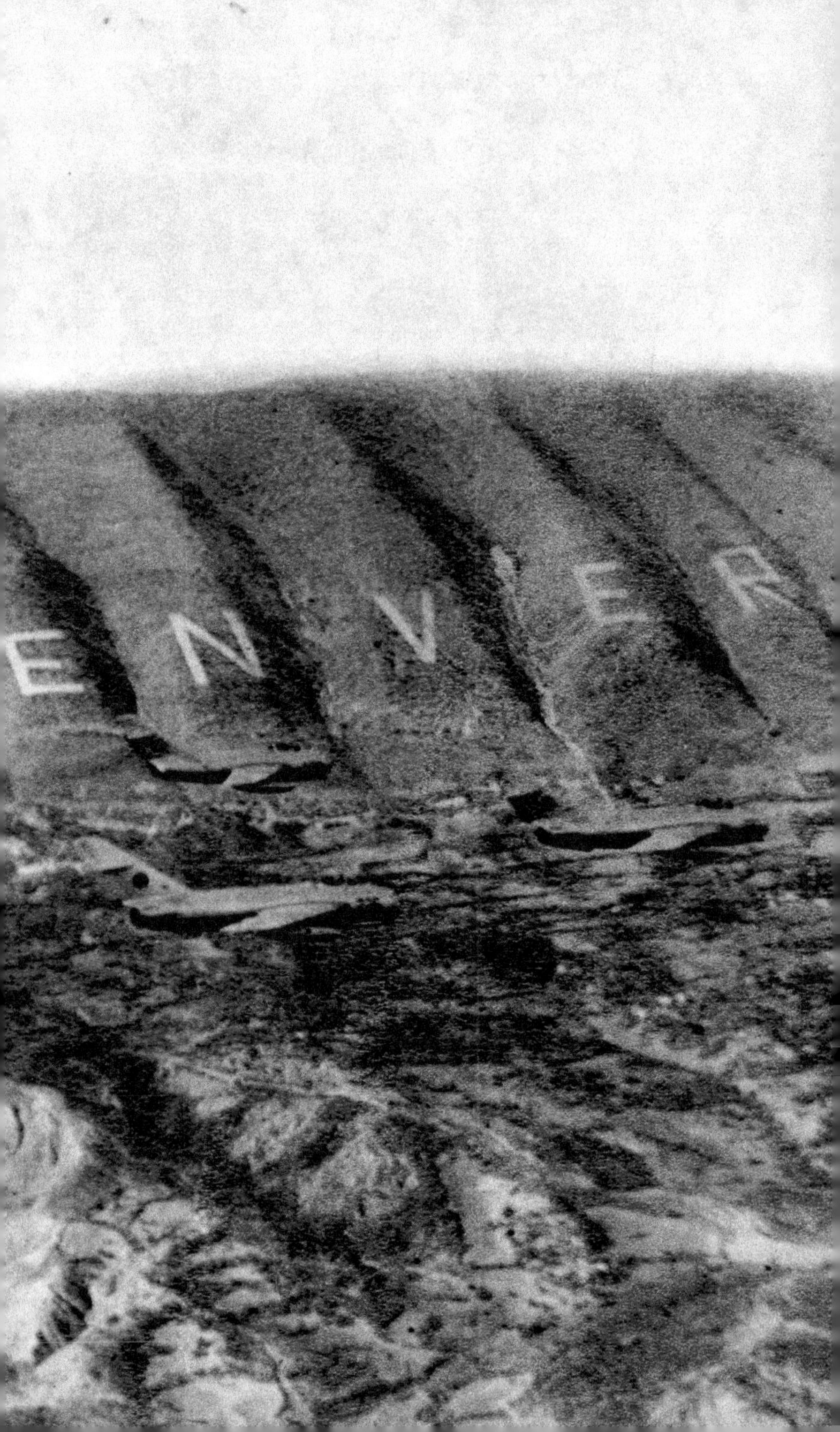

E N V E R

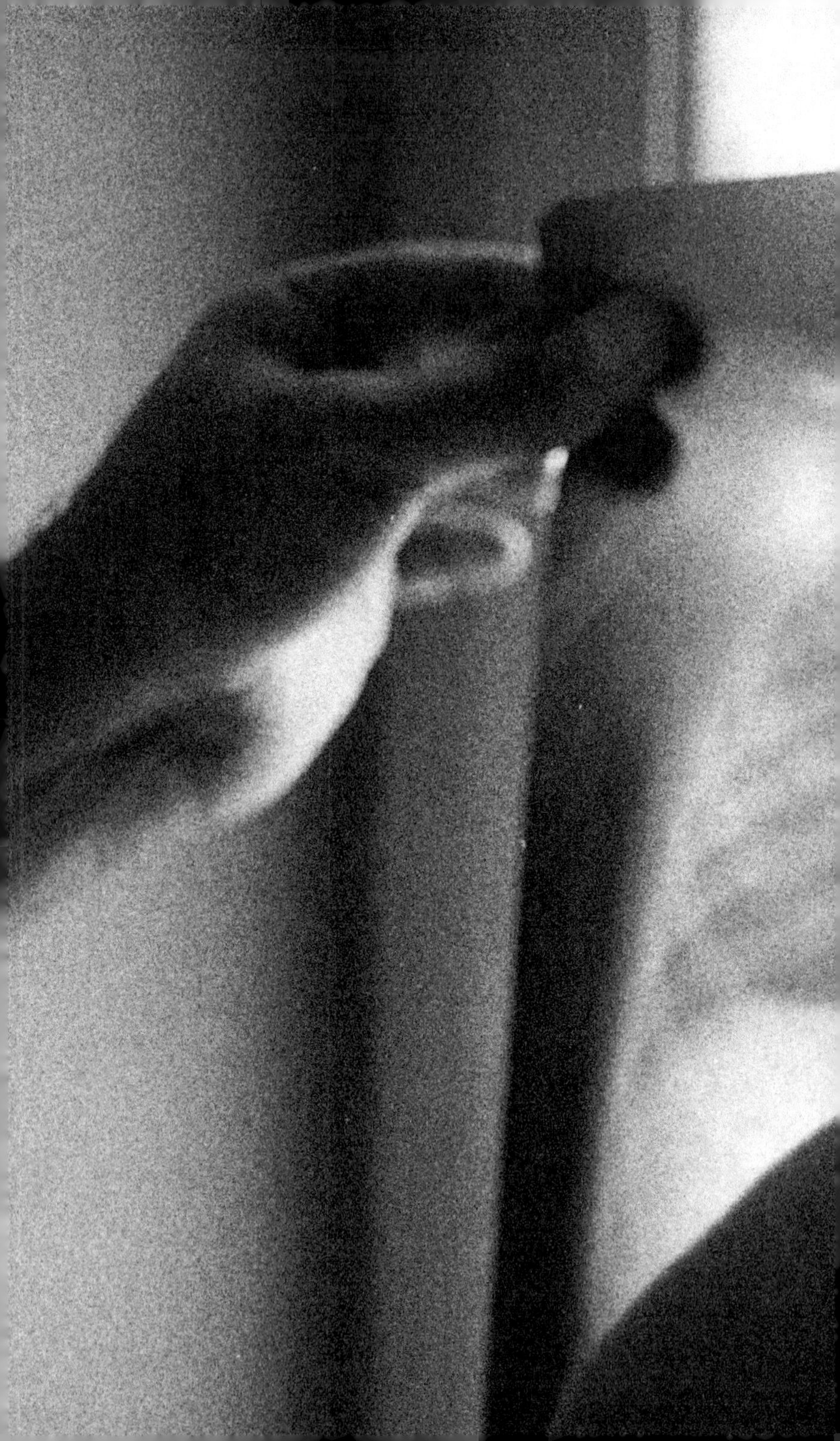

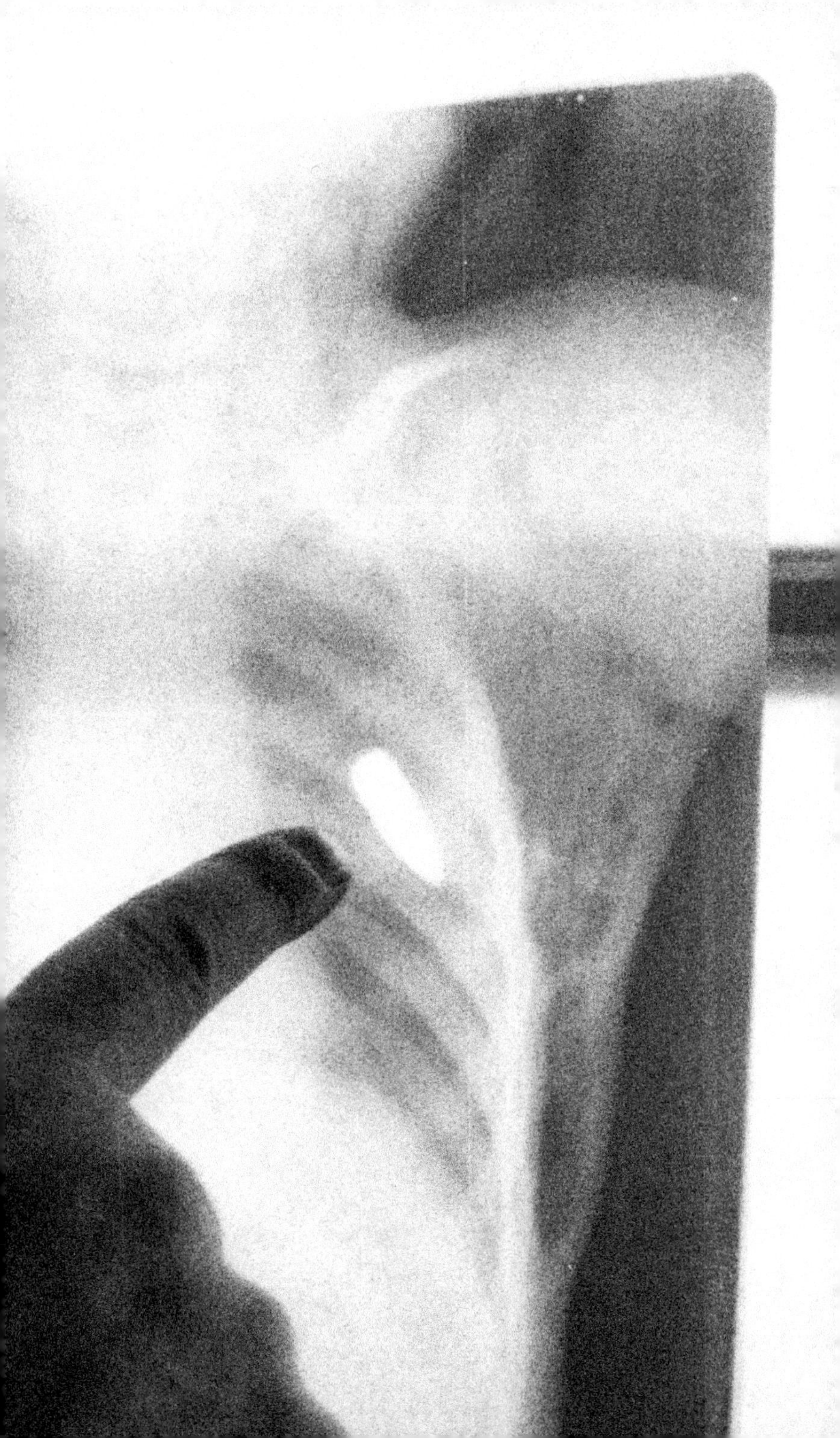

Fig. 1. DESERTION ARCHIVES by Armando Lulaj, 2017.
Photo taken on July 13, 1990 in Brindisi, Italy, by Agim Kubati.
Courtesy of DebatikCenter of Contemporary Art.

Fig. 2. Kronikë '97, 1996–97. Frame from "Kronikë '97".
Unrealized footage directed by Kreshnik Hashorva,
DOP Bashkim Asllani.
Courtesy of National Albanian Film Archive.

Fig. 3. ENVER Slogan, 1976.
Armando Lulaj's personal archive.

Fig. 4. Kronikë '97, 1996–97. Frame from "Kronikë '97".
Unrealized footage directed by Kreshnik Hashorva,
DOP Bashkim Asllani.
Courtesy of National Albanian Film Archive.

ブロークン・ナラティヴ

アルマンド・ルラーイ

マルコ・マッツィ

このインタビュー／対話はオープン形式で行われた。質問はアーティストに送付され、諸処にある我らが現代刑務所内にて折々に書き起こせるよう、回答は録音された。

トラック01

1997年：なぜ、君はこの日付からこの証言を始めることにしたのか？ その当時に何が起こったのか、1997年とは何なのか？ また、なぜ、その年は現代アルバニアの歴史にこれほど深く刻み込まれたのだろうか？ アルバニアで実際には何が起こったのか？ そして、君個人としては何を覚えているのか？ 多くの歴史家はおそらく、政権崩壊の時期、1990年代初頭においてアルバニア現代史を開始させるであろう。君は、なぜ、後年を選択するのだ？

僕は1980年生まれだが、当然ながら僕の記憶に刻まれている'90年代の主要なエピソードは、共産主義政権の崩壊に関連している[1]。これらの記憶は、僕にとっては、君が言うところの歴史的

---

1 読者諸氏に、1985年エンヴェル・ホッジャ死去（Enver Hoxha）以降のアルバニアでの政治的沿革について概括的な参照枠を提供するために記す。 1991年の共産主義体制終結後、ホッジャの後継者ラミズ・アリア（Ramiz Alia）の下、アルバニアは大統領制共和国に変貌を遂げる。1997年に国家を無政府状態に陥れたネズミ講[訳注：伊語ではピラミッド型金融制度と呼ばれる]危機による破綻にいたるまでは、首相

事象と並行して起こった出来事に関連したイメージとして目に浮かんでくる。　エンヴェル・ホッジャの壮麗な黄金像がティラナ(Tirana)のスカンデルベグ広場(sheshi Skënderbeu)でデモ隊によって破壊された時を、　とてもよく覚えている。　それと時を同じくして、　街の大通りで母と僕が郊外の自宅に帰るための安全な道筋を見付けようとしていた矢先に、　戦車が行く手を阻んだので、　そのことを覚えている。　戦車の天辺にいた兵士は機関銃を握りしめていた：　砲塔はある角度で停止するまでゆっくりと回転し、　その砲身はまさに僕らに向いており、　僕らは身をすくめ石のように棒立ちになった。

　国外へ脱出しようと、　諸外国大使館の高々とした塀をよじ登っていた人々の激烈で劇的な興奮を映し出していたテレビの画像を、　非常によく覚えている。　僕はこのテーマに関する両親の議論を覚えている：　僕らも国を離れるべきだったのか否か？　僕の父は軍隊に所属していたので、　立てた宣誓に違反することはできないと言った。　このため、　僕らは国を去らなかった。　大衆が鉄の船を身一つで、　自らの素肌で覆い尽くした時にも、　同じ論議が僕らの家庭内で再提起された。

アレクサンダー・メクシ(Aleksandër Meksi)とともに、　民主党党首サリ・ベリシャ(Sali Berisha)が複数回に渡る大統領任期を務め、　政権を掌握。　その後の総選挙で、　アルバニアは議会制共和国となり、　首相ファトス・ナノ(Fatos Nano)率いる社会党が台頭、　1998年にはパンデリ・マイコ(Pandeli Majko)が首相に就任。　社会主義勢力の衰退に伴い、　他の政治的組織が発足し　2005年にはサリ・ベリシャが権力の座に返り咲く。2013年の選挙では「欧州アルバニアのための同盟」における「統合のための社会主義運動(SMI)[訳注：伊語原文ではLSI]」に連携した野党社会党が勝利を収め、　社会党党首エディ・ラマ(Edi Rama)が首相に就任、　現職を務める。

　測深機を近年の歴史の深淵に投げ込んだなら、僕の思春期前の記憶に刻み込まれた最もショッキングなイメージにすぐにも拘泥するだろう。それは1992年のことだ。国の南部、フィエル（Fier）の地での兄弟二人の公開絞首刑。事件は僕の12歳の誕生日の翌日、6月25日に発生したため、よく覚えている。その執行に関して紛糾していたのは、体制交代直後に執行されたということであり、改変前の国家司法組織とされていた前政権により何とかして課された「最後の」死刑であった。だが、ことさら重要なのは、それが新しい民主主義制度の最初の死刑判決であったことだ。これは、未来、この未来にとって、国の進歩そして実際1997年にピークに達した民主主義制度の発展にとって、非常に意義深い兆候だった（未だにそうである）と思う。

　ジャン・ジュネについての逸話があるのだが、それは僕の同国人の国外脱出に関するイメージにまたもや関連づくものだ。その画像は、現代美術デバティクセンターの不可欠なパートである「Archive of Desertion」に含まれている[2]。1990年7月13日、ドゥラス（Durrës）の港を出航した最初の船は、ドイツ及びイタリア大使館に避難していた4,000人以上のアルバニア人を載せて、

2　2003年にアルバニアの若手アーティストや知識人によって設立された「DebatikCenter of Contemporary Art(現代美術デバティクセンター)」は、自らが掲げる目的の一つとして、芸術機関の包含と排除のメカニズムについて疑問を呈する。同年、第2回ティラナ・ビエンナーレのオープニングでのパフォーマンスでデビューを飾った(https://debatikcenter.net/index)。現在の構成では、現代美術デバティクセンターは大学の研究員、活動家、建築家、芸術家、架空及び実在のグループ、批評家、キュレーター、ジャーナリスト、翻訳者などの集団であり、これらの実践に光を当てるだけでなく、代替となる未来と「現状」への抵抗戦略を想像するのに必要なツールの提供にも努めている。

ブリンディジ（Brindisi）に到着した。その日、重要な瞬間が記されたのだが、それは、その場にいたメディアによってではなく、その同じ船上に居合わせた、ロシアブランドのカメラを持参していた一人の移民によって記録された。その写真は、メディア機構によって流布されているものとは大きく異なる。アルバニア人について構築されたナレーション［訳注：語られる話］、主としてメディアの常套句に基づいた叙述を、何らかの形で丹念に作り込もうとすると同時に忌避しようとするイメージだ。

　このリヴァース・ショットでは、異国の地に達したばかりの船艇の別角度からの眺望、撮影者である彼自身が反対岸に到達し、その地に踏み入らんとする直前に、メディアによって不朽にされた瞬間を我々は目にする。写真家や外国人カメラマン達のレンズの間を前進する半裸の躯体は、我々の近年の歴史における重要な瞬間を記録している。その身体は歴史のレンズを通り抜けようとしており、極めて正確な瞬間に捉えられた。身体は歴史に足を踏み入れているようであり、同時にそれから逃げ出そうとしているように見える。この画像において、脱出要因を増幅する要素、つまり我が国の現代の状態の重要な箇所は、投錨された船である。船は鏡像であり、過去を反映していると同時に未来を、我々に示している存在である。それは、僕の作品にもよく現れる、絶え間ない逃亡の状態を強調している。

　僕の祖国は独自の創造力を有しており、いつだって、時の中に穴を穿ち、省略や併発する出来事を創り出す奇妙なナレーションの蒐集家の如きものだった。常に公式のナラティヴ［訳注：語り］とはかけ離れたパラレル・ストーリーを構築する能力を持った、未だ発見されていない奇妙なアーカイブ群を有する「コレクター」国家。

　例えば、現代史上、疑いようのない人物、科学者や革命家、重要な国家元首達が、謎に包まれた状況でごく短期間アルバニアを訪問したと言われている。そのうちの幾つかは、ナレーションのみが残っており、エルネスト・チェ・ゲバラの実証されていない訪問のように、アルバニアの地に実在する証拠はなく、文書も写真もないが、証人の話のみが存在する。その他の場合には、若き日のヤセル・アラファトの事例のように書類が存在する。彼は国内で過ごしており、当然ながら共産主義体制下でのことだった。これらの訪問は文書化されていてもいなくても、我々のアイデンティティの構築に根付いているが、そのアイデンティティはまだ未完成のままだ：これは先程述べた、ジャン・ジュネの事例でもある。

　後の天才たる彼の犯罪事始めは意義深い徴候だが、この国の発展に意味深長に関係は「ない」。僕にとっては、ドゥラスから出航しブリンディジに上陸する半裸の躯体のイメージが、ジャン・ジュネの1936年7月にアルバニアに向けて出立した旅と、奇妙な二義的繋がりを持っている。ファシスト達が国に侵攻する3年前、別の船がこの度は反対方向に、ブリンディジから出発しアドリア海を渡って、ドゥラスに錨を下ろした。その船上に、年若きジュネが乗り合わせていた。彼は軍隊から脱走したばかりで、偽名で取得したパスポートで旅をしていた。彼の思惑は、より冒険に満ちたはずの他の地へ向かう中継地点として、アルバニアを使うことだった。アルバニアの地に降り立った後、彼はドゥラスで数日間過ごし、そこで家畜を盗んだとも言われている。車の都合を付け、ドゥラスから首都ティラナに到着した。メインの広場であるスカンデルベグ広場では、その怪しげな風貌のため憲兵の目に留まり、パスポートを調べると偽物だと気付かれた。そのため、パスポートの記載でいうところの「ゲイエッティ氏」は、さらなる確認のため憲兵詰所に連行された後、国外退去に24時間の猶予が与えられた。さもなければ逮捕されるところであった。南下してギリシャのケルキラ島到達を試みたが失敗し、北に向かい、ユーゴスラビアを目指した。その地で彼はスパイ容疑をかけられ、逮捕・投獄された。さらに、彼の物語は続く…

　僕は、この国のアイデンティティの別の土壌を構成する、これらの二義的な繋がり、これらのイメージ、これらの（探し求められた）隠喩に非常に興味を持っており、今後も持ち続けるだろう。

　1990年と1997年の主な違いは、1990年には我々は過去からのある種の象徴的分離を被ったのに対し、変化の歴史的ピークを印した1997年の出来事は、新自由主義への道を「永劫に」固めたということである。この全てに、万人の側から、ある種の拒否、抵抗があったことを付け加えなければならない。何らかの方法で、1997年に我々は未来を呑み込む前に吐き出そうとしていた。

　1997年の歴史的事象は、事象の問題性の様々なレベルの連立と、それに巻き込まれた主体が各々の事実の意味を、個別にまたは全体として調査及び理解する難しさに関与している。その年は、独自性と固有の能力を持っていたし、今なお持っている。それは何らかの形で時間をブロックし、抗い、消去する能力だ。その年について、アナス・ホリビリス（Annus horribilis [訳注：(ラテン語)おぞましき年]）、「完全破壊の年」「呪い年」「ピラミッド年」「詐欺の年」「忘れ難き年」あるいは「忘却すべき年」「衝撃の年」など、多くの定義が付与された。誇張されて愚かにも「原爆なしでのヒロシマ」という名や、シンプルに、ナインティーン・ナインティセブン（Nineteen Ninety Seven）という呼び名まで。これらの決まり文句は、主にメディア、地元及び諸外国の政治家、非政府組織、国内に潜入した宗教活動家や暗躍する強力な世界的組織の発現により伝播された。その年の混乱と衝撃は、その前後に引き起こされた状況のように、他国で実施された経済ショック療法と同様の、特別に組織化された計画の影響だったと思う。

1970年代、ジェフリー・サックスとデヴィッド・リプトンは、国の社会主義経済を市場経済に転換することを目的とした、ミルトン・フリードマンのチリに対する計画を一夜にして策定した。アルバニアの場合、緊急性はそこまで高くなかったと思う：我が国のためだけでなく、バルカン諸国、とりわけ'90年代初期から既に戦争に巻き込まれていた地域のためには、様々なレベルでよく考え抜かれた地理戦略的な計画を調整するのに多くの時間があった。今日、一般的な確信によれば、その計画はアメリカ人の手によるものであり、1992年初頭に国内で運用を開始したピラミッド・スキーム[3] の導入によっても発展し始めたというものだ。その後1996–1997年の2ヶ年に爆発的状況となり、コソボ紛争とともに1999年に続いた。

その時期に、ほとんどのアルバニア人は職を失った。主たる生産活動は終焉を迎え、産業は崩壊した。工場は閉鎖され、機械設備はスクラップとして売却された：多くの企業は、取るに

3　「ピラミッド・スキーム」という用語は、マーケティング・モデルまたは投資モデルを指す。このモデルでは、いわゆるネズミ講[伊語：聖アントニオの連鎖]の運用と同様、各投資家の儲けは他の出資者を募ることに直結している。後述で言及される「ポンジ・スキーム[Ponzi伊語発音：ポンツィ]」は、実際にはこのモデルの不正バージョンであり、その収益は、生産製造や金融活動の収益からではなく、新規投資家によって支払われた出資金からのみ派生する。

足らない金額で民営化された。当時、人々は貯蓄を全てポンジ・スキームに預け、家を売却した。人口の大部分は、ピラミッド・スキームで生み出された金銭と海外及び移民からの援助金によって生計を立てていた。人々は政府によって、この巨大なマネーロンダリング・マシーンに「クリーンな」身銭を注ぎ込むよう、繰り返し奨励されてきたが、ある日のこと、そのマシーンは弾け飛んだのだ。言われた通り、経済は「緊急治療室に担ぎ込まれて」そこで崩壊した：あの日が到来し、アルバニア国民の貯蓄は永遠に消滅した。特別法により、議会はピラミッド企業の活動を禁じ、彼らの協力者の一部を逮捕したが、その資産を凍結はしなかった。人々は自らの金銭の返還を求めて抗議し始めた。返還は全ての政党によって広く公約されたが、決して実現することはなかった。残ったものはといえば、抗議行動の勃発に始まり、弾薬庫が空になり、世に言う無政府状態と国家に対する反乱の出現にいたるまで、既に書かれた台本のように見えた。ピラミッド詐欺の側に組みしていた民主党の腐敗政権は、抗議を鎮圧しようとしている最中に崩壊した。この国は、当時の反対派に支持された犯罪グループの手中にあり、後に極めて短期間で政権を掌握した。綿密な統計は未だに存在しないが、1997年の出来事の間に3,000人以上の民間人と360人の警察官が殺されたと試算されている。5,000人の民間人が負傷し、ピラミッド・スキームで12億米ドルが蕩尽された。

　当時、我々はCNN効果を体験していた。大抵、外国のチャンネルを視聴し、外国のラジオ局を聴いていた。統制されていた我々の放送局よりも、信憑性が高いと思われていたからだ。'90年代初頭の僕の記憶は遥かに鮮明であるのに比べ、1997年については、極僅かの、ぼんやりとしたエピソードしか覚えていない。僕にとって、依然として深遠なるブラックホールのようなものである。君の質問に答えるならば、これが1997年の事象に、僕がこれほどまでに興味を抱いているもう一つの側面である。僕の心に焼き付いているイメージは、ほぼ丸一年に及ぶ暴力的な出来事の数々に比べると極僅かだ：その時期の僕の経験は何らかの方法で凍結され隠蔽されている。それらは僕の頭に閃くのだ、無秩序な細切れフィルムのフレーム内に、連続的に反復する冴えた音に伴われて。ある空間の内部に身を置くようなものだ。そこでは、あの時代のとあるイメージを伴って、明瞭な音が永続的に再現される。だが – 奇妙なことに – 必ずしも1997年のアルバニアのとあるイメージではなく、複数の他のイメージ、パラレル・ストーリーの投影なのだ。僕が思うに「電気ショックの年」（と僕は呼んでいる）は、我々が糧にした、あらゆる種類の支離滅裂なイメージや文献・資料を大量に生成したとはいえ、イメージよりも音に関連している。

　これは僕らが子供の頃にやっていたことを思い出させる。1990年よりも以前、いやそのすぐ後も、同世代の大多数の者と同様に、僕はカセットプレイヤーを常用していた。テープのダビングが出来なかったので、幾つもカセットがない場合には、僕らが所持していた唯一のカセットを繰り返し再生した。録音の中で僕らが最も気に入っていた箇所を何度も聴くためや、歌詞やリフレインの言葉を聴き取ろうとして、再生と巻戻しのボタンを押していた。往々にしてテープがレコーダーの中で詰まることがあり、僕らは内部メカニズムからそれを取り出さなくてはならなかった。その後、また再生するためにテープを巻き直して修正を試みたが、「Play」ボタンを押した時には、無音のポーズやひずみの生じた一節が聞こえることがあった。何らかの方法により、楽曲の内部で前後の音の間に生成したこれらの無音の間（ま）は、もはや失われた「オリジナル」の一節の記憶を強固にしていた。そして旋律とひずんだ言葉は、僕らにとって、より際立って明確になっていたのだった。オリジナルの音を強固にする力があるが、何か異なるものを生み出すためにその音を除去することも可能な、この無音の空白。その空白を、1997年に関して突き止めようと未だ僕は試みているのだ。

　1997年、何ヶ月もの間、我々のほとんどが、国内のありとあらゆる都市や村で同一の音を聞いた。同一の音が反響し、テレビとラジオから流れ出た。音というのは記憶するための、忘却するという我々の意志に反して使われるための、適切な鍵なのだと思う。実に恐ろしいと同時に勇気づけられるのは、人々の精神の中には、何が起こったのかについての沈黙の調和のような、共通の理解があることだ。だが（まだ）明確な集団理解、即ち、直近の過去の歴史的認識ではない。この「沈黙」は侵犯すべき空間となってしまった。そこでは、記憶は粉砕される傾向にある。言わば、国際通貨基金の公式の事実譚に置き換えられ、腐敗したメディアの画像やプロパガンダ文書に追い払われるのだ。記憶は、我らが守護天使であり神の右の御手であるアメリカ合衆国の利益や、我々の新自由主義政府のプロパガンダ、特定政党の民族主義的思想、近年の政治史の組織体である諸国の特定の政策によって、駆逐されてしまう。記憶は時間によっても操作されるが、僕が壊滅的だと思うのは、政治によって教唆された大衆が、忘却に陥りつつあることだ。そうすることで政治家階級は、民衆を操られるがままの木偶の群れと化す。オーケストラのお偉い指揮者様が口述した、その台本を演じるお偉い腹話術師殿の手の内の、操り人形へと変換することができるのだ。この眺望には、芸術家、政治活動に従事していた映画監督、調査ドキュメンタリー制作者の声が完全に欠落している。

今日と1997年。イタリアと西側のメディアは、アルバニア国家が1997年に経験した無政府状態に至らしめた真の原因については、相対的に見て、ほとんど報道していなかった。密入国の不法移民、犯罪などの話題のみ取り上げていた。多くの人々が、イタリアでは現在でも、1997年の危機は共産主義政権の悪政によるものであったと考えているが、我々は、非常事態と暴動の責任は共産主義の過去とはあまり関連がなく、むしろ「民主的」な性質の経済モデルの爆発的普及に関していたことを知っている。共産主義的経済から現在の経験への移行について話してもらえるだろうか？ この移行を君ならどのように定義する？ 何が経済的に変わったのか？ 何が起きたのだ？

世界のメディアは1997年の出来事を大々的に報道した。彼らは独自のバージョンを流布した：主として結論は前政権の悪政に言及し、常に独裁政権を非難。明るみに出ておらず、まだ解明しなければならない異なるナレーションについては、ほとんど言及していない。先述のように、提案されたと言うより、むしろ御仕着せの、現時点でも絶頂を極めるモデルは新自由主義であるが、実際にそれが分析されたことはかつてない。1997年を象徴的な状況として、若干、1990年のように扱おうとする向きがあるが、僕の意見ではそうではない。また、今日のシステムを崇め奉るために、過去のシステムを悪魔呼ばわりしようとする。これは反省すべき無邪気なアプローチだ。つい最近になって初めて、近年の政治経済での発展に伴い、 ベールが剥ぎ取られつつある。 今日の政治・経済的発展に関連して、 まさにその当時アルバニアで確立された経済モデルを見直しているのだ。 主として国内外の若手研究者達が真摯に取り組んでいるのだが、 当時の複数のモデルについて関連付けがなされ、 詳細な分析が行われるようになってきている。

　エドワード・サイードは自著『文化と帝国主義』[4] に「20世紀末期の独立に対しての新しい電子媒体の脅威は、 植民地主義そのものよりも深刻である可能性がある[…]。 新しいメディアは、 これまでの西洋のテクノロジーのいかなる顕示よりも、 ”受容的な”文化に深く浸透する力を有している。 」と書いている。

　1990年代以降、 我々は目新しいものの一大「受容体」となった: それはひとえに、 ブルガリア・韓国・ドイツ・イタリアそしてトルコ製の家電製品の爆発的普及から始まった。 新しいカラーモニターが各戸に鎮座し、 衛星放送のパラボラアンテナが各建物のバルコニーや窓に咲き誇った。 テレビ映像へのこの渇望、 永続的で恒常的なその現実に対する熱望は、 新しいエレクトロニクスへの希求とともに、 かつてないほどに今日も存在し続けている。

　1997年に生まれて始めてのコンピュータを入手した。 それはPower Macintosh 8500 だった。 当時、 僕はそれをどう扱えばいいのか分からなかった。 僕らの両親は、 コンピュータに取り組んで 使いこなすよう、 僕と姉に仕向けたが、 どのように役立てたも

4　Edward W. Said, Culture and Imperialism (New York: Alfred A. Knopf, 1993) [訳注: 日本語版は、 みすず書房より『文化と帝国主義』(エドワード・W・サイード著、 大橋洋一訳、 1998年: 第1巻、 2001年: 第2巻)として出版。 本文では伊語原文をもとに訳している。]

のか僕には皆目見当がつかなかった。当時の僕の初期のビデオでは、コンピュータは電源が入っていたりいなかったりで、ほとんどの場合、フレームの奥の方にあって、その当時に作った短いエチュード(études)の端役に過ぎなかった。

　僕が当時住んでいたのは、最大の弾薬庫の一つ、シュコラ・エ・バシュクァル(Shkolla e Bashkuar「統一学校」の意)、アラファトが訪問し訓練も受けた、軍でも最重要とされる訓練センターの近くだった。僕はその総合施設を熟知していた。そこは、僕達が軍事演習を行うために頻繁に集まり、訓練をする兵士達を見ていた場所だった。武器庫が解体された時、僕の隣人や友人のほとんどは武装するためにそこに駆け付けた。僕は行かなかった。僕は武器を取ることに興味がなかった。父は銃を所有していたので、銃器が何であるかを僕は正確に知っていた。僕の家のバルコニーから、僕の友人達が大量の軍需品を運びながら、家の狭い通りを下っているのを見た。何人かは、かの有名なロシア製の12.7×108 mm弾丸の箱だけを略奪していた。他の地区から来た別の者達は、ライフルと機関銃の部品だけを運んでいた。これらの武器を機能させるためには、人々の間の協力が必要だった：まず武器に対する弾薬の交換が始まり、売買行為が続いた。短期間のうちに皆が武装していた。あっと言う間に、銃器は家庭用電化製品よりも広範に行き渡り、より重要になった。

　無意識のうちに生まれた反乱、怒り、興奮は、非常に異なる何かに対してだったのだと思う。僕が保つあの記憶の微細な断片の中、あるいは僕が見たあの幾千もの光景の中には「純粋な」正真正銘の要素が存在している。それは一般的な作り込まれたナラティヴからはこぼれ落ち、さらに興味深く大いに異なった「ある」革命の思想に、より一層関連性がある。僕はしばしば、皆が銃口を向けたこの敵は誰だったのかと自問することがある。 その最も適切な解答は、 資本主義そのもの、 現実であり、 もはや暴かれた未来だったのだろう。

　1997年に関しては様々なナレーションがあるが、 最も普及しているのは国際通貨基金［訳注：International Monetary Fund, 略称 IMF］によって用意されたものだ。 クリストファー・ジャーヴィスの報告書[5] は、 政権崩壊直後に始まった主要な経済的時事から1997年までを再構築している。 この報告書によると、 また1997年以降発表の複数の報告書にもよると、 本題は、 経済危機は何をさておき金融市場の熟知不足によりもたらされた、 ということである。 形式だけの金融システムとほぼ全ての形態の私有財産を除外していた経済を有する国、 その国の市場へのアクセス不能を引用しながら、 ジャーヴィスは論を続ける。 報告書は、 共産主義体制の崩壊後、 同国で営業していた三つの銀行は民間部門に応じるに足らなかった、 と断言する。 民間部門は著しい成功を収めて成長しつつあり、 非公式な融資会社の台頭を助長した、 と。 1992年以降これらの融資会社は皆、 ピラミッド・スキームに変貌し始めた。 彼らは政府の全面的な支持を得て、 多数の国会議員だけでなく政党を、 また明らかにされているように、 これらのスキームによって私腹を肥やした政府高官達を「後援する」ことにも加担した。 IMFによると、 政府は、 ピラミッド・スキームが勃興する最中 – 崩壊過程でも – その危機の受動的な傍観者であった。 その

5　Christopher Jarvis, "The Rise and Fall of Albania's Pyra-mid Schemes," Finance and Development 37, no. 1 (2000). オンラインで閲覧可能：www.imf.org/external/pubs/ft/fandd/2000/03/jarvis.htm　［訳注：後続の引用は伊語原文をもとに訳している。］

バブルのエスカレートは経済的には壊滅的なものだったが、IMFによれば短期的であり、言うなれば統制されていた。それにひきかえ、市民の暴動は社会に長期的な影響を及ぼし、未だに尾を引いていると言える。

　これらの年は地元の犯罪組織や外国マフィアにとっては、まさに濡れ手に粟だった。ピラミッド・スキーム内で汚れた金を還流させ、不法移民を統治し、後には武器・麻薬密売を支配した。ピラミッド・スキームの利子が毎月30％まで増加し始めた時に、崩壊の危機迫るという警鐘が鳴った。1996年のスキーム崩壊は、ジャーヴィスによって、なかなか生彩に富んだ表現で描写されている：「アルバニア人はネズミ講に投資するため家屋を売却し、農夫は家畜を手放した。その当時の風潮は、市民の一人によって生々しく捉えられた。日く、1996年の秋、ティラナは屠殺場のような臭気と騒音がしていた。ピラミッド・スキームにつぎ込むため、農民が手持ちの家畜を売り払いに市場へと曳き連れていたから」。

　先に述べたように、報告書では地政学的側面に関する何か、その何かが、意識的に蚊帳の外に置かれた、という印象を僕は持っている。アルバニアは、戦乱地域の安定要因と常に考えられてきた。弾圧や大量虐殺、宗教的憎悪などの悲劇的な出来事によって、しばしば苦汁を飲まされてきた。その地域を統制し平穏を保ちつつ発展拡大を目的とした、当時の様々な地政学的な政略、それらは現在でもバルカン諸国で活発な状態なのだが、それらを念頭に置くと、きっかりとした瞬間に遠隔操作で爆発する準備万端のより広大なチェス盤に、それを補完する一部分として1997年の出来事を我々は結び付けずにはいられない。

　1997年の出来事が未来に及ぼし得た社会的影響は「Kronikë '97」(クロニック・ノントディエット・シュタットゥ)という題

名の、 未完に終わった並外れた映画素材の道標となった。 この作品素材は、 共産主義政権時代に旧Kinostudio（キノストゥディオ）で働いていた人々のグループによって制作された。 これはひとえに、 体制側の数多くの映画作品を撮影したカメラマンと、 過去にKinostudio制作作品を数多く指揮した監督のおかげであった。 同監督は1994年のジャンニ・アメリオの長編作品『Lamerica（ラメリカ）』にも携わっていた。 国立映画資料館に保存された、 8500メートルにも及ぶ35mmフィルムなのだが、 地元や外国のメディア及び記者とはまったく違った何かを捉えていた。 これまでとは異なる、 だが経済的「ショック療法」戦略に深く相関する起因を求めて、 このグループは数ヶ月に渡る撮影旅行を完遂。 素朴派の手法で撮影されたこの資料には、 様々なロケ先でグループが行った収録が含まれる。 彼らが被ったショックの深度と、 発生した出来事が社会の将来に及ぼし得た影響を調査するため、 精神病院で医師へのインタビューを行い、 入院患者を撮影した。 その後、 動物が受けたストレスの度合いを理解しようと、 檻に入れられた動物達を撮影しに動物園へと向かったり、 警察犬学校に行き、 訓練士に同じ質問をしたりした。 彼らは、 聾唖者施設や視覚障碍者施設、 考古学公園、 破壊された美術館・博物館、 刑務所、 地元の墓地や、 第一次・第二次世界大戦戦没者の外国人墓地で調査を続けた。 31幕からなるこの映画は、 編集されたことはなく未完作品のままだ。 この資料は、 1997年の日付の、 この我が国で署名された「レディメイド（ready-made）」第1号である。 ある種の複雑な調査に取り組もうとした、 おそらく唯一の素材であり、 そして、 歪んだ教唆に満ち満ちた、 特にメディアによって提案されたイメージ描写のさらに先へ踏み込んで、 異なる証言を探した試みである。

　「空気の奥底は黒い。」

　僕は1998年10月にアルバニアを去り、10年以上イタリアに在住した。僕はイタリアを、別天地に移住するための可能性と必要書類を僕に与えることができる、通過点の港だと常に考えてきた。僕達は留学生だったのだが、権利を持たない移民あるいは尊厳のない外国人労働者として暴力的に扱われた。空気中に息衝いていたこの暴力は、とりわけ警察で具体化された。警察は非常に人種差別的で、いわゆるヨーロッパの規則、即ち武力と暴力の行使を叩き込むことに熱心だった。

　僕の同胞の多くが、その社会に変節し隠れていたという事実は、許しがたいが理解はできる。1997年の最も悲劇的な出来事の一つに関して、苛立ちを覚えるエピソードを記憶している。僕がフィレンツェ（Firenze）に到着してからわずか1ヶ月後、僕の親しい友人の叔父を訪ねた。彼は長年その地に住んでいたが、自分自身や妻、年若い息子のための滞在許可証などの書類を一切持っていなかった。1997年3月28日に、イタリア海軍のコルヴェット軍艦シビッラ号（Sibilla）に衝突されオトラント海峡に沈没し、女性と子供を含む81人の犠牲者と数十人が行方不明になった船、カトル・イ・ラドゥス号（Katër i Radës）について、僕達は話題にしていた。彼の妻は、イタリア人がアルバニア人の船を沈めたと言った。その場にはアパートの所有者であるイタリア人も居合わせていた。すると彼女の夫は憤懣をぶちまけ、彼女に言明を訂正するように言い付け、これらの嘘を誰にも、彼女自身にも決して繰り返さないよう命じた。それどころか、彼はイタリアのメディアの説を言及しなければならなかった。それによると、この事件は避けようのなかった不運で、即ち「正当化された」事故であった。アパートの所有者も支持したのと同じナレーションだ。僕は女性の方に同意していたので、自分の意見を述べようとした。こうして、僕はそのアパートには招かれざる客となったことを理解した。この一般的な態度は存続し、反駁されるべきであるのに、イタリアに住むアルバニア人現代アーティスト達によってすらも異を唱えられることはなかった。我が民族の暗黙のタブーのままだ。

「イタリアでは、アルバニア人はまず始めに未来の移民である」とスーザン・ソンタグは「ニューヨーク・タイムズ」紙に掲載された記事で書いたが、1999年のコソボ紛争について語るためにバーリ（Bari）に在住していた。この発言はかなり的を射ていると僕は思う。この女性作家は南イタリアに長く滞在し、その10年間で彼女が好んだ映画の一つが『Lamerica』だった。1998年の春、彼女は1997年の惨事から再浮上したばかりのアルバニアを訪れた。彼女の訪問を企画し、同行していた当時のアルバニアのソロス財団の理事が、アルバニアの風景や人々を観察することで何を思ったかと彼女に尋ねると、彼女は「20年後にこの場所がどうなっているかを考えています…」と率直に答えた。そして「変えるのは難しいでしょう」と付け加えた。

我々は、その訪問からちょうど20年が経過した現在も、同じ政治家階級を相手にしている。政治家達には、上辺を取り繕い、ハードディスクを消去し、新章を上書きすることで、最初から、ゼロからやり直したいという、この不条理な欲求が常にある。

先程述べたように、1990年代に始まった新自由主義の拡大は、衝撃の最大力であるピークを1997年に迎えた。この政策 – 何よりも時事問題に僕は言及している – は、この国を完全に食い潰している。全ての公共財の民営化、競争の欠如、憲法に違反する寡頭政治家達の濫用のために可決された特別国会法、汚職、そして何より、贅沢三昧の現政府の支出による債務増加。犯罪組織とマフィアは政府とともに権力の座に着き、この国は国際的な麻薬ビジネスの重要な担い手に成り果てた。マフィアとアルバニア政府の間には、この政府以前にも常に繋がりがあったが、決してこれほどまでに公然としてではなかった。今日、マフィアはバルカン諸国を東西の架け橋として利用している。アルバニアはヨーロッパのゴミを埋める場所、アフガニスタンやラテンアメリカからヨーロッパの中心部に向けて送り込まれるコカインの中継地となり、同国自体が大麻の大規模生産国になった：これらのプランテーションの一部が、ISIS（過激派組織IS=イスラミック・ステート）などの原理主義組織の資金源になっているのではないかという疑いがある。

　2013年に政権を握る前、社会主義者達は、共産主義崩壊以来この国が目にしたうちで最も右翼の政府を形成し、その象徴に「ルネサンス」を掲げ、まさに1997年の英国総選挙の勝者であるトニー・ブレアの新生労働党（New Labour）からそのアイディアとプログラムを盗用した。この単語はブレアと新生労働党のペテンに似つかわしい。19世紀から1912年の［訳注：オスマン帝国からの］独立宣言にかけての当国史の期間を指す、リリンディア・コンブターレ（Rilindja Kombëtare）あるいはアルバニア・ルネサンスとして知られる［訳注：民族意識高揚を目的とした］我々の歴史的運動に、結び付けたいのであろうが。短期間で「復興を遂げた」社会主義者達は、我々の現代史において最大級の如何様師である実体を曝した。彼らの指導者エディ・ラマをアディダスやコカ・コーラのような、一種の国家的ブランドに仕立て上げることで、彼らは腐敗と犯罪の巨大機構の正体を現した：そして、先に述べた我々の国外脱出への姿勢は大きく勢いを増した。欧州のどこか他の国でのより良い生活を求めて、 この立法府の間に約50万人が祖国を後にした。

《NEVER》[6] について。 イデオロギー、 経済： おそらく、 これらが二つの異なるタイプの「ナレーション」なのだろうか？ 君ならイデオロギーを、 そして経済をどのように定義する？ 芸術的観点から、 イデオロギーをどのように探究し、 どのように取り組んでいるのか？ そして経済については？ 君の作品は概して、 現代の政治的ナレーションのイデオロギー的上部構造、 及び、 経済構造の両方を探究することを目的としているように私には思われる。 とりわけ、 君のビデオ作品《NEVER》 を念頭に置いている。 それについて詳しく話してもらえるだろうか？ 「制作手法」の観点からも《NEVER》 について話してほしい。 君は、 現代美術において長い伝統を持つ道具としての言葉を用いた。 このビデオ作品は、 具体詩とコンセプチュアル・ライティングの偉大な一例と見做すことが可能だろうか？

6　ビデオ作品《NEVER》(2012年、 22分、 モノクロ及びカラー) は、《It Wears as It Grows》(2011年)及び《Recapitulation》(2011年)とともに、 2015年のヴェネツィア・ビエンナーレでルラーイが発表した《Albanian Trilogy: A Series of Devious Stratagems》の一部である。 参照： Armando Lulaj, Albanian Trilogy: A Series of Devious Stratagems, ed. M. Scotini(Berlin, Sternberg Press, 2015). [訳注： 展示作品の3冊組カタログ]

Fakt(アルバニア語)=Fact(英語)/Fucked(英語)=I shkërdhyer, të shkërdhyer(アルバニア語).

　英単語「Fucked(たぶらかされた、 呪われた、 台無しにされた)」の発音は/fʌkt/である。「Fucked」の音は、 アルバニア語の「Fakt(事実、 つまり真実の、 実在する何か: 英語では Fact)」の音と非常によく似ている。 それゆえ我々が「Fucked」と言うと、 アルバニア人は「Fakt」と理解する。 これは「事実上(In Fact)」我々は「たぶらかされて(Fucked)」いる、 と僕に言わしめる。

　我が国のような国の現代的認識は – 僕が何度も言及したように – 歴史的瞬間にその国を訪れた、 カメラマン達の写真報道によって作り出されたイメージを介しても広範囲に形成された。 そのようにして、 アルバニアとその民の現代史を象徴する紋切り型の手法を「でっち上げた」のだ。 この操作手法は '90年代初頭に確立され、 さらにメインストリームのレベルにも拡大する。 ベネトンの広告キャンペーンは、 私物化行為・独創性・形成の重要な一例である。 ベネトンが使用した写真は、 アルバニア人写真家によって撮影されたものだ: オリジナルはモノクロだが、 キャンペーンではレタッチされ、 全世界にカラーで発表された。 広告的表現法を用いた、 白黒からカラーへ、 現実から知覚への移行は、 精神性の形成が可能な概念的操作だった。 写真は超越する力、 極端な威力を有している。 その影響力は – 大企業やその他の強力なメディアで使われただけでなく – 過去には政党によっても利用されたが、 現在ほどではなかった: なぜなら今日では、 写真は政治の表現において新たな役割を担ったからだ。

　全ての芸術運動はいかに反抗的なものであっても、 常に社会運動あるいは政治的イデオロギーと繋がっている。 アルバニアの現代美術に対する世界的な関心は、 まさに1997年に生まれ、

そのわずか数年後にはヴェネツィア・ビエンナーレへの参加をもっ
て具現化したと言わなければならない。政治と、当時そして今現
在もこの国で活動する諸外国の民間財団が、極めて重要な支援
的役割を果たしてきた。この戦略について、僕が未だ賛同しな
いでいるものとは、不合理な虚偽の側面を晒す、作られたナレー
ションだ。この小国は、最も公然と露出し、要職に就く力を有し
た輩によって提示された、単一のナレーションのみを作り出して
はならなかった。芸術界の多くの人物がこのナレーションの構築
に参加し、そのためにアルバニアではかつてないほど芸術と政治
が密接になり、一種の理想郷的な成功を宣言した。僕は全く逆
だと思う。アルバニアの芸術システムの一部をなすが、公式版ナ
ラティヴの構築に協同しなかった、その他の少数の人々にしてみ
れば、この国では芸術と政治がかつてないほどに隔たっている。
対極にあると言えるだろう。その虚偽の構築には、世界の他の国
々で '60年代にも表出していた何か、今ではしかし芸術家にではな
なく政治に役立っている何かに関する、非常に興味深い側面があ
る。アーティスト達が国や社会の戦慄的な状況に立ち向かうため
には、シュールレアリスム的な「スキャンダル」群を生成し、相交わ
る必要がある。それらが総体において再生と革新の動きに命を与
えるのだ。ここアルバニアでは全く逆のことが起きる。堕落した国
家は、度を越した腐敗という形で「スキャンダル」(超現実主義者)
を自ら生み出し、今日の芸術と建築により煽られた「現代ルネサン
ス」という宣伝装置を通して、全てを濾過する。若いアーティスト
だけでなく、古参ですらも(成功を続けている二人のアーティストの
過去は曖昧なままだ)、政府の芸術の追随者あるいは使者となり
さがった。彼らはこの堕落国家の産物であるがゆえ、何も面白い
ものを生み出さない。この国は、組織化・フィルタリング・振興が

可能な芸術システムが存在しない国である：発展に極めて重要な要素、即ち独立した戦略が今なお欠けているのだ。

　《NEVER》を実現するため、僕は大勢の人々、政治関係者や政治家自身に会わなければならなかった。当時、山のある村、自治体、政府そのものは、三つの異なる組織の「所有物」であった。それらの組織は、国内で最重要な三つの異なる政党によって管理されていた。僕が必要としていた許可を与えるために、彼らが共同できるとは到底思えなかった。後に気付いたのだが、明らかにそのアイディアは、彼らにとって芸術としてよりも商業的なものとして興味深かったのだ。なぜなら、僕に許可を与える名目で、それぞれの党の宣伝に利益をもたらすよう彼らのグループを組織することを望み、ある者は自社の燃料を何トンも売り付けようとし、またある者は知人を雇いたがり、終にはイメージをも利用したがった。僕は脅迫じみて来た圧力を取り除こうとした。彼らの誰とも共同せず、単独で行動することを選択したのだ。完全に戦略を変更し、言わば「アンダーグラウンド(underground)」で作業して、いかなる許可も利用せず、許可なしで済ますことにした。運営するのは実に骨が折れた。

　僕の作戦では、ベラァトゥ市（Berat）のあらゆる場所から目視可能な、36,000平方メートルのスペースを占める巨大な文字表記を想定していた。1960年代に共産主義者によって大きな石で作られた、シュピラッグ山（Shpirag）の巨大な文字表記を変換するという象徴的な行為には、長い歴史がある。それはもともと僕の発想ではなく、1994年にその表記を破壊し、永久に排除しようとした民主党員の思いつきですらなかった。それは、共産主義の独裁者エンヴェル・ホッジャの名前の綴りを目にして、ベラァトゥ市長に別の文字を追加する提案をした、あるアメリカ人外交官の妙案だった。 外交官はコロラド州のデンバー（Denver）出身だったので、（僕の国で、 全ての外交官、 外国からの植民地支配者がそうするように）独創的で機知に富んでいると思い込み、 彼はその名前の前に「D」の文字を追加することを提案した。 当然ながら、 これが実現することはなかった。 1994年に民主党員だか右派だかが石を吹き飛ばし、 その石は山肌を転がり落ちて農民達の家屋を破壊したものの、 独裁者の名前を完全に消し去ることはできなかったからだ。 彼らはナパームを使用し、 山に火を放った。 この作戦で二人の兵士が重度の火傷を負った。

　当初のアイディアは、 1994年の山火事を制御された形で再現し、 燃料を使用して山の急斜面に文字の輪郭を焼き付けることだった。 僕達は小規模な実験を行った：惨憺たる結果。 それは典型的な軍事作戦であり、 僕には利用可能な手段が一つもなかった。 もう一つの課題は、 山が雑草で覆われていて、 蛇がウヨウヨしていたということだ。 そのような状況下では風向きの予測ができず、 火炎の制御は不可能だったため環境を損なう危険性があり、 その手のことは一切できなかった。 数ヶ月後、 僕は農民達に会いに山に戻った。 僕に手を貸すよう、 彼らを徹底的に納得させるには、 何ヶ月にも渡る交渉と説得を要した。 映像に登場する彼らの内の一人は、 表記が実現された1968年当時は少年で、 石を並べる作業に参加していた。 途轍もない挑戦、 それはラバを使って石を運んだ軍隊によって始められ、 若き共産主義者達 – 僕達の生き証人はその内の一人 – によって完成された壮大な作品。|若者達は、 軍隊によって配置された岩を石灰で白く塗り上げた。 老人は、 消失してしまった文字の位置を完璧に知っていた。 なぜなら1997年に、 アルバニア共産党の依頼で、 彼は他の

者達とともに草木を刈って、元の位置に文字を書き直し、それら
の文字を地面の上に石灰で塗ることに成功していたからだ。

　僕は農民達に、名前をそのままに書き直したいのではな
く、外交官の「D」及び共産主義者のアイディアの両方に対し
て、抜本的な変更を導入したいと説明した。僕は、最初の
二文字の配置の入れ替えを望んでおり、そうして「ENVER」は
《NEVER》になった。一つの行為。さらに別の行為。現実に根
差した事実の模倣は、だがしかし、この意味でのみ認識される
べきではなかった。付け足す、あるいは減らす／埋没する行為の
いずれにせよ、同じ名前を書き直したり、その意味を完全に変更
したりする全ての場合において、関連付けと類似性は避けられな
い。新たな単語はその内に否定を隠し持っていた。だが、誤って
何度も書かれたような、アイディアやイデオロギーの否定ではなか
った。この言葉は、この未来、この奪われた未来に、再浮上させ
られることを望まない過去からのメッセージを隠している。

　2012年にこのモノクロ画像を作成した時、僕に手を貸してく
れた皆に言った。この作品は、これほど誇張されんばかりに目
に留まるとしても、知覚されるようになるのは10年くらい経過して
やっとか、あるいは、おそらくそれが跡形もなくなり始める瞬間、
時間によって再び覆い隠される時だろう、と。僕が探究に関心を
寄せている過去には、拒否の兆候が明確にあるのだが、我々が
生きているのとは異なる未来の兆候もある。

　公営の資料館では、石の表記に関する極僅かの資料しか見付
からなかった。全てが消失したかに見えたが、僕はそれを全くも
って信じていない。それらは全て、これらの機関に勤務していた
人々や、書類や写真にアクセスし、私（わたくし）した者達の個人
のアーカイブに隠されている。国立映画資料館には、表記が登場

するカラーフィルムがほんの数秒間と、 独裁者の名前が撮影され
た、 こちらもカラーの写真が僅かに数枚ある。

　これらの年代記とドキュメンタリーは、 1960年代末から'70年
代初頭のものであり、 主に空軍に関連している。 資料館の同じフ
ォルダにある、 当時の他の年代記や報告書は、 主として共産主義
イデオロギー下での建国、 世界的な共産主義レジスタンス運動、
アルバニアでの共助と活動家の訓練、 ベトナム戦争、 パレスチナ
問題、 アフリカの恒久的破壊についてである。 それらには、 紛争
地帯における米国の惨憺たる政治・経済・軍事的存在が伴ってい
た。 これら全てのシークエンスは、 この未来に影響を与え[なか
っ]たと思われる「ループ」の内にいるが如く、 プロパガンダ装置を
介して繰り返されていた。 それらは、 分析されるべき[ではない]
集合的記憶の、 遥か遠[くではな]い過去の一部のように思われ
る。

　人間は思考によって自分自身を生み出し、 この過去を置き
換え得るのは別種の「ループ」だけだ。 我々が晒されているこの
新たな「ループ」は、 1960年代初頭にKUBARKマニュアル[7]で説
明・分析されたものと同等の、 ロボトミーを生成する一種の拷問
である。 明らかに今日は全てが遥かに複雑だ。 なぜなら、 真実
と現実を操作する手段は、 非常に異なり洗練されているからだ。
マルクスは記している:「手段は結果のように、 真理の一部であ
る。 同様に、 真理の探究は真でなければならない。 真の探究と

7　『Kubark Counterintelligence Interrogation(KUBARK対敵防諜
　　尋問)』は、 拷問などの極端なテクニックをも用いる尋問実行用の詳細
　　マニュアル。 1963年にCIA諜報員の便宜目的に開発され、 1997年に
　　周知されるようになった。

は説かれた真理であり、 その散在していた構成要素が結果において集結する[8]。 」

　当時のアルバニアにはゴダールもマルケルもいなかったが、 映画素材を絶対的真実として編集し、 独自のナレーションを生み出す、 映画撮影の国家機関だけはあった。 炎上し得るあの導火管を再び装填しなければならない。 この政治資料を再利用し、 再び編集し、 書き直し、 パレスチナやイスラエル、 イランについて、 さらにアフガニスタンとイラクにおけるアメリカの存在について、 我々が今日有する認識と関連付けなければならない。 自由と民主主義を語る悪辣な虚言を擁護した上で、 これらの戦争へ我々が参加したことは分析されるべき変遷である。 これまで想像不可能だった方法で情報を総合し、 国政の集合的記憶を書き換える必要がある。 過去はこれらの正当な理由を擁護してきたが、 現在はそれらを否定している。 現在は真実を殺めるもの、 殺人的イメージの作り手としての様相を呈している。

　《NEVER》には、 1990年代以降に根本的に変化・変容し始め、 経済及び監視の両方に関連する、 風景の概念についての別の側面もある。 まさに連続殺人犯の手の込んだ犯行のようだ。 殺人者は、 観客とともに創作したゲームの快楽のためだけに、 意図的に手掛かりを残す。 だがそのゲームの中では常に二歩先を行き、 ますます複雑な殺人を犯し続けるがゆえに、 決して捕まることはない。 ここで僕が話題にしているのは、 民間企業が環境

8　Georges Perec, Things: A Story of the Sixties / A Man Asleep, trans. David Bellos (London: Vintage, 2011) [訳注： 日本語版は、 白水社より『物の時代・小さなバイク』(弓削三男訳、 1978年)として出版、 復刻版『物の時代小さなバイク』が文遊社より2013年に刊行。 本文では伊語原文をもとに訳している。]

に及ぼした壊滅的な生態学的影響や、自然に与え続けている損害についてだけではない。ティラナ、ドゥラス、フィエル、ヴロール（Vlorë[伊語名ヴァローナValona]）などの大都市を変貌させた請負契約と汚職の癌についても話していないし、建設業界マフィアの計画を依怙贔屓するために「特別に」作られた法律についても話していない。僕は、凝視する眼差し、全方位から監視する視線について話しているのだ。これは現在、各個人に及ぶものであり、我々を自覚のある囚人、風景の均質な部分となす。足立正生氏[9]は「物質としての人間の存在さえも風景に変換されてしまった[…]。グローバルな均質化のため、また、今では全てが産業及び市場経済の目的の支配下にあるため、我々の考え方は変化に適応しようと摸索している。したがって、風景論の続編作品としては、映画は本物の人間を忍耐強く記録することから始めるべきである」と的確に述べている[10]。実際には、風景を眺め観察するのは我々だけではなく、風景そのものが、我々を観察しているのであり、意識を介して、我々を凍りつき静止した社会にしてしまう矛盾を実現するのだ。

　「Unable to Perform なぜなら Unfree to Perform。」

　状況を変えるには、我々がルールを書き換えなければならないと思う。もはや出来事を撮影したり記録したりするべきでは

9　足立正生（あだちまさお,1939〜福岡出身）は、パレスチナ民衆解放戦線への賛同で知られる日本の映画監督兼脚本家。日本赤軍メンバーだった彼はレバノン及び日本で投獄され、その後、国外居住権を剥奪された。

10　Empire and Revolution: Conversation Between Masao Adachi and Takashi Sakai［訳注：引用は伊語原文をもとに訳している。］(http://eigageijutsu.blogspot.com/2009/03/empire-and-revolution-conversation.html).

なく、 撮影されたドキュメントの変革のためには、 乱闘の中に身を投じ、 そこで我々の役割を果たして、 新しい集団性を作り出す必要があるのだ。 新たなる動画を制作するためには、 カメラを投げ捨て、 出来事を撮影せずに、 何か他のことをする。 カメラが知覚できる画像を超える、 別の事象を生成する。 我々は、今までとは違うタイプの証拠、 新奇のイメージを作成する必要があるのだ。 そのイメージは全く異なる方法で構築しなければならない。 これを実行するには、 秘密裡に地下で作業する必要がある。

　この数年間、 僕は地図を作成し、 山肌の名前が辿った具体的な変遷を記録した。 1968年の「ENVER」からの移行は、 2013年あるアーティストが《NEVER》の改変希望の表明をした暁には「FEVER(フィーヴァー： 熱狂)」(経済的な意味合いで、 と僕は思う)へと向かったが、 物理的には実現することなく、 概念上でのみに終わった。 他の者達は2018年に、 副詞「EVER(エヴァー：常に)」を山の上に残そうと「N」の文字を焼き払うことをシミュレートした。

ENVER	1968
DENVER	1993
	1994
ENVER	1997
NEVER	2012
FEVER	2013
EVER	2018
NEVER	2021

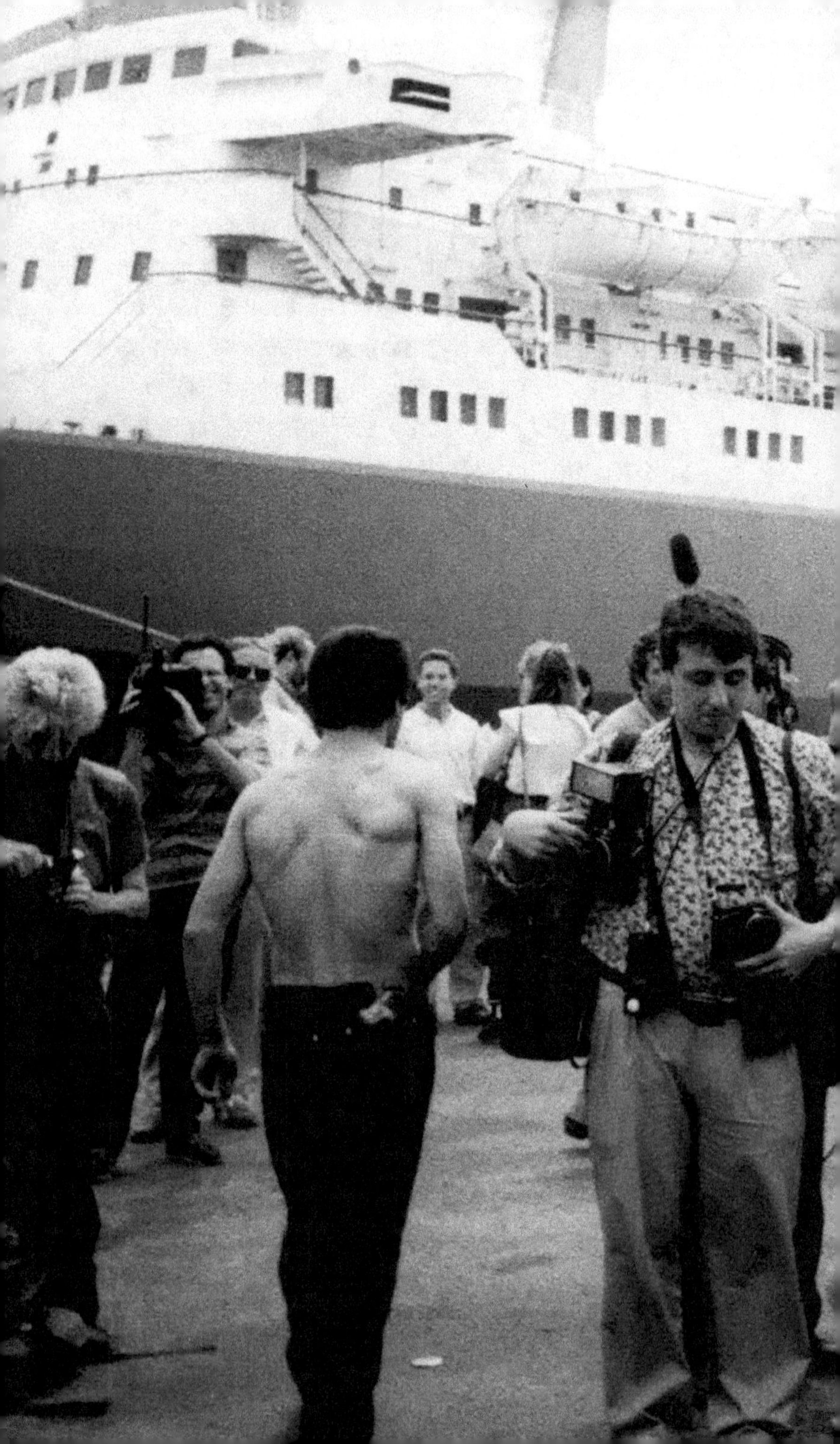

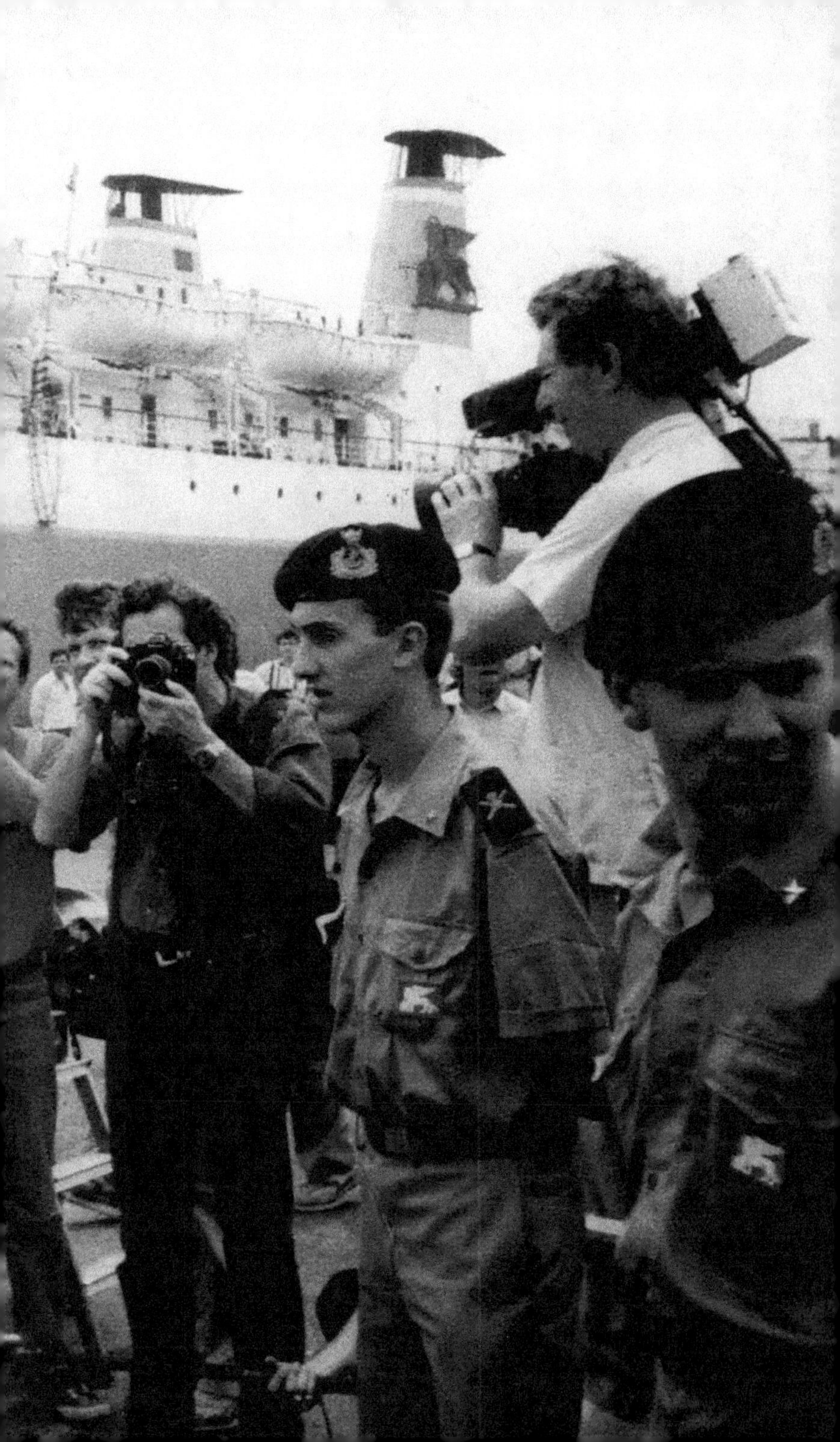

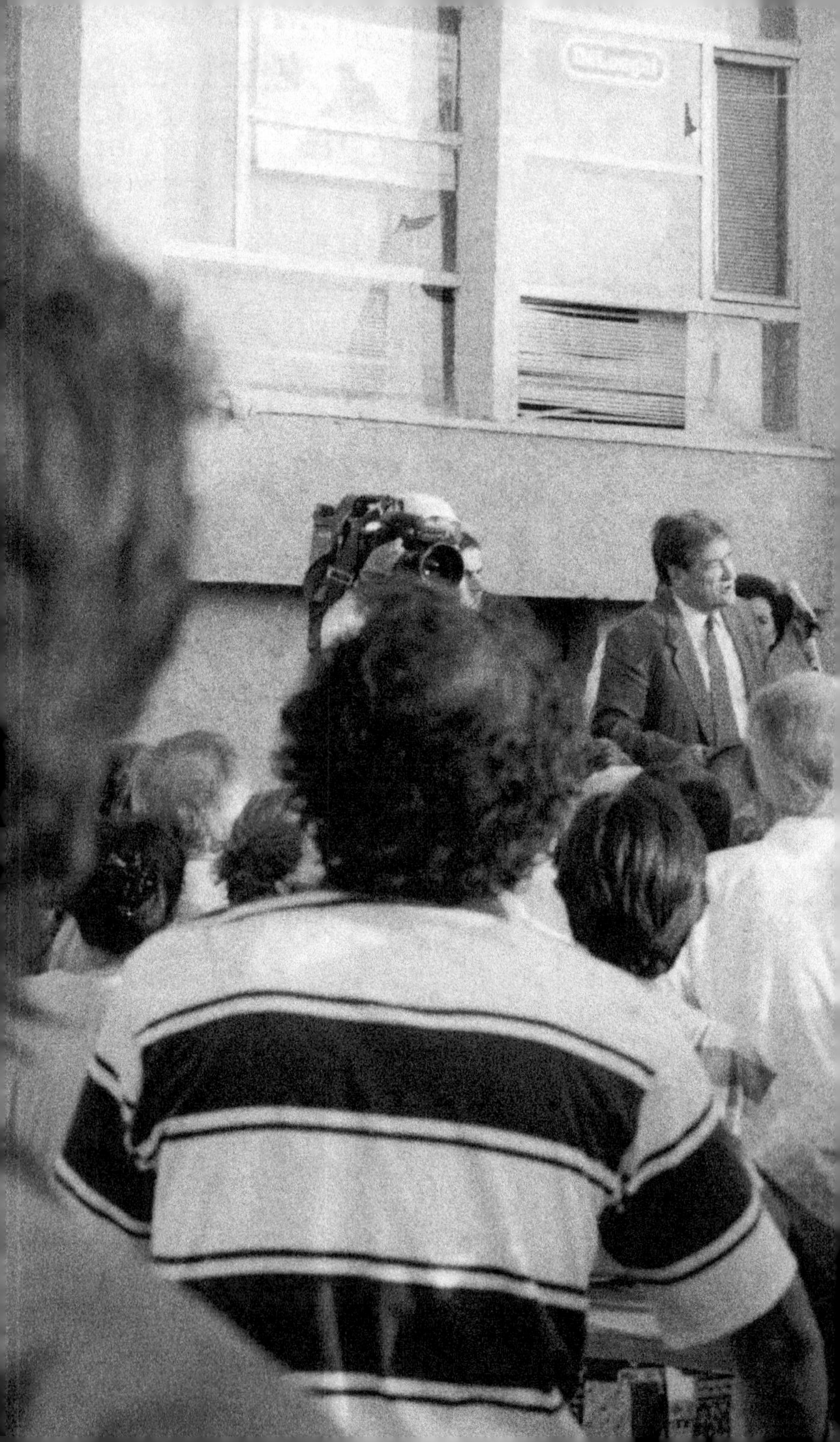

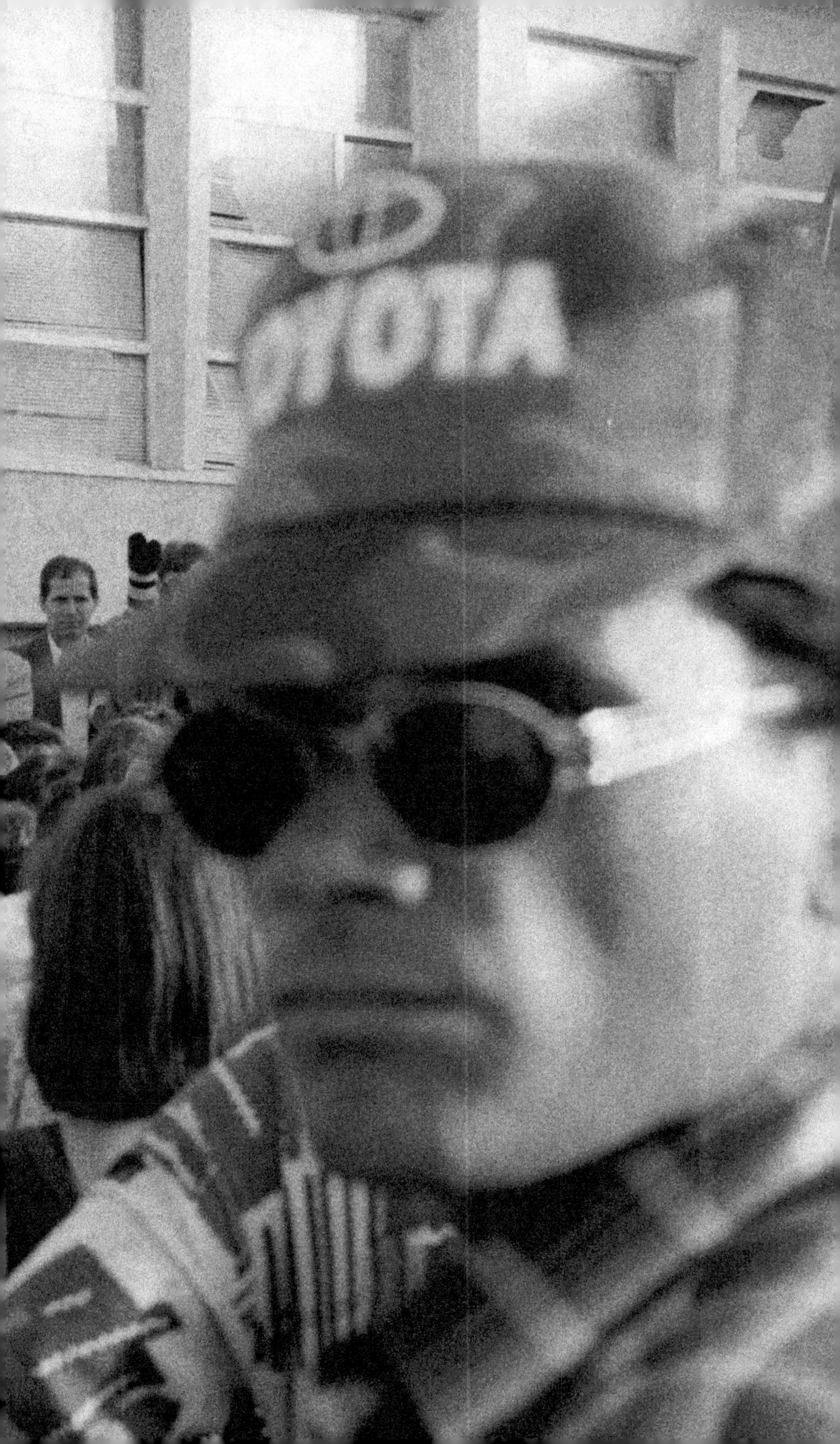

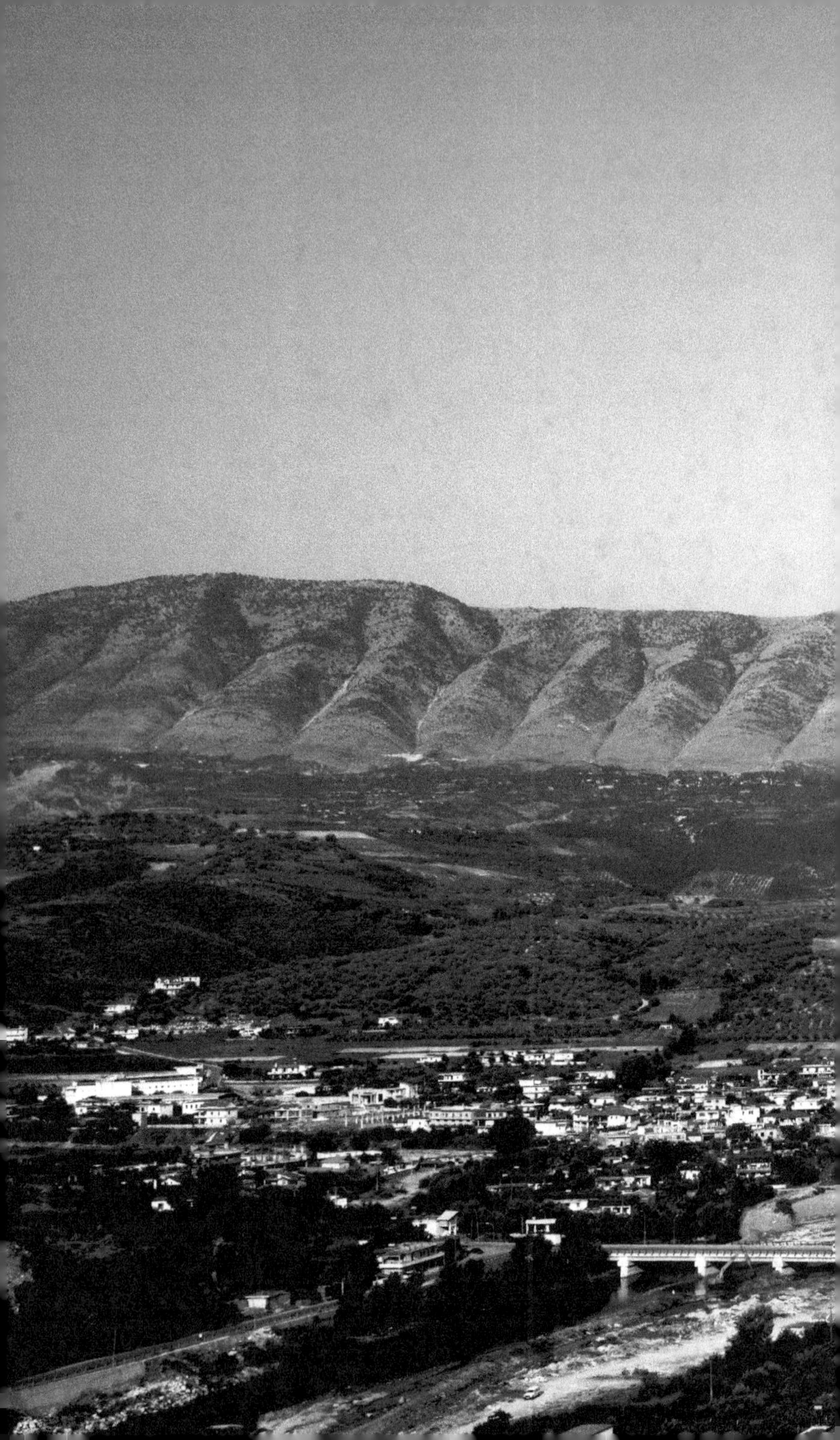

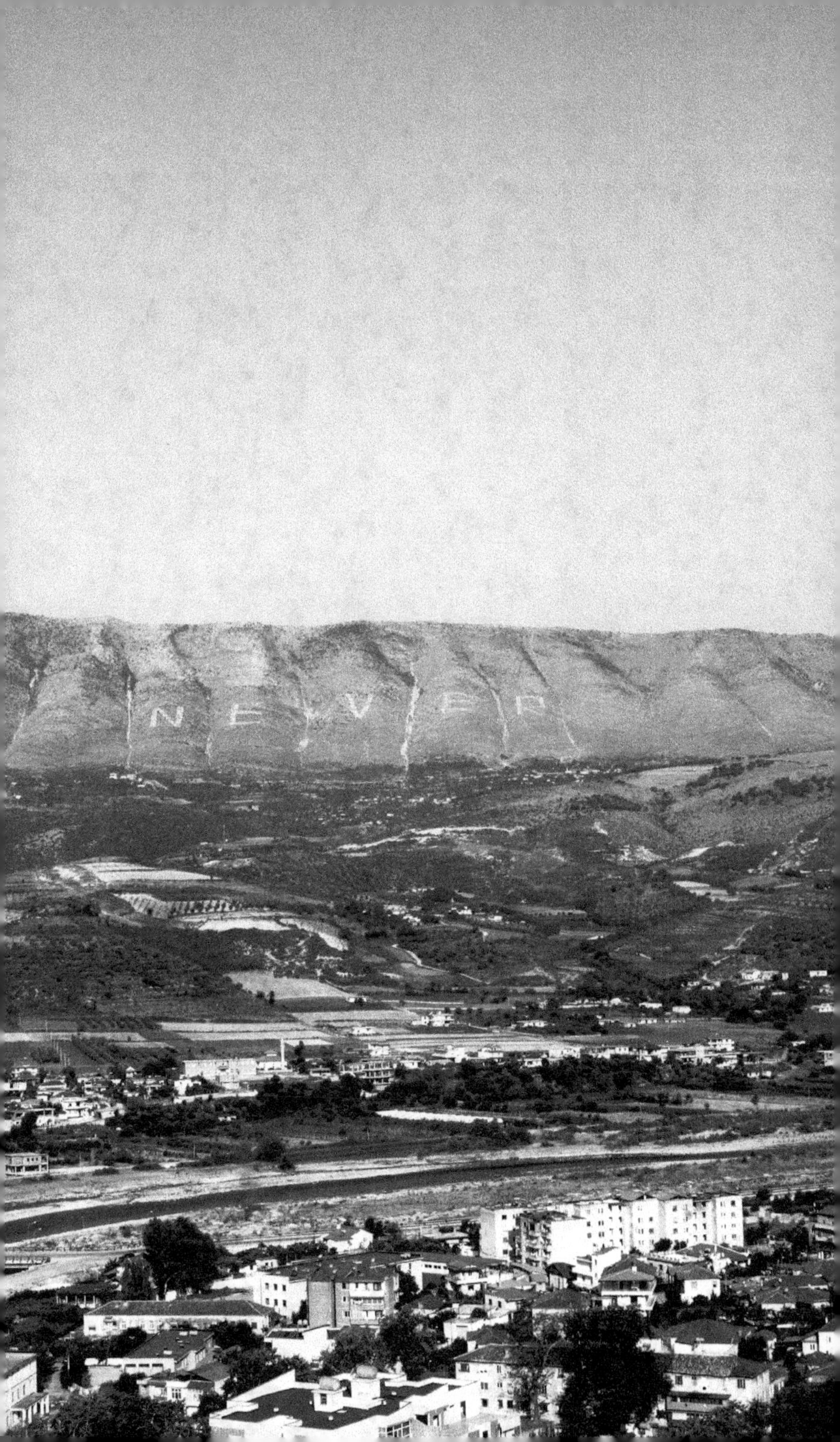
NEVER

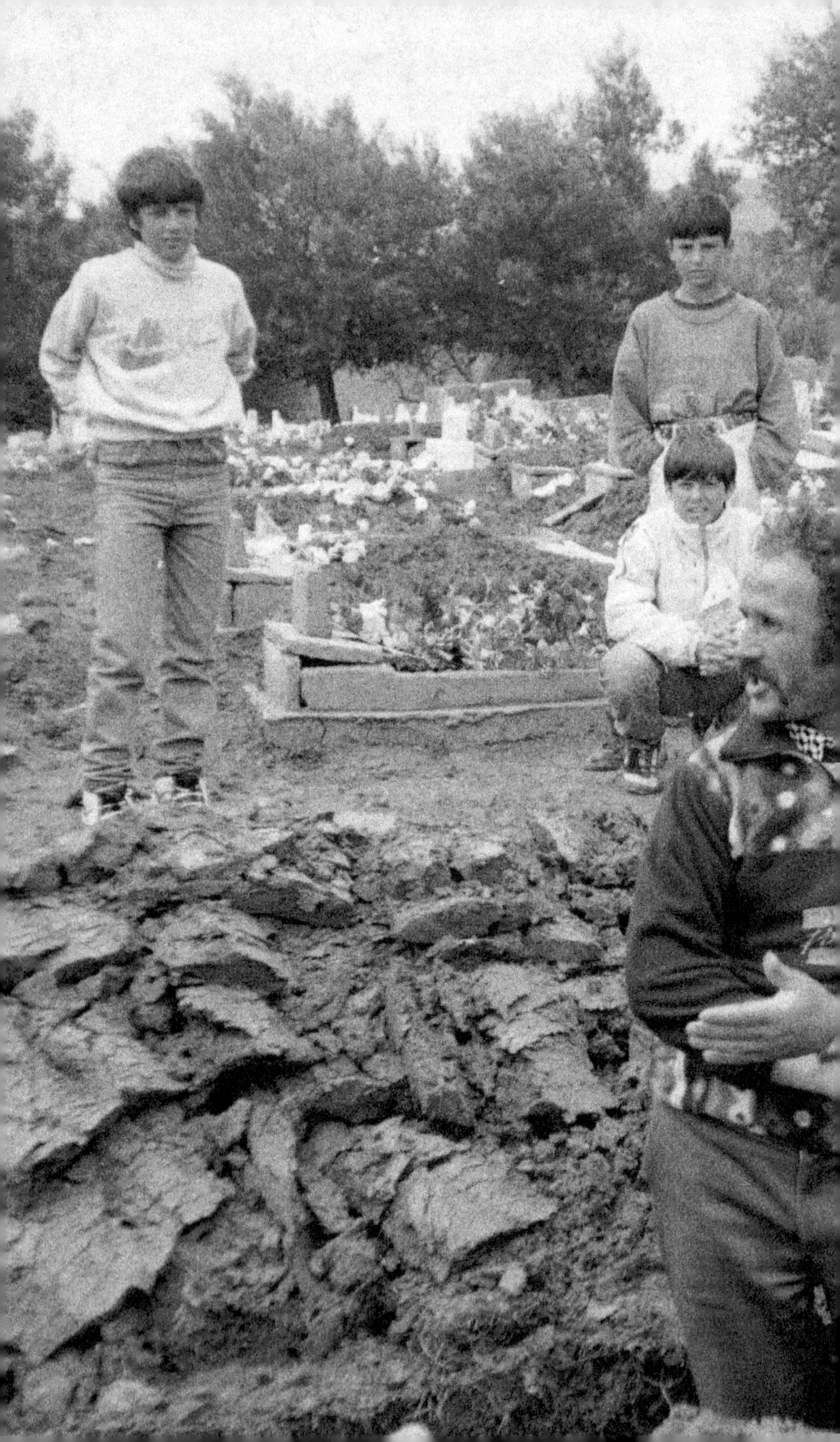

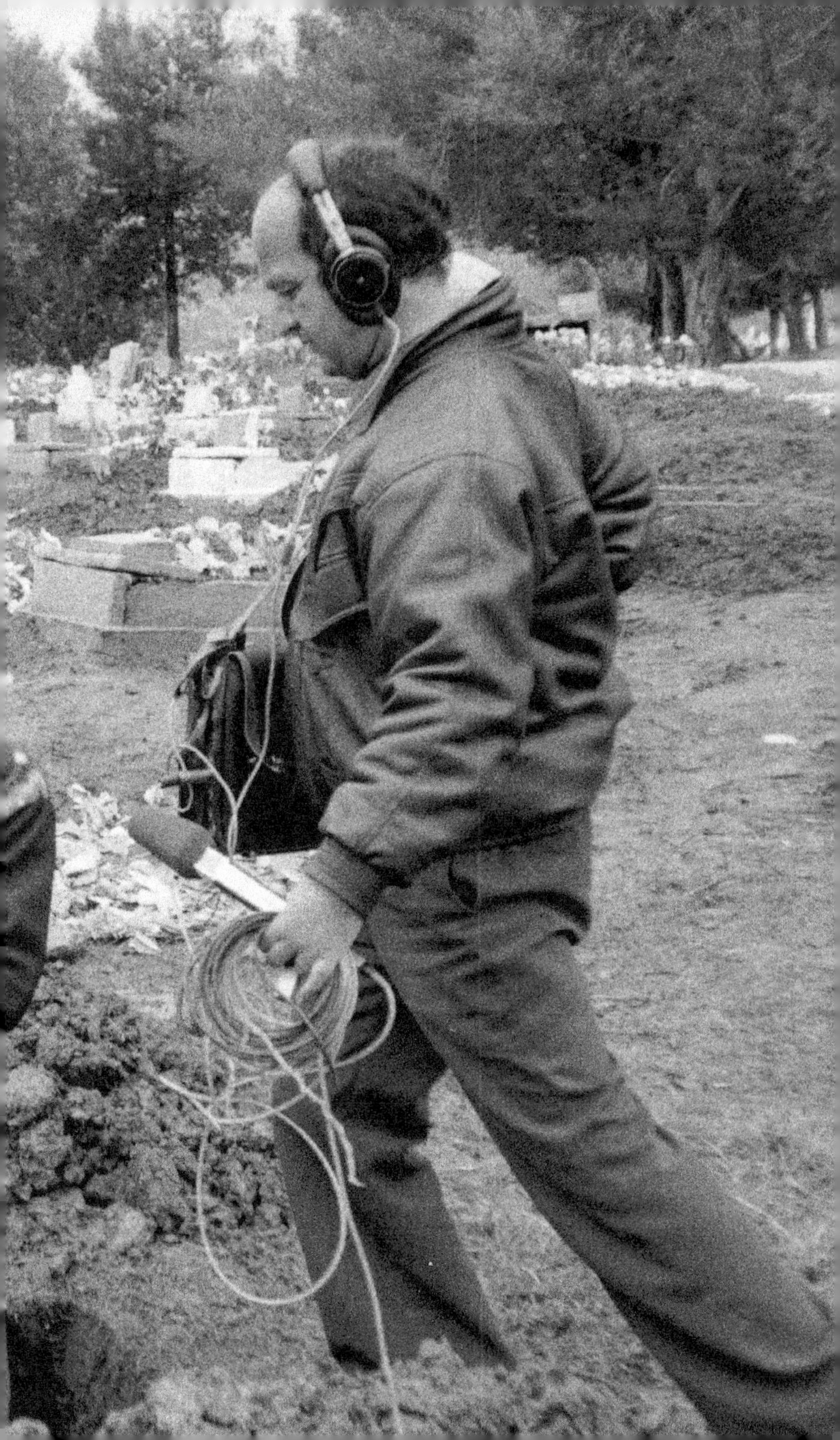

Fig. 5. DESERTION ARCHIVES by Armando Lulaj, 2017.
Photo taken on July 13, 1990 in Brindisi, Italy, by Agim Kubati.
Courtesy of DebatikCenter of Contemporary Art.

Fig. 6. Kronikë '97, 1996–97. Frame from "Kronikë '97".
Unrealized footage directed by Kreshnik Hashorva,
DOP Bashkim Asllani.
Courtesy of National Albanian Film Archive.

Fig. 7. NEVER by Armando Lulaj, 2012.
Video, Full HD, B/W and Color, Sound, 22'.
Courtesy of DebatikCenter Film and Paolo Maria Deanesi Gallery.

Fig. 8. Kronikë '97, 1996-97. Frame from "Kronikë '97".
Unrealized footage directed by Kreshnik Hashorva,
DOP Bashkim Asllani.
Courtesy of National Albanian Film Archive.

TRACK 02

The sinking of the Katër i Radës. *The tragedy of the channel of Otranto. I'd like to start out from this event to talk about narrative. What can you say about this event? What do you remember? This event is very significant because with the Albanian exodus to Italy in the late nineties we witness the beginning of a long series of tragedies in the Mediterranean. Here, in my opinion, there really is a question of "narrative." Back then in Italy the center-left was governing and this tragic event has in fact always been treated as a "tragic accident." The news was quickly archived, with the result that very few people remember it today. What really did happen? How did people talk about this tragedy in Albania? How was the problem of Italian responsibility in this "accident" treated? Do the official Italian narrative and the official Albanian narrative show significant differences?*

I've always loved the sea, but I've always been afraid of deep water. I don't clearly recall when I saw it for the first time, but it must have been in Durrës because that is where my family and I spent our summer holidays. I remember that every year, like all the other vacationers, we took a boat ride for a short excursion of 30–40 minutes into the open sea. It was an old, double-decker white boat that could carry a hundred people or so. I remember that I held onto the railing, trying to distract myself so as to forget my nausea.

The first time I undertook a long trip was to the United States in 1996, and I saw the ocean from up high. It looked flat, motionless but powerful. Chilean filmmaker Raoul Ruiz speaks very interestingly about the sea from above, which can be compared to the frame, to film, and to cinema. He says, "the sea remains a powerful enigma for me. For example, when I travel by air and cross the ocean, I see it immobile as if it were made of hard material," like the frame.[1] "But, instead, you know it moves," like film.[2] "And when you've seen this, you're never completely sure of anything around you, you know that, like the sea, everything moves, is liquid,"[3] like cinema. Further on he says, "Cinema is always moving, or better, we could say it alters, it's a system of alteration of frontiers and borders."[4]

It must have been toward the end of 1997, when I had just started to attend an art class with a private tutor, that during our first lesson the teacher informed us that only a few of us would be able to see the treasures hidden at the bottom of the sea. It was his recurrent metaphor for the development of artistic depth, and to give an example he referred to Leni Riefenstahl's *Impressionen unter Wasser* (*Impressions of the Deep*).

Expel them! Reject them! Throw them into the sea! This is the language of power in our day, when the permanent crisis is moving toward ever deeper abysses. "They should be thrown back into the sea. And when they shoot at our law enforcement […] their ships should be sunk." These words, published on the day of the sinking of the Albanian ship, were heard all over the world: they bear the signature of a political personality who was important at the time, the former President of the House of Representatives, who was a member of the Northern League.[5] The ramming of *Katër i Radës* by the *Sibilla* constituted the first naval blockade against immigrants in the Mediterranean. The tragedy also gave new connotations to the narrative of the

---

1 Raoul Ruiz, *Ruiz faber,* ed. Edoardo Bruno (Rome: Minimum fax, 2007), 140.
2 Ibid.
3 Ibid.
4 Ibid., 141.
5 This was Irene Pivetti, President of the Italian House of Representatives from 1994 to 1996.

thousand-year-old confrontation between East and West. The collision of the two ships was treated (again) as a clash between two different civilizations. On the one hand, the defenders, represented by western seamen, and on the other hand, the others. The political VIPs were not involved in the subsequent criminal trial, even if they had always endorsed the order to strike. The question also concerned international law, the United Nations Convention on the Law of the Sea, signed in 1994, because the collision occurred in international waters.

Everything was enshrouded in a cloud of legal quibbles that managed to catapult the responsibility of the Italian state in various directions. In the month of March, three days before the tragedy, an agreement concerning immigration and the responsibilities and duties of the parties involved had been signed by Albania and Italy. During the trial it came out that at the moment of the incident the agreement had not yet been signed by the President of the Republic of Italy; in this way any and all responsibility by the Italian state was avoided. The criminal trial amounted to an evasion of the real responsibilities, with only the two commanders of the ship being charged and convicted. In that trial, though, what was missing were the corpses that should have been there in the courtroom. It was a trial of numbers, a cloud of numbers. Money. Victims. Survivors. Hundreds. Numbers and figures dividing and multiplying. At the end of the trial, one of the survivors, like a realistic prophet, told the media that they should dive down below, to the bottom of the Adriatic Sea, because the sea floor was strewn with bones. No more secrets, no more wonders: the treasures of today's Impressions of the Deep are the poor remains of our fellow humans, people just like me, just like you. The trial was shrouded in the language of power — difficult, ambiguous and evasive, bottomless and impenetrable, as legal language often is — it carried you back in time, foreseeing a future no one wanted to face.

In republican Rome it was the custom that in cases of disaster or future dangers, predicted or imminent, the Sibylline oracles would be consulted. It seems that these powers also held a surprise future for the *Katër i Radës. Katër i Radës* means "The

Fourth of Harbor"; it was a former Soviet PT boat built in the fifties, one of ten passed on to the Albanian navy between 1957 and 1960. That night the PT boat, which in the seventies had been turned into patrol boat A-451, with a number for a name, was not loaded with torpedoes but with more than 120 people trying to escape from extremely hard conditions in their country. They wanted to escape from that year, from that precise year, to leave behind once and for all the turbulent history of Albania and find truth in exile.

The narratives of the versions upheld by the two countries, Italy and Albania, were very different at the time, but I don't think they still are today. The phenomenon of the crisis of the Mediterranean returns, repeats itself like the same wave breaking on the same coast. Today no one believes in this grotesque idea of Europe, this monetary pact of states full of corrupt bureaucrats, this new Europe that supposedly protects liberty but isn't able to protect human lives, which only pretends to deal with the current immigration emergency, which lets people drown, abandoning human beings at the bottom of the sea and taking no responsibility, which is guilty of wars and financial crises inflicted all over the world.

The affair of the ramming of the *Katër i Radës* by the corvette *Sibilla* closely mirrors today's history, which is stained by similar and even more criminal episodes, like the sighting and abandonment of immigrants at sea, or the political decisions of this Europe. Whenever I read news of sightings and abandonments I don't know why but I always think of "The Vulture and the Little Girl," the picture taken by Kevin Carter in Sudan in March of 1993, and what was said about it.

In the twenty-sixth act of *Kronikë '97*, which was filmed in Italy, the survivors and relatives of the victims of the *Katër i Radës* find themselves in the middle of the sea facing the crane of another big ship that is bringing the sunken PT boat to the surface. I've always thought that something was lost on that voyage… When the sunken boat comes to the surface, harmless now with its soaked cartridges, you can see in the survivors' eyes that something is missing. You can see that something gets detached at that moment, something that may have already been foreseen before the first disembarkation in 1990. Something that many of them still living abroad, immigrants or exiles, want to recover, to reach. At that moment we lost our Self again. We shut ourselves in again. A deep dive into the abysses of our history, into that epic past full of fascinating ghosts, of unsettling religious comings and goings over five centuries, of massacres, isolation, and absolute negation, always searching for another convincing proof of identity. Instead the proof, the contemporary scientific evidence, is to be found right in front of us all, covered over by a cloth comparable to the veil that the West wants to violently tear off the East and vice versa.

That collision was proof of the loss of a political possibility that had been simmering for years in Albania, and that had to do with the future of a westernized national identity, the breakaway from communism, the flight from the East and the current efforts to separate ourselves definitively from Orientalism…, the so-called matrix of evil, of the dark past and wickedness in the world, nourished by western fascism. We have to tear off the veil. Take off the mask of the real murderers. The historians. The politicians. We can't rush toward the West by annihilating the so-called forces of evil, like Afghanistan, Iraq, and very soon Iran. We can't continue to uphold this narrative.

The problem of the Albanian exodus and expatriation: With the downfall of communism thousands of Albanian families looked for refuge in Italy and Greece. Here, again, "narrative." Participating in the Venice Biennale in 2015, you carried the skeleton of a sperm whale from Albania to Italy and you photographed the voyage to create a film made up of pictures of the transport. But it didn't seem to me to be simply documentation. It is a work in itself, in my opinion. Can you talk to us about this work in relation to the problem of the exodus and crossing the sea? Why did you shoot the transportation of that "piece" of your work?

The problem you pose is constantly moving, and it is structured exactly like a narrative that goes to pieces here to be recomposed in another part of the world. It is a global problem, a consequence of global politics. I'm especially interested in certain underpinnings of the powerful structure that is able to shape identity.

In an interview in 2002, a year after I was expelled from the Florence Academy of Fine Arts, I was asked a question concerning Franz Kafka's *Der Bau,* comparing my work, or to be more exact my being, to the main character in the story. On re-reading it I realized that the intention of the question about a particular work of mine made in 2001 was not only aimed at understanding. Rather, it revealed historical prejudices and clichés regarding immigration. The question touched my being and my past as well as my stereotypical future, and came out of the same perspective that constructs the narrative of all the others who cross the border.

When I was a little kid I heard my family talk about Kafka and every time I heard that name it made me anxious. In Albanian *kafka* literally means "skulls" (the singular is *kafkë*) and I didn't understand why they were talking about skulls. Since Kafka is such a cerebral author, I've always loved that assonance and the play on language it creates. In the past I looked for a hidden, deep semiotic connection to explain the symmetry between our contemporary condition and the architectural structure inside the head (skull) of Kafka's character. But in fact things are a lot simpler, not nearly so complicated.

At the beginning of my academic studies I was free of the system's conventions and traps. I'd written a manifesto titled *Underground Movement,* which talked in general terms about what we should do in the academic world and how to behave vis-à-vis the institutions. We were to act according to two key concepts: to be precise and perfect like Fontana's slash and complex like Duchamp. In 1999 we began to produce our first group works, conceived as events that appeared and then faded out. Together with a close friend, Riccardo Comitini, a disciple of Marcuse who owned an iMac G3, we did a remake of a graphic novel for schools in the seventies, which was interpreted by the children. The reworked graphic novel was made into a black book titled *Amore Mio*, like the famous seventies show,[6] where we added the prison universe to that of the school. We presented it at my friend's final exam, accompanied by a video loop bearing the same title, which we played at full volume in the auditorium of the Academy. It was a video montage of black and white horses mating. No one liked it, not even our fellow students, who made up the audience. We could have anticipated the teacher's irritation but we didn't understand the refusal of our fellow students who were in the same academic year as us.

Generally speaking, unlike contemporary art which has a much smaller but also more educated public, literature has a much wider distribution and so a broader public. The contemporary art public is very conservative and closed-minded compared to that of literature. The reading public is generally larger, if more mediocre, because readers are often looking for normalcy, since they want to find themselves in what they read.

Joseph Brodsky's text, *The Condition We Call Exile*, speaks of the condition of the exiled writer who always has his compass pointing toward his home country, addressing a real as well as an imaginary public.[7] In many cases, this type of writer feels superior and doesn't want his condition to be compared to that of simple immigrant workers forced to disguise themselves in the new society (from which, however, the poet or the artist draws inspiration). Instead, the writer struggles to become the "rooster

---

6   The group show *Amore Mio*, organized by self-invited artists under the supervision of Achille Bonito Oliva and inaugurated on August 6, 1970 at Palazzo Ricci in Montepulciano, had an original formula: "To inaugurate different behavior, a first in the history of cultural custom: to affirm for each artist the direct responsibility of presenting himself critically without the customary mediation of the art critic."

7   Joseph Brodsky, "The Condition We Call Exile," *The New York Review of Books*, January 21, 1988, https://www.nybooks.com/articles/1988/01/21/the-condition-we-call-exile/.

in the henhouse" populated by these compatriots, these "others," whether real or imaginary.

I have recently come across an Albanian poet who lives abroad in a state of exile. Like so many other contemporary authors, he writes in two languages, his native language and the language of the country where he is living. Thinking of his original language like an army that has been left behind, an armored suit of identity, the case of the poet Gëzim Hajdari is especially significant.[8] In the past, some of our great poets were able to capture the image of their times, whereas our contemporary poets are still searching for an image powerful enough to express the spirit and condition of society in our day. That image evades them still. It is a fugitive. Again and again…

Self-crucified, literally crucified by his colleagues from the communist times as well as by his country's younger poets and writers, who nonetheless are lapidated with untiring coherence in his verse, what interests me about Hajdari compared to other poets is that his life and his truth are welded to be offered as a complex proof of our collective memory in its unending strife to create this image. Expatriated in 1992 in seemingly incredible circumstances, this fugitive poet has never returned to Albania. His poems about Albanian history are almost unknown and intentionally left in the shadows, with the justification that his version is excessively subjective, while on the contrary this is the essential matrix of his poetic language.

Images have the power to construct history, and Hajdari creates a multifaceted image. At times it is too singular for bad cinema, but for a good director it offers a unique image that befits the real culture of the country alongside our stereotyped perception of it. He creates an image that is at one and the same time present and remote. It is as if he was trying to make a timeless image whose memory has been lost come out of

---

8   The Albanian poet and translator, naturalized Italian, Gëzim Hajdari, born in Lushnjë in 1957, was forced to leave his country for Italy in 1992 because of the threats he received for repeatedly denouncing corruption and the collusion that existed between organized crime and politics.

the caves and place it here in our midst, to reactivate it. What interests me most is how he persists in reconstructing the forcibly forgotten image by activating our dormant testimony in order to recompose the recent past. In these paradoxes, complex but at the same time incisive, the contemporary Albanian spirit seems to be captured.

As regards what we said above, we should also remember the torpedo killing of a whale that occurred off the coast of Patok in 1963.[9] The story has lived on and grown year after year, along with the progressive neglect of Tirana's Museum of Natural Sciences. Erected in the 1930s during the fascist era, the building was deliberately left to deteriorate until it was torn down to make room for the appetites of the contemporary architecture of unbridled capitalism. Inside that now non-existent space was displayed the scientific proof, the metaphor, of a head-on collision. The building was originally planned as an airplane hangar; in 1948, after the Second World War, it was transformed by the communists into the Museum of Natural Sciences. The Museum had a famous debut, which reflected political relations with the Soviet Union at the time. Indeed, the first embalmer was Russian, and his works of taxidermy, including a wolf and an owl, are still perfectly preserved and are among the most beautiful pieces in the collection. Many of these objects are embodiments of stories connected to specific episodes and periods in the country' political history. The owl was named after Nikita Khrushchev in 1958, when bilateral relations between Albania and the USSR ceased, and a pelican killed by Enver Hoxha himself was placed by its side. Another, smaller pelican was in the same showcase; it is said to have been killed by the communist regime's Prime Minister, Mehmet Shehu, who was forced to commit suicide by Hoxha.

Instead, the remains of the sperm whale told a far more epic story connected to the Cold War. In 1963, the whale was hit off-

---

9   Today the Lagoon of Patok is a large nature reserve on the northern coast of Durrës. The area is marked by continual conflicts between various criminal organizations and important political figures.

shore by one of the eleven PT boats gifted to Albania by the Soviet Union. I haven't found any documents about the number of the boat that shot the whale, or whether it was the *Katër i Radës,* the *Zero* or the *Treti i Radës* (The Third of Harbor). However, it is said that the Albanian navy, in the grip of paranoia and terrified at the idea of an imminent attack coming from the coast of Italy, where there was a US base, sighted an enormous object at sea. The PT boat, patrolling uninterruptedly, got in touch with the high command and immediately received the order to shoot. With torpedoes. The presumed American submarines were in fact a pack of sperm whales, also known as cachalots (*Physeter macrocephalus*). They killed them all, then tied one behind the boat and dragged it to shore, where it was buried by the sailors themselves. Years later its remains were dug up by the museum staff. Every bone down to the smallest was carefully cleaned and prepared and the skeleton perfectly reconstructed by the technicians of the Museum of Natural Sciences. Mouth wide open and shouting as though to instill fear but also to testify to that violent collision at sea, the eleven-meter-long beast killed by the Albanian navy, nicknamed the "American Sub," was exhibited on a pedestal of veneered wood, where it remained for decades to tell a political story that could travel further.

The demolition of the Museum was meant to destroy these narratives, the politics of memory that the museum itself, and that building in particular, had created over the years. It really does seem that the neoliberal spirit wants to cancel all memories, principal or collateral, and that it's doing this using the primitive technique of beheading. This story was the subject of my 2011 film, *It Wears as it Grows,* the first episode of my *Albanian Trilogy: A Series of Devious Stratagems.* In 2015, in order to continue the narrative generated in that political space, a narrative already hinted at by the film's title, I decided to present the skeleton to a different public and even put it on a different pedestal in an art show with the title *All the World's Futures.* I decided to bring the skeleton to Italy, where I exhibited it in the Albanian pavilion at the Venice Biennale. It was displayed inside the Arsenale as one of the main pieces in the show, where besides narrating its past it could now also speak about the future, the ideologies, the body of power itself, the state, art, and the market. Or, to cite Marx, it could speak of the alienating power of humanity.

To do this we dismantled the reconstruction of the whale made in the sixties, cutting the skeleton into pieces and putting them into wooden crates. I didn't want to make a "real" film with the documentation of the voyage, but simply to leave traces for the near future. I photographed the bones separately. I had the skeleton — and its background story — officially registered as a national relic at the Center for the Registration of Works of Art. Then I completed the extremely complicated customs procedures and finally the skeleton sailed across the sea. I documented each step, from the mounting to the dismounting in Venice. At the end of the Biennale, during the dismounting of the whole show, I hired two sculptors who worked for days inside the exhibition space to make perfect molds of the skeleton pieces, which I then cast in iron in a foundry. This was all documented either by me or by others involved in the various steps of the process. In this way we created what seem to be the beginnings of films originating in different places. The photos, the videos, the documents, the skeleton itself, and the iron copies may have triggered the mechanism which in the cinema is called a "shadow film" or "parallel film," which is one of the best things in cinema. The skeleton went back to Tirana, where it is no longer only the matrix of the historical account narrated in my film. Today it tells a new, evolving story in a different language, inside the new museum, a restored building located on the outskirts of the capital, the former headquarters of the Army Orchestra during communism.

Privatization. The "narrative" of privatization. As you say in your comments to my notes, after the collapse of communism Albania went through a process of privatization that is still ongoing, very potent and very "intrusive." What sort of "narrative" has accompanied this process? How is contemporary art used in Albania to legitimize or in any case "go along with" these choices?

Privatizing the future.

The interest of the Albanian "renaissance" government is focused on two main aspects of the development of contemporaneity, namely (contemporary) art and architecture. The former would seem to have achieved the goals proposed for it, at least for those who think they will be the ones to carry it forward and decide who will take part in this contemporaneity and who is out. Paradoxically, the alternative they impose amounts to being either in or out of history. Even if recent contemporary art seems to find itself in a blind alley, and there are many who say that it may have exhausted its real mission, since it has become a red carpet for the corrupt state, it has opened the way to the second, far more interesting phase of development — the drive toward contemporaneity found in architecture. In contrast to the previous stage, this most recent stage really does seem to be a well-structured business plan carried out by a board of administrators with precise ideas for today's market. It should be said that many parts of this political plan have been stolen from the New Labour program. Indeed, it is not by chance that Tony Blair and Alastair Campbell are currently the advisers to the government and the Prime Minister. However, in contrast to New Labour, which introduced the freshness of change also by exploiting the success of the participation of famous artists and pop singers, who later jumped ship and continued their careers on their own, here the opposite is true. There is bitter competition among young artists, who are literally elbowing one another to climb onto the visibly disastrous ship of power. The fraternizing of these artists and architects with the government has grown more and more intimate. They are authentic Brothers in Crime.

To the credo of business-states that there is no salvation without globalization we have to add another commandment that has become a constitutional principle with us, namely the alliance with organized crime. Along with its artists and its architects, this government seems trapped inside a Möbius strip and cannot survive without organized crime.

The majority of the exhibitions organized in the country are not the product of research, or even of an interest in Albanian problems; rather, they come out of a rapid assimilation of the official narrative. Albania, and the capital city itself, are used in many cases as a post-historical display. Artists are always perceived to be a highly courteous and cultivated bunch who are not supposed to be actively involved in politics. They mustn't criticize; on the contrary, they must justify the precocious ejaculation of the expositive concept. They mustn't use real language, like the poor, beautiful, violent language of reality. Rather, being perennial slaves of society and politics, they have to invent a language to disorient the masses of people who seem to be ready to explode. This reality is both banal and dangerous.

The government's sermons and apologias don't convince anyone anymore, not even the swathe of people obliged to vote for the governing Socialist Party so as not to lose their jobs. It should be said that this right-wing "socialist" government has gone far beyond the right-wing Democratic Party, which is still at a rudimentary stage of development. For the Albanian socialists, to govern means to profit. The change they promise can't come about in reality, but can only be represented in 3D. What governs this structure, which also includes control of the media, involves looking for and hiring many foreign curators as well. This is one of the worst things to have happened in the contemporary art world; it can be seen as the *true Tirana Conspiracy,* instead of the infamous incident that took place during the first Tirana Biennale.[10] These shows are good for the lazy tourist but never for the curious explorer. The lazy tourist is always a victim and an arm of neoliberalism and these shows are looking for exactly this type of public.

Let's admit it: there's something very interesting in all this, I'd even say intriguing. On the one hand the substratum is being eliminated by making it hard to discern, but this very act

---

10 The Tirana Conspiracy will be discussed on Track 04. See p. 240, n. 11.

produces situations that undermine these schemes, opening up cracks in the official narrative and making these cracks visible for the first time. The official narrative is slowly being deflated to expose its skeleton to one and all. The large paving stones with the pyramidal apex in Skanderbeg Square seem to have been laid there only as upside-down mental barriers. Now they are lying in the square but they should be removed, hurled against the institutions, not made to keep people from taking possession of them but to destroy doors that are always kept locked.

The people seem to have become immune to the scandals produced by the political elite. Nothing seems to change this attitude. The conservative form of art that has recently been imposed in the country and described as the only possible form, in fact contradicts reality. Art is used to hide the daily corruption, to throw a veil over this reality. Lately the system, meaning the institutionalized scene, works only on imported projects rather than on ideas rooted in our country's reality. My way of working is exactly the opposite: to be more imaginative and scandalous than reality and the things imported. To stimulate the public and make it react. Imagination and tactical operations. Taking inspiration from what is left out, what is "cleared away" from the scene. Taking inspiration from the growing number of ill people with mental illness who live on the street because they are homeless. They are an inspiration to me. I think it's important for the people to get ready to experience a great work that contradicts "their" narrative, a heresy strong enough to break up that narrative into little pieces.

In this context, a very interesting artist, Scarlet Hori, recently told me she was about to leave for Africa. She said that after carrying out prolonged research she'd decided to go there to meet an important sorcerer who can work spells. She wanted to put a special hex on all of our parliamentary representatives, all the members of the government, the President, and the Prime Minister. It seemed like a fantastic idea to me. I'd like the archives and productions of DebatikCenter of Contemporary Art to be dedicated to this type of work, for it to become our next focus.

Architecture is the battle-horse for inscribing the future, and this is why the present government has concentrated on it. Social change is taking place only through the polluted mechanism of politics. It's not the product of culture, which really does seem to be experiencing the end of history. The change is produced with violence, rather like the impact that contemporary art has on a person foreign to it when they encounter it for the first time. Ultimately, what we notice from the start is the political madness injected into urban design and architectural projects. There's a hodgepodge of themes, symbols, cultural references, and financial interests that can change the design of buildings already approved or in the works. Rather than working in harmony, they fight each other, creating friction and discord. There is a profound hatred of the complexity of the simple. Destruction becomes a spectacle, staged as if performed by military specialists, in the presence of the media. Shock therapy becomes live performance. This seems to be the only moment when, along with the annihilation of memory, the construction of a false contemporary identity, golden and gleaming, is being documented. What can be more beautiful than building new homes using red and white bricks again, as in the past? Those who survived call them rat holes, cells, chicken coops, and pigsties, but in all this urban folly they are the only buildings that stand with their heads held high, even if they're old and have become run-down with the passing of time. Why is it that no one manages to (re)produce on another level the simplicity and rationality of the past, which can speak to us more clearly than the future, instead of making these stupid things with strident colors that are destroying the city?

There is always friction in architecture. There is attrition between the architecture of the socialist period and our contemporary architecture, and this is only normal in a growing city. There is contrast between fascist architecture and the architecture of recent years, and we can actually feel a struggle for identity and a competition among buildings. The new structures don't communicate with the past, but the most significant thing is that they don't communicate with each other — on the contrary, they create conflict. They repel each other, they attract each other, they create bumps in the squares. In the city of Tirana it feels like the ground isn't stable any more, it's moving. It really feels like being on high sea.

These are some of the themes we should be treating, maybe in a show of a different sort, one that can bring to light the gaps in the narrative and open up new directions. I have yet to see a show that deals with this confusion. We're still trying to simulate order and hide our social problems. Curating a show is thought of rather like tidying up, not as something conceptual, but something merely spatial. This expositive space is comparable to the rooms of a private hospital and not to the public emergency room. Who are these people that lie to the public so shamelessly? Who are these critics and curators that can't even conceive of a different space? What is this art scene that teaches artists not to use "vulgarities" when they speak in public or to the public? Who composes this fictitious, ignorant audience, this self-proclaimed public of the art scene, who imposes these rules? In the name of what public are they speaking? The only interesting public in this country is the mass of people they call vulgar, who are precisely the ones I want to address. Why are artists afraid to repeat certain gestures made by their predecessors, or go beyond them? Why do architects talk about economic progress, and why are they comparing this fictitious progress with China? The absurdities I hear every day are fit for a psychiatric ward. We shouldn't be doing shows to teach good manners, but to make people reflect, to make them react. Shows that can change your way of thinking. A show that doesn't have this characteristic can have only one title: *Shkërdhatokracia.*[11]

---

11 The term *Shkërdhatokracia* can be translated as "cratocracy," meaning power based on power itself, the dictatorship of cast. It was coined by the Albanian writer Dritëro Agolli (1931–2017) to designate the outcome of the country's politics after the fall of the communist regime.

What is DebatikCenter of Contemporary Art? How does it fit into the context of Albanian "political aesthetics"? Is the DebatikCenter project an alternative way to do politics by using "aesthetic strategies"? And how does it work? How do you use images? What types of image, and of the theory of the image if you can call it that, do you uphold individually and as a group — politically — with the DebatikCenter?

The DebatikCenter of Contemporary Art is an initiative taken by people from different backgrounds, ranging from academics to the world of art, journalism, etc. The collaborators of the DCCA are activists, architects, filmmakers, real and imaginary collectives, critics, curators, translators and lawyers. The term DEBATIK, which sounds a lot like "debate," is the acronym for *Djemtë e Bashkuar Antëarë të Idealeve Komuniste,* meaning "Union of Young Boys with Communist Ideals." The original DEBATIK group was created during the Second World War. It was made up of young people who stood with the communists in the struggle against Nazi-Fascism. Many of them were killed during the war, without living to see the ideals of the organization come to life, which in reality no one managed to do. It was to them, to those lives abruptly cut off, to their broken ideals, to the nostalgia for a past which might have become a better future, that we wanted to turn when we decided to use this acronym again. The actions of the DCCA are aimed especially at young people, the generations to come, who need to adopt a critical approach toward the past and the changes of the future.

There is a struggle going on concerning the past and how to start writing the future based on that past. The way in which Albanian historians and politicians have approached that problem has been to try to "reclaim" the past, leaving certain periods intact and rewriting others. This is still the case and will be so for a long time.

The nostalgia I'm referring to relates to our past, the utopian promise of a better future which was shown to be unreal and impossible, with the result that we've all embraced this horrific future. I think it's really important to be nostalgic these days and to feel regret for a collective possibility that has vanished into thin air. I'm interested in taking another look at the things we've left behind, in continuing to scrutinize the past and bear witness to this unnatural mutation.

The DebatikCenter of Contemporary Art, with its collaborators from various backgrounds, is trying to record this mutation, which is obviously all over, but is more clearly visible in small countries like ours. We are trying to create ideas by using images of the past from different parts of the world that can transcend the present, challenging it in order to capture the spirit of our times. To give an example, *Moving Billboard* is a project we carried out in 2018. It consists of twenty-four advertising billboards spread all over the country, from north to south, starting from mountain tops and forests and arriving at the main and secondary roads of various cities. Showing the kind of images mentioned before, the project was structured to cover twenty-four hours. Every image coincided with a particular hour of the day or night, remaining at the predetermined site for just one hour. At the end of exactly one hour it was dismounted by an itinerant team. With the idea of a moving spectator in mind, with little probability of seeing all the images from the first to the twenty-fourth, we wanted to leave open the possibility of constructing different narratives starting from the combinations that each spectator would be able to see in twenty-four hours. The project included different kinds of images, ranging from economic corruption to police brutality, environmental collapse, contemporary geopolitics, immigration, the war against terrorism, and so on.

I would describe the aesthetic strategies you refer to as tactics designed to pierce the aesthetic shield of politics, whose main purpose is to use art to hide behind. For me, art has never been a shield to hide myself. I've never seen it as something to speculate on. And I'll never be able to accept the prevailing utopian fable of the artist-politician recounted in certain artistic circles. That's a lie and it will always be a lie.

The peculiar thing about this country that makes it so attractive to foreign artists isn't the enormous difference separating art from politics and vice-versa; on the contrary, it is the fake convergence of the two. Outside the country the perception and the story told is that the goal is to eliminate this distance completely, to remove all obstacles that divide art and politics, so that each will come ever closer to the same nucleus. The nucleus itself is clearly in sight, by now just a short distance away. This narrative is banal and superficial, just a propagandistic gimmick that can't (yet) serve as the foundation for this beautiful idea.

We are living through a crisis of representation. People don't feel represented anymore, and this is happening all over the world. The words used to name today's politicians have lost their power. It seems that no word can really correspond to their role in our times. You can call them thieves and corrupt, as they indeed are, but to society this will seem naive and impotent. There is a rule in this country, often referred to as free, unsolicited advice. It comes mainly from my parents' generation, but also from colleagues and foreigners who live and do business here. It says you should never criticize the government, you need to stay on the sidelines, horizontal, never get mixed up with politics — and if you really can't avoid it, then grab as much money as you can and get out. Some of these people are important people at the head of large companies and in their role this is understandable. Others, instead, are at the head of important NGOs, intellectuals, and human rights activists, and this is where the problems begin. Still others, less protected and more sincere, are our relatives.

My concern has always been to find escape routes. I'm always looking for people and collaborators who live in the country and occupy a vertical position. People who consider resistance only as resistance, and not as a foothold to raise their profiles and have a pretext for organizing projects that can get state funding.

All this has to do with the stolen future. We are led by people, politicians, and political parties that are always trying to steal the future, everywhere and anyhow, from people who aren't able to imagine any future here. Being stolen, this future, or better still these futures, travel like packages containing information bits that in all probability are not wanted.

An elementary line of reasoning comes to mind when I think about the future of my country and the past of other countries, like Italy, Germany, or the United States, whose futures we are stealing. Actually, we can only steal something that happened in the past, and so these damaged futures contain adulterated information. This intuition creates a truer and more genuine aesthetics, very different from what exists now. Was Hakmarrja për Drejtësi[12] a real threat or only a mediatic fragment that emerged clandestinely in the mid-nineties? Perhaps these stolen futures hold splinters of information about the Red Brigades, The Weathermen Underground Organization, or the Baader Meinhof group? It is precisely this abstraction, which in reality isn't so abstract, which interests me.

---

12 Hakmarrja për Drejtësi is the name of a dubious and perhaps phantasma-goric subversive terrorist group discovered in 1996 in Albania, accompa-nied by a lot of media clamor. The affair ended after twenty years of trials with the full absolution of those indicted.

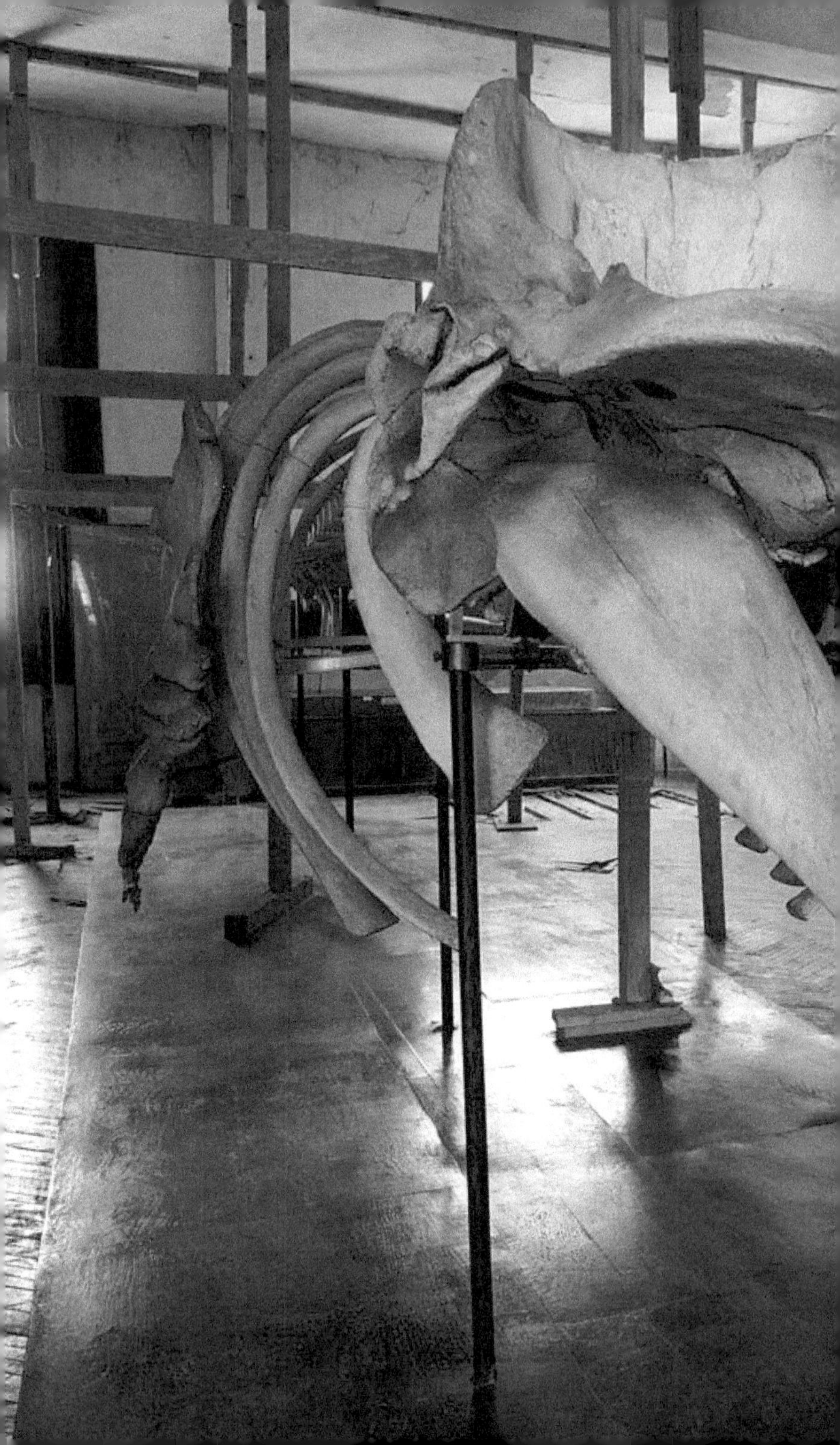

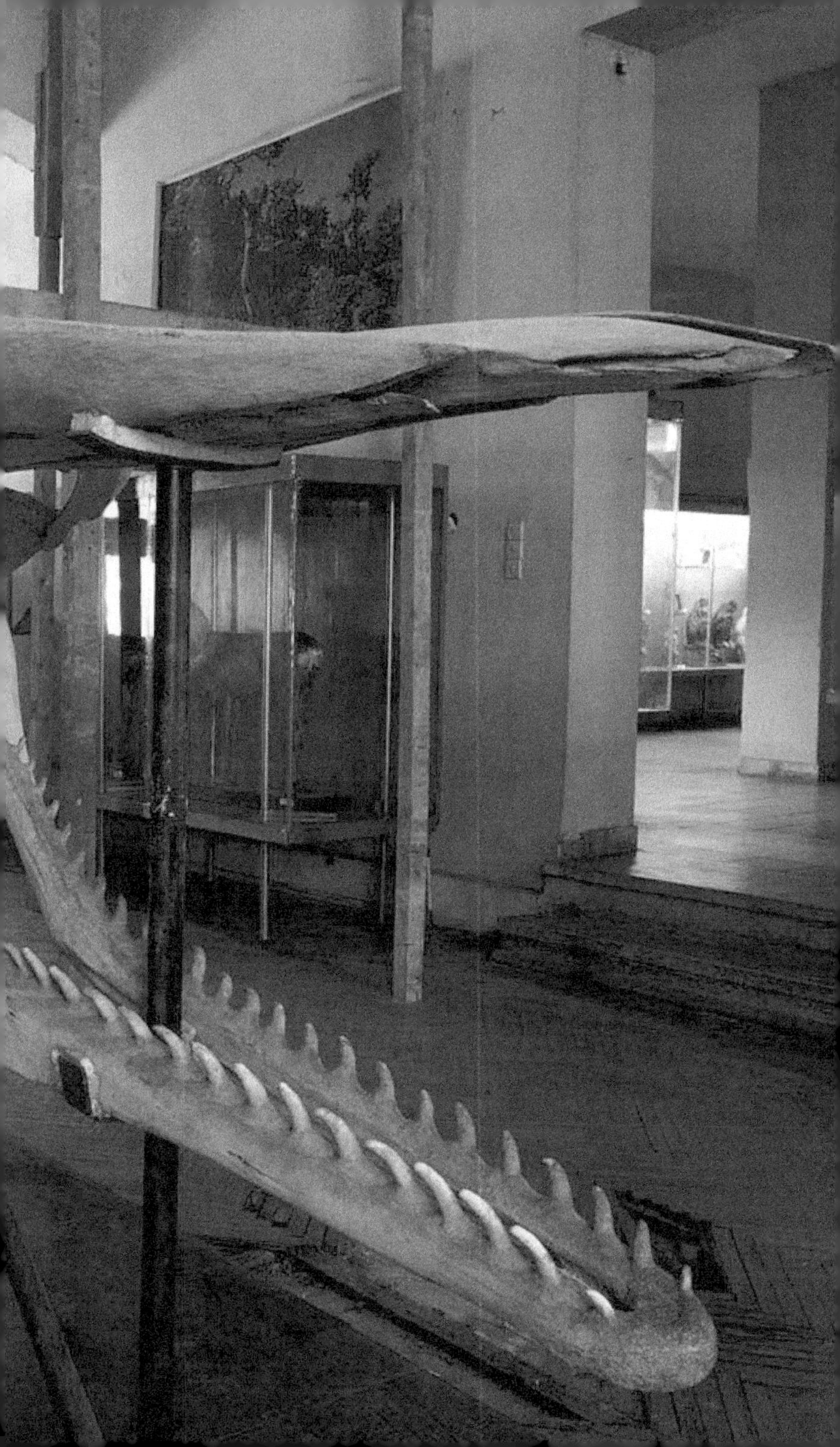

Fig. 9. It Wears As It Grows by Armando Lulaj, 2011.
RED transferred in Full HD, B/W and Color, Sound, 18'.
Courtesy of DebatikCenter Film, Artra Gallery and cinqueesei.

トラック02

カトル・イ・ラドゥス(Katër i Radës)号沈没。オトラント海峡の悲劇。この出来事を手始めに、ナレーションについて話題にしたいと思う。この出来事について、君は何を発言できるだろうか? 何を覚えている? この出来事は重要である。なぜなら、'90年代末におけるイタリアへのアルバニア難民流出により、地中海での、長きに渡る一連の悲劇の序章が目撃されることになるからである。私の見解では、ここでこそ「ナレーション」が問題となる。イタリアでは、当時、中道左派が政権を握っており、悲劇的な出来事は常に「悲劇的な事故」として扱われ、ニュースはすぐにお蔵入りにされたため、今日それを覚えている者はほとんどいない。本当のところは何が起こったのか? アルバニアでは、この悲劇はどのように語られたのだろうか? この「事故」におけるイタリアの責任問題に、どのように対処したのか？ イタリア版とアルバニア版の公式ナレーションには違いがあるか？

僕は常日頃から海を愛してきたが、深みに対する恐怖を常に抱いていた。初めて海を見たのがいつだったかは、よく憶えていないが、他でもないドゥラスだったはずだ。なぜなら、家族とともに夏期休暇を過ごしていたのがその地だったからだ。毎年、全ての避暑客らと同様に、湖で30–40分程の短い周遊をするために汽船に乗ったことを憶えている。二層式の全体が真っ白な古い船で100人くらいを乗せることができた。吐き気を忘れるために気を紛らわそうと、船艇の船縁にしがみついていた記憶がある。

　初めて長旅に出たのは1996年、アメリカ合衆国行きで、上空から大洋を見下ろした。平坦で、不動ながらも力が漲っているように見えた。ラウル・ルイスは「Conversazioni 1988–2002(対話1988–2002)[1]」の中で、上空から見た海洋について、1コマ、フィルム、映画と対比しうる方法で、非常に興味深く語っている。

　「…海は私にとって非常に強堅な謎のままである。例えば、飛行機で旅をして大洋を横切る時、海はあたかも固い素材の如く不動に見える…」[1コマの如く]。「だが、動くのだと君は知っている」[フィルムの如く]。「これを見た時には、君の周りにあるもの全てに確かではいられなくなる。海のように、全て動くのだと知っている、液体なのだ…」[映画の如く]と言う。その上さら

1　Raoul Ruiz, Ruiz faber, ed. Edoardo Bruno (Rome: Minimum Fax, 2007)に収録。Raoulの綴りでも知られるラウル・ルイス・ピノ(Raúl Ruiz Pino, 1941–2011)は、1974年パリに亡命したチリの監督。亡命先では、オリジナルで革新的な映画作家の比類なき才能を表現する機会を得た。

に「映画は常に動く、と言うよりむしろ、変質させると言えるだろう。境界や限界の変質システムなのだ」と言う。

1997年の年末頃だったか、プライベートの芸術コースに通い始めた時、僕達の講師が初回の授業で、僕達のうちの極僅かの者のみが海底に潜むお宝にお目にかかれるだろう、と言った。それは、芸術センスの発達について、その講師がよく使っていたメタファーで、例として、レニ・リーフェンシュタールの『ワンダー・アンダー・ウォーター原色の海(Impressionen unter Wasser)』を挙げた。

奴らを追放せよ！撃退しろ！海に放り込め！恒久的な危機がさらに底知れぬ深淵へと向かっているゆえに、これが今日の権力の言い様である。「彼らは海に投げ戻されるべきだ。また、彼らが我々の法執行官に発砲する時[…]彼らの船は撃沈されるべきだ。」この表明は、アルバニア人移民船の沈没の日に拡散され、世界中に知れ渡った。これは、当時の重要な政治家、北部同盟(Lega Nord)に属する元下院議会議長[2] の発言である。シビッラ号によるカトル・イ・ラドゥス号への衝角激突は、地中海の移民に対しての最初の海軍封鎖となった。悲劇はまた、東西の千年に及ぶ対立のナレーションに新たな意味も与えた。2隻の船の衝突は、二つの異なる実体の激突として(またしても)扱われた。一方には西側の船員に代表された防衛者、そして、他方には移民に代表された占拠者。上座を陣取る大物政治家達は、常に攻撃命令を支持していたにもかかわらず、その後の刑事裁判には巻き込まれなかった。この問題はまた、国際法である1994年調印の国連海洋法条約(United Nations Convention on the Law of

---

2　1994年から1996年まで下院議会議長だったイレーネ・ピヴェッティ
　　(Irene Pivetti)のことである。

the Sea）にも関係していた。 なぜなら、 衝突が国際水域で発生
したためだ。

　イタリア国家の責任の所在を、 うやむやにしてしまった法廷
での丁丁発止の暗雲に、 全てが包まれていた。 その年の3月、
悲劇の三日前に、 アルバニアとイタリアの2カ国間で、 まさに移
民及び関係者の責任と義務に関する協定が調印されていた。
刑事裁判で判明したのは、 この協定が事件発生の時点では、
大統領官邸での署名がされておらず、 イタリア国家の一切の責
任を回避していることだった。 刑事裁判は、 実際の責任からの
逃避だった。 それは2隻の船長のみを相手取っての訴訟となり、
後に彼らは有罪判決となった。 しかし、 その裁判では、 法廷の
ど真ん中に、 そこに置かれるべき遺体の山はなかった。 それは
数字の、 数字だけで搦め捕られた裁判だった。 金銭。 死者。 生
存者。 セント刻み。 分割し、 乗算した数字と金額。 裁判の終盤、
生存者の一人は、 まるで現実主義の先見者のようにメディアに伝
えた。 メディアは、 アドリア海の底まで潜るべきだった、 なぜなら
海底には人骨が累々としていたから、 と。 もう神秘でも不可思議
でもない、 今日の「水中の印象(Impressioni subacquee)」のお
宝とは、 我々の仲間、 君や僕と変わらない仲間達の哀れな残骸
なのだ。

　権力の言語 – 難解で曖昧模糊、 つかみどころがなく、 底知れ
ず不可解な、 しばしば法律用語がそうであるような – に包まれた
裁判は、 君を連れて時を遡り、 何人（なんぴと）も直面したくない
未来を予告した。

　共和政ローマでは、 災害や将来の危険が予測されたり差し迫
ったりした場合に、 シビュラ達の神託(l' oracolo delle Sibille)

を仰ぐのが慣習だった。これらの力は、カトル・イ・ラドゥス号にも、驚愕の未来をとっておいたようだ。

Katër i Radës は「投錨地の4番目」を意味する：'50年代に建造された旧ソ連の魚雷艇で、1957年から1960年の間にアルバニア海軍に譲渡された11隻の船団のうちの1隻であった。あの晩、'60年代に哨戒艇A451に改造され、名前代わりの数字が振られた魚雷艇は、魚雷は搭載していなかったが、窮地に立つ自国から逃れることを望んだ120人以上の人々を乗せていた。彼らはあの年から、まさにあの年から逃れ、アルバニアの動乱の歴史ときっぱりと袂を分かち、亡命先で真実に巡り合うことを望んでいた。

イタリアとアルバニアの2カ国が主張していた複数のナレーションやバージョンは、当時は大きく異なっていたが、今日ではそうではないと思う。地中海の危機という現象は再来し、同じ海岸線に打ち寄せては砕ける同じ波のように繰り返される。今日、このヨーロッパの馬鹿げた考えを信じる者はいない。腐敗した官僚だらけの国家間の通貨協定や、自由を守るはずが人命を救えず、現在の移民の緊急事態に取り組むふりをする、この新たなヨーロッパ。それは人々を溺死させ、人間を海の底に見捨て、いかなる責任も負わずに、様々な国に被らせた戦争と金融危機の罪を犯している。

コルヴェット軍艦シビッラ号によるカトル・イ・ラドゥス号の衝突問題は、海上での移民の目撃と放置、このヨーロッパの政治的決定といった、さらに犯罪的なエピソードで彩られた今日の我々の歴史に密接に関係している。目撃と放置のニュースを読むと、なぜだか《ハゲワシと少女(The Vulture and the Little Girl)》が脳裏に浮かぶ。 1993年3月にスーダンで撮影されたケビン・カーターの写真画像、 そしてその作品について言われたことを想起する。

　イタリアで撮影された「Kronikë '97」の第26幕では、 カトル・イ・ラドゥス号の生存者達と犠牲者の家族が、 沈没した魚雷艇を水面に引き揚げている別の大型船のクレーンの前で海水に浸かっている。 あの航海で何かが失われたと僕は常々考えていた。 水浸しの薬莢の如き人身が搭載されていたため、 今では害をなさない難破した魚雷艇が水面に現れる時、 生存者の眼差しの内に、 何かが失われたと分かる。 その瞬間に、 何かが剝離したのが分かる。 おそらく既に1990年の最初の上陸の時から、 予告されていた何かだ。 今なお外国で生活している彼らの大部分、 移民や亡命者の多くが取り戻したい、 到達したいと望んでいる何か。 あの瞬間に、 我々は再び自我を失ったのだ。 我々は再び自らを封じ込めてしまった。 我々の歴史の奥底へ深々とダイブ。 魅惑的な亡霊に満ち満ちた、 5世紀に渡る宗教上の撹乱した錯綜、 大虐殺、 孤立、 絶対的否定の壮大な過去に、 何か別の「説得力のある」アイデンティティの証拠を常に探し求めて潜没する。 ところが、 その証拠、 現代の科学的発見は、 我々全員の目前にあったのだ。 それらは、 西が東から、 また逆も然り、 荒々しく引き剝がさんとするベールに匹敵する素地で覆われていた。

　その衝突は、 アルバニアで長年沸き立っていた政治的な可能性が、 喪失された証拠であった。 それは、 西洋化された国民的アイデンティティの未来や、 共産主義からの離脱、 東からの逃亡、 そして、 西洋のファシズムに煽動された世界の暗黒の過去と邪悪の元凶、 いわゆる諸悪の根源である[...]オリエンタリズムから決定的に分離する今日の努力と関係があった。 ベールを剥ぎ取らなくてはならない。 真の殺人者から仮面を毟り取るのだ。 歴史家。政治家。我々は、アフガニスタン、イラク、そして早々にイランでのように、俗に言う悪の勢力を壊滅させることによって西側に駆け寄ることはできない。我々はこれ以上、このナレーションを支持し続けることはできないのだ。

アルバニアの国外脱出と出国問題。共産主義の崩壊により、幾千ものアルバニア人家族がイタリアとギリシャに避難先を求めている。ここにおいても「ナレーション」が関わってくる。2015年のヴェネツィア・ビエンナーレへの参加に際し、君はマッコウクジラの骨格をアルバニアからイタリアに搬送し、移送時の写真で構成された映画を作成し、道行きを撮影した。だが、それは単なるドキュメンテーションではないように私には思えた。私の意見では、それ自体が作品である。国外脱出と渡航の問題に関連付けた上で、この作品について我々に語ってもらえるだろうか？ なぜ、君の作品のあの「部分」の搬送を撮影したのか？

君が提起する問題は変動し続けており、いかにも、ここで粉々に砕け散っては、世界の別の場所で再び結合するナレーションのように構造化されている。それは地球規模の問題であり、グローバルな政治の結果である。僕は特に、アイデンティティの形成が可能なこの強力な構造の、ある種の下部構造に興味がある。

国立フィレンツェ・アカデミア美術学院から除籍された翌年の2002年のインタビューで、フランツ・カフカの「巣穴(der Bau, The Burrow)」に関して、僕の実体験、もっと正確に言えば、僕という存在と物語の主人公とを比較しつつ質問をされた。 その短篇を読み返してみて気付いたのだが、 質問の意図は、 2001年に行った僕の仕事に関連しての認知的なものであっただけではなく、 移民に対しての歴史上の制約やステレオタイプを含んでいた。 僕という存在、 過去、 そして紋切り型に填められた僕の未来に関わる質問は、 国境を越える全ての人々のナレーションを構築するのと同じ視点によるものだ。

　僕が子供の頃、 家族がカフカについて話すのを聞いたことがあった。 僕はその名を聞くたびに不安に喘いだ。「Kafka(カフカ)」の綴りはアルバニア語で複数形の「頭蓋骨」（単数形はkafkë）を意味し、 それゆえ僕には、 なぜ頭蓋骨について話しているのかが分からなかった。 カフカはまさに頭脳派（cerebrale）の著者なので、 僕はこの音韻の類似性とこの言葉遊びが成り立つことをずっと気に入っていた。 過去に、 僕は現代の我々の状態と、 カフカの登場人物の頭（頭蓋骨）の内部に構築された建築との対称性を説明するため、 隠された、 あるいは、 深層にある記号論的な繋がりを摸索してきた。 だが、 物事はずっと単純でそれほど複雑ではないのだ。

　僕の学問事始めでは、 慣例やシステムの謀略に囚われずに行動していた。 僕はアカデミアで何をすべきか、 体制に対し、 どのような態度を取るかを大枠で扱った「Underground Movement」という題名のマニフェストを書いた。 二つのキー・コンセプトの下に取り組まねばならなかった。 フォンタナの切り口のように正確かつ完璧であること、 デュシャンのように複雑であること。 1999年に僕達は、 出現と消失を繰り返すイベントとして考案された最初のグループワークを始めた。 僕の親しい友人、 iMac G3を装備したマルクーゼの信奉者こと、 リッカルド・コミティーニ（Riccardo Comitini）と一緒に、 子供達が演じる1970年代の学校向け写真劇画のリメイクを作製した。再編された写真劇画は、'70年代の有名な展覧会3と同名の「Amore Mio(アモーレ・ミオ)」というタイトルの黒い本となった。僕達は、学校の要素に刑務所の要素を追加した。その作品を友人の試験で発表して、僕達は同じタイトルのビデオを「ループ」で再生し、アカデミアの講堂にてフルボリュームで上映した。黒と白の馬達の交尾のモンタージュ。その試験での発表を好評価するものは一人もいなかった、観衆だった同級生達でさえも。僕達は、女教授の苛立ちは予見できたが、同学年の学生達の拒絶は解せなかった。

　一般的に言えば、往々にして学のある、遥かに限定された鑑賞者を有する現代美術と異なり、より広い分布を持つ文学はより多くの読者を持つ。現代美術の鑑賞者は非常に保守的かつ閉鎖的なままで、文学の読者とは異なる。大衆は読むことで自分自身を見出したいと考えるため、正常性の側にいることが多い。それゆえ、文学の読者層は凡庸ではあるが一般的により幅広いのだ。

　ヨシフ・ブロツキイのテクスト「我々が亡命と呼ぶ状態」4は、移住/亡命作家の状況を語っている。その作家は常に祖国に向けられた羅針盤を持ち、現実の、だが想像上の大衆を相手にしてい

3　アキッレ・ボニート・オリーヴァ(Achille Bonito Oliva)監修で、自主的に集結した芸術家達により運営され、1970年8月6日モンテプルチャーノのリッチ宮殿で開催された合同展覧会「Amore Mio(我が愛)」は「文化的慣習の歴史上、前例なき異なる行動の幕を切って落とす：アーティスト各人のため、芸術批評の因襲的媒介の圏外に、批評的に自らを形成する直接責任を肯定する」というオリジナリティ溢れるモットーを掲げていた。

4　このテクストはイタリアの出版社アデルフィによって、ジルベルト・フォルティ(Gilberto Forti)翻訳で、1987年ノーベル文学賞受賞者である、反体制派のこの作家により発せられた二つのスピーチとともに

る。多くの場合、このタイプの作家は自分自身を優越する者と見做し、自らの地位が、この社会で偽装せざるを得ない一介の移民労働者や亡命者の境遇と、横並びにされることを望まない（しかし、作家や詩人、芸術家は、その社会から着想している）。だが、実在か想像かに関わらず、この同胞達、これらの「他者」がひしめく「鶏小屋の雄鶏」たらんと奮闘している。

僕は最近、亡命者として国外在住のアルバニア人詩人と接触した。他の多くの現代作家のように、彼は2カ国語、母国語と居住先の国の言語で執筆している。出身地の言語を、今となっては我々の背後にある軍隊、アイデンティティの鎧と考えると、詩人グズィム・ハイダーリの受難[5] は重要なケースとなる。その昔、我らの偉大なる詩人の幾人かは彼らの時代のイメージを捉えることができたが、現代詩人達は、我々の社会の精神と今日の状態を表現し得る、強烈なイメージを未だに摸索している。そのイメージはさらに逃亡する。そのイメージは潜伏するのだ。幾度となく…

自主礫刑、共産主義時代の同僚達によって文字通り礫にされ、さらに自国の若い詩人や作家によっても同様の仕打ちを受けたが、彼は自らの詩句で飽くことなき一貫性を持って叱責の礫を浴びせる。僕が興味深いと思うのは、他の者達においてよりも、彼の人生と彼の真実が一つとなり、このイメージを構築しようと不断の追求をする集合的記憶の複雑な証拠として提案される

『Dall'esilio（亡命先から）』（1988年）に発表された。［訳注：本文中のテクスト題名は伊語名からの翻訳である。］

5　イタリアに帰化したアルバニア詩人兼翻訳者であるグズィム・ハイダーリ（Gëzim Hajdari）は、1957年ルシュニェ（Lushnje）生まれ。地下社会と政治との間の腐敗及び結託を繰り返し告発したことで受けた脅迫のために、1992年に自国を去りイタリアに渡ることを余儀なくされた。

ことだ。小説まがいの状況で、1992年に故国を離れた逃亡者の詩人は、かの地に戻ることは二度となかった。アルバニア史に関する彼の詩は、過度に主観的なバージョンを与えているとの弁明で、ほとんど世に知られておらず、自発的に影に捨て置かれている。その主観的バージョンが、詩人の語彙の本質的な特徴でもある。

　イメージには歴史を築く力があり、ハイダーリは多面体のイメージを築き上げる。時にそれは、粗悪な映画にとっては風変わりだが、優れた監督にとっては一種独特でもある。国の実際の文化に相応しく、それでいて、国に対して抱くステレオタイプの認識にも適したイメージだ。現在であると同時に、遥か昔のイメージを創り出す。まるで、記憶から失われてしまった、時代を超越するイメージを洞窟から出て来させようとし、我々の間に据え直し、それを再び活性化するかのように。僕が興味を持っているのは、この「強制的に忘れ去られた」イメージの再構築に見られる執拗さであり、詩人はこのように近年の過去を再編成するため、我々の「休眠状態にある証言」を活性化することで、そのイメージを達成する。これらの複雑でありながらも鋭いパラドックスの数々に、現代のアルバニア人の精神が捉えられているようだ。

　上記に関して、1963年にパトクトゥの沖合[6]で発生した、魚雷によるクジラ殺害のエピソードについても考察できるだろう。そのナレーションは、ティラナ自然科学博物館を舞台に語り継がれ、切迫する劣化とともに、年を経るにつれ尾鰭が付いた。ファシズム時代の'30年代に建設された建物は、意図的に放置さ

―――――――――

6　パトクトゥ潟（Laguna e Patokut）は今日、ドゥラス北部の海岸にある広大な自然保護区である。この区域は、様々な犯罪組織と重鎮の政治家との間の絶え間なき対立によって影響を被った。

れ徐々に劣化していたが、とどまる所を知らない資本主義の現代建築への渇望に、その地を明け渡すため最近になって解体された。もはや存在しないその空間の内部には、科学的な証拠、ある正面衝突の隠喩が展示されていた。建物はもともと飛行機の格納庫として設計され、第二次世界大戦後の1948年、共産主義者達によって自然科学博物館に改築された。博物館は、ソビエト連邦との政治的関係も反映した名立たるデビューを飾った。博物館の初代剥製師はロシア人で、彼の剥製作品、特にオオカミとフクロウは、今日でも大変良好に保存されており、収蔵品の中で最も美しい作品とされている。これらの物品の多くは、国の様々な政治的期間に関連する物語の担い手だ。フクロウは、アルバニアとソ連の二国間関係が終了した1958年に、ニキータ・フルシチョフと渾名を付けられ、その傍らにエンヴェル・ホッジャの手によって殺されたペリカンが設置された。別の小さなペリカンが同じ展示ケース内にあり、一説では共産党政権のメフメット・シェウ首相（Mehmet Shehu）によって殺されたと言われている。そのシェフ首相は後にホッジャによって殺害された。

それにひきかえ、マッコウクジラの残骸は、冷戦に関する遥かに壮大な物語を語っていた。1963年、マッコウクジラは、ソビエト連邦から譲渡された11隻の哨戒艇のうちの1隻に外海で襲われた。マッコウクジラを撃った船の番号 – それがカトル・イ・ラドゥス号、ゼロ号（Zero）あるいはトレティ・イ・ラドゥス号（Treti i Radës 投錨地の3番目）だったのかどうか – については、いかなる文書も見つからなかった。しかし、米軍基地があるイタリアの海岸からの緊迫した攻撃の恐怖で、偏執妄想状態のアルバニア海軍は、海で巨大な物体群を目撃したと言われている。間断なきパトロール中の哨戒艇は、最高司令部と連絡を取り、即時攻撃を命じられた。 魚雷発射。 アメリカの潜水艦と疑われたのは、 マッコウクジラあるいは「キャシャロット[7]」の一群だった。 群れは全滅。 彼らは哨戒艇の後部にクジラの1頭を縛りつけ、 岸まで運んだ。 そこでクジラは船員達自身によって埋葬され、 数年後に博物館のスタッフによって掘り起こされた。 全ての骨片は丁寧に洗浄・準備され、 自然科学博物館の技術者達によって骨格が完璧に組み立てられた。

大きく開かれた口で咆哮を上げ、 恐怖の念を抱かせるかのように、 はたまた海上での激突を証言するかのように、 アルバニア海軍によって命を奪われた海獣は「アメリカ潜水艦」と渾名を付けられ、 その体長は11メートルに及んだ。 ベニヤ板の台座の上に展示され、 何十年もの間そこに留まり、 遥か彼方に置き換え可能なこの政治にまつわる物語を語り続けていた。

博物館の解体に伴い、 博物館自体が、 特にその建物が長年に渡り生み出してきたナレーション、 記憶の政策をも消滅させることが望まれた。 新自由主義の精神はまさに、 主要であれ傍系であれ、 全ての記憶の消去を望むようであり、 斬首の原始的手法を用いてそれを行う。 この物語が、 僕の2011年の映像作品《It Wears as it Grows》の主題だった。 僕の《Albanian Trilogy: A Series of Devious Stratagems》の最初のエピソ

7　マッコウクジラ（抹香鯨Physeter macrocephalus）は、 有歯のクジラ目であるハクジラ亜目Odontocetiの中で最大である。 フランス語では"cachalot（キャシャロ）"（英語でもかつては使用されていた名称、 現在は廃語）、 スペイン語では"cachalote（カチャロテ）"と呼ばれ、 おそらくポルトガル語の"cachola（カショラ）"に由来するとされる。 カショラとは頭を意味する口語的な語彙で、 これらの動物では頭部が体長の3分の1を占める。

ードである。2015年、映像作品タイトルにも予告されるように、政治的な空間によって生成されたナレーションを継続するため、僕は骨格を別の観衆に委ねたいと思い、「All the World's Futures(全ての世界の未来)」という名を冠したアート展覧会で、それをさらに異なる台座に置きたいと考えた。

　僕は骨格をイタリアに持ち込もうと決意し、ヴェネツィア・ビエンナーレの主要展示作品の一つとして、アルセナーレ会場スペースにあるアルバニア・パビリオンに展示することにした。そこでは、骨格が自らの過去を物語ることに加えて、イデオロギー、権力の実体そのもの、国家、芸術、市場について：あるいはマルクスの言葉を借りれば、人間の疎外する力についても語ることができた。

　これを全て達成するために、'60年代の構造を切断し、骨格を多くの部分に分割して木箱に収めた。僕は道行きの記録で「本物の」映画を作りたいとは一度も思わなかったが、近い将来に痕跡を残しておきたかったのだ。骨を個々に撮影した。僕は骨格とその歴史を国の遺産として、歴史的発見及び芸術作品の登録センターのアーカイブに初めて登録した。その後、非常に複雑な税関手続きを経て、最後に海での航海を続けた。組み立てプロセスからヴェネツィアでの解体まで、全てのステップをドキュメンタリー撮影した。ビエンナーレ閉会時、展覧会場全体の撤去作業中に、僕は、展示スペース内で数日間働いていた二人の彫刻家を雇った。彼らは骨格の様々な部分の完璧な石膏の鋳型を作り、その後、僕は鋳造場でその鋳型に溶けた鉄を投じた。この全ては、僕自身またはプロセスの様々な段階での関係者によってドキュメンタリー撮影されており、異なる場所で生まれた「映画」の始まりのようなものを構築している。写真、ビデオ、書類、骨格そのもの、鉄の複製品が、映画芸術の中で最も美しいものの一つである「シャドウ・フィルム」あるいは「パラレル・フィルム」と呼ばれるメカニズムを引き起こしたのかもしれない。ティラナに再び戻った骨格は、もはや僕の映像が語る歴史物語の単なる発生源ではない。今日では、新博物館内で、進化中の新たな物語を異なる言語で語っている。その修復された建物は、共産主義時代に陸軍オーケストラの本部を擁していた、首都の郊外に位置している。

民営化について。民営化の「ナレーション」。私のトラックへのコメントで君が言うように、共産主義崩壊後、アルバニアは未だ進行中の、非常に強力で非常に「干渉的」な民営化プロセスを経験した。このプロセスにはどのような「ナレーション」が伴ったのか？アルバニアでは、これらの選択を正当化するため、あるいはいずれにせよ、それに「寄り添う」ために、現代美術はどのように用いられているのか？

「未来を民営化する。」
アルバニアの「ルネサンス」政府の関心は、現代の発展の二つの主要な側面、即ち（現代）芸術と建築に非常に集中している。前者は与えられた目標を達成したように見える。少なくとも、芸術を推進していると考え、誰がこの現代性の内に在るべきで、誰がその外に留まるべきかを決定する者達の側では。奴らによって課された二者択一は、逆説的に、歴史の内にいるのか外にいるのか、ということと同等だ。最近の現代美術は膠着状態にあるようであり、腐敗国家の赤絨毯と成り下がり、おそらく本来の使命を使い果たしてしまったのではないかと言う人も多いが、建築によってもたらされる現代性への衝動という、より興味深い発展の第2段階への道を開いた。以前とは大きく異なり、この最新の使命は、今日の市場に対する正確なアイディアを持った経営陣によって遂行される、しっかりと練られたビジネスプランのように見える。この政治計画の多くの部分は、新生労働党プログラムから「盗用」されたと言わねばならない。今日の政府と首相の顧問が、トニー・ブレアとアラステア・キャンベルであることは偶然ではない。重要なアーティストやポップシンガーの成功と参加（後に乗り掛かった船を見捨て、彼らは自身でキャリアを築き続けたが）を利用して「変化の新鮮さ」を導入した新生労働党とは異なり、ここでは逆のことが起こる。見るからに沈みかけた権力の船に乗り込もうと、文字通り、押し合い圧し合いしている若いアーティスト達の間には、熾烈な争いがあるのだ。これらの芸術家や建築家と政府の友愛関係はさらに強固になっている。彼らはまさに、兄弟盃を酌み交わした「Brothers in Crime(共犯者達)」である。

グローバル化の他に逃げ道はないという企業国家の信条に、憲法の原理原則に取って代わるもう一つの戒律が我が国では付け加わる。組織犯罪との同盟に関するものだ。この政府は、芸術家とお国の建築家とともに、メビウスの帯に閉じ込められているように見え、組織犯罪なしでは生き残ることができない。

国内で開催される展覧会の大半は、研究やアルバニアの問題への関心からではなく、公式のナレーションの急速な学習から生じる。アルバニア、そして首都そのものが、多くの場合、ポスト・ヒストリカルな展示として使用されている。アーティスト自身は常に、教養があり行儀の良い個人と見做される。積極的な政治活動をしてはならず、展示コンセプトの早漏を批判するのではなく正当化しなくてはならない。現実の、飾り気がなかったり、美しかったり、乱暴だったりする言葉遣いのような、真の表現法を用いてはならない。だが、今にも爆発しかねない、一触即発に見える大衆を当惑させるために、社会と政治の永久奴隷として、それらしい表現法をこしらえなければならない。この事実は陳腐であると同時に危険なものである。

　政府の説法や弁明はもはや誰をも納得させず、働き口を失わないためだけに投票を義務付けられた大衆さえも説き伏せない。社会主義者達の政府は、初歩的な段階に留まっている右派の政府に比べると、遥かに先を行っていると言わなければならない。アルバニアの社会主義者にとって、統治することは利益を得ることを意味する。彼らが掲げる変化は、実際には到来することが叶わず、3次元のレンダリングでしか表現され得ない。メディア統制も含むこの構造を支配するものは、多くの外国籍キュレーターの発掘と雇用をも左右する。これは現代美術の分野で起こった最悪の事態の一つである。これは第1回ティラナ・ビエンナーレの陰謀ではなく、まさしく「ティラナの真の陰謀」のようだ[8]。これらの展覧会は怠惰な観光客には向いているが、好奇心旺盛な探究者には決して適していない。怠惰な観光客は、常に新自由主義の犠牲者であり武器であり、これらの展覧会はまさにこのタイプの観客を求めている。

　それを認めようではないか：この全てには興味深い要素がある。好奇心をそそると言えよう。なぜなら、知覚困難にすることで基体を排除しようとする一方で、これらの枠組みを弱体化させる状況が生み出され、それらの状況は公式のナラティヴに亀裂を入れ、初めてこれらの亀裂を可視化するからだ。公式のナラティ

8　Il vero Complotto di Tirana：後述の脚注50を参照。

ヴはじわりじわりと分解し、その骨組みを全ての者に曝け出す。スカンデルベグ広場に設置されたそれらの巨石は、ピラミッド状の頂点からめくれ落ちて逆さまになった精神的障壁としてのみ、そこに置かれているようだ。今、それらの石は広場に横臥しているが、撤去されるべきであり、体制に投げ付けられるべきである。人々がそれらを所有するのを妨げるためではなく、常に閉じられたままの扉を破壊するためのものであるべきだ。

　人民は、もはや政治によって生成されたものを、スキャンダルだと騒ぎ立ててはいないようである。何事もこの態度を変え得ないようだ。国内で、最近確立された芸術の保守的な表現形式は、分かり易い唯一の形式として説明されており、現実と矛盾している。芸術は日常茶飯の腐敗を隠蔽し、この現実を糊塗するために使用されている。近頃では、システム即ち制度化されたアートシーンは、この現実に根差したアイディアではなく、国外から輸入されたプロジェクトでのみ機能する。活動する方法において、僕の意見は真っ向から反対だ。現実や輸入されたものよりも、想像力とスキャンダラスさを増すこと。観衆を刺激しリアクションさせる。創意工夫と計算された作戦行動。脇に追い遣られたもの、シーンによって「通関された」ものから着想を得る。増加の一途を辿っている精神障碍を抱えた路上生活者達から閃きを見出す。彼らは僕にとってインスピレーションの源である。「奴らの」ナレーションに逆らう重大な作品、ある種の異端、あのナレーションを打破し得るほどに強烈な異端作品を、じっくりと鑑賞する準備を整えることが民衆にとって肝要だと思う。

　この件に関して、最近、非常に興味深いアーティスト、スカァレット・ホーリ（Scarlet Hori）がアフリカに向けて出立しなければならないと述べた。彼女は長い探究の後、まじないをかけられる重要な呪術師に会うためにもその地へ赴くことを考えていたと僕に語った。彼女は、我々の国会議員連中、政府の全構成員、大統領と首相に特別な魔法をかけたかったのだ。そのアイディアは僕には素晴らしく思えた。DebatikCenter of Contemporary Artのアーカイブや制作、僕達の次のテーマがこのタイプの作品に捧げられることを望む。

　他方では、建築は未来を銘記するための主力であり、今日の政府はこの実践に焦点を合わせている。社会の変革は、政治の汚染された仕掛けを通してのみ起こり、文化のおかげではない。文化は歴史の終焉を本当に体験している最中のように見える。変革は、事情に疎く問題とは無関係の門外漢が、現代美術に遭遇した時の衝撃に似た暴力で、もたらされる。最近、すぐに目に付くのは、都市デザインと特別な建築プロジェクトに注入された政治的狂気である。認可されたばかりの建物や、建設中の建物のデザインを変更可能なテーマ・シンボル・文化・経済的関心の寄せ集めがあり、互いに争って協力せず、反対に軋轢と不協和音を引き起こす。シンプルなものが持つ複雑さへの、根深い憎悪がある。メディアの面前で、軍事専門家による遂行の如く火薬を装填され、一大スペクタクルと化した破壊行為は、記憶の消去とともに、黄金色に光輝く偽の現代的アイデンティティ構築をも記録する、唯一の瞬間のように思われる。かつてのように、再び赤や白のレンガ造りの家を建てるよりも美しいものには、一体何があると言うのだろうか？ 生き残った家々を、あばら屋・独房・鶏小屋・豚小屋と人々は呼ぶが、それらは、この都会の狂気の中で、時の流れによって老朽化はしていても、頭（こうべ）を高く掲げて屹立する唯一の建物である。なぜ、誰一人として、都市を破壊し調和を乱す色彩で愚行を働くのではなく、未来よりも雄弁に我々に語りかけることのできる過去のシンプルさと合理性を、別のレベルに進展させることができないのだろうか？

　建築には常に摩擦がある。社会主義時代の建築と現代の建築の間に軋轢があるが、これは成長中の都市では全くもって当たり前のことである。ファシスト様式建築と近年の建築との間にコントラストがあるのは、アイデンティティをめぐる鬩ぎ合いや、建物同士での競合をも知覚するのが事実であるためだ。新造の建築物は過去とはコミュニケーションを取らない。それどころか、最も重大なのは、新築建造物同士で疎通せずに、相克が発生することである。相手を押し退け、時には引き寄せ合い、諸処の広場に凸凹と隆起を成す。ティラナの街では、地盤はもはや安定せず動いているように思える。それはまさに沖合にいるかのようである。

　これらは、願わくはナラティヴの空白を明らかにし、新たな道を拓く異なる種類の展覧会を通して、取り組むべき課題の一部である。この混迷に取り組む展覧会は未だ見かけたことはない。秩序を装い、社会問題を隠蔽しようとする試みが未だに行われている。展覧会を監修/ケアする［訳注：curare監修・編纂する、治療・看護する］とは、概念的にクリーンにするのではなく、空間的にのみ清掃活動をするようなものと想像されているふしがある。展示スペースは、私立病院の各室との比較がこぎれいさにおいては成り立つが、現実の難局を反映している公立の救急病棟とは比べようがない。これほど厚顔無恥に大衆に嘘をつく、この者どもは誰なのだ？別の空間を想像できない、この批評家達やキュレーターとは何者だ？アーティストや俳優が公で、あるいは観衆に向かって話す時に「卑俗さ」を用いないようにと教えを垂れる、このアートシーンとは一体何なのだ？この架空の無知なオーディエンス、その手の規範を強要

するアートシーンの、 この自称観客を構成しているのは誰な
のか？ 彼らはどの観衆の名の下で話しているのだ？ この国で
唯一の興味深い観衆とは、 奴らが野卑と呼ぶ大衆である：僕
はそれに反して、 その大衆とこそ相まみえたいと思っている。
アーティストが先人達の特定の行いを繰り返したり、 さらに先
へ進んだりすることを恐れるのは、 どうしてなのか？ なぜ、
建築家は経済の発展について語り、 なぜ、 彼らはこの架空の発
展を中国と比較するのか？ 僕が毎日耳にする不条理は、 精神病
院に相応しいものだ。 教育目的で展覧会を設営する必要はない
が、 人々に考えさせ、 反応させるために展示を制作しなければな
らない。 君の考え方を変革することが可能な展覧会。
　この種の特徴を持たぬ展覧会には、 シュクルダートクラツィア
(Shkërdhatokracia)[9] という一つのタイトルしかありえない。

「DebatikCenter of Contemporary Art(現代美術デバティ
クセンター)」とは何か？ アルバニアの「政治的美学」というコン
テクストに、 どのように組み込まれるのだろうか？ デバティクセ
ンター・プロジェクトは「美学的戦略」を活用し政治を行う別の方
法なのか？ また、 どのように活動しているのか？ 君達はどの
ようにイメージを使用しているのか？ 定義することが可能であ

9　伊語「Cratocraziaクラトクラツィア」即ち「権力そのものに基づいた権
　　力、 カースト制独裁」と翻訳可能なShkërdhatokraciaという用語
　　は、 アルバニア人作家ドリテロ・アゴーリ(Dritëro Agolli, 1931–2017
　　)によって、 共産主義政権崩壊後の国内での政治の結果を示すために
　　考案された。

れば、どのタイプのイメージ及びイメージ理論を、君と仲間達はデバティクセンターを介して – 政治的に – 擁護しているのか？

DebatikCenter of Contemporary Art［訳注：以下、DCCA］は、学術・芸術界やジャーナリズムなどの異なるバックグラウンドを持つ個人達によって立ち上げられたイニシアチブである。DCCAのコラボレーターは、活動家、建築家、映像監督、架空及び実在の集団、批評家、キュレーター、翻訳者、弁護士だ。「dibat-titoディバッティト」［伊語：討論、ディベート］と非常によく似た単語「Debatikデバティク」はDjemtë e Bashkuar Antarë të Idea-leve Komuniste（ディエムトゥ・エ・バシュクァル・アンタール・トゥ・イデアーレヴェ・コムニステ）の頭文字であり、「共産主義理想メンバーの統一少年団」を意味する。元祖のDebatikグループは第二次世界大戦中に発足。彼らはナチス・ファシズムとの戦いで共産主義者を支援した6〜19歳の少年達だった。彼らの多くは、組織の理想を体現できずに戦時中に命を落とした。実際のところ、誰一人もその理想を体験することは叶わなかった。この頭文字を再び使用することにした時、僕達が込めた想いは、まさに彼らに、突如として毟り取られた命に、砕け散った理想に、より良い未来であったかもしれない過去へのノスタルジアに向けられていた。DCCAの活動は、特に若者達、過去に対する分析的アプローチを持つべきこれからの世代、及び未来の変革を対象としている。

　過去と、その過去に基づいてどのように未来を銘記し始めるか、をめぐる継続的な戦いがある。アルバニアの歴史家と政治家がこの問題にアプローチした方法は、過去の「土壌改良」を試みること、特定の期間はそのままにして、他の期間を書き換えようとすることだった。 これは存続しており、 今後しばらくの間も深刻な大問題が残るだろう。

　僕が話しているノスタルジアとは、 その我々の過去、 より良い未来の理想郷的な約束に関するものだ。 その約束はその当時口火を切られ、 この恐ろしい未来を我々が「受け入れた」がために、 非現実的で不可能であることが明らかになった。 これらの時代に郷愁を抱き、 霧散してしまった集団的可能性を後悔することは、 非常に重要だと思う。 僕は、 置き去りにされたものをさらに見返し、 過去を注意深く観察し続け、 この不自然な突然変異を証言し続けることに興味がある。

　DebatikCenter of Contemporary Artは、 様々な分野からの協力を得て、 この突然変異を記録しようとしている。 これは言うまでもなく広範囲に普及しているが、 我々のような小国ではより顕著である。 また僕達は、 我々の時代の精神をも捉えるために、 時間に抵抗し挑むことが可能な、 世界各地からの過去の写真画像を使用してアイディアを構築することも試みている。 例として、《Moving Billboard》は、 2018年に実施したプロジェクトである。 このプロジェクトは、 山の頂上や森林部を起点として、 様々な都市の幹線道路及び二級道路にいたるまで、 北から南へと全国に点在する24枚の広告用看板で構成されている。 前述のタイプの画像を含んだ上で、 プロジェクトは24時間に分割された。 各画像は日中もしくは夜間の特定の時間帯に一致し、 予め定められた場所に1時間だけ設置された。 きっかり1時間を終了後、 巡回チームによって、 画像ポスターは看板から撤去された。 移動中の鑑賞者と、 その者が1から24番目までの画像全てを目にする確率が非常に低いことを念頭に置いて、 僕達が想定したアイディアは、 各々の鑑賞者が24時間の間に見ることができる組み合わせから、 異なるナレーションを構築する可能性を残しておくことだった。 このプロジェクトは、 経済的腐敗から警察の残虐行為、 環境破壊/汚染、 現代地政学、 移民、 戦争、 テロリズムなど、 様々なタイプの写真画像で構成されていた。

　君が言及している美学的戦略は、 僕が戦術的戦略と呼ぶもので、 即ち政治の美学的防御を貫通可能な戦術である。 政治の主たる目的は芸術を利用し、 その背後に身を潜めることだ。 僕は芸術を、 僕自身を隠す盾とは一度も考えたことはない。 金儲けをするものとして見たことがない。 従って、 芸術の取り巻きの間で語られる芸術家-政治家の、 今では主流となった理想郷の夢物語を、 僕は決して受け入れることができないだろう。 それは嘘偽りであり、 虚言であり続けるだろう。

　外国の芸術家達にとって非常に魅力的に映るこの国の独自性は、 芸術と政治を隔てる天と地ほどの距離ではなく、 両者の架空の近接である。 国外での認識とナレーションでは、 芸術と政治それぞれの中核により一層接近するために、 この隔たりを完全に排除し、 二者を分断する障害を野放しにしないという意思があるとされる。 中核そのものがありありと見え、 今では極めて至近距離にある。 これは陳腐な表面的なものに過ぎない。 この素晴しい理念の礎で(この先も)あり続けることは不可能な、 プロパガンダの思い付きに他ならない。

　我々は代議制の危機に瀕している。 人々はもはや代表されているとは感じておらず、 これは世界中の至る所で起こっている。 今日の政治家を意味する言葉はその力を失った。 この時代に、 彼らの役割に実際に合致し得る単語はなさそうだ。 彼らを泥棒、 汚職者と、 事実その通りなのだし、 呼ぶこともできるが、 社会にとって、 これでは無邪気で無力に思える。 この国には、差し出がましい無償の助言として言及されることが多いルールがある。主に僕の両親の世代からだが、同国在住でビジネスをしている同業者や外国人からも言われることがある。政府を決して批判してはならない、前に出ずに横並びであれ、決して政治に口を出してはならない、と言う：万が一、どうしてもそれを実行しなければならない場合は、可能な限りの金を儲けて、こっそりとずらかるのだ。これらの人物の何人かは、大企業に携わる非常に重要な人々であり、彼らの役職からすればこの言い分は頷ける。他方、別の者達は大規模なNGO（非政府組織）を率いる知識人、人権活動家であるのだが、諸問題はここから始まる。最も保護されておらず、最も誠実なその他の人達は、我々の親類縁者である。

僕の懸念は常に解決策を見付けることだった。僕は常に国内在住で縦割りの地位にある人々や協力者を探している。抵抗を、声を荒げるきっかけとしてではなく、いわんや国家資金獲得を目的とするプロジェクトを組織するための口実を得る詭弁としてでもなく、抵抗を抵抗としてのみ考える人々を僕は求めている。

これは全て、奪い去られた未来に関係している。何処であろうとおかまいなしに、何が何でも未来を絶えず盗み取ろうとする者ども、政治家、政党によって我々は率いられている。彼らはこの地にいかなる未来も想像することができない。盗まれたがために、この未来、いやむしろ、これら複数の未来は、含めたくない情報の断片を内包する一纏まりとして、まことらしく過ぎ去っていく。

我が国の未来と、イタリア・ドイツ・米国など、我々が未来を盗用している他の国の過去を考えると、初歩的な推論が思い浮かぶ。実際、我々は過去に起こったことを盗むことしかできないため、これらのひび割れた未来には歪曲された情報が含まれている。既存のものとは非常に異なる、より現実的で真実の美学を創出する直感。ハクマールリィア・プル・ドレトゥスィ(Hakmarrja për Drejtësi)[10] は現実の脅威だったのか、それとも1990年代半ばに違法に表面化したメディアの断片だったのか? これらの盗まれてしまった未来には、赤い旅団(Brigate Rosse)、ウェザーマン(Weather Underground)、またはバーダー・マインホフ・グループ(Baader Meinhof)に関する情報の欠片が含まれているのか?僕が興味を持っているのは、まさにこの抽象化であるのだが、抽象と言うほど空論的ではないのだ。

---

10 Hakmarrja për Drejtësi(正義のための復讐)は、アルバニアで1996年に、メディアの轟々たる非難を浴びて発覚した、胡散臭く、おそらくは幻の破壊的テロリストグループの名称である。事件は20年に渡る裁判の後、被告人全員が完全無罪で解決した。

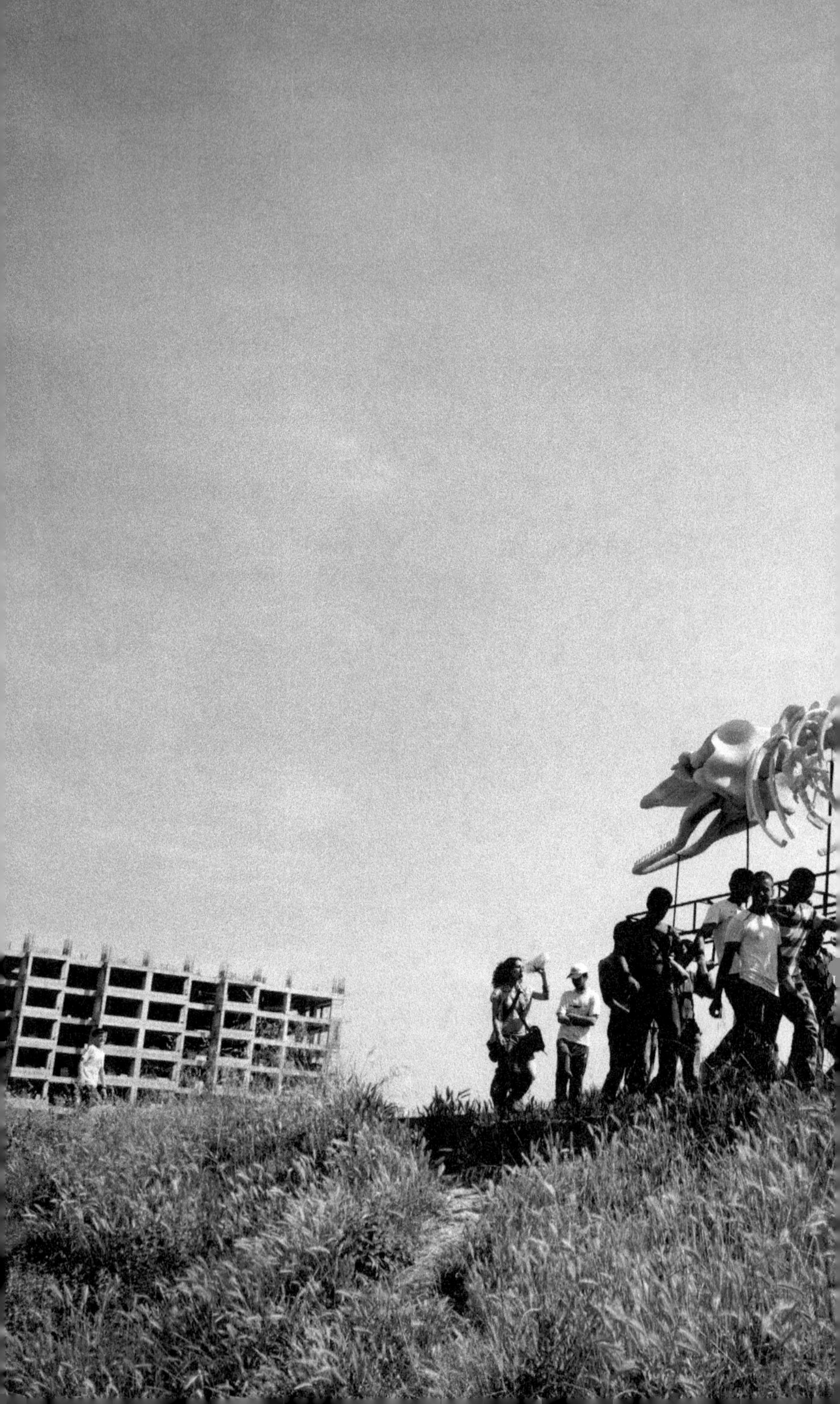

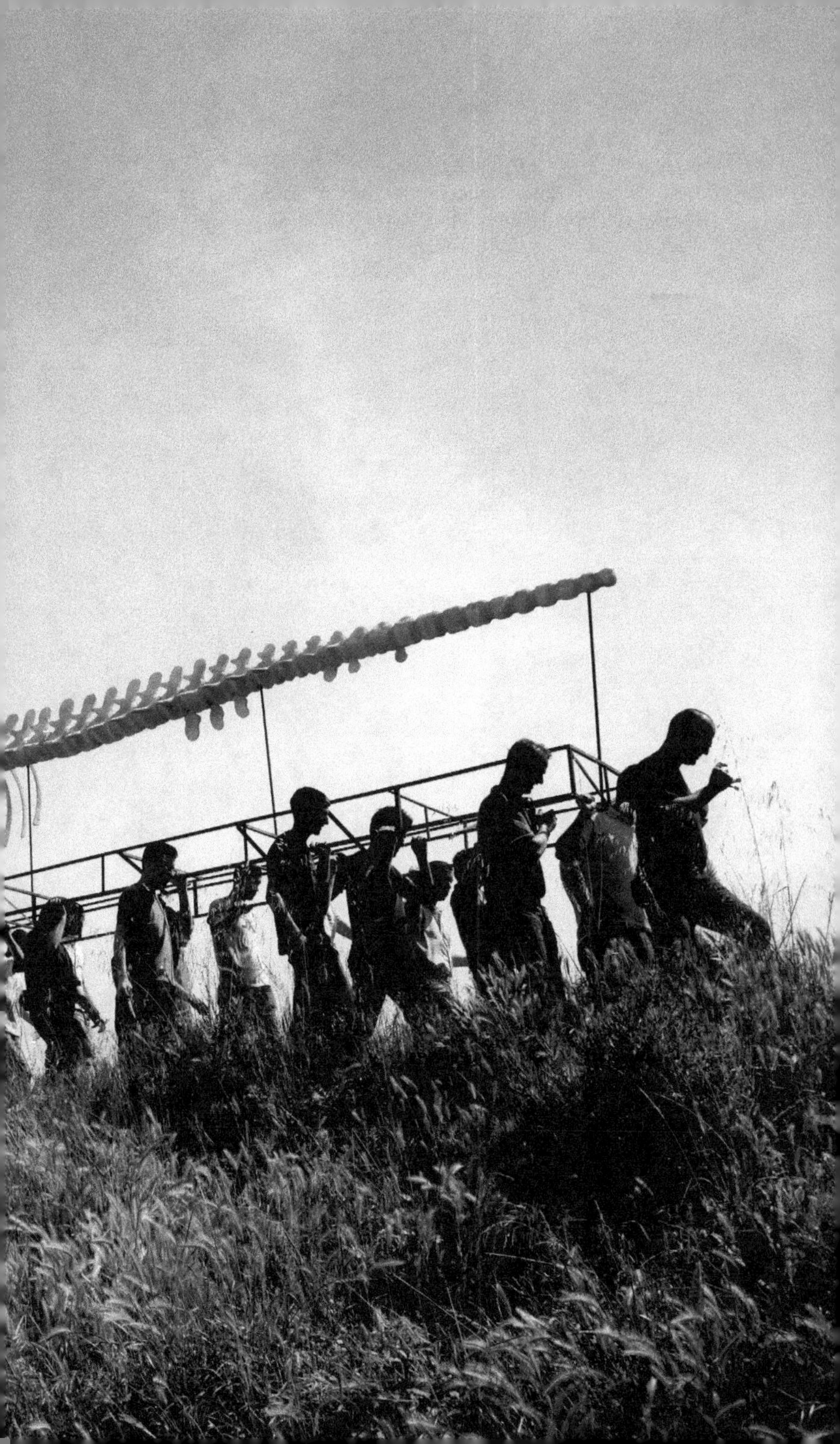

Fig. 10. It Wears As It Grows by Armando Lulaj, 2011.
C-print. 200×140cm. Production photo by Massimo Sciacca.
Courtesy of DebatikCenter Film, Artra Gallery and cinqueesei.

TRACK 03

Breaking Stones *is a performance you've made into an online video.*[1] *Can you tell us how* Breaking Stones *was conceived, how the video was conceived? What was (is) going on (historically, politically) at that (this) moment in time in Albania?*

For some time now I've been collecting stories and transcribing events based in everyday reality. They are unmistakable traces of the here and now that are still difficult to interpret. Or, to be more precise, the interpretation of these events can come about only by using various strata and levels of interpretation. They are events that surface as marginal exorcising responses, and they tell about a country — the words that come to mind are those of a much-loved author — that has to vomit on itself to escape dying. These stories look like theater pieces. Example: an old woman in slippers, who looked like she'd just gotten out of bed, was staring at the apex of the 4EverGreen Tower in Tirana, which was still under construction and will be one of the highest buildings in the Balkans. She was holding a bag full of rotten garbage. Gesturing to the tower custodian, she insisted that she absolutely had to go up to the top. The custodian feared the worst, but the old woman only wanted to go up the tower to lean out over the highest platform and throw down her bag of garbage. This story made me think of what Susan Sontag had

---

1   Armando Lulaj, *Breaking Stones* (2017), *DebatikCenter,* https://debatik-center.net/strikes/breaking_stones.

said about Albania when she spoke about garbage and the future of the country.

Another story seems to perfectly encapsulate the toxic reality of the country's media and politics. Some time ago, a politician went on all the television shows threatening other politicians. He held a large, black briefcase crammed, in his words, with compromising material, both audio and video, about his opponents, who were high-ranking government officials. The talk shows and other programs of that kind exploited him just as much as he exploited them. The media used and encouraged this blackmailer, a politician who was part of the 2013–17 governing coalition, but never investigated the compromising material he claimed to possess. This story is reflected in the marginal reality I'm talking about. It reminds me of a man who lives near the United States Embassy. Pleurad Xhafa[2] recounts that every morning a man of about thirty comes out of an alley beside the Embassy holding two black VHS cassettes up to his ear. He walks alongside the yellow wall of the Embassy, mixes in with the city and disappears into the crowd. He repeats this ritual every day, with no precise purpose, or at least that's what it seems. It makes for a truly exceptional performance.

Another boy, who lives near the Foreign Ministry, or the Ministry for Europe and Foreign Affairs as it called today, for a long time now has been pushing a brick down the street with his feet. He always takes the same route, and while he's carrying out his ritual he always drinks a bottle of Coca-Cola. Another man, about forty years old, appears every morning at the corner of the main square of a small suburban town, near the stop where the buses that leave for Tirana are stationed. Turning his back to the departing buses, he beats his head against the wall over and over again.

---

2   Pleurad Xhafa (b. 1984), is a visual artist and filmmaker who lives and works in Tirana. He graduated from the Academy of Fine Arts of Bologna in 2012, and is one of the founders of the DebatikCenter of Contemporary Art.

These acts happen by the hundreds and taken together they open a sort of curtain behind which we can see the part of reality that is on the verge of exploding. The foundations of these acts are purely political, and the energy of the gestures expresses today's problems better than all the artists working in the country now. *Breaking Stones* is closely connected to the curtain that unveils this reality.

For some time now I've been collecting crime news with the aim of producing a history book made up of 1,001 cases, starting from 1992. Before the nineties, under communism, no Albanian newspaper had a column reporting news of crimes — it wasn't allowed, though we should also say that there really wasn't much crime. Mine will be a book of the thousand and one nights, dealing with the evolution of society through crime in democratic times, and it will begin exactly on June 25, the day of the public hanging of two brothers in the town of Fier.

All these extracts of reality, like the cases mentioned before but also the crime news, are situations on or beyond the edge. Media coverage of these events, ferocious crimes, and even suicides would lead one to believe that what connects them all is the constant presence of the figure of the mentally ill person. The recurring trope of the "abnormal" is itself suspicious though, suggesting that there is something going on that "they" want to prevent us from finding out. In the majority of cases, the media don't investigate on their own and mental illness is, indeed, listed as a leading cause for these murders and suicides in the police reports. The number of cases is so high, however, that mental illness cannot possibly account for all of them. So the picture they paint is not the whole truth. The events have been altered: they've been edited in institutional offices. This ruse, upheld even by the victims' families, who for cultural reasons feel ashamed of, say, a suicide in the family, allows the authorities to camouflage reality.

In the cases I'm talking about we discover a substratum that reveals a parallel territory, a completely different country. In a certain sense they explain the reason for the desertion and abandonment that (unfortunately) have become the only politics and the only truth of our day.

Breaking Stones is one of the first works that was uploaded on the DCCA web platform, which we reactivated in 2017. The video is part of a section we call *strikes,* which includes only actions performed with precise purposes in precise places. The first ideas for *Breaking Stones* came out of this accumulation of stories. In my opinion, these acts go far deeper than any historical, political, or social narrative I could offer about this country. I'll only answer by saying that I'd really like someone to associate *Breaking Stones* with an act like the ones I've described, and for someone else to interpret it (also) by associating it with what has been happening here recently.

From the historical-artistic point of view, Breaking Stones *is certainly also a "nocturne." Why did you choose the night?*

The night has great evocative power, it is in fermentation, always waiting for something that might arrive, something that might happen. I'm fascinated by waiting, silence, stray animals, and a certain type of void that becomes more perceptible at night.

The void I'm talking about comes out of the collision and accumulation of many different situations and stories. It is the void formed in the instant an act is carried out, but it often remains suspended and indecipherable. The reverse sensation which is created by information doesn't interest me at all. I'm interested in what is formed but is indecipherable, what cannot be immediately interpreted. I call it the sensation of a void that comes out of a suspended act captured at the precise moment in which it must occur. During the night this sensation becomes even more visible and tactile. I like to associate the act carried out in *Breaking Stones* with a diving board into the void.

Art and crime. Breaking Stones *makes us think deeply about crime and vandalism. What difference is there between being an artist and being an "outlaw" or "criminal," as it were? In your life what relationships (even only conceptual) have there been with the concept of crime and criminality? According to you, how does the artist interpret the concept of crime and punishment? Crime and prison? Do we find this in* Breaking Stones?

The Société Spectrale, a collective that collaborates with the DCCA, recently carried out an operation condemned as vandalism. Their gesture was a precise consequence of a violent act carried out by the central government, which, along with city hall, has decided to build a new road just over two kilometers long at the stratospheric cost of forty million euros — a great piece of corrupt business on the part of this government, involving also the falsification of the signature of a US Senator. Before the work can begin, many houses and shops built after the nineties will have to be demolished. Most of them are lacking title deeds, even if they were constructed over twenty years ago and the inhabitants pay their taxes regularly. The government doesn't want to compensate the latter but simply evict them with the pretext that they erected their houses illegally. Over and again, these people have been called Neanderthals, unworthy of being citizens of the reborn capital. The authorities went so far as to spray-paint red crosses on the outside walls of their houses and the local shops, a gesture that infuriated the inhabitants. The Société Spectrale went to this suburb, bought cans of spray paint from a shop marked with a red cross and headed for Skanderbeg Square, which had recently been spiffed up as a symbol of government propaganda. The performers held their forearms in front of the enormous rocks that surround the plaza, middle fingers raised, and proceeded to liberally spray paint their rough surface, transforming the rocks into spectacular contemporary cave paintings.

The cave paintings were considered acts of vandalism, whereas the red crosses that the authorities painted on the houses of the citizens, which remind us of terrifying episodes in the horrific history of the 20th century, weren't. Prejudice and bigotry remain little-studied phenomena in this country and we don't talk about them much. For example, the marginalized communities in the country, people who by and large came from rural areas and moved to large towns in the early nineties, are referred to by names and adjectives such as "Chechens," Neanderthals," "faggots," "Talibans," "ISIS members," etc. This sort of language is copied mainly from the vocabulary that the country's politicians use on a daily basis; it has become *culture*. Recently, the Société Spectrale began to build a library called *The Essential Library*. It is comprised of books, articles, and other materials about Chechnya, the Chechens and their history; about the meaning of the word Taliban and the region it belongs to; about the struggle of LGBTQ+ people; about misogyny — which is deeply rooted in this country; about the evolution and life of the Neanderthals; and obviously about terrorism and ISIS. The titles, names, and words that appear in this *Library* are always used in derogatory terms, triggering hatred, nourishing prejudice and bigotry, and sparking off local conflicts. These words have changed our way of looking at others, at strangers, as it were. It is time to remove this terminology from the Albanian language and replace it with this essential bookstore. The *Library* will be a space for discovery, but also for discussion about the significance of the words used.

While I was working on the idea for *Breaking Stones* I discovered a meaningful connection between the artistic lyceum I'd attended until 1998 and Tirana's Penitentiary 313. As a matter of fact, these two institutions located in the capital have the same name, "Jordan Misja." Born in Shhkodër in 1911, Jordan Misja was a patriot and a communist hero. He was a painter, having enrolled in the Florence Academy of Fine Arts in 1940. In 1942 he was killed in the north of Albania by the fascists. In any case, I don't think this is something to ignore, the fact that the institution that is meant to prepare artists and the penitentiary have the same name. Through my research I also discovered that the name "Jordan Misja" was given to the penitentiary after 1997, and this is another example that shows once and for all the importance of that year and the direction the country took back then.

Most of the footage in *Breaking Stones* was in fact shot near Penitentiary 313. The police car that appears in the second frame continuously patrols the area surrounding the prison, which is obviously under constant surveillance.

In this period of the country's history, the figures of the artist, the politician, and the criminal merge. Today's reality has gone beyond what was envisaged, it has overreached the intended experimental utopia. This can be best understood and deciphered by studying the link between contemporary art and organized crime. To speak about the fusion between contemporary art and (Albanian) politics is by now only a polite way to designate this new connection. I'm fascinated by these latest developments, because I've never believed in any of these politicians, who are supported by a handful of successful artists. The idea of working toward a utopian fusion between art and politics has never really come to life in this country. The artists, curators, and architects associated with this organization need to inform themselves better. What makes me laugh even harder is to see artists whose work isn't actually trite support this farce left, right, and center. *What the fuck was Douglas Gordon thinking?*

I think our Prime Minister has actually ruthlessly violated many of these people, but he's done this with velvet gloves so to speak. The connection I'm talking about can be considered the second Tirana Conspiracy, or the second Tirana Affair. The first is generally thought to be the incident that took place during the first *Biennale di Tirana* in 2001, which we'll talk about later. That made the failure of a certain organizational structure clear. This second case, which is still very much actual today, has reached a new level: politics, organized crime, and contemporary art are governing a state.

This new level also represents the beauty and the success of a foretold failure, which for the moment none of the subjects involved seem willing to accept. It seems to be a well-thought-out artistic enterprise, and I don't believe that the person or the people behind it will ever produce anything of this magnitude again. They've made a large contemporary social sculpture. They've planted sick palm trees on toxic land.

Albanian politicians are aware of this, because they flaunt this connection, they illustrate it using mafia codes in their press conferences. They seem proud of this new association, this language: they're not afraid of being unmasked because they've taken off the mask themselves, and they have a mission. The mission of this government is very interesting, and it is succinctly described by Jonida Gashi[3] when she says, "Taking after the leaders of the original Albanian National Renaissance movement, who at the end of the 19th century sought to launch the country into modernity, the members of today's Renaissance movement (which in actual fact is a faction inside the Socialist Party) are trying to launch the country into contemporaneity; and they want to do this at any cost and by any means whatsoever."[4]

Between today's artist, today's politician, and the perennial criminal, I'm most interested in the criminal. I'd never choose the artist and still less the politician. Nothing about politicians has ever interested me and there is nothing that can interest me in today's artist. They're both bygone figures. Today's artists are like turkeys fattened for the butcher on Thanksgiving Day, at the auction, the fair, or political events. In our day being an outlaw is a privilege; as a matter of fact, artists in general have always been fascinated by crime and illegality. The criminal mind is always mobile, suspicious of everything and everyone, always searching for different ways and means to achieve its purposes. However, between the actual criminal act (of/by a criminal) and the *potential* one of/by a "normal" person, or what we like to

---

3   Jonida Gashi is a researcher at the Institute of Cultural Anthropology and the Study of Art (Academy of Albanian Studies) and one of the founders of the DebatikCenter of Contemporary Art. Her research focuses on the newsreels and documentary films of the Albanian communist show trials, and the artistic experience of post-communism in Albania.

4   Personal communication.

call a normal person, I'm more interested in the latter because they're the most unpredictable and can commit far more original crimes or misdeeds.

I'm fascinated by the methods of serial killers. The perfection of the act, the understanding of space, the procedure that is more and more perfect, the hidden traces, the entrance on stage and the exit, the things included inside the scenario of the crime (or of the work of art) and those excluded: all this tends toward perfection, and that's why this figure fascinates me, and why after all it is very close to the figure of the artist, who loves art because he's always attempting to kill his own work.

The majority of artists today don't believe in the mission of art, they don't even believe in the role of the artist anymore. They are predictable, mediocre killers who follow a code out of a manual. Their works are stillborn and can't be brought back to life. They have a different mission, one that is totally banal. They're faithful to the religion that glorifies them. I want to believe in tomorrow's artist. The greatest artist of tomorrow may be the one who has already defected, who abandoned everything at the right moment, and not the one who continues to act between the lines.

All the artists who remain afloat today are trying to penetrate deeper and deeper into the heart of the game. An artist will always make this kind of effort, by any means necessary, and therein lies the relationship with power that needs to be analyzed in these terms as well. My current attitude is a bit different in that it is closer to the figure of the spectator who doesn't go to shows. For the moment I have only intuitions about a future reality I'd like to stimulate and incite in order to speed up the collision. Accelerate and crash, says my friend Giovanni De Donà![5] This attitude may well cause the accident that will lead to situations we don't yet know and should perhaps follow or

---

5   Giovanni De Donà (b. 1974), graduated in philosophy from the University of Bologna. He is a performer, author of installations, producer of kooeditions.art, an experimenter and avant-garde artist, and owns a patent related to multimedia technology.

else completely abandon. Even though I still think we should go ahead without calculating the damage inflicted and incurred over the years, simply following our instincts. The accident is caused by forces and fears that no one can control. I don't know if there's a limit, but if there is an imposed limit that allows us to connect these situations it is the presence of the penitentiary.

In fact, it is a sort of limit, the penitentiary.

The politician tries to avoid it all his life, and in the majority of cases he is able to because he controls the system. He knows very well that it is his future home, where he would never want to live, because he is destined to disappear in the criminal. Like a very bad conceptual escapologist, he performs tricks that are by now well-known to everyone and so becomes something impossible to believe in. By contrast, the artist really wants to perform the number, to possess the penitentiary, to challenge it, and embody it in a certain sense, and then to evade it each time, repeatedly, like a criminal.

Breaking Stones is based on the unexpected. Passing cars, the world that "happens," the city that "exists." I also find it to be a particularly "religious" work. In fact, beating a stone very clearly recalls lapidation. But instead of hitting the body of a stoned martyr, the stone hits the road surface, sharply and desperately. Besides, the phases of the video, the beginning, the middle, and the end, make us think of a via crucis, a procession toward the Calvary. The vertical structures (and there are many) in the video, like the light poles etc., make us think of crosses, of a crucifixion. Is there a religious echo in this work? A ritual aspect?

The stone breaks before it cracks the asphalt, which represents the power structure. Breaking Stones is a ritual, a repetition, a loop, because only in this way, very slowly but insistently, can the structure be cracked. At least, these were my intentions. In the technical script I wrote for the work, the ending is different from the video — it continues with another dark road with an individual who repeats the same gesture coming out of it. It should be said that the piece concentrates on a single gesture, on the ritual and not on the individual. In a certain sense the work happened by itself, because I found the stones on the road, I didn't bring them onto the scene. The frames themselves were composed as a response to the stones I found. There's a double repetition of the act, because the stones were brought by someone else and I just used them, I broke them up to make them more manageable, perhaps, to make them manageable for the following day, the day of the uncontrollable and unannounced protest that could (have) happen(ed) and one day will. That's why I also speak about a missing or suspended act, because it's aimed at the preparation of the next scene, which we don't see. I don't find much of a religious component in the video. During communism, we were the only constitutionally atheist country in the world. Personally, I was born an atheist and still am one, but I am fascinated by cults and by paganism, for example. Various aspects of religion interest me, for instance that of a ruling and controlling power. After the fall of communism it became possible to practice religion in Albania once again. The three largest faiths, along with a dozen or so suspicious sects, took control of this confused society again.

Many of my classmates from the art lyceum, some of them talented people, have become members of these suspicious foundations. The current mayor of Tirana belonged to one. I don't know what they learned in them, but judging by their careers I think they grasped the true religion of our times. Various aspects of the narratives and characters of Christ and Mohammed fascinate me, but I remain a Marxist as far as religion goes.

The signs I see around my city, which are also very clear and unmistakable in *Breaking Stones,* have mainly to do with economic power, the real religion of our day. As far as symbols and figures of a religious nature, you refer to the Stations of the Cross. It might look that way, but it wasn't something I intended, though undoubtedly the work could be another in another register. These passages, these cuts, also serve as a curtain. In one sequence of the video, on a wall that is hidden by trees and shadows cast by yellow streetlights the word "ALLAH" has been written in capital letters. It's an improvised mosque, a clandestine neighborhood mosque that also serves as a car-repair shop. Regarding stoning, but not martyrdom, a young Albanian artist named David Kampi has made a video about a very famous artist. Actually, just like the Muslims when they perform the hajj, for hours he stoned three oil cisterns that look a lot like the works of Richard Serra and like the new buildings in the Mecca, which represent evil. Ironically, the work is titled *Stoning a Richard Serra.*

> *Breaking Stones and the concept of impotence. The idea of furiously breaking a stone into pieces also recalls the repression of anger and sexuality. What type of repression of drives do you find most humiliating and dangerous for the individual? In what way are anger and sexual instinct controlled in Albania today? The death instinct and Eros?*

Obviously, the work is linked to impotence in relation to the political and economic reality, the impotence of our generation, trapped in the system, and the inability to radically change things. I'm interested in the attempts made to carry out this difficult enterprise. The component of impotence is also related to another phenomenon that is widespread in the country and that I find very interesting, namely that of wasted energy, understood as impotence. If there is a level in the work that presents impotence in the broadest sense, it may have something to do with the recent global political landscape as well as with the meaning of art today: the impossibility to create art and the feeling of impotence in the face of global reality.

A while back I said that Albanian artists suffer from premature ejaculation, but the metaphor referred to society in general. I didn't mean to say they don't know how to wait or to explore the duration that pleasure can have. Rather, their knowledge, and here I mean the revolutionary struggle, remains premature, because the revolution was never completed, since it was interrupted halfway through. This is the crux of the problem, in my opinion. In the context of this phenomenology, the work that treats these problems gets lost, because it doesn't offer different dimensions and is not experienced as it should be. The repetition of this "premature ejaculation" is a problem for our whole society and isn't merely something that concerns the work of art and the artist. The artist is called into question because they have to act in this context. But even those who have lived abroad and attempted to do something there have problems in grasping the sense of this society. It's clear that there's some confusion in all this, but we have to go on trying, to create mechanisms, even fictitious ones, to keep on learning, so as to get to the heart of the question, not only as regards this aspect of society but also the more general ones.

The depths that this country hides are still clouded. Recently an unknown artist from Vlorë completed a new work that gave me food for thought. It's a small sculpture made in 2013. This delicate sculpture has the exact shape of a life-size used condom. The aged and hardened purple-colored object is titled *Bad Seed*. At no cost does the artist want to exhibit this work, nor does she want to explain its meaning. This especially interested me, as did the visionary procedure, the choice of the object. Her works deal with violence, societal rape, systemic repression, racism, the perverse way (never discussed in academic texts) of feeling Aryan, of racial purity; they are about discrimination, misogyny, and extremely violent, sharp machismo.

Unfortunately, these works can't earn much visibility here, because the whole apparatus of the state and of art will never face up to these problems in Albanian society. I feel very close to this artist's choices and the themes she deals with concerning society's conscious and unconscious drives, which also relate to psychic processes. When I arrived in Italy my first works touched closely on these themes, on Freud in particular, on the pleasure principle, which I subsequently abandoned you could say because my research turned to different problems. Those works, made between 1999 and 2000, began as studies and sketches, and they were roughly ten meters long. Built as architectural platforms, with pornographic figures and real characters who were members of the Academy, they turned into life-sized tombs in the end, the tombs of the teachers at the Academy. In these pieces, which still lie buried in the attic of a house in Tuscany, the anger expressed, understood in light of the violent institutional relationship between student and teacher, actually referred to something else — namely, what had happened in Albania in 1997.

Inside that institution all the events from the past were repeated, represented by the figures of the psychoanalyst/ teacher and the patient/student, who always desire something different from each other. The theme of premature ejaculation, or impotence, is always tied to recent history and to system change. We are living in very interesting times, where the form of mass protest — the swathes of people who desire change — is described by the state and the Prime Minister as a failed erection. These are the terms that the Prime Minister uses to refer to the people. The Albanian people are represented as a male being that cannot have a real erection. The only erection the Prime Minister sees, or rather, doesn't see, and here I can't blame him, is that the rebellion, which he himself provokes and incites, never arrives. It seems that everything is buried in the past, in the turbulent period between 1990–1997, and that society has become so atrophied that it can't explode in any meaningful sort of public gesture.

Let's see what the younger generation will do, if they will be able to sum up the present. I think this is also the task of the artists who live here. Artists have to react, because they can sum up this "interesting" moment we are living through better than anyone else.

Breaking Stones and Italian contemporary art. Your relationship with Gino De Dominicis[6] and the idea of limit. Not only

---

6   Gino De Dominicis (1947–1998) was a controversial and multifaceted protagonist of the Italian art scene, besides being an architect and philoso-

the whale skeleton, but also and above all the Breaking Stones *performance. There are many elements in common between* Breaking Stones *and De Dominicis's videos* Tentativo di volo *and* Tentativo di formare quadrati invece che cerchi in acqua. *But the fundamental difference is that De Dominicis presents an impossible act. Man cannot fly, it's a law of nature, just as he cannot create squares by throwing stones in water. How can an artist relate to the concept of limit? What do you share and not share of De Dominicis's view of art and the artist? In this work what is the importance of the idea of a "conceptual art"?*

The performance *Breaking Stones* could be understood as an overture, the preparation for a future protest. We have to stop scratching our scabs and try to look past those who caused them. There's nothing there anymore. The postconceptuals have stolen it all. We have to open new wounds, and these wounds have to go much deeper. The point is always to stay one step ahead of the game: if you're not a pioneer, then you are nothing, you're only good for filling corners in collective shows. These I really hate, because they put you in the condition of protecting the others, the more powerful artists, while in reality you're destroying yourself. Collective shows are made to promote another figure, no longer the figure of the artist (and this has been true for some time now) and not even that of the curator, as De Dominicis maintained, but an extremely important reality like collecting. Collective shows have become traps for artists. It's not exciting to get yourself noticed in a collective show anymore. It's like driving on dry asphalt. Conceptual art is itself a trap, and Duchamp was a great inventor of traps. De Dominicis understood this.

-----

pher. He shrouded himself in mystery to void being labeled and judged by the critics. His production is divided between the installations and sculptures done in the sixties and seventies, which focus on the relation between time and eternity, and the figurative paintings he did almost exclusively afterwards, up to the time of his precocious death under circumstances that made many think of suicide.

To go on doing conceptual art is like wanting to go on driving safely. I'm always ready to play the game, but when the game becomes accessible to everyone you have to get out. By now everyone understands the perfection and the naïveté of the conceptuals. *Screw their Bible.*

We need to write a new book, but first we need to do something else. As US artist David Hammons says, to overcome this obstacle first of all we have to open a center for detoxifying from Duchamp. I think Hammons is sincere when he says this, because he himself fell into a trap. Conceptual art is like a cross. In order to toss this cross, this trap, into the sea, I called one of my cats Marcel Duchamp and in 2018 we made *Plumb në zarf (Bullet in Envelope)* with that cat. It's a work that aims at initiating a missing dialogue.[7] Like all cats, Duchamp is a magnificent feline, and I'm waiting for him to surpass the artist by not becoming another postconceptual copycat, like those postconceptual altar boys who never challenge their church, even when they're grown up, choosing instead to become priests themselves.

The only thing that interests me about De Dominicis is his death. Death in general fascinates me, and his death was a great work of art. I'm not interested in writing a sentimental letter full of cheap mysticism and unveiling fake secrets to approach him. The imprint of Duchamp's sperm as an act of love definitively surpassed the pathetic letters written by artists. Gino De Dominicis's death is on another level. I also say this because for sometime now I've been trying to carry out an idea. I'd like to sign the body of a suicide immediately after they perform the act (in a gallery or elsewhere). I ought to have signed the immobile body of Gino De Dominicis. I ought to have done it in 1998 when he died and I arrived in Italy. Sign the body of a suicide. Steal suicide.

---

7   Armando Lulaj, *Plumb në zarf* (2018), *DebatikCenter,* https://debatikcenter. net/strikes/bullet_in_envelope.

Breaking Stones is also a work about the mortality of the body. At the beginning there is a powerful detail, the barking dog. Then the street noises. And, obviously, the sound — extremely loud — of the stone hitting the ground. What is the importance of sound in this video? What relationship do you have, in your work, with contemporary music? Can Breaking Stones also be interpreted as a piece of "concrete music"?

With sound I've always had the same relationship as the funeral march written to be played at the funeral of a great deaf man. Trapped!

The soundtrack in *Breaking Stones* is all field recording. I placed the unidirectional mic with the camera and followed the action. There is no manipulation in the studio, no post-production, everything comes from the environment. My intention was to follow a precise idea, which came out of the circumstances found at the scene. The prisoners, along with the people living in the surrounding houses, could hear what was going on outside. They couldn't see it, but they could imagine it, and that interested me.

Breaking Stones makes one think a lot about your national hero, Gjergj Kastrioti (Skanderbeg). The idea of a "rebellion" underway is definitely present in the video. Do you think this reading is possible? Who occupies, socially and politically if not physically, the "soil" of Albania today? Against what and in what way is it possible and necessary to rebel?

Today's politics, everywhere, consist in occupation of the public sphere, and rebellion occurs when there is a widely shared perception that the territory has been occupied. For this reason everyone traces historical parallels between occupiers in the past and those in the present, whether they be institutions, foreign armies, political forces, or today's wealthy elite.

They say that the first movie filmed in Albania, by a troupe from Turin, has a very meaningful title, *Albania ribelle* (Rebel-

lious Albania). Over the years we've mythicized the power of re-bellion and pushed it away, distancing ourselves from it, and we still fight it even now. Rebellion can't be real if it is kept within the frame of conceptual art, as art tends to do. Rebellion is not a form to be put on show — in my opinion it can't be put into an archive or given a label: it's not exhibitionism, but rather an uncontrolled act of courage that has to dare produce something unmistakably new, otherwise it's just a purposeless catwalk show.

I'm still waiting for the development of the impossible protest, but I'm not sure what that means today. The way I imagine it, it would be impossible to carry out, even if to me it seems realistic. If it happens, today's artists should only stand and watch, not interfere, if we want to achieve something that can be compared to that impossible idea. Even today the idea of rebellion is conceived of and situated as an isolated phenomenon, impossible because no longer realistic, relegated to a corner in an out-of-the-way abandoned house. I think this is still a profound and complex idea that we should achieve, because it involves freedom.

In this corner of the world we are living through the era of a third love story, after the one for the Soviet Union and the one for the People's Republic of China.

If we had a hidden love during communism, acknowledged by everyone, it was the love for the West, the love for America, in the days when for the state apparatus America was the enemy, the symbol of every evil. After the fall of the regime I witnessed the landing of the United States in this country. People rolled out carpets they'd brought from their homes over the tarmac where James Baker[8] and the American motorcade passed to reach Skanderbeg Square. America as a symbol of democracy

---

8   James Addison Baker (b. 1930), lawyer and member of the US Republican Party, was Secretary of the Treasury during the presidency of Ronald Reagan and Secretary of State in the final months of the presidency of George W. Bush. He played a primary role in the period after the fall of the Berlin Wall and the Soviet Union. His official visit to Tirana in June of 1991, the first by a high-profile representative of the US executive to Albania, was

and prosperity was the missing future. But things have changed recently. After twenty-seven years of love, the American diplomats, the Embassy, or even an anonymous American in the city, are no longer automatically perceived as a friend ready to pat you on the back, but rather as a subject or institution to fear. A warning, an alarm from the past is ringing. Because of the speed in the spread of information and the wars in Afghanistan and Iraq, which recall the atrocities in Vietnam so vividly present for my parents' generation, the notion of America is changing.

In 2013 we witnessed the first and only symbolic protest to have taken place so far in front of the us Embassy in Albania. The protest focused on the Syrian chemical weapons that our government was secretly negotiating with the United States government to bring into the country in order to be dismantled at a location very close to the capital. At the time, in order to stir up a more violent reaction on the part of the population, the leader of the opposition Democratic Party, vaguely but effectively claimed and repeated non-stop that the negotiations should end. Following this line of reasoning and citing the "obscure" history of the United States, he evoked the civil rights movement of the 1960s and the more recent Black Lives Matter movement. Even if it is perhaps still early, it seems that the seeds of doubt have been sowed. The United States has a more pervasive presence here than any other foreign country. The stars and stripes always wave when political parties protest, but the younger generations have very different ideas. Nowadays America is like the ex-lover that you hate and love at the same time, that you want to cancel, excise, and burn, eliminate from the pages of your diary, but that you can't in the end because it's alive inside you. It dwells in our minds, and the mind is the real territory that needs to be liberated.

---

greeted by over 300,000 people, who crowded the streets to acclaim him and his delegation.

Breaking Stones and the concept of "martyrdom." Who are to-day's "martyrs" in the Albanian culture and mentality? Who is a "martyr" today?

Right after 1990, the first room in the house to be modernized was the bathroom. In droves we substituted the stone slabs of the Soviet period with low-quality white and grey ceramic tiles imported from abroad. We also put in a bathtub, a shower with an electric boiler, a French-style toilet, and a bidet, all illuminated by cold neon light. Once the bathroom was done, the rest of the house was gradually decorated with new tiles. Later on we turned to the building itself, opening new windows or enlarging existing ones, adding new rooms by taking over ("occupying") common areas.

Tiles are important to us, because their value isn't only private but also historical, representing political transformation. I think that the architects who designed the new plan for Tirana's main square, Skanderbeg Square, had this use of the past in mind.

From the private space of the bathroom, this brand-new tile flooring moved outdoors to the public space of the main square, which was — but is no longer — an important symbol of the country's memory. The large stone tiles paving the square come from all the places where Albanian communities live, from bordering states but also from the diaspora (at least that's what they say). The idea of a united nation represented by the tiles in this square is an aestheticizing idea of unity that also involves another type of unity, namely that of identity. It is a populist idea of unity implying continual transformation, which is in fact tied to neoliberal politics.

As someone has very astutely said, albeit in an ironic way, in the future those tiles will supply material for pedestals for the martyred poets who sacrificed their lives to protect the collective memory against the recent destruction of the square. Immediately after we finished shooting *Breaking Stones,* on that very same day, I went to the square at dawn and I made UNTI-TLED *(Pissed Off)*.[9]

In the history of our country the martyr is obviously considered a person who died for the fatherland, a partisan for example. Now, however, we are experiencing an absurd historical-political conflict that leads to a rewriting of the past and the elimination of these historical figures just because they are associated with communism. This absurdity continues and expands, also because we try to combat it with individuals, namely historians, who are fundamentally incompetent as well as basically speaking on behalf one political party or the other.

After 1990 we erected false martyrs, false democratic martyrs and false socialist martyrs and we even resuscitated the martyrs of the Church out of the past — in an exceptional performance in the spirit of today's Europe. Like so many historical falsifications, today's martyrs are honored more than those who were killed in Kosovo, to give just one example. Personally, when I think of martyrs I think much more about those who haven't arrived yet, who are still to come. Tomorrow's martyr will come from the future, and will (perhaps) be only an idea that exists online. This narrative interests me: the country needs to start imagining and resuscitating the martyr of the future.

---

9   Armando Lulaj, *Pissed Off* (2017), *DebatikCenter*, https://debatikcenter.net/strikes/Pissed_Off.

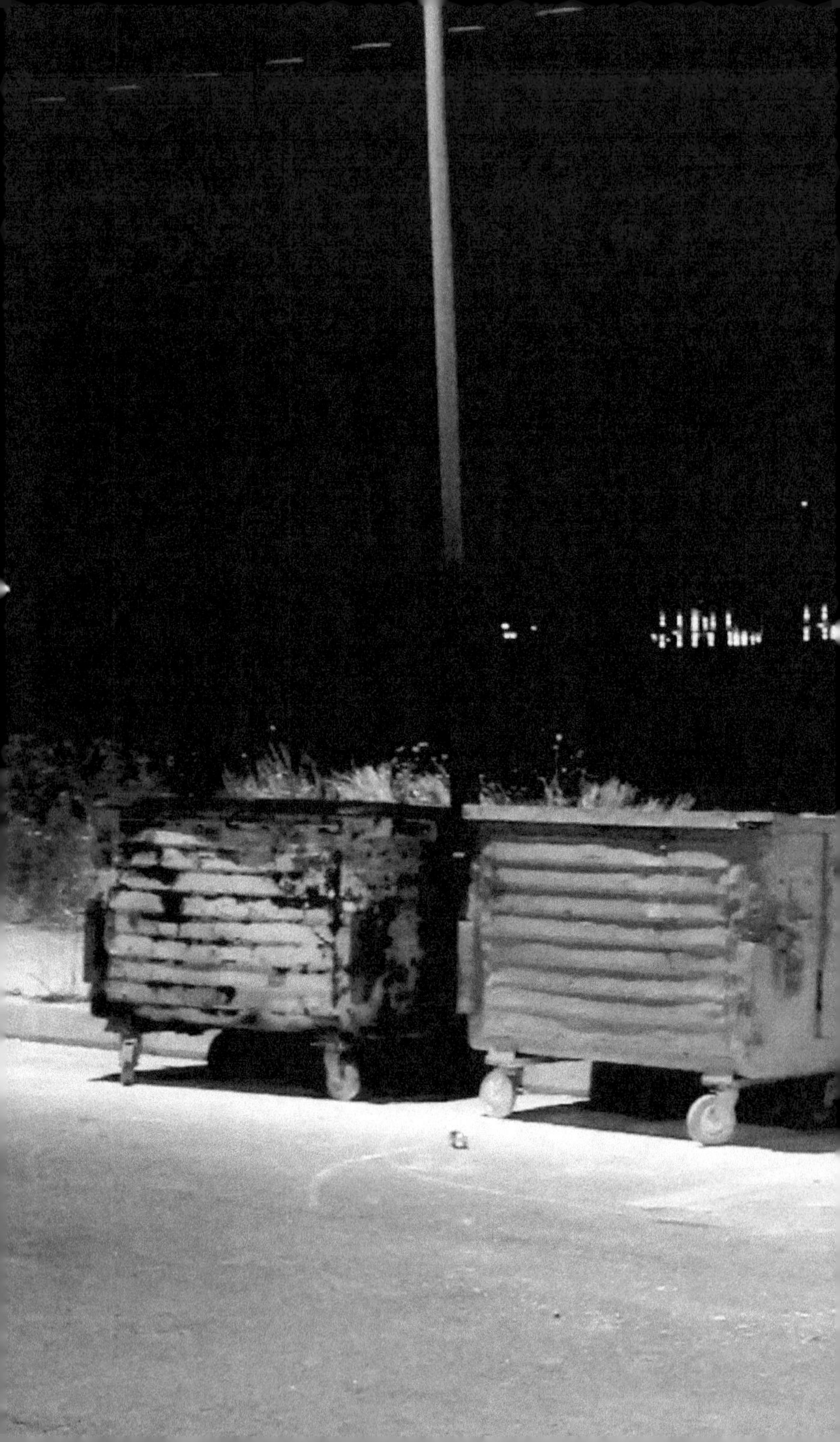

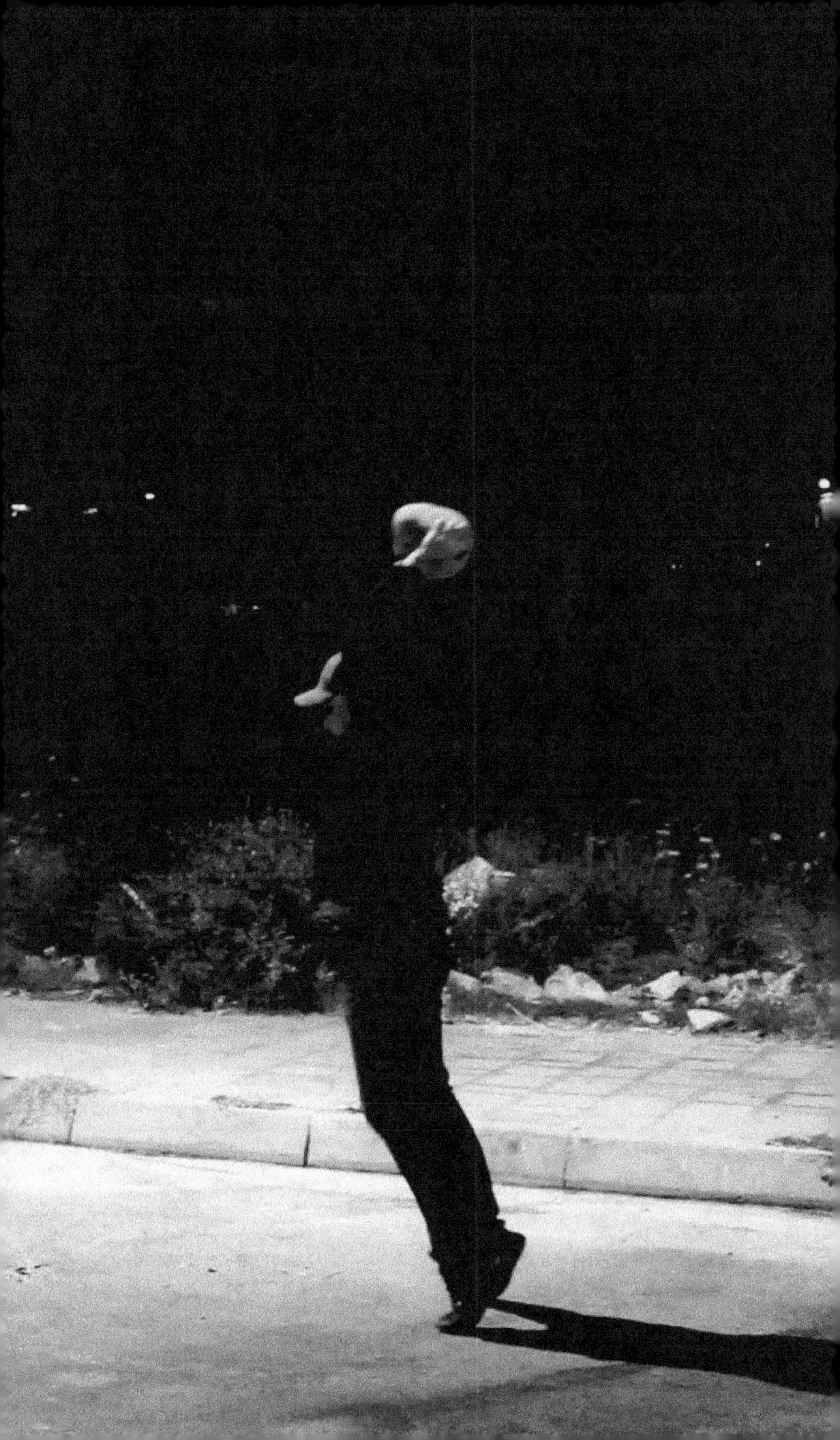

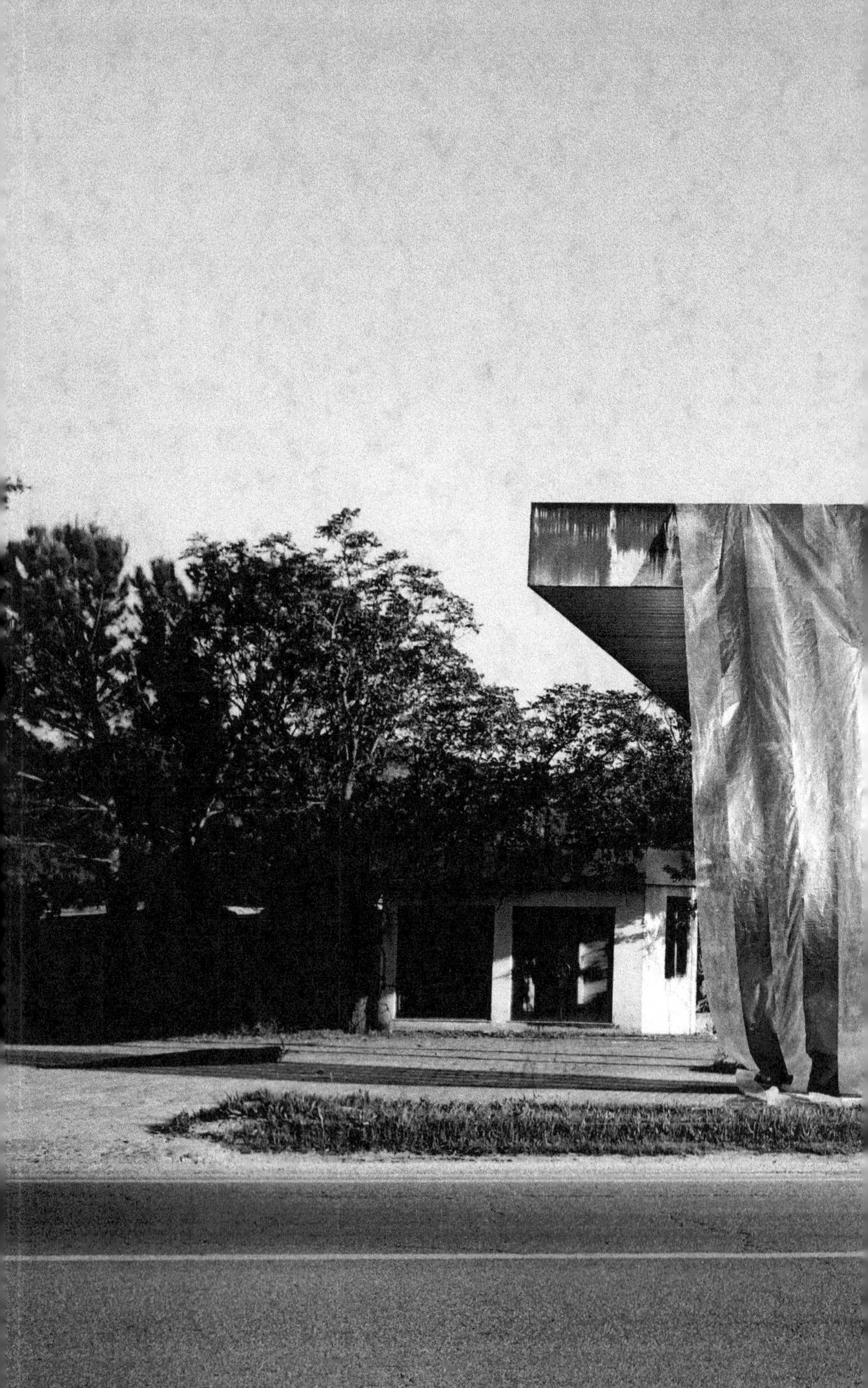

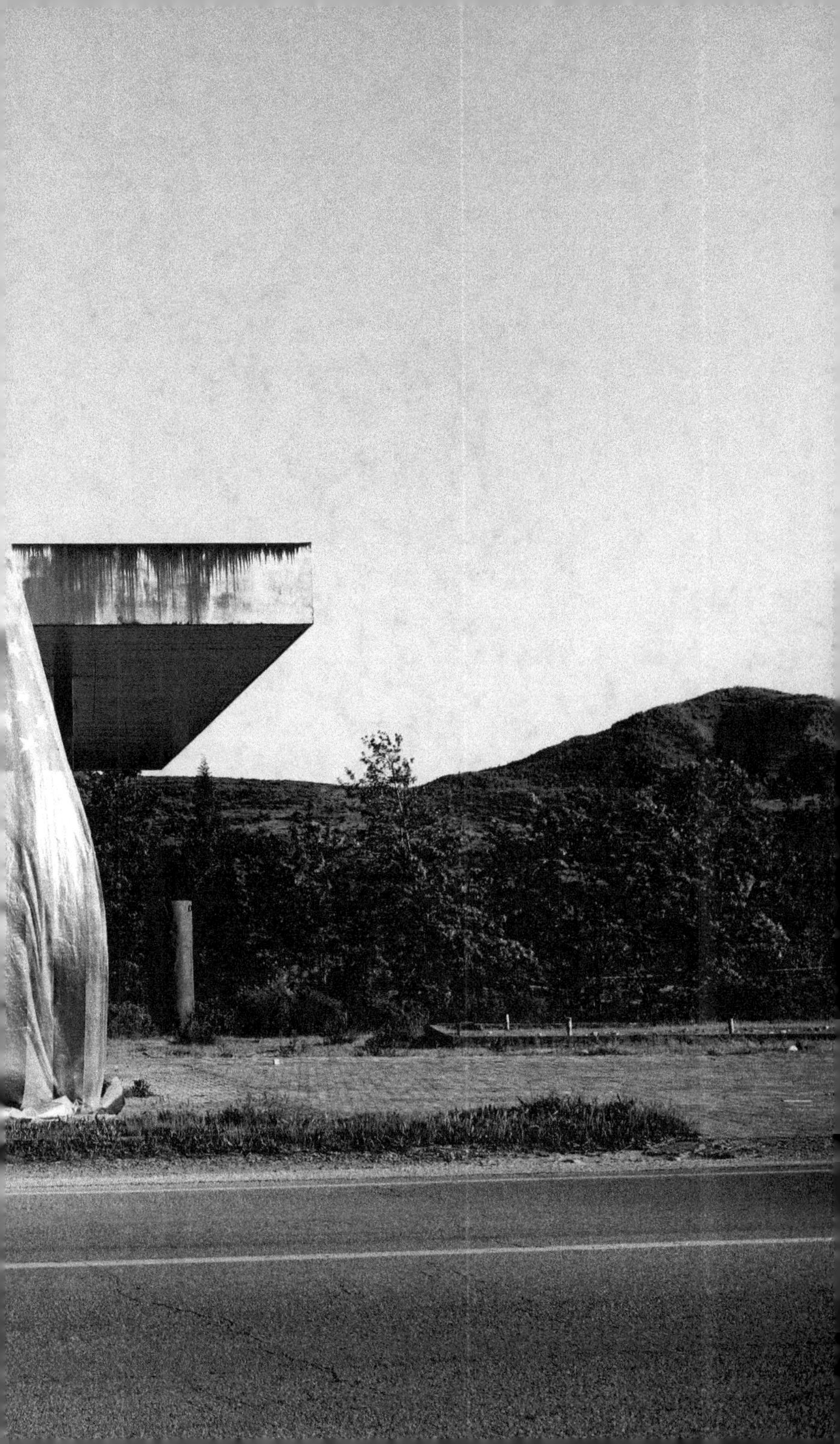

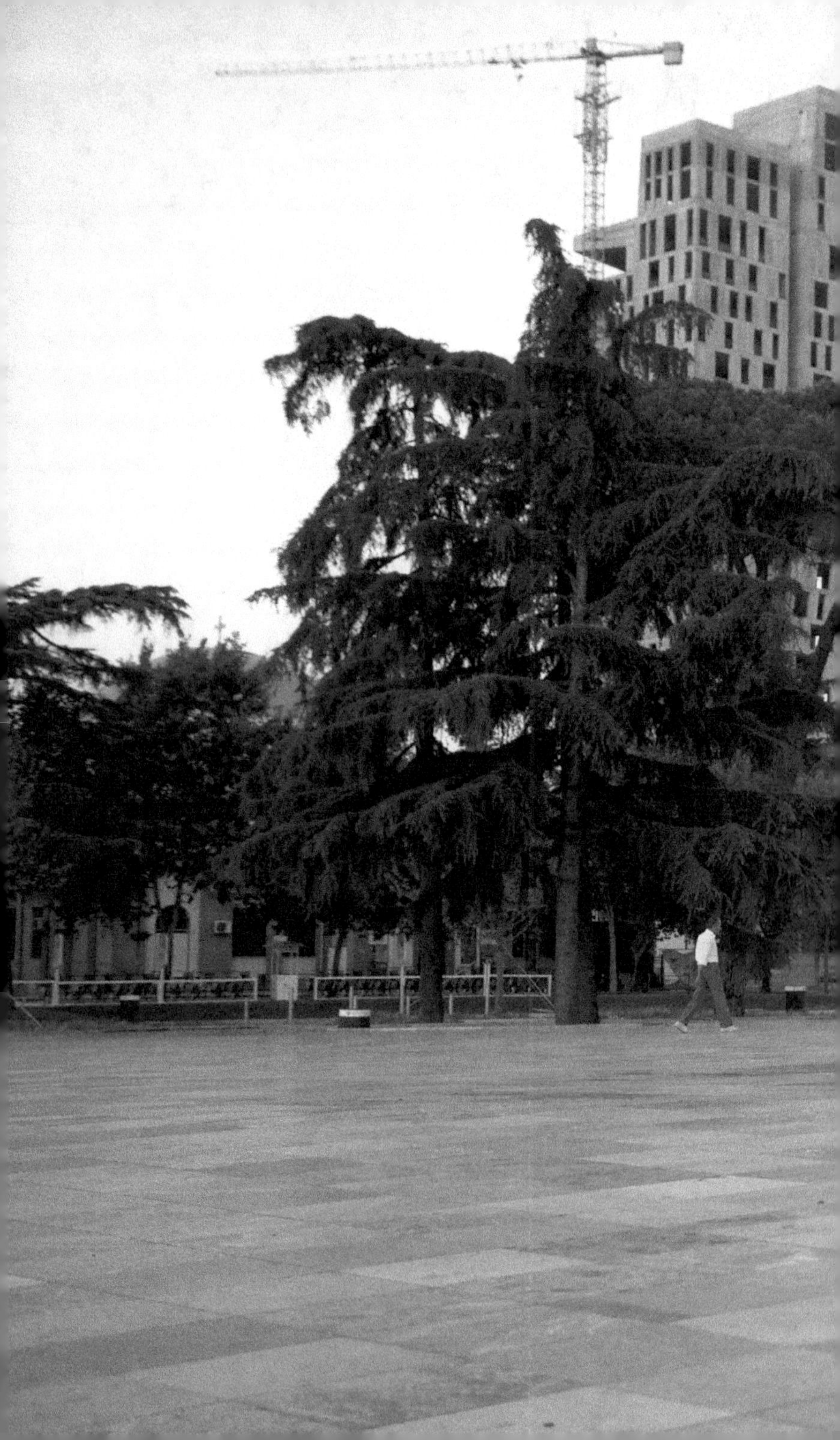

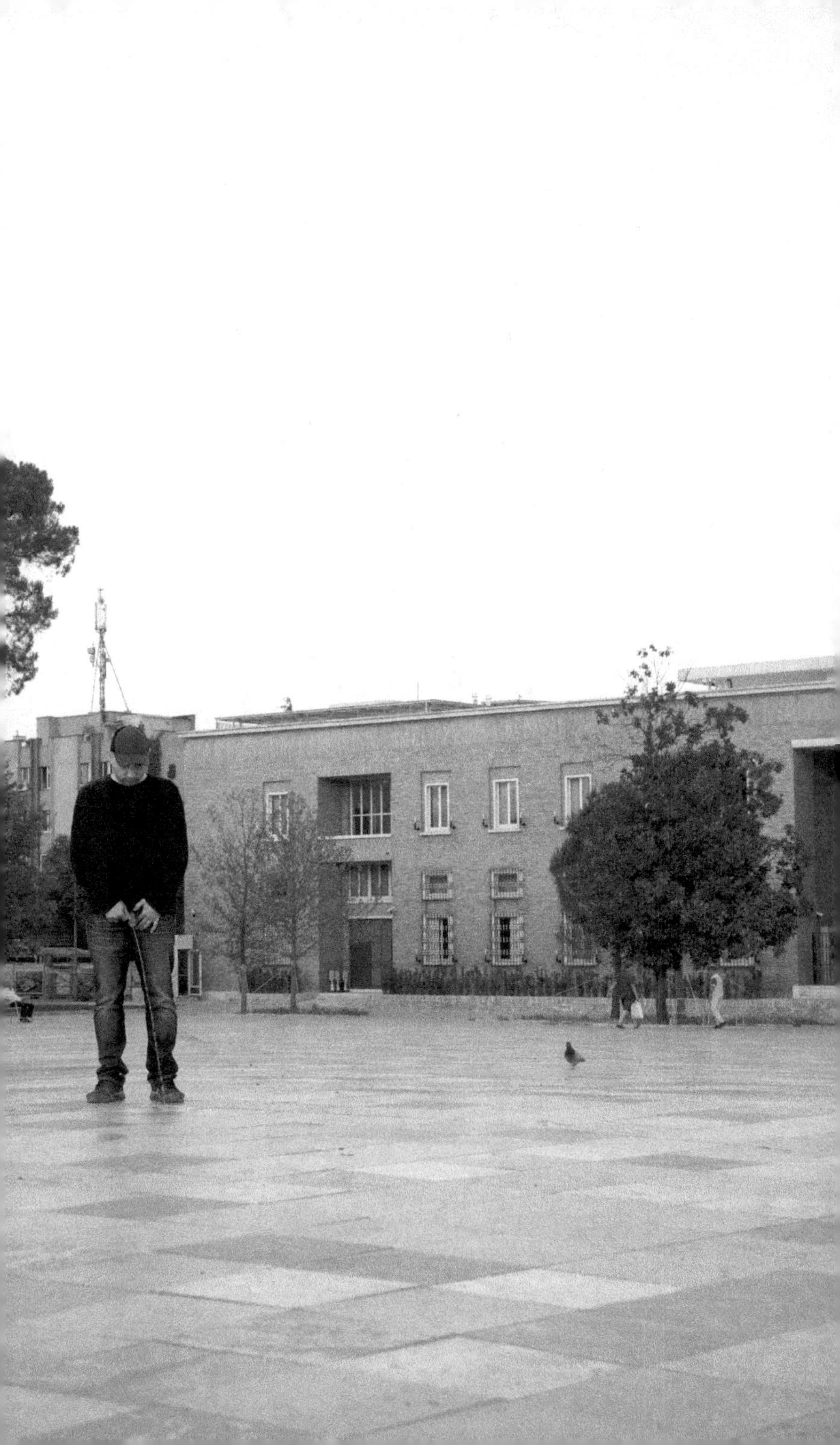

Fig. 11. Breaking Stones by Armando Lulaj, 2017.
Video. Color. Sound. 10'31".
Courtesy of DebatikCenter of Contemporary Art.

Fig. 12. FALLEN (american neanderthal) by Armando Lulaj, 2016.
C-print. 140×140cm. Production photo by Marco Mazzi.
Courtesy of Paolo Maria Deanesi Gallery and DebatikCenter of
Contemporary

Fig. 13. UNTITLED (pissed off), by Armando Lulaj, 2017.
Documentation of the performance on the highest point of the not-
so-slight inclination of the new Skanderbeg square, Tirana, July 22,
2017.
Production photo by Pleurad Xhafa.
Courtesy of DebatikCenter of Contemporary Art.

トラック03

《Breaking Stones(ブレーキング・ストーンズ)》[以下、 BS]
は、 インターネット上でビデオ公開したパフォーマンスである[1]。
BSがどのように生まれ、 ビデオがどのように生まれたのかを語
ってもらえるだろうか? その当時/その瞬間に、 アルバニアで何
が(歴史・政治的に)起こっていた/いるのか?

僕はしばらく前から見聞きした話を収集しており、 日々の実生活
で起きた出来事を書き記している。 それらは、 その時とその場所
の紛うことなき痕跡であり、 解釈するのが未だに困難だ。 換言す
れば、 これらの出来事の解釈は、 解釈の様々なレベルと異なる
レイヤーを用いた場合にのみ成り立ち得る。 これらの出来事は、
被魔的で、 限界ギリギリの反応として出現し、 –僕が敬愛する作
家の言葉を借りると–「死を免れるため己の身に反吐を吐かねば
ならぬ」国について我々に語って聞かせる。 これらの話は舞台の
稽古に似ている。 例えば: スリッパを突っ掛けた寝起きのような姿
の老女が、 バルカン諸国で最も高いビルの一つ、 ティラナで建設
中のフォーエヴァー・グリーン・タワー(4EverGreen Tower)の天

1　参照: https://debatikcenter.net/strikes/breaking_stones

辺を見上げていた。その手には、腐ったゴミがぎっしりと詰まっ
た袋が握られていた。ビルの管理人に向かって身振り手振りで、
なんとしてでも上に登りたいと言って聞かなかった。管理人は
最悪の事態を想定したが、老女はただ天上デッキから見晴ら
して、ゴミ袋を眼下に投げ捨てるためにビルに登りたがったの
だ。この話は、スーザン・ソンタグが国の未来と廃棄物について話
した時に、アルバニアに関して発言した一節を思い起こさせた。

　別の話はまさに、メディアと政治に毒された現実からの投影
のように思える。しばらく前、とある政治家が、ありとあらゆるテ
レビ番組に出演し、他の政治家達を脅しまくった。彼はパンパ
ンに膨らんだ大きな黒いブリーフケースを手にしており、彼によ
ると、それは彼の対抗勢力、政府代表者達の沽券を脅かす音
声・映像資料ということだった。トーク番組やその手の放送は、
彼が彼らを利用していたのと同じやり方で彼を悪用した。メディ
アはこの脅迫者、直近の政府の一員であるこの政治家を取り上
げ、助長していたが、この者が所持していると言っていた、政敵
の政治生命に関わる資料についての調査は行わなかった。この
件は、僕が述べているこの限界ギリギリの現実に反映されてお
り、アメリカ大使館の近辺に住むある男のことを僕の脳裏に思い
浮かばせる。プレウラッド・ジャファ[2] が語るところによれば、齢三
十くらいの男が毎朝、手に持った二つの黒いVHSカセットを両耳
にあてて、大使館脇の路地から出て来るという。大使館の黄色い
壁伝いに歩き、街中に紛れ、雑踏の間に姿を消すのだそうだ。

2　1984年生まれのプレウラッド・ジャファ(Pleurad Xhafa)は、ティラナ在
　　住、同地で活動するヴィジュアル・アーティスト兼映画製作者。2012年
　　ボローニャ美術学院卒業。現代美術デバティクセンター創設者の一人
　　である。

男はこのルーティンを連日繰り返し、少なくとも明確な意図はないようだ。パフォーマンス効果は絶大である。

また別の、成年間際の少年は、外務省、今日では欧州外務省と呼ばれる官庁の近隣に住んでいるのだが、しばらく前からレンガを足で蹴って引き摺りながら徘徊している。いつも同じ道順で、自身の日課をこなす際には常にコカ・コーラのボトルを飲んでいる。別の男は四十絡み、郊外の小さな町の広場の片隅、ティラナへ行くバスの停留所に毎朝出没する。発車するバスを背にして壁の方を向き、その壁面に何度も何度も頭を打ちつけている。

何百と発生している、これらの行為をひとまとめにしたならば、言わば、ベールを剥ぎ取るのだ。ベールの向こうには、現実のあの一部、爆発寸前の部分が姿を現す。これらの行為の根底に潜むのは純然たる政治的なものであり、これらの行為のエネルギーは、今日抱える問題を、国内で近年活躍するどの芸術家よりも雄弁に語る。《Breaking Stones》は、その現実を我々に開示するこのベールに密接に結び付いている。

しばらく前から、僕は1992年以降の1001件の報道記事からなる歴史書を編纂する目的で、犯罪記事になった事件を蒐集している。'90年代以前、共産主義時代には、アルバニアの新聞で犯罪記事を扱う紙面は一切なかった：許可されていなかったのだ。犯罪自体が非常に少なかったとも言わなければならないが。これは犯罪を通して、民主主義時代の社会の変遷を扱う千夜一夜の書となるはずで、フィエル市で兄弟二人の公開絞首刑があった、あの6月25日にまさに始まる。

先述の事例のような、これら全ての現実の縮図は、それに犯罪ニュースも、限界ギリギリにあるか、限界を突破する状況だ。新聞やテレビのニュースにおいて、これらの出来事、凶悪犯罪、 さらに自殺事件に共通するものは、 精神障碍者の人物像の恒常的な存在である。 精神障碍者のこれほど繰り返される存在は、 疑わしくも明白な事実、 現在進行中の、 我々には隠しておきたい何かの証拠となった。 これらの事件のほとんどの場合、 新聞は調査せず、 警察の調書では大抵、 殺人の容疑者や自殺者は精神障碍者であるとされる。 報告された事件の数が多いことは、 精神障碍者の人物像に結び付けられた凶行の数の多さを正当化するものではない。 これは全ての真実ではない。 事件は改変され、 機関のオフィスで編集されたのだ。 被害者家族、 例えば、 文化的な教えでも自殺行為を恥じる人々からも裏付けされた、 この誤摩化しにより、 当局は現実を偽装しようとしている。 僕が話題にしている事例では、 パラレルな領域、 全く異なる国について我々に語りかける基体、 ある意味で、 脱走と放棄の理由を解説する事例に遭遇する。 脱走と放棄は（残念なことに）この時世の唯一の政策と唯一の真実になってしまった。

　《Breaking Stones》は、 僕達が2017年に再開したDCCAのWebプラットフォームの初期作品の一つである： ビデオは「strikes」と呼ばれるセクションの一部であり、 そこには特定の場所で特定の目的で実行された活動のみが含まれる。《Breaking Stones》を構成した最初のアイディアは、 この数々のエピソードの蓄積に由来する。 僕の意見では、 これらの行為は、 この国について僕が為し得る歴史・政治・社会的ナレーションのいずれよりも遥かに深遠なものである。 僕は、 誰かが《Breaking Stones》を僕が描写したような行為に関連付けてくれ、 また別の誰かが、 それを国内で最近起こっていることと関連付けることで（も）解釈してもらえるなら嬉しい、 と言うに留めて君への回答とする。

歴史的・芸術的観点から見ると、BSは確かに「夜景」作品でもある。なぜ、君は夜を選んだのか?

夜は徴候に満ちていて、不穏で、生まれ得る何か、起こり得る何かを常に待っている。僕は、待つこと、静寂、彷徨う獣達、そして夜間にさらに知覚されやすくなる、ある種の空白に魅了されてやまない。

僕はいつも空白に魅了されてきた。僕が言及しているこの空白は、多くの状況と多くのエピソードの衝突と蓄積によって形成される。それは行為の瞬間に形成されるが、中断されて判読不能なままだ。情報によって完結される感覚の逆転は、僕には全く興味がない。僕は、形成されるが解読できず、すぐに読み取れないものに興味がある。僕はそれを、実行されるべき正確な瞬間に捕捉された、一時停止の行為の空白感と呼んでいる。夜になると、この感覚はさらに「可視化」され、手触りが伝わってくる。僕は《Breaking Stones》を空白への跳躍台に連想付けるのが気に入っている。

芸術と犯罪。BSは、犯罪性と破壊行為について非常に考えさせる。アーティストであることと、いわゆる「無法者」「犯罪者」であることとの間には、どんな違いがあるか? 君の人生において、犯罪行為や犯罪性というコンセプトとの関係(概念的のみでも)はどのようなものであったか? 君の意見では、芸術家は犯罪行為と刑罰のコンセプトをどのように解釈するのか? 犯罪と刑務所? これはBSに出現しているのか?

DCCAと協同する団体である「Société Spectrale(ソシエテ・スペクトラール：［訳注：実体のない］幽霊結社)」は、最近、破壊行為と糾弾された作戦を実行した。彼らの行為は、政府による暴力行為の明確な帰結であった。政府は市役所とともに4000万ユーロという巨額な費用を投じ、全長たった2km強に過ぎない新設道路の建設を決定した。この政府による大掛かりなビジネスの腐敗には、あるアメリカ合衆国上院議員の署名偽造も含まれる。工事を着工するには、1990年代以降に建設された相当な数の家屋と店舗を、まず取り壊さなければならない。これらの建物の多くは20年以上前に建設されており、住民達は定期的に税金を払ってはいても所有権証書がない。政府はその住民達への補償を望んでおらず、20年以上前に無許可で建設されたため立ち退かせたいだけだ。彼らは幾度も、生まれ変わった首都の市民であるに値しない、洞窟居住者どもと呼び捨てられた。当局はスプレーで赤い十字を描き、彼らの家や店舗に印を付けた。これは住民を激怒させた所業である。Société Spectraleはこの郊外地区に赴き、赤い印の店の1軒でスプレー塗料を購入し、最近、再整備されたばかりの、政府のプロパガンダの象徴であるスカンデルベグ広場に到達した：パフォーマー達は広場を取り囲む未加工の巨石の上に、中指を立てた「Fuck You」のポーズで手を載せ、スプレーで型取りして、壮大な「ケイヴ・ペインティング(cave paintings)」、現代の洞窟壁画を作成した。

　彼らのケイヴ・ペインティングは破壊行為と見做されたが、一方、20世紀の悲惨な歴史の身の毛もよだつ行為を彷彿とさせる、当局によって市民の家に記された赤い十字印はそうではない。この国では、人種差別は僅かに研究された現象に過ぎず、それについては、ほとんど語られていない。例えば、婚姻後、'90年代初頭に大都市に移住した国民の一部、主に農村部出身の辺境少数民族を指すには、「チェチェン人」「ネアンデルタールの男達」「同性愛者」「タリバン人」「ISIS」などの渾名や表現が使われる：この言葉遣いは、主に国の政治家達が日常的に使用する語彙に由来し「文化」となった。最近、Société Spectraleは「Essential Library(エッセンシャル・ライブラリ)」という図書館の構築を開始した。扱うテーマは：チェチェニア、チェチェン人、その歴史。単語タリバンの意味とそれが属する地域。同性愛者の解放。－この国にこれほどまでに根付いている－ミソジニー。ネアンデルタール人の進化と文化。そして当然ながら、テロリズムとISISに関する書籍、記事、その他の資料で構成される。このライブラリに表示されるタイトル・名称・用語は、侮蔑的な文脈で常に使用され、憎悪を活性化し、人種差別を助長し、地域の紛争に火をつけている。これらの用語は言わば、我々の他者や外国人に対する認識方法を変えてしまった。アルバニア語からこの用語用法を削除し、この本質的なライブラリに置き換える時なのだ。ライブラリは発見のためだけでなく、使われている用語の意味に関する議論のためのスペースにもなるだろう。

《Breaking Stones》の制作中に、僕が1998年まで通っていた芸術高等学校とティラナの監獄、313刑務所との間の、意味深長な繋がりを発見した。首都の二つの機関には同じ名前「Jordan Misja」が付いている。ヨルダン・ミースィヤ(Jordan Misja)は1911年シュコドラ(Shkodër)生まれ、愛国者であり共産主義の英雄だった。彼は画家であり、1940年にイタリアの国立フィレンツェ・アカデミア美術学院入学。1942年にアルバニア北部でファシストによって殺害された。それにしても、芸術家を養成する機関と刑務所が同じ名称であるというのは、黙視すべき事案ではないと思う。僕の調査の中で、ヨルダン・ミースィヤの名が刑務所に付けられたのは1997年以降だったことも発見した。これは、あの年の重要性と、この国が辿ったその余波とを今一度反映している、また別の事例である。

《Breaking Stones》の素材の大部分は、まさに313刑務所のすぐ近くで撮影された。セカンドショットに現れるパトカーは牢獄のエリアを常に巡回しており、その界隈は当然ながら厳重に監視されている。

国史の今この時、芸術家・政治家・犯罪者の姿は一つに溶け合っているように見える。今日の現実は予想のその先へ行ってしまい、この地で創出することを望まれた実験的な理想郷を逸した。現代美術と組織犯罪の間の結び付きを介することで、現在というものがなお一層、推定・解読され得る。現代美術と（アルバニアの）政治の融合について話すことは、今となってはこの新しい繋がりを示すためのお上品な方法に過ぎない。僕はこれらの最新の動向に魅了されている。なぜなら僕は、二、三人の順調なキャリアのアーティストに支持された、これらの政治家達を信じたことがかつて一度もないからだ。この国では、芸術と政治のユートピア的融合に向けて取り組むという考えが生まれたことはなかった。この組織に関連するアーティスト、キュレーター、及び建築家は、しっかりと情報を取得する必要がある。さらに僕に苦笑させるのは、作品に平凡ではない要素があるアーティスト達が、この茶番劇を其処彼処でサポートしているのを見ることだ。What the fuck was Douglas Gordon thinking?[3]

3　ダグラス・ゴードンは一体何を考えていたのだ？ダグラス・ゴードン（Douglas Gordon）は1966年グラスゴー生まれ、ビデオ・アーティスト兼ドキュメンタリー制作者。彼の作品は主として記憶と相互影響に焦

　我々の首相は自覚を持って暴力的に、彼らの多くを強淫したと信じている。ただし避妊具を装着した上で。僕が言及する繋がりは、アルバニアの「第二の陰謀」、あるいは「第二の事件」と見做すことができる。第一弾は、2001年の第1回ティラナ・ビエンナーレのイベントであると広く考えられており、これについては後で話そう。そのイベントは、とある組織構造の不首尾を明らかにした。今も進行中のこの「第二の事件」は、政治・組織犯罪・現代美術が国家を統治するという新たなレベルに達した。

　この新たなレベルは、前触れのあった破綻が見事なまでに結実したことも意味するのだが、今のところ関係者の誰もその破綻を受け入れたくないようだ。よく計算されたアート・オペレーションのように思えるが、それを実現した者もしくは者達が、これほど重大なことをまた仕出かすことはないと思う。彼らは壮大な、現代の社会彫刻を作り上げた。彼らは有毒な土地に病んだ棕櫚の木を植え付けたのだ。

　アルバニアの政治はこのことを認識している。なぜなら、その代表者達はこの結び付きを誇示し、記者会見でマフィアの掟を遣いそれを例示しており、彼らはこの新しい繋がり、この表現方法を誇りに思ってすらいるようだ。自らでその化けの皮を剥がしたが故に、彼らは正体を明かされることを恐れず、一つの使命を担っている。この政府の使命は実に興味深いものであり、ヨニダ・ガシ

　点を当てる。ベルリン在住、同地で活動。超長編実験的フィルム『24時間サイコ(24 Hour Psycho)』(1993年)とドキュメンタリー『ジダン: 神に愛された男(Zidane: A 21st Century Portrait)』フィリップ・パレーノ(Philippe Parreno)との共同監督作品を制作したことで有名。

ィ[4] により寸分違わず位置付けられた。 曰く「18世紀末に国を近代性に向かわせたアルバニア復興の推進者達に続き、 今日の"ルネサンス(Renaissance)"メンバーは、 国を現代性に向けて発進しようとしている：それを彼らは達成したいのだ、 どんな代価も厭わず、 あらゆる手段を尽くしても。」

今日のアーティスト、 今日の政治家と件の犯罪者の中では、僕は犯罪者に一層の関心を寄せている。 アーティストを選ぶことも、 政治家を選ぶこともないだろう。 僕は政治家に一度も興味を持ったことがなく、 今日のアーティストに心を引かれることは決してないだろう。 どちらも地に落ちた人物像だ。 今日のアーティストは、 感謝祭やオークション、 見本市、 はたまた政治イベントで血祭りに上げるための、 ぼってりと肥やすべき七面鳥と見做されている。 我々が生きている時代では、 アウトローであることは特権であり、 概して芸術家は犯罪性や違法性にいつでも魅了されてきた。 犯罪者の頭脳は常に作動しており、 常に全てのものと人を疑い、 常に目的を達成するための様々な手段と方法を探している。 しかし、 犯罪者の行為と、 普通の人あるいは普通と我々が呼ぶ者の「起こしかねない」行為とでは、 僕は後者に興味がある。 なぜなら、 それは最も予測不可能であり、 犯罪者の行為よりも遥かにオリジナルな犯罪や凶行を犯す可能性があるからだ。

僕はシリアル・キラー達の手口に魅了されている。 行為の完璧さ、 空間の読み方、 完全犯罪の手順、 隠された手掛かり、 殺人

---

4 ヨニダ・ガシィ(Jonida Gashi,現代美術デバティクセンター創設者の女性メンバーの一人)は、 ティラナにあるアルバニア研究アカデミーの、 文化人類学・芸術学研究所の研究者。 彼女の調査は現在、 ワールドシネマの観点から仔細に分析された、 アルバニア共産主義体制の政治裁判に関するニュースとドキュメンタリーに向けられている。

シーンへの入場と退場、犯罪シナリオ（または芸術作品の中）に含まれるもの、及び除外されたもの。このプロセスは全て完璧さを目指す傾向があり、このことが、僕がこの人物像に魅了される理由であるが、やはり、その人物像は芸術を愛するアーティストの姿に近接している。アーティストも自らの作品を、完成の域に達するために常に抹殺してやまないのだ。

今日のアーティストのほとんどは芸術の使命を信じておらず、芸術家の役割さえも信じていない。彼らは、マニュアル式の掟を適用する予測可能な二流の殺人犯である。彼らの作品は生まれながらに絶命しており、もはや蘇生することは叶わない。彼らの使命は全くの別物で、全くもって陳腐だ。彼らは自身を賛美する宗教に忠実である。僕は明日のアーティストを信じたい。明日の偉大な芸術家とは、おそらく既に脱走した者、適切なタイミングで全てを放棄した者であり、もはや陰に隠れて行動し続ける者ではないだろう。

現在上手く立ち回っている全てのアーティスト達は、ゲームの中心にどんどん自らの駒を持ち込もうとしている。アーティストは、あらゆる手段で常にこの手の試みを行うが、ここに権力との関係が位置付けられる。権力はこういった側面でも分析する必要がある。僕の現在の立ち位置は、展覧会に行かない観客像の方により結び付いているため、若干異なる。今のところ、僕はある一つの現実の未来への直観しか持っていない。その現実が衝突点に一刻も早く到達するよう、僕が挑発を仕掛けて、火蓋を切りたいと思っている。僕の友人ジョバンニ・デ・ドナ[5] は言う：加速と

―――――――

5 ジョヴァンニ・デ・ドナ（Giovanni De Donà）は1974年ベッルーノ（Belluno）生まれ、ボローニャ大学哲学部専攻、パフォーマー兼インスタレーション制作者である。kooeditions.artのプロデューサーである彼は

クラッシュ！この立ち位置はおそらく、未知の事態に繋がる事故を引き起こすだろう。おそらく我々はその事態に従わねばならないか、あるいは根本的に放棄しなければならない。被むり耐え忍んだ、積年の損害を演算するのではなく、前に進むべきで、直観にのみ従う必要がある、と僕は思うのだが。その事故は、何人（なんぴと）にも制御不能の、誘発された力と恐怖によって引き起こされる。制限があるかどうかは分からない。だが、これらの状況を関連付けられるようにする、課せられた制限があるのだとすれば、それは刑務所の存在である。

　刑務所、それがある種の制限/限界だ。

　政治家は一生涯そこを避けようとする。大抵の場合、彼がシステムを統制しているので逃げ果せる。そこが将来の住処、下手をすれば終の棲家だとよく分かってはいるが、決して居住したいとは思っていない。なぜなら、犯罪者として消え失せることを運命付けられるからだ。手際が悪すぎる、頭でっかちのエスケープ・アーティストのように、今では誰もが知っているトリックを彼は実行し、全く信用の置けない実体に成り果てる。アーティストは一方、実際に脱出劇を実行し、刑務所/限界を手中に収めたいと望む。ある意味で、それに果敢に挑み、取り込んで、その後、犯罪者のように毎回、何度でも脱出することを望んでいるのだ。

　BSは不測の事態に基づいている。通り過ぎる車、「生じる」世界、「存在する」都市。また、BSはことさらに「宗教的な」作品だと私は思う。実際、石の連打は投石のテーマを鮮烈

実験者でありアヴァンギャルド実践者。マルチメディア技術に関する特許の所有者でもある。

に連想させる。だが、投石される殉教者の躯体を打つ代わりに、石は道路の舗装を強硬に絶望的なまでに打ち付ける。さらに、ビデオの行程、開始・進行・終了は、十字架の経路、カルヴァリオの丘への歩みを思わせる。電柱など、ビデオ内の(多数の)垂直構造は、十字架、磔刑を思い起こさせる。この作品には宗教的な言及があるのか? 儀式的なものはあるか?

アスファルトを割る前に、石は砕ける。アスファルトはまさに権力の構造を象徴している。《Breaking Stones》は儀式、反復、「ループ」だ。なぜなら、このやり方でのみ、少しずつだが粘り強く、今日の構造を真っ二つにできるからだ。少なくとも、これらが僕の意図であった。僕がこの作品のために書いた技術テクストでは、これはビデオのようには終わらず、同じジェスチャーを繰り返す別の人物が登場する別の暗い路上で続いていく。作品はそのジェスチャー、その儀式にのみ着眼したものであり、個人についてではないと言っておかねばならない。ある意味では、作品は独りでに展開した。なぜなら、僕が石を発見したのは道すがらで、それらを現場に持ち込んだ訳ではないからだ。フレーミング自体も、僕が見付けた石に呼応して構成されていた。石は誰か別の者によって持ち込まれ、僕はただそれらを使ったが故に、行為の二重の反復がある。僕はそれらの石をより扱い易くするために砕いたのだ。おそらく、明くる日に扱い易くするために、一切の前触れもない、あの無制御の抗議のために。その抗議行動は起き得たし、起き得る、従って、いつの日か到来するのだろう。この理由から、僕は未遂に終わった行為、または中断された行為についても話している。なぜなら、その行為は、まだ我々が目にしていない次の場面に向けられているからだ。ビデオ作品中に、宗教的な要素がそれほどあるとは僕は思わない。共産主義時代、憲法によると、我々は世界で唯一の無神論国家だった。僕個人としては無宗教として生まれ、今現在もそうであるが、例えば、諸々の宗派や多神教信仰などに惹かれている。僕は、統治権力の側面や制御といった様々な観点から、宗教に興味を持っている。共産主義の崩壊後、国内では宗教活動が再び可能になった。三大勢力の信仰［訳注：イスラム、カトリック、正教］に加えて、両手に余るくらいの胡散臭い教団が再びこの混乱した社会を牛耳った。

　僕の高校の同級生で才能ある者達の多くは、これらの疑わしい教団の構成員になった。ティラナの現市長も然り。そこで彼らが何を会得したのか皆目見当がつかないが、彼らのキャリアを見る限り、我らの時代の真の宗教を学び取ったのだと思う。種々の観点から、僕は、キリストとムハンマドの人物像とナレーションに魅了されてはいるものの、宗教に関してはマルクス主義者のままだ。

　僕の街で目にする兆候は《Breaking Stones》でも、非常に存在感があり歴然としているが、そのほとんどは今日の真の宗教である経済力に固有のものだ。宗教的なシンボルや人物について、君は十字架の道の留（りゅう）を呼び覚ましている。そのように見えるかもしれないし、間違いなく別のレベルの解釈でありえるとしても、それは意図したことではない。これらの行程やカットは場面転換の緞帳の機能も果たしている。ビデオのシーケンスでは、木々と黄色がかった街灯から投影された影で隠された壁面に、大文字で「ALLAH（アッラー）」と読み取れる。それは即興のモスク、その界隈の「秘密裡の」モスクだが、自動車修理工場としても機能している。殉教ではなく投石に関しては、アルバニアの若手アーティスト、デヴィッド・カンピ(David Kampi)がある高名な芸術家についてのビデオを作成した。かいつまむと、悪を象徴する、メッカの新しい建築に似ているだけでなく、リチャード・セラの作品にも非常によく似た3基の石油タンクに向かって、イスラム教徒が「ハッジ(Hajj)」を行う時と同じように何時間も、彼は石を投げつけた[6]。この作品は、風刺を込めて《Stoning a Richard Serra》と題されている。

> BSと不能のコンセプト。石を激烈に砕くというアイディアは、怒りと性の抑圧をも思い出させる。どのタイプの欲動抑圧が、個人にとって最も屈辱的で危険だと君は考えるか? 今日のアルバニアでは、怒りと性的本能はどのように制御されているのか? 死の本能とエロスとは?

明らかに、この作品は政治・経済的現実に関する不能、システムに閉じ込められた我々の世代の無力さ、そして物事を抜本的に変革する能力の欠如と結び付いている。僕はこの困難な企てを実現する試みに興味がある。さらに不能の包括的な要素もあるのだとすると、それは国内に蔓延している別の現象と関係がある。僕の意見では非常に興味深いもの、不能として理解されている、浪費されたエナジーの現象である。狭義での不能を示す作

---

6 アメリカのパフォーマー、彫刻家、ビデオ・メーカーであるリチャード・セラ(Richard Serra, 1939〜サンフランシスコ出身)は、金属製の巨大モニュメント作品で知られている。「Hajj(ハッジ)」とは毎年イスラム暦第12月に行われるメッカ大巡礼のことで、それを締めくくるのが象徴的な悪魔への石投げ行為である。

品中に、 一つのレベルがあるとするならば、 それは、 おそらく最近のグローバルな政治的形成に関わる何かであり、 今日、 芸術活動をする意味にも関係するものだ。 芸術活動をすることの不可能性と、 グローバルな現実を前に無力さを感じること。 アルバニアの芸術家達は、 早漏に苦しんでいると先程言ったが、 この隠喩は社会全般に対してのものだった。 僕は、 彼らが待つことを知らず、 快楽の持続時間を探求したくないのだ、 と言うつもりだったのではなく、 彼らの知識が、 ここでは革命のための闘争という意味で、 早熟のままであるということだった。 なぜなら、 革命はこれまでに完遂されたことはなく、 途中で分断されたからだ。 僕が思うに、 ここに問題がある。 この現象学の中では、 これらの問題を扱う作品は、 異なる次元を提供せず、 然るべく体験されないが故に、 無駄に消え失せてしまう。 この「早漏」の繰り返しは、 我々の社会全体にとっての問題であり、 芸術作品や芸術家に関する懸案なだけではない。 アーティストが引き合いに出されるのは、 この全体的情況において行動に移さねばならないからだ。 しかし、 海外に住み、 その地で何かを試みた者でさえ、 この社会の意味を理解することは困難だと感じている。 この全てに混乱があることは明白だが、 社会のこの側面だけでなく、 その他のより広範な側面についても核心に迫るために、 挑戦し、 架空でもいいから装置や仕掛けを創出して、 貪欲に学ぶ必要がある。

　この国がひた隠す奥深さは、 未だぼんやりとしたままだ。 ヴロールの無名の女性アーティストが最近新しい作品を完成したのだが、 その作品に僕は考えさせられた。 彼女が2013年に作った小さな彫刻だ。 この繊細な彫刻は、 原寸大の使用済みコンドームの正確な形状をしている。 実際、 使用済みのコンドームである。 古ぼけて硬化し紫がかった色のオブジェに、 アーティストは《Bad Seed》(悪い種子)というタイトルを付けた。

　彼女はいかなる理由でも作品の公開を望まず、 その上、 その意味を説明したがらない。 説明を望まないということは実に僕の興味を引きつけ、 予知夢的な進展、 オブジェの選択、 そして作品を展示しないという決定も然り。 彼女の作品は、 暴力、 社会的強淫、 組織的抑圧、 人種的偏見、 アーリア人であるという(学術文書では全く詳しく説明されていない)倒錯的感覚、 純粋な血統、 差別、 ミソジニー、 超暴力的で激烈な男性優位主義について述べている。

　アルバニア社会のこれらの問題に、 国家や芸術機関が組織ぐるみで取り組むことはまずないため、 残念ながら、 こういった作品が我々の目に触れることはない。 僕は、 この女性アーティストの選択と、 彼女が取り上げたモチーフに大いなる親近感を抱いている。 そのモチーフ、 この社会の意識的・無意識的な欲動についての主題は、 まさに精神的プロセスに関わってくる。 僕がイタリアに到着した頃、 最初に手がけた作品群はこれらのテーマ、 特にフロイトや快楽原則に関連していた。 その後、 僕の探究は別の展望に向けられたため – と言うか – 見切りをつけたのだが。 1999年から2000年の間に作成された、 当時の作品群は、 習作・スケッチとして生まれ、 長さは約10メートルに及んだ。 それらの作品は、 猥褻な挿絵と実在の人物・アカデミアのメンバー達を描いたデッサンと共に平面的な台座群として組み立てられ、 三次元の実物大の墓、 アカデミアの教授陣の墓石群に仕立てられていた。 トスカーナの家の屋根裏部屋に今でもひっそりと埋もれているこれらの制作物では、 怒りが教育機関の内に、 学生と教師像との間に、 暴力的な関係へと屈折していったが、実際には、別の何か：1997年にアルバニアで起こったことに対して向けられていたのだ。

　その学院内では、精神分析医/教授と患者/学生の姿を借りて、過去の全ての出来事が繰り返されていた。患者は常に精神分析医から何か別のものを望んでおり、その逆も同様だ。早漏や不能の主題は、近年の歴史とシステムの変化に常に関連している。我々は実に興味深い時代を生きている。そこでは大衆 − 変化を望む国民 − の抗議の形は、国家と首相によって、試すべくも実現しなかった勃起として描写される。首相はこれらの言い回しを用いて、国民に言及する。アルバニア国民は、真の勃起ができなくなってしまった雄性体として表されている。彼が目に浮かべる唯一の勃起とは、まさに決して蜂起することのない反乱であり、それについては彼の言い分が間違っているとは言えない。彼自身が、その反乱を挑発し煽動している。全てが過去に、1990年から1997年の受難の中に埋もれているように見える。いかなる大衆の行為としても爆発できないほどに、社会は萎縮してしまったようだ。

　新世代が現在を概括できるようになるのなら、彼らが何をするか見てみようではないか。これもこの地に生きるアーティスト達の務めだと思う。アーティスト達は、我々が経験しているこの「興味深い」時代を、誰よりも上手く要約できるからこそ、反応を示さなければならないのだ。

BSとイタリア現代美術。 ジーノ・デ・ドミニシス[7]と君との関係、 限界の概念。 マッコウクジラの骨格だけでなく、 とりわけBSのパフォーマンスも。 BSと、 デ・ドミニシスのビデオ《Tentativo di volo(飛行の試み)》及び《Tentativo di formare quadrati invece che cerchi in acqua(水面に円環ではなく正方形を形成しようとする試み)》の間には、 多くの共通要素がある。 だが、 根本的な違いは、 デ・ドミニシスが不可能な行為を示していることである。 人間は飛ぶことができない。 それは自然の摂理である。 同様に、 水に石を投げて正方形［訳注: の波紋］を形作ることはできない。 アーティストはどのように限界の概念に関わることができるのだろうか? デ・ドミニシスの、 芸術及びアーティストについてのヴィジョンのうち、 君は何を共有し、 何を共有しないのか? この作品BSにおいて、 コンセプチュアル・アートのアイディアはどれほど重要なのか?

《Breaking Stones》 のパフォーマンスは、 ある序曲、 将来の抗議の準備と理解することができる。 瘡蓋を掻きむしるような真似は止めなくてはならない、 傷を負わせた者達のその先を見据えようとすることで。 そこには、 もはや何もないのだ。 ポストコンセプチュアル派の輩が全て盗み去ってしまったのだ。 新しい傷口を

7　ジーノ・デ・ドミニシス(Gino De Dominicis, 1947–1998)は、 イタリアのアートシーンにおける論争的で多面的な中心人物であり、 建築家兼哲学者。 批評家の判断とレッテルから逃れるために、 謎に包まれていた。 彼の作品は、 '60年代から'70年代に制作されたインスタレーションと彫刻に大別され、 時間と永遠の関係に焦点を当てている。 具象絵画は後にほぼ専業的に従事し、 誰しもが彼の自死を疑った状況での早すぎる死を迎えるまで制作していた。

切り開かなくてはならない、 そしてこれらの傷はより深くなければ
ならない。 ゲームでは常に一歩先にいることが肝要だ： もし君が
先駆者でないのならば、 何者でもたり得ない。 僕が実際のところ
忌み嫌っている共同展覧会、 その片隅のスペースを埋めることが
できるに過ぎない。 なぜなら、 君は他者、 もっと強力な者達を守
る立場に置かれ、 実際には君自身を壊滅に追い込んでいるから
だ。 共同展覧会は別の象徴を振興するためだけに開かれる。 デ・
ドミニシスが言っていたように、 （もはや随分以前から）アーティスト
の姿ではなく、 キュレーターのそれでもない、 組織的収集といった
最重要な実体を振興するためだ。 共同展覧会はアーティストにとっ
ての罠になってしまったのだ。 共同展覧会で注目を集めようとする
のは、 もう刺激的ではない。 乾いたアスファルトで車を運転するよ
うなものだ。 コンセプチュアル・アートそれ自体が罠であり、 デュシ
ャンは罠の偉大な発明者だった。 デ・ドミニシスはそれが分かって
いた。

　コンセプチュアル・アートを作り続けることは、 安全運転を続
けたいと思うようなものだ。 僕は常にゲームに心惹かれている
が、 このゲームに皆が手を出せるようになってしまったら、 退散
しなければならない。 今となっては万人がコンセプチュアル・ア
ーティスト達のナイーヴさ（naïveté）と完璧さを理解できる。 One
should fuck their Bible.[8]

　新たなる書を記さねばならない、 だがその前に何か別のこと
をしなくては。 デイヴィッド・ハモンズ[9] が言うように、 この障害を克
服するには、 まず、 デュシャン毒を抜くための療養センターを開

8　奴らのバイブルを台無しにせねば。

9　1943年スプリングフィールドで生まれたデイヴィッド・ハモンズ（Da-
　　vid Hammons）は、 アメリカの芸術家、 彫刻家、 パフォーマー。 '70

設する必要がある。 そう言う時の彼は非常に真摯だと思う。 なぜ
なら彼自身、 その罠から抜け出せないでいるからだ。 コンセプチ
ュアル・アートは十字架のようなものだ。 この十字架、 この罠を海
に投げ入れるために、 僕は飼い猫達の1匹をマルセル・デュシャン
と名付けた。 その猫とともに2018年、 実現しなかった対話を始
めることを目指した作品《Plumb në zarf, Bullet in Envelope》
を僕達は制作した[10]。 デュシャンは、 他の全ての猫達と同様、 偉
大なネコ科生物であり、 彼がアーティストを超越するのを僕は待ち
望んでいる。 一人前になっても彼らの教会に楯突くことなく、 同じ
ような司祭と成り果てる、 ポストコンセプチュアルの侍祭達のよう
な、 ポストコンセプチュアルの別の「コピーキャット[11]」にはならない
よう、 僕は期待しているのだ。

　デ・ドミニシスについては、 僕はその死にのみ関心がある。
死は概して僕を魅了し、 彼の死は素晴らしい一つの芸術作品だっ
た。 彼に近付くために、 小遣い稼ぎにもならないような神秘主義
に満ち満ちたセンチメンタルな手紙を書いたり、 偽りの秘密を打
ち明けたりすることに興味はない。 愛の表明としての、 デュシャン
の精液の素描［訳注:《Paysage Fautif罪のある風景》(1946年)］
は、 芸術家達の手でしたためられた感傷的な書簡を永遠に凌駕
した。 ジーノ・デ・ドミニシスの死は別のレベルに設定される。 と
いうのも、 しばらく前から、 僕はとあるアイディアを実現しようとし

年代及び '80年代のニューヨークとロサンゼルスにおいての作品と活躍
　で最もよく知られている。

10 参照: https://debatikcenter.net/strikes/bullet_in_envelope

11 コピーキャット (Copycat)、 特に学校用語では(他人の宿題を)書き写す
　生徒」を意味する。 だが、 伊語への翻訳では「キャット(猫)」と直前に言
　及した飼猫デュシャンとの言葉遊びは喪失されている。

ているからだ。ギャラリーで自死行為に及ぶ自殺者の遺体に署名したい。ジーノ・デ・ドミニシスの不動の躯に署名すべきだった。彼が亡くなり、僕がイタリアに到着した当時、1998年にそうしておくべきだった。彼の自死の躯に名を記す。自殺行為を盗み取るのだ。

《Breaking Stones》のビデオは、身体の致命性に関する作品でもある。冒頭に、強烈な要素、吠える犬がいる。さらに往来の音。そして当然ながら、地面に打ち付けられた石の – 非常に激烈な – 音。このビデオの音響はどのくらい重要か？君の作品において、現代音楽とはどのような関係を持っているか？ BSも「具体音楽(musique concrèteミュジック・コンクレート)」の一作品として読み解けるか？

僕は音響とは常に同じ関係性を持っていた。かの葬送行進曲が音に対して持つ関係、葬儀のために作曲された、偉大な聴覚障害者のための曲［訳注：アルフォンス・アレーAlphonse Allaisの作品に言及］。してやられたり！

《Breaking Stones》のサウンド・トラックは全て「フィールド録音」である。僕は単方向マイクをカメラと一緒に配置し、アクションに従った。スタジオでのいかなる調整もポストプロダクションもない。全ては撮影環境から由来している。僕の意図は厳格な目標に従うことだったが、それは現場に存在する状況によって提供されたものだった。

被拘留者達は、周辺のマンションや家屋の住民達と同様、塀の外で起きていることを聞くことができた。彼らは見ることはで

きなかったが、 想像することができた。 このことに僕は興味を抱
いている。

　《Breaking Stones》は、 貴国の国民的ヒーローであるジェル
ジ・カストリオティ・スケンデルベウ(Gjergj Kastrioti Skënderbeu)について非常に考えさせる。 進行中の「反乱」のアイディ
アは確かにビデオに存在する。 この読み解き方は可能だと思
うか？ 今日のアルバニアの「大地」を物理的にではなければ、
社会・政治的に占めているのは誰か？ 何に対して、 どのように
反抗できる/すべきなのか？

今日の政策は、 何処であろうと、 公的領域の占領であり、 領土
がもはや占領されていると広く共有された認識がある時に反乱が
起こる。 このため、 機関、 外国軍、 政治勢力、 あるいは今日の
富裕層であるかどうかに関わらず、 過去と現在の占領者達の間
で、 万人が歴史的なパラレルを描く。
　アルバニアで撮影された初の映画は、 イタリアのトリノからのク
ルーの手によるもので、 『Albania ribelle(反乱のアルバニア)』と
いう非常に意味深長な題名だと言われている。 反乱の力は伝説
化され、 何年かの間に我々自身の手で遠ざけられたものの、 今
もなお、 常に我々自身によって格闘が続けられている。 反乱が、
コンセプチュアル・アートの枠組内に、 芸術それ自体の保守傾
向の如く保持されているならば、 反乱はそのものたり得ない。
反乱は展示できるような表現形式ではなく、 僕にとっては、 それ
はファイリングもラベル付けもできないものだ。 反乱は露出主義で
はなく、 無制御な勇気の行動であり、 さらに前進し 言うまでも

なく、何か新しいものを生み出さなければならない。さもなければ、何の目的もないショーの催し物でしかない。

　僕は今でも、不可能な抗議行動の展開を待っているのだが、今日それが何を意味するのかは定かではない。僕にとっては極めて現実的に思えても、僕が想像する方法は実行不可能だ。これが生じた暁には、今日のアーティスト達はただ静観すべきで、その不可能なアイディアに匹敵する何かを得たいのならば、彼らは介入すべきではないだろう。反乱の思想は、今日でも異例の現象として考えられ、もはや現実的ではないために不可能なものと位置付けられて、町外れの廃屋の片隅に追い遣られてしまっている。僕にとっては、この思想は深遠で複雑な理念であり続け、自由に関するものであるからこそ実現すべきものである。

　世界のこの片隅で、我々は、ソビエト連邦との親密な関係、そして中華人民共和国との蜜月に続き、3番目の恋物語の時代を生きているところだ。

　共産主義の間に万人が認識していた、秘めた愛があったとするならば、それは西側への愛、アメリカへの愛だった。国家組織にとって、アメリカは敵、諸悪の象徴だった当時のことだ。政権崩壊後、米国がこの国に上陸したのを僕は見た。人々は自宅から持ち出した絨毯を、アスファルトの上に敷き広げた。その上を、ジェイムズ・ベイカー[12] とアメリカ人達の行列が、スカンデル

---

12 弁護士で共和党員のジェイムズ・アディソン・ベイカー（James Addison Baker, 1930〜ヒューストン出身）は、ロナルド・レーガン大統領の任期中に財務長官、そしてジョージ・W・ブッシュ大統領時代の最後の数ヶ月に国務長官を務め、ベルリンの壁崩壊及びソビエト連邦崩壊後の期間に指導的役割を果たした。1991年6月ティラナへの彼の公式訪問は、米国政府幹部の権威あるメンバーのアルバニア初訪問であり、彼

ベグ広場に向かって通過して行った。 民主主義と繁栄の象徴としてのアメリカは、 欠けていた未来だった。 しかし、 最近は状況が変わった。 27年間の「熱愛」の末、 アメリカの駐在員事務所や大使館、 あるいは市井の無名のアメリカ人でさえも、 もはや親しげに君の肩をポンと叩いて来るような、 気さくな友人と同等だと無邪気に見做されることはなくなった。 むしろ、 恐れるべき人物や機関のように思われている。 警告、 警鐘が過去から鳴り響いている。 僕の両親の世代が経験した時代の、 ベトナムでの残虐行為を彷彿とさせたアフガニスタンやイラクでの戦争、 及び、 情報の伝達速度と帝国主義の拡大が原因で、 アメリカの概念が変わりつつある。

　2013年、 我々は米国大使館前での唯一の象徴的な抗議行動を初めて目撃した。 抗議はシリアの化学兵器に対するもので、 我々の政府はその兵器を自国領へ輸送し、 首都の至近距離にある場所で解体するために、 合衆国政府と密かに交渉を進めていた。 当時、 野党であった民主党の指導者は、 住民からより暴力的な反応を惹き起こすために、 非常に曖昧だが効果的な方法で、 交渉は中断すべきだと延々と持論を繰り返した。 彼はこの論議をしながら、 米国の「暗黒の」歴史を引用し、 ’60年代の人種隔離、 及び「Black Lives Matter(ブラック・ライヴス・マター)[13] 」の

とその代表団をともに讃えようと沿道に集った30万人以上の人々によって迎えられた。

13　「Black Lives Matter」は、 逐語伊訳では"Le vite nere contano"(黒人の命も価値がある)。 イベントとデモを開催することで、 有色人種に対する人種差別及び偏見と戦うために、 アリシア・ガルツィア(Alicia Garzia)、 パトリッセ・キュラー(Patrisse Cullors)、 オパル・トルネーティ(Opal Torneti)により、 2013年アメリカ合衆国で発足された国際的な運動。

最近の取り組みを呼び覚ました。 まだ時期尚早ではあるが、 この
テーマに附随する諸問題は際立ってきつつあるようだ。 領土内の
他のいかなる外国籍の存在と比較しても、 米国はより浸透した存
在感を放つ。 諸政党が抗議する時、 星条旗は常に揺らぐが、 新
世代の者達はかなり異なった考え方をしている。 アメリカは今や、
君が憎むと同時に愛している元恋人のようなものだ。 君の日記
の頁から消し去り、 切り取り、 焼き払って、 排除したいと望んで
も、 君の中で生きているが故に、 結局はそう出来ない。 それは我
々の脳裏に住み着いており、 我々の精神が、 解放されるべき真の
領域なのだ。

《Breaking Stones》 と「殉難」のコンセプト。 今日のアルバニ
アの文化と精神性における「殉難者達」は誰なのか? 今日の「
殉難者」とは誰か?

1990年の直後、 インテリアに関して僕らが改装した、 家庭内での
最初の環境はバスルームだった。 人民は群をなして、 社会主義
時代の石板を、 外国から輸入された白とグレーの粗悪なセラミッ
ク製タイルに置き換えた。 さらに、 バスタブ、 電気ボイラー付きシ
ャワー、 フランス式トイレ、 ビデを追加した。 これらの家具調度品
は全て、 冷ややかな蛍光灯の光で照らされていた。 バスルーム
が完成すると、 家の残りの部分が徐々に新しいタイルで覆われて
いった。 その後さらに、 僕らは改築に取り組んだ。 新しい窓を増
設、 既存の窓も拡大し、 共有スペースをふさいで何室か新しい部
屋を追加した。

　タイルは我々にとって重要だ。　なぜなら、　私的な価値があるだけでなく、　政治的変革という歴史的な意味も有するからだ。　ティラナの中央広場であるスカンデルベグ広場の再整備を計画した建築家達は、　過去のこのような利用法を念頭に置いていたと思う。

　バスルームといった私的空間から、　新品のタイル張りは大規模に屋外に移動し、　中央広場の公共空間に到った。　そこはかつて - 今ではそうではなくなってしまったが - 国の記憶の重要な象徴であった。　広場を舗装する大型の石のタイルは、　アルバニア人共同体が居住する全ての場所、　近隣諸国からだけでなく、　ディアスポラからも産出している(と、　少なくともそう言われている)。中央広場のタイルで表現された統一国家の思想は、　統一性の唯美主義的思想であり、　それは、　また別のタイプの統一にも関連する。　国のアイデンティティ的な、　ポピュリズム・タイプの、　永続的な変革の統一だ。　それは、　新自由主義政策にまさしく関係するものである。

　非常に明敏なある者が、　皮肉を込めて僕に語った。　将来、これらのタイルが、　殉難詩人達の礎石を建立するための材料を供与しなければならない、　と。　詩人達は自身の命を犠牲にしても、　先達ての広場の破壊という集合的記憶を守らんとして亡くなったのだ。《Breaking Stones》の撮影終了直後、　その同じ日の明け方に、　僕は広場に行き《UNTITLED (Pissed Off)》[14] を制作した。

　当国史において殉難者とは、　歴史上、　故国のために死没した者と認識されている。　例えばパルチザンのような者のことだが、　たとえ、　今現在、　不条理な歴史・政治的対立を我々が体験しているとしても、　だ。　その歴史・政治的対立では過去を書き換

____

14 《無題(怒り心頭)》。

え、共産主義に関係があるというだけで、この歴史上の人物を排除しようとする。この不条理が継続し、さらに拡大してしまっているのは、あまりにも専門知識が足りず、政治的に同調した歴史家達という個人が立ち向かっているせいでもある。

1990年以降、我々は偽りの殉難者達、偽の民主主義殉難者や偽の社会主義殉難者を祭り上げた。また、－今日の欧州精神の異例のパフォーマンスにおいて－過去のカトリック教会の殉教者達をも蘇生させた。歴史上の多くの「虚偽」と同様に、今日の殉難者は、一例を挙げるならば、コソボで殺された者達よりも栄誉を授けられている。僕個人としては、殉難者について考える時、僕はまだそこにいない者達、来たる者達に一層の思いを馳せる。明日の殉難者とは、未来から来たる殉難者であり、（おそらく）オンライン上に生きる観念に過ぎなくなるだろう。僕はこのナレーションに興味がある。なぜなら、国は想像力を働かせ始める必要があり、未来の殉難者を蘇生させなければならないからだ。

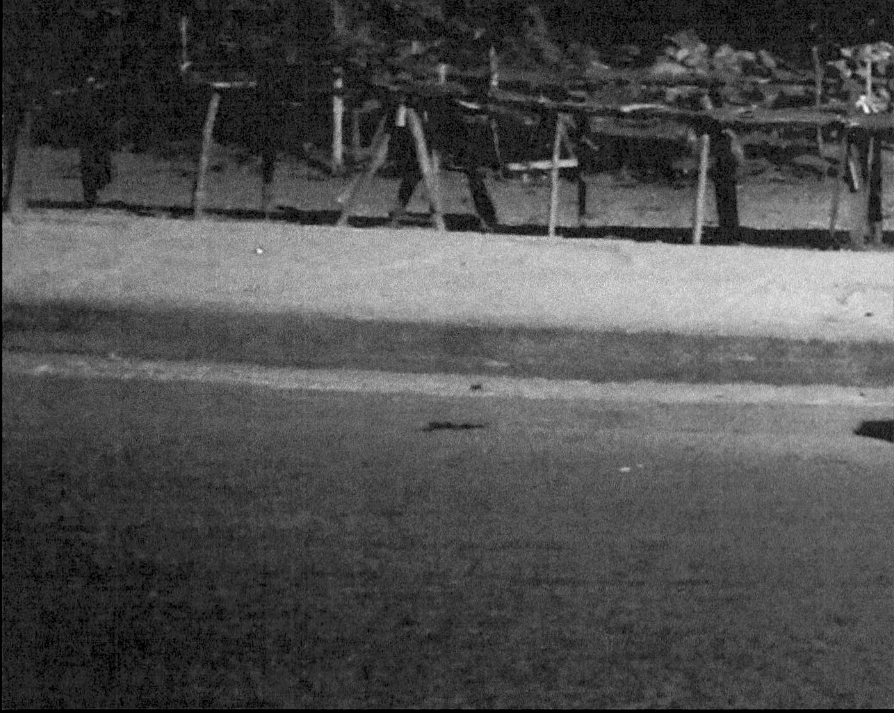

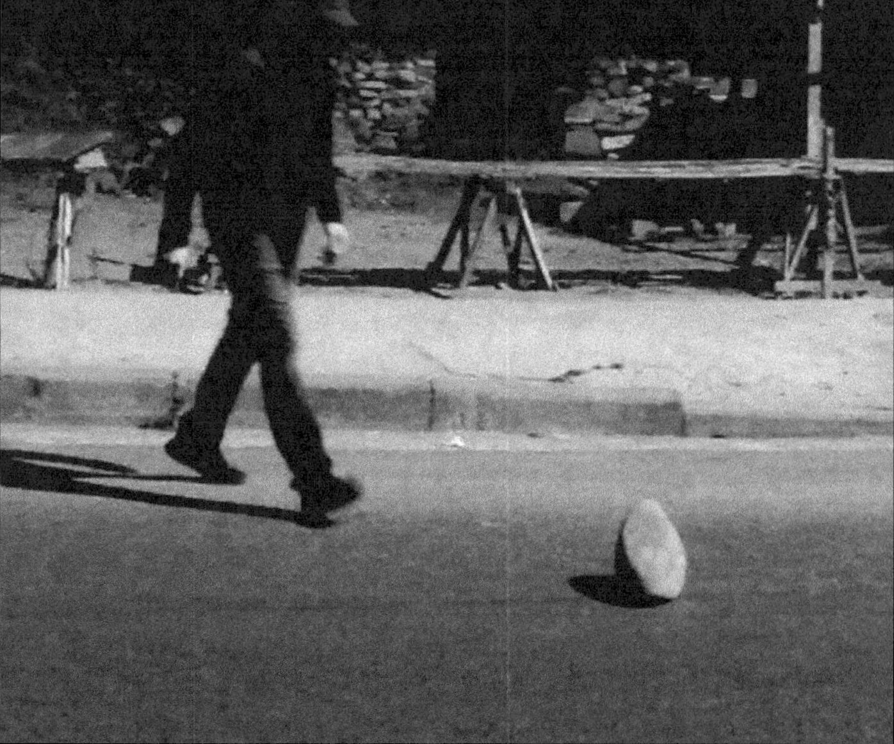

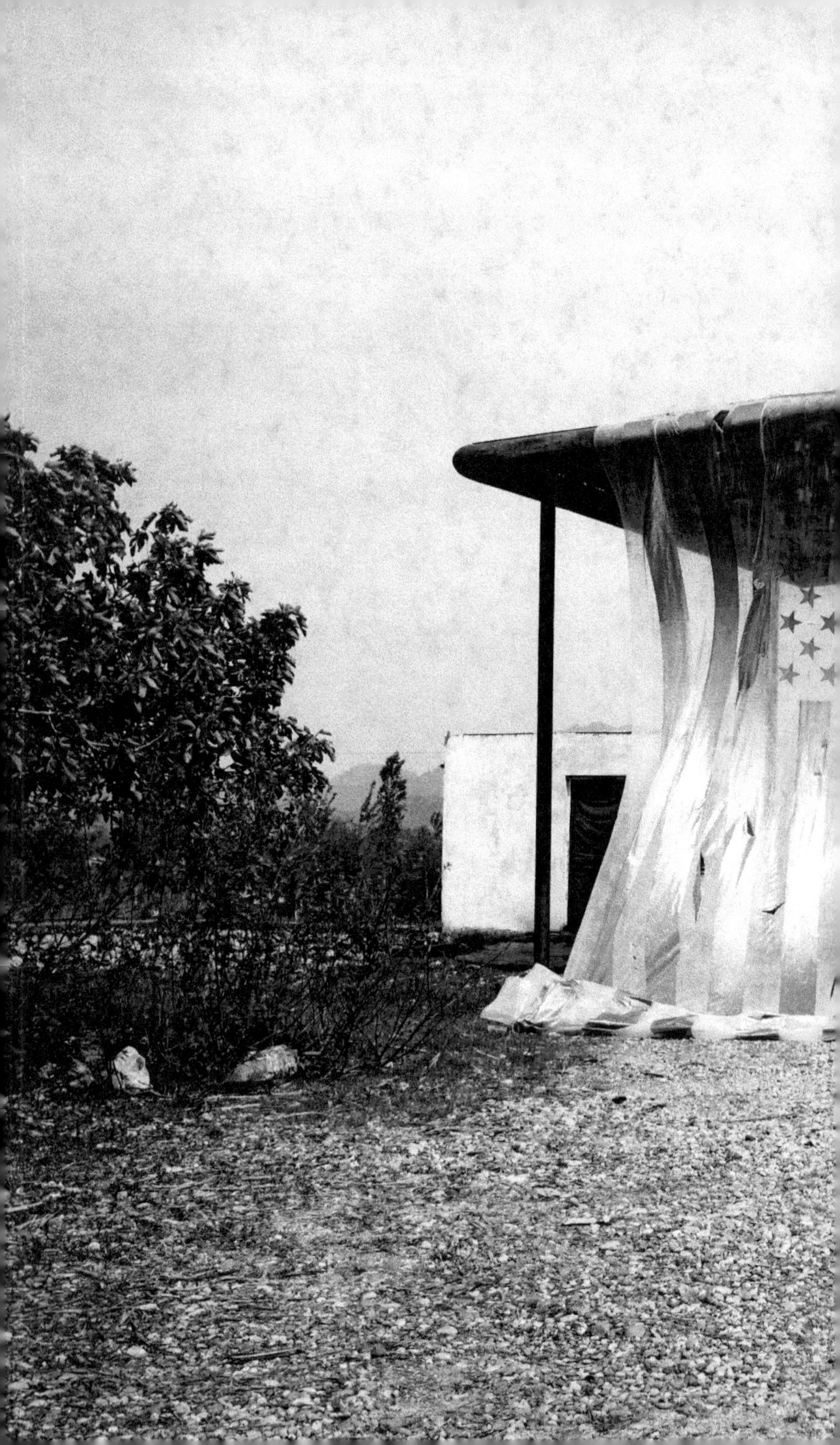

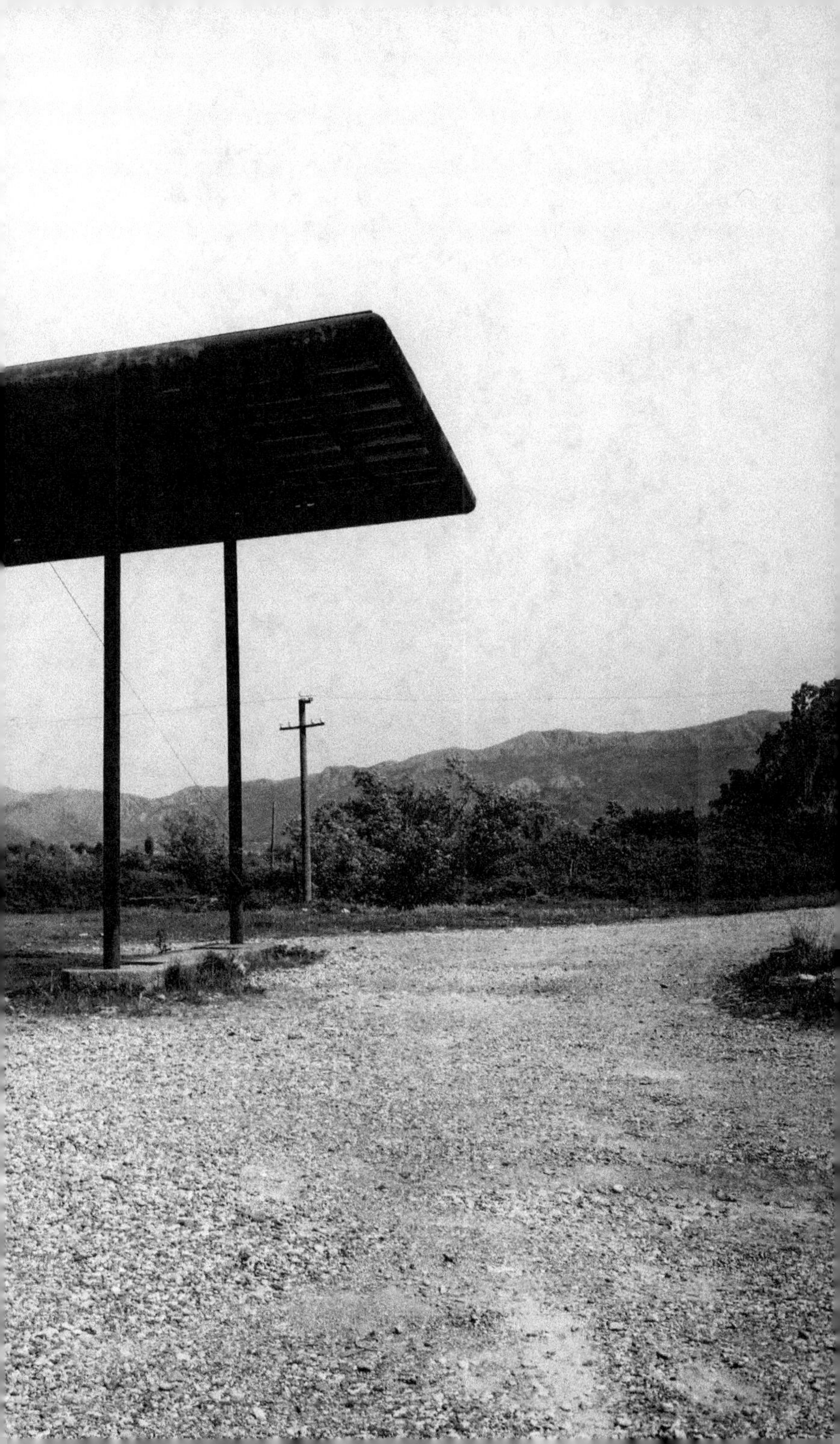

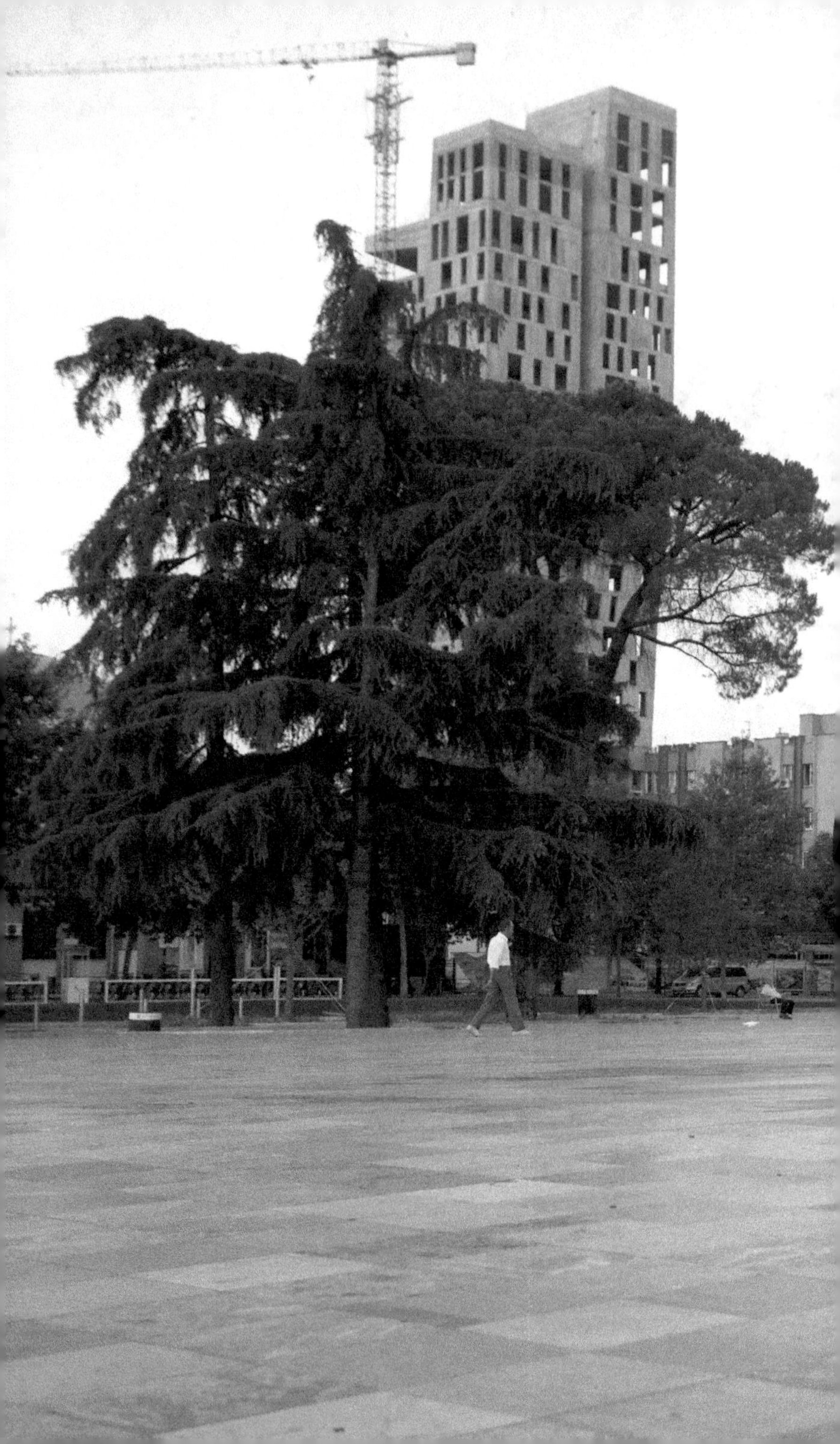

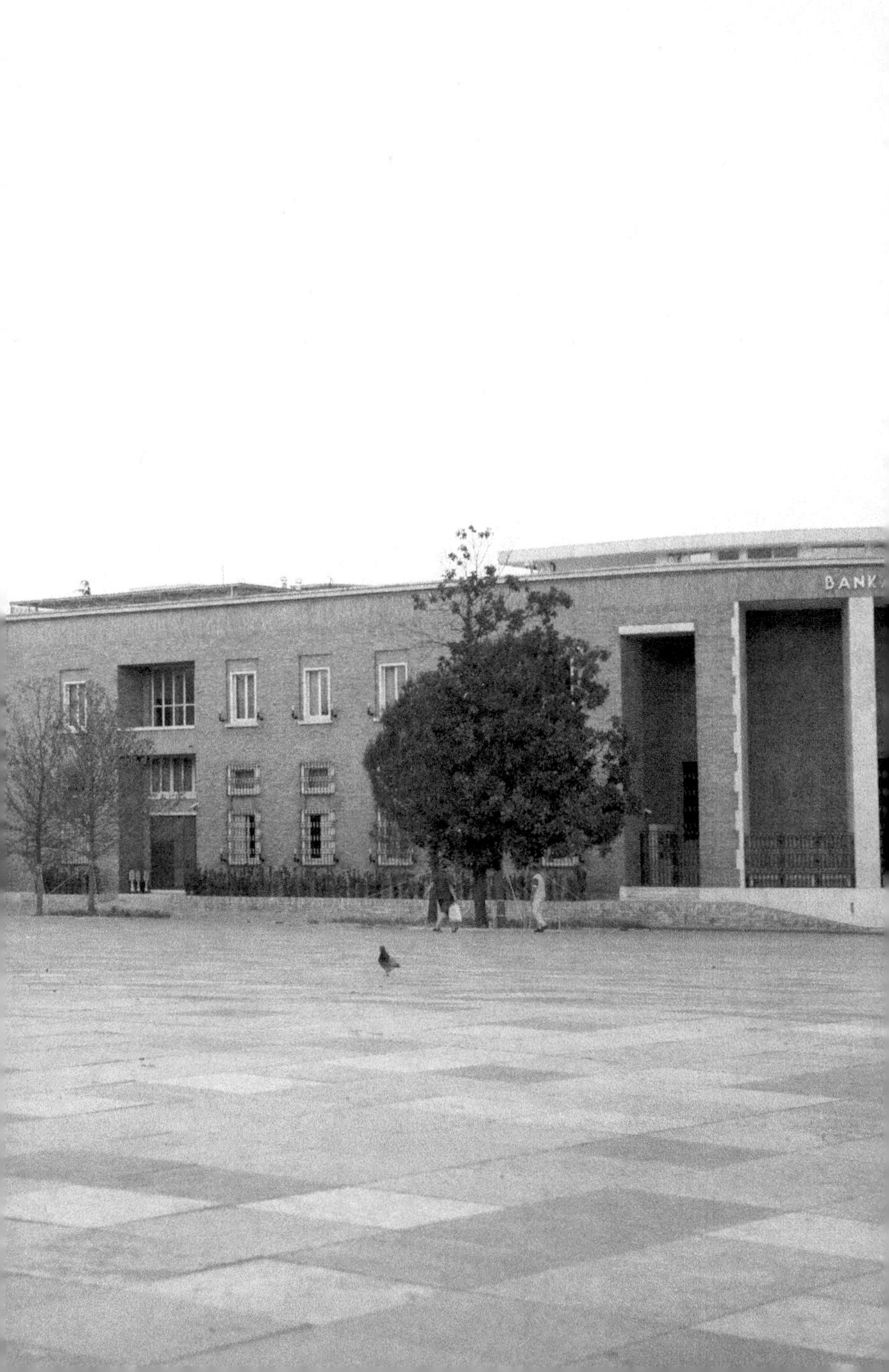
BANK

Fig. 14. Breaking Stones by Armando Lulaj, 2017.
Video. Color. Sound. 10'31".
Courtesy of DebatikCenter of Contemporary Art.

Fig. 15. FALLEN (american neanderthal) by Armando Lulaj, 2016.
C-print. 140×140cm. Production photo by Marco Mazzi.
Courtesy of Paolo Maria Deanesi Gallery and DebatikCenter of
Contemporary

Fig. 16. UNTITLED (pissed off), by Armando Lulaj, 2017.
Documentation of the performance on the highest point of the not-
so-slight inclination of the new Skanderbeg square, Tirana, July 22,
2017.
Production photo by Pleurad Xhafa.
Courtesy of DebatikCenter of Contemporary Art.

TRACK 04

You and censorship. How have you been censored in Italy and in Albania? Have there been any episodes of explicit censorship? Can you expand on this? What happened to you (even recently with Bullet in Envelope*...)?*

It's not exactly news that different groups and/or entities attack an artist to control their work and freedom of expression. Today censorship is still a very widespread phenomenon, which obviously concerns above all activities that tend to express criticism by showing the reality of power in all its forms, starting with the government and arriving at a denunciation of the workers' conditions at the Guggenheim in Abu Dhabi, for example. It should be said that today we are faced with a situation that seems uncontrollable, because increasingly power tends to exert censorship from the start, cutting criticism off at the bud so as not to allow it to flower. In all these years, in my experience, there have been many situations that illustrate this. But there is a difference when we are talking about other countries because, I believe, my origins have played an important role. As compared to my native country, the censorship structure in other countries is more complex, more stratified and with more levels. Except for very few exceptions, which according to me really should be the norm, art in Albania, as well as investigative journalism, is controlled exclusively by the government. If an artist deals with issues that involve the way the country is governed, for example the corruption of the government, they are to all intents and purposes classified as an opponent and put on what they actually refer to as "the blacklist."

Recently the government's structure of control — even if control of these phenomena has a much longer history, beginning in the communist period — has become far more effective. If in the past, namely in the 1990s, it stooped to brutalities like burning a book or the offices of a national newspaper, today's specialists are much more sophisticated. Today's situation makes me think of the events of 1997 and the state of emergency we lived in for months. There are so many things that the current way of governing has in common with 1997. For example, the state has total control of the judiciary. For a long time now, the so-called judicial reform has blocked the formation of the Constitutional Court. The executive branch governs primarily through decrees of the Council of Ministers or by special laws, which seem to be proposed exclusively by oligarchs. All these anomalies, which have by now become the norm, are connected to censorship and the government's use of the media, but also art.

Toward the end of 1997, the public broadcaster produced a program with high school art students which I also participated in. The purpose of the program was to try to analyze the role of art and the artist in the development of society. It was one of many TV programs trying to assuage the shock people had suffered. In that program they talked about the role that the artist should have, the structure of this institution and the need to reform it, but also about the role that artists had inherited, an imposed role, oriented by politics, which clearly suffocated every level of creativity and liberty of expression. When the program was aired the next day, we discovered that they had cut out most of our provocative statements. Though I was very young, I felt like I'd been amputated. For the first time I sensed a certain marginalization, due also to the position taken toward us by some of the teachers and the majority of the other students in the school. It was on that occasion that for the first time I perceived how narrow-minded an artistic institution could be. One year later, in 1998, together with two of my friends who had also been on that television program, I left to study in Florence, where I carried on, or at least I still think I did, something that was rooted in that program.

At the Florence Academy of Fine Arts, before making *Walking Free in Harmony* (2001) I made two other works, *Guasto (Out of Order,* 2000) and *Acqua due volte al giorno* (*Water Twice a Day,* 2000). It was a very intense time because something was stirring in the city, it was as if a new wind was blowing. In the Academy, the echo of discussions that found no answers from among the teachers lingered in the air. The classroom was full of paintings, second-rate drawings, and copies of other artists' works, things we'd already done at the beginning of high school. It was a suffocating environment. That was why I made *Guasto.* Right in the middle of the easel-painting class, when everyone was silently at work, I picked up the classroom fire extinguisher, took off the safety valve and transformed the room into a white space. When the white powder had settled on the floor and the room had become something decidedly different, a sort of white cube, I wrote the word *Guasto* in black on the extinguisher, which is also the title of the work. After *Guasto* I almost never went back to class. In the morning I handed out leaflets and in the afternoon I went to the Biblioteca Nazionale (National Library) to read Ludwig Wittgenstein, whom I liked a lot at the time. That meant I was making too many absences and risked failing the year, but I wasn't worried. In the corner where I worked in I'd placed a houseplant on top of my stool, a *Spathiphyllum* or peace lily, as it is known in English, and alongside it a note. On the note I'd written the name of the plant with a felt-tip pen along with instructions for its care — water twice a day. I thought it was the teachers' duty to water the plant, something they never did, and so the plant died.

In the end, the Florence Academy created problems for me. Besides being traditionalist, it was organized mainly for foreign students, Americans and Europeans that is, who wanted to study the Renaissance. In the Academy's administrative office I felt the pressures of a border-police station. The non-western students, the ones from the so-called third world (in those days there were no students from the fourth or fifth worlds), were really treated very badly. This imposed, controlled, and forced submission to an administration that considered us third-class citizens made me sick to my stomach. What was at stake was my very identity. That's why I felt that more than censoring my work they were trying to censor my identity. I say this because at the time the gesture of *Walking Free in Harmony* was not seen as a work of art at all. In what was said against it there was always an implicit condemnation of my origins, including absurd, almost fascist arguments having to do with the landings of immigrants in the nineties and the clichés formed after 1997. A few days after my expulsion my fellow students in the Academy staged a goodbye concert in the courtyard of the institute, a very noble gesture on their part and one that was very encouraging for me.

After Florence I went to Bologna — I had no choice. At the time of my move there, in 2002, Bologna was a very vibrant city, full of lively debate. It was a left-wing town that allowed considerable freedom, but then things gradually changed.

One of the first things I saw there — I was shaken by it for a long time, and still am — was a fresco in Saint Petronius Cathedral, specifically the 15th-century fresco by Giovanni da Modena, where the prophet Mohammed is depicted naked in hell. The image is compelling — it is one of the most powerful I've ever seen. The Cathedral was always guarded because after September 11th there had been several terrorist attempts and every time I went back to see the fresco, which isn't well-placed for viewing it frontally, the police were present.

From 2004 onward I created works in various strategic spots in the city. These included the TPO in Piazza Verdi (a well-known center of social gathering, afterward torn down to "gentrify" the neighborhood by putting up new residential quarters), a vibrant space that was also important in the city's political history; and the Cavour Gallery, an area under the portico that houses the city's most expensive shops. I transformed all these spaces into stages for interventions dealing with the city's political and cultural problems, but not only that. In 2004 they removed my neon installation *L'élégance du Temps,* which was placed on the facade of the TPO building. Using the three colors of the Italian flag the neon announced the opening of a center for kamikazes and skyjackers. In 2007 I was invited to make another neon installation in Piazza Verdi along with other artists. I created two texts, *Piazza SSenza Valori* in white neon, and further back a much more optimistic and romantic title in red neon, *But Let Us Yet Put Forth Courageously,* a phrase taken from T.S. Eliot's early poem "Departure and Arrival." The white neon was situated at the beginning of the colonnade, near the wall of the church, beside the ceramic plaque with the name of the piazza, while the red neon continued underneath the colonnade. The installation was sabotaged. First they cut off the electricity, then they cut the wires. It was attacked both by center-left and center-right organizations, by the Church as well as by the city government. With this particular work, besides talking about the past and the future, I also wanted to show the (extreme) overload of values that a conflict in a square brings forth, and also to imagine a square without them. Curator Hans Ulrich Obrist has spoken about the significance of a square of this kind, whether or not such a square can be constructed and what that would mean. Not by chance, but out of the extreme volition of an aesthetics which I don't share, such a square was in fact constructed in Tirana, a city that Obrist seems very close to: Skanderbeg Square is the perfect example of the uprooting of memory. The square was designed as a pyramid, as though to suggest the idea of lowering the value of the collective, the masses, and raising that of the individual. According to the architects and politicians who planned that square, it is the individual who should be placed at the top, while the masses should be situated far beneath.

In 2014 some misunderstandings of my work UNTITLED upset the Jewish community. Having been invited to exhibit by the Bologna Art Fair, I decided to show a work previously planned for a museum under the colonnade of Galleria Cavour. The installation is the exact copy of the iron sign bearing the words *Arbeit Macht Frei* found over the entrance to Auschwitz, made by the inmates. The copy is made in neon, but the words are backwards, just as they would be if read from inside the camp. The rabbi of Bologna gathered in front of the work with members of the Jewish community, in this central space that explodes with wealth, and threatened to destroy it because they considered it anti-Semitic. The work was debated in the media, by city hall bureaucrats, and also by the director of the Bologna Art Fair, who wrote to the Jewish community to explain the purpose of the operation. What they failed to deal with or even mention, however, were the real aims of the work, which were to challenge both the meaning of the museum space and of racism toward immigrants. In this case, but also in all the others, my intention was not to cause discord, but to dig below the surface in order to reveal the interweaving of history and power, the fabric that a visual image can sum up better than a thousand words.

Since 2012 I've been living in Tirana again. It might seem that a lot has changed in the art world here. But once you scratch the surface and dig a bit deeper, you realize that we are (I am) still inside that 1997 television program, where the aim isn't to make a clearly focused analysis, but instead to move further and further away from the heart of the problem. This country is very interesting, very complicated and often difficult to perceive; for many people it's almost incomprehensible. The truths are so difficult, but at the same time so transparent, that bringing them to light is an arduous task.

For my latest works, to arrive at the perfect meaning of things and create a deep wound on top of the wound made by the capitalist system, I am (again) using dangerous ingredients that can be misunderstood if not analyzed with care, calmly and objectively. I'm not sure if these are the right words, but I believe that by pushing harder to go beyond the status quo, a different reaction can be triggered. I'm aware that this is difficult to achieve and that the responsibility is very great, for every artist knows that s/he could fail and so the message could be misunderstood. In that case, it is the artist who must be the first to take all responsibility.

Bullet in Envelope is a work consisting in details conceived in relation to the current social and political situation in Albania. It is addressed to the country's most important artistic institution, the Albanian National Gallery of the Arts, whose name has been changed now to the National Museum of the Arts. Starting from the idea of what a museum ought to be today and the premise of protecting it from the concept of franchising spreading all over the world and insinuating itself here as well, I tried to stretch the limits and show the real face of this institution as it undergoes the ordeal of this… transformation. The people who worked there used to represent the avant-garde of openness, while now they are partisans of narrow-mindedness. They've become bureaucrats. Though still public, this institution functions as though it were private, following certain vague rules of the market and opposing the idea of any alternative artistic world.

"This new museum is nothing other than a cheap whore," exclaimed a cultural journalist while storming out of a press conference in a rage…. The main components of the work *Bullet in Envelope* are the ogive of a bullet shot in an unnamed place and a letter that is impossible to read without looking through a scientific police microscope. These two objects were put inside a white envelope that held various pieces of information, addresses, linguistic and humorous games, all produced in collaboration with Duchamp the cat. The envelope was then sent to an institution able (but also not) to "sniff out" all the elements borrowed from the history of art but also those borrowed from social history. But no, the work was unanimously — that is, by the artistic establishment and the director of the institution — denounced to the state police as a violent gesture against public morals because it used criminal language which, according to the verdict of artistic officialdom, cannot be considered art.

This paradox and the problems that characterize the work still puzzle me. Both the head of the criminal police, by pure chance an artist-turned-policeman because he couldn't support himself through art, as well as the public prosecutor in charge of the case examined the evidence carefully and, like good curator-dogs, they "sniffed" well before coming to the conclusion that my work was certainly a work of art and absolutely not a threat, because it lacked all the elements of a threat, contrary to the interpretation and declaration of the artistic institution. According to the police and the prosecutor's office, all the requisites that constitute a threat were lacking, and so they decided to dismiss the case. The work deals with the institution of art and the current government, which seems determined to launch the country into contemporaneity. Its focus is just this *explosion of the contemporary* and the vision for the future announced in 2013 by the socialist government — a government that in fact has never shown, and will never be able to show, any rebirth whatsoever, any reawakening, any explosion or real democratic openness in its institutions. On the contrary, all the institutions have grown stiffer, more rigid. Institutional art is increasingly tied to politics and the government and has withdrawn into itself, while the real explosion has already taken place and continues to take place on the street, far from the walls of the Museum / Ga(o)l(lery) / Government.

A week after I mailed *Bullet in Envelope,* student protests erupted in virtually every public university in the country and in every faculty of the biggest university of them all, the University of Tirana. It is very significant that the protest broke out in the School of Architecture and then spread to all the others, including the Schools of Law and Social Sciences. The denunciation of the National Gallery only confirmed an intuition. Even if they were threatened and divided into many groups, the students performed a hugely significant symbolic act. Once and for all they destroyed the powerful government propaganda machine and unmasked the Prime Minister, the socialist artist, who was thought of rather like the way workers used to think of the utopian Brazilian president Lula. The students' unanimous political act was to not have a leader, and to not negotiate with the government, especially not with the Prime Minister. This signal should be analyzed in depth, because besides demonstrating for the umpteenth time that the government had reached rock bottom, it also showed a degree of stratification and complexity that we'll have to reckon with very soon in the future.

The rules of this generation have changed, precisely because the rules of this government never change — arrogance, control, police, threats, gangsters, reclusion, rape, drug trafficking, contemporary art, design, architecture.

This institution, the National Gallery, is a public body that has played a fundamental role in the transformation of art in the country, both before and after communism, but which has recently adopted the extreme arrogance of the government. The government imposes its control over the institutions of art. It has erected a system, a *re-education camp* that supports the political system and exhibits only art it has approved. This artistic institution is increasingly comparable to death row in maximum-security prisons. The system works according to the famous saying "fight fire with fire." Aimed at destroying all truth, thousands of misleading messages are sent about the same question, to exhaust you and demolish the authenticity of every fact and, in the end, to exercise what I believe to be the most dangerous kind of censorship: to prevent a concept from developing, a work from starting, a critical book from being published and distributed, or an investigative film from being financed. People are talking more and more. "They" can't hide the truth, they can't hide the evidence, kill you and bury you in the garbage like they did with sixteen-year-old Ardit Gjoklaj,[1] but they can create another truth and slap it on the pages of all the newspapers worldwide, paying to do it. But people have started talking, and this can't be stopped.

---

1   On August 7, 2016, the body of the sixteen-year-old Ardit Gjoklaj was discovered underneath the garbage in Sharrë, a newly revamped landfill site for disposing of most of the refuse of Tirana. He was a night-shift worker and there were indications of an attempt to cover up the accident. The investigation revealed that on November 25, 2015, 48-year-old Mirvete Duka, a mother of four, had fallen victim to a workplace accident at the same site. In this case, too, there had been an attempt to keep a lid on the affair. The inquest uncovered only a series of administrative irregularities and inadequate recruitment procedures and safety measures for the prevention of accidents.

This is the current scene and the substratum of *Bullet in Envelope,* a work that for the time being can be found in the collection of the prosecutor's office, which I'll have to write to ask to borrow if I want exhibit it, obviously in a future show in the National Gallery (Museum) of the Arts.

Albania and Brazil. Many people say and write that the art scene in Brazil after the recent elections has been devastated. In some ways Brazil reminds me of Albania. Have you got anything to say about this? What sort of limitations are there in Albania? What similarities are there between the Brazilian extreme right and the Albanian system?

If you analyze the Albanian right and left wings today, you won't find any real differences between them. If we compare ourselves to the rest of the world, one fundamental difference is that here there don't (yet) exist extremist parties or organizations like in the rest of Europe or, further away, in the West or the East. Everything is still being compared to the previous regime, the dictatorship and its extreme "drawbacks," while the "benefits" that can only be produced by a common ideal, such as the idea of communism, are never discussed. There's a phrase I like very much that illustrates the thinking of the majority concerning the difference with the past: *From prison to poison is like from poison to prison.*[2] This position has to be handled with gloves, not only because it is complicated but also because it implies a distinction between types of negativity, making it seem that people would prefer prison rather than neoliberal poison. And here by prison is understood security, work, and less criminality.

Albanian society remains conservative and closed and the concept of freedom is still not well understood. This is one of the serious limitations that the country has to face. The politicians have well understood this particular characteristic of our soci-

---

2   See Victor Strato, *From Prison to Poison from Poison to Prison* (2019), DebatikCenter, https://debatikcenter.net/strikes/from_prison_to_poison.

ety, which is why they can do what they do so blatantly. The Socialist Party was able to construct a narrative predicated on the elimination of these limitations. While ostensibly being a party that assists the most disadvantaged classes in society, in the end the Albanian Socialist Party did not go down this road, instead opting to squeeze these sections of the population even harder. As I've said before, the figure of the current Prime Minister has been strongly upheld and supported both inside and outside the country not only for the program he presented, national Rebirth and European (re)Renaissance, but also because, being an artist, he was sold to the people as a reformer who could change the degenerate system installed by the right wing. The current Prime Minister was seen by the masses very much like the union representative Luiz Inácio Lula da Silva was seen in Brazil, who was beloved by the people and the rest of the world and who governed for years, but whose government turned out to be a den of corruption. There are many similarities between Lula's government and the current Albanian government that are worthy of analysis. But whereas Lula is now in prison, the problem seems to have been solved by our government, because its intensification of control over institutions continues to have the support of the international community, even if this means that the latter are losing credibility by becoming the historical enemy of the people, which is a real paradox.

Like the right-wing government before it, the current one controls most of the media, along with the judiciary and penitentiary systems. Every time the (current) government is criticized, the propaganda machine responds by comparing it to the previous right-wing government which is responsible for killing four civilians during a violent protest in 2011, whereas they (the current government) haven't killed anyone directly yet. This defense is also shared (and repeated) by the country's artists and curators. But the Socialist government, which in reality is a privatized government, has imprisoned a lot of people whose only crime was being too poor to pay for electricity because they were unemployed and didn't receive any state benefits either. Many of these people committed suicide, and in fact the number of suicides is growing rapidly. This government is also responsible for another national tragedy: its politics has triggered the second largest exodus in Albanian history. Poverty has increased, the middle class is disappearing, and the only segment of the population favored by this government are the ultra rich. Wouldn't you agree, then, that these are crimes, these are murders committed by the current government?

As far as art is concerned, all the promises made to artists about a cultural explosion have evaporated into thin air. The only artist to come to the fore in this period, the only one able to find a market and be presented in international shows as the single emerging Albanian artist is the Prime Minister himself.

In an interview that Edi Muka[3] gave to an Albanian journalist — in which, as usually happens, his claims were neither challenged nor contested — Muka talked about the questions that ought to interest today's artists, referring mainly to the young Albanian artists who find themselves at a crossroads and don't seem to know what path to take. To illustrate, he gave examples of the issues artists should explore, such as the right wing regimes in Brazil, Turkey, Trump's United States, etc., where dictatorship, censorship, and racism are prevalent, as well as other issues like immigration and climate change. I find it really important to deal with these global issues but only if we examine them in depth, so not with the aim of hiding the urgent problems facing our country but, on the contrary, in order to shed light on them. So it would seem that the example doesn't fit. The local situation already reflects global issues, and this is what we should be talking about.

If there is a problem our contemporary artists have never seriously confronted that is identical to Brazil's it is that the crimes committed by the dictatorship have never been addressed adequately. Contemporary artists don't want to deal with this prob-

---

3   Edi Muka, born in Albania in 1968, is a naturalized Swedish curator. He was formerly a lecturer in the Academy of Arts in Tirana and co-founder of the Tirana Biennial. In 2007 he was the artistic co-director of the Göteborg International Biennial of Contemporary Art.

lem. The artists working in Albania with official support don't concern themselves with legality, the use and misuse of power, corruption, the government's justification of rape, or with ad hoc "special" laws like the one used to demolish the National Theater. Why is it unthinkable that courageous artists who are ready to exhibit their research into the murder of Ardit Gjoklaj, the minor killed by the state apparatus whose body was found buried in a rubbish heap, will never be invited to do so in the rooms of the Museum/Gallery? Why will an investigative project on the crimes committed in the past by Members of Parliament and members of the government never be exhibited? We all know that a large number of Socialist MPs are criminals, traffickers, men guilty of rape. Why doesn't the Museum show projects that examine the production of drugs by the state itself, and the involvement of the government and the police in this scheme? Why won't the most well-known curators in the country ever accept the idea of exhibiting works concerning the construction and financing of the Prime Minister's house, or its commercial and architectonic value? Why will they automatically refuse a project that predicts a little tremor of an earthquake in the vicinity of that house, which represents power? Why will they object to an exhibition based on the conjecture that in Surrel[4] (read Surreal) it could rain for months on end, and lightening could strike one of the four buildings that make up the Prime Minister's residence? To avoid this kind of question by treating other problems and making comparisons with global issues seems to me intentionally cunning, like comparing every evil to a greater evil so as to make our own reality seem less serious. Why should the barbarian reception given to Judith Butler in Brazil in 2017[5] be more important than the gang rape

---

4   Surrel is located near Tirana, on the road to Mount Dajti. It is one of the favorite vacation spots for the inhabitants (and the VIPs) of the capital, including the Prime Minister, who lives there in a large house which is completely out of proportion to the country's standard of living.

5   When philosophy Judith Butler was invited to participate in a conference in Brazil in November 2017, she was met with violent hostile demonstrations on the part of locals opposed to gender theory. These demonstrations

committed by Socialist mayor Elvis Roshi? Why has the Prime Minister, that contemporary artist, defended this act for years, justifying it as a youthful mistake, and why has no artist or curator, man or woman, spoken up about it? It is above all art that pursues these kinds of questions that finds no space to exhibit anywhere.

If we want to avoid falling into the populist trap of the shows that surround us today, and that send a puerile message on the level of Journalism 101, these are the main issues Albanian artists ought to be dealing with now. In my opinion, the day when we produced shows and artistic projects under the shadow of feeling inferior to other countries is long gone. Albania is no longer a country where works seen over and over in other countries should be presented. On the contrary, it is now a country where we can and must develop new proposals, a New Wave to launch beyond our borders. This is what we need to talk about, because no other urgency exists. As I said before, between the right and the left there is no real difference as far as results are concerned, only the way of operating remains (for now) different. Both systems are very effective, so "Fuck them both."

I hate to have to admit that the Albanian right-wing seems more sincere and more to the left than the left-wing in this country, which is actually more to the right than the country's right-wing parties. We are governed by a right-wing party that is left-wing in name only.

Censorship of the right and censorship of the left. Is there any logic in making this distinction? Is censorship, after all, censorship tout court? Are there types of censorship that differ in these two systems or are the strategies the same? How has the model

---

culminated in a bonfire where a puppet of a witch resembling her was burnt. See Ruptly, "Brazil: 'Take your ideologies to hell' - Judith Butler haters burn effigy outside Sao Paulo seminar," *YouTube*, November 7, 2017, https://www.youtube.com/watch?v=dhlDqBM9vYU.

of control and censorship that was present in the communist period changed, how has it adapted itself to today's situation?

As Giorgio Agamben says, today's governments produce crises everywhere, and crisis is a strategy produced by governments themselves. Crises increasingly express the illegality of the system, they justify and legitimate decisions taken by those in power. Censorship is an integral part of this system. The rules of control aren't always the same, they become ever more refined and interconnected, but they are still violent, because crises evolve. Government propaganda uses all possible means to try and conceal the truth and the scandals produced by institutional corruption. People are terrified of this and they increasingly withdraw into themselves, because everything is directed against them. Very serious events have occurred, world-class scandals, like the explosion at the former munitions depot in Gërdec in 2008. Women and miners were working there and twenty-six people died. The affair also involved the son of the then-Prime Minister, Sali Berisha, the government itself, the Pentagon, and the American Department of State. And there are other situations the current government has been involved in. As I said before, due to the shortcomings of the courts and thanks to ad hoc laws passed to favor the oligarchs and so on, this government has for some time now acted following the parameters of a state of democratic emergency. To plant cannabis all over the land was a decision made by the left-wing government. Together with the state police, criminal gangs controlled the plantations and the politicians took their share. We now see them all putting this money into real estate speculation. The monument to police casualties erected in front of the Ministry of Internal Affairs at the time when the police and the Minister himself were involved in drug trafficking, which looks just like a copy of the memorial to American police casualties, ought to have the silvery silhouette of the cannabis plant instead of silver stars. The death of the sixteen-year-old who worked off the books in the Tirana garbage dump, which took place under the watch of the local government, since Tirana City Hall is responsible for the landfill site in question, produced another enormous scandal that the state covered up by awarding sub-contracts to relatives of the public prosecutor who was in charge of the investigation. Skanderbeg Square is proof of this rampant corruption. There are some journalists who try to investigate and get to the bottom of these issues, even if their reporting is completely ignored by the TV channels. They are systematically censored, fired, and even threatened, as in the case of a journalist whose house was the target of mob bullets, or shall I say state bullets? Non-governmental organizations and the voices of civil society seem to be inexistent, because they're always funded by the government, so in a certain sense they work for it. Even artists who are only occasionally activists can't get into the handful of shows that are organized, and if they do succeed in exhibiting their work they use weak instruments like icons, or images, and never investigation. If you do research these issues the first to condemn you, even before the state, are the artists and curators themselves. They accuse you of being part of the opposition faction and of destroying the narrative created over the years, according to which Albanian contemporary art has been a success story that has produced personalities who have brought honor to the name of the nation all over the world. And so we must go on in their wake and honor this past.

This country's elegance is always misunderstood. It can't be represented in a meaningless, unintelligent way, in the way the perfect, custom-made frame and museum glass are used, for example. I believe that beauty is hidden intelligence, which the educated eye of contemporary art cannot see anymore. There is a very clear element of censorship in all the artists, actors, filmmakers, and other members of the art system in this country (which I don't belong to), and that is self-censorship. It may seem trite to refer to this type of censorship once again, but there is more to it than meets the eye. It's a matter involving education, training, and the desire for integration. Recently, theater actors have staged a protest against the state's project to tear down the National Theater building which was built by the fascists in the thirties, and to replace it with a new contemporary theatre designed by an important architectural studio and funded by an oligarch connected to the death of the sixteen-year-old in the landfill site. The government has approved the project by a special law. The actors' cause is right. What is at stake is far more than protecting the city's identity. The actors' understanding and use of language, which has evolved from the ineffective way they used it at the start of the protest, are gradually growing more radical. In the beginning, if someone came closer to reality and the way(s) in which it should be articulated using new, stronger language, they were reproached by the other actors themselves, who even had written rules about how to speak. It was fascinating to see how actors you'd seen in important roles and had imagined differently did not possess a language of their own. It was sad to see actors who didn't understand the power of gesture, didn't know how to be effective offstage. It was sad to see actors who lacked the use of gesture.

Observing the current National Theater situation, with its imminent destruction to make room for new buildings to launder the money of criminal gangs and high-standing politicians, I noticed that the use of "proper" language led to even more "proper," totally empty and useless discussions. This "propriety" was defined as a synonym of civility, integration, and democracy. I believe that being civilized is an entirely different thing: I am opposed to integration (referring to the figure of the artist) and that is what we have to struggle against…. The saddest thing of all is that this "propriety" seems to have become common practice. If artists are to teach something, the first thing they have to do is change their behavior. They have to tear away this mask to show something urgent — urgent behavior in an urgent situation calls for urgent means.

To provoke a different reaction, at the start of the actors' protest I sent them a written text to perform there in the square where they were protesting, titled *Kori* (*The Chorus*), a sophisticated pièce consisting of a long orgasm. It was a text as a play without words, which I'd written for the generation of actors active before 1990, but also for their students, the same actors we see protesting now. A collective orgasm for an hour a day, until this political scum and all the other ghosts that wash their money in cement get off that public ground.

> *Painting and politics. Action Painting—in the United States—was an artistic current exported all over the world and made to pass as "the art of freedom," in contrast to the art of political oppression of the Soviet Union and China. But we now know that Action Painting was a farce, a form of art supported to communicate the idea of a "free" America in opposition to an "enslaved" Russia, etc. What is more, abstract art doesn't have any explicit political component in the visual content of the painting. What is political in abstract painting? How can abstract painting be political?*

For a long time now I've been composing a different narrative about the presence of the United States in Albania. I call it *The Third Love Affair.*

One of the first works I did after being expelled from Florence's Academy of Fine Arts, which I later put into this archive, was *Powershift* CIA (2001), the photographic documentation of a performance done in the vicinity of the Amerigo Vespucci airport in Florence. When I showed it in Tirana the following year, an American diplomat asked my father for information about what the three letters in the title of the work, CIA, stood for. In the photo you can see an American pitbull terrier jumping over an obstacle that has a torn red Albanian flag on top. I'm not sure what my father answered, but what he advised me then, and went on repeating for years, was to never get involved in politics or mention politics in my works, especially American politics.

What I wanted to communicate at the time was simply what I felt, which was that politics—especially American politics, which then as now wields the most influence in this country—was decisive in the distribution and control of power. The plans for regime change in the nineties, but also the events of 1997, seemed to me so well-structured and effective that only one organization would be able to carry them out. At the time all these suppositions were only provocations, and my evidence was not very well-founded.

Political interest in art and culture was strategic for all the foreign forces that operated — and operate — in the country. A constant presence that right from the start has supported artistic activity was the foundation of the philanthropist George Soros, whose organization has funded numerous art shows, artists and musicians, festivals, and so on. The fact is that many of the artists and even politicians who went on to have successful careers were and are still supported by that foundation. My first and rather reckless performance, entitled *Performing Soros, A Friendship Cycling Tour* (1997–1999), was precisely about this interesting and ubiquitous presence in the field of art.

In 1997, in a state of total emergency, the Soros foundation had started a project called Journey of *Hope — Friendship Cycling Tour.* I took part in it because a cousin of mine who worked for the foundation and was the manager of this project had invited my sister and I. The foundation gave everyone (or almost) a Bianchi road bicycle. Along with a group of other cyclists who were taking part in this project, including people from Mexico, Protestants from Honduras, American filmmakers, Spaniards etc., we were to ride our bikes through Albania, Italy, and Greece. I remember that they didn't give me a bike, though they did to everyone else, and so I decided to make the trip on my own mountain bike. In Albania we were escorted by the police and often by soldiers from the multinational military mission present in the country.[6]

During the trip, which lasted a month, the foundation produced a documentary where this experience is filmed, with all its risks, its failures, conflicts within the group, and also a few love stories that blossomed on the road — in brief, the utopia

---

6   The Alba mission, which was initiated by Italy and sanctioned by the UN and the OSCE, as well as the Silver Lake and Libelle missions, which were implemented by US and German military units respectively and whose main goal was the safe evacuation of their nationals, intervened in Albania at the height of the crisis that followed the collapse of the pyramidal financial schemes in the country.

of togetherness. I remember that the film was then shown in a gala celebration at the Convention Palace (Pallati i Kongreseve) in Tirana in the presence of politicians and foreign diplomats. During the trip, I befriended the Albanian police officers who escorted us in Albania, and to avoid staying on the bus I rode with them in their cars. Meanwhile, I took photos of the journey with the tourist camera I'd bought in the States a year before. I took shots of the police, the army, the participants in their biker's clothing, the bag full of money carried by my cousin. I photographed the group pedaling along the roads of a country in the grip of chaos, one that seemed like an alien river running over newly burnt land. I shot a great many photos. I didn't realize at the time that this project was a highly political operation, narrating something that was an integral part of a reality created and conditioned by various influences that I only understood afterward. We were dummies, puppets tied to a short leash inside a political operation, and we didn't know it. For this reason, to challenge the lack of awareness I had at the time, I made the journey again on my own in 1999. Putting the photos from 1997 alongside those from 1999 I created my first slide composition.

I've given this long introduction because I think the time has come to fully understand the reasons for the political support that a certain type of art that evolved in Albania after the fall of the communist regime has enjoyed for almost thirty years, and how this type of art has influenced social perceptions and domestic politics.

To respond to what can be sensed between the lines in your questions, which create a very evocative parallel, I remember that when Frances Stonor Saunders's article "Modern Art Was CIA 'Weapon'" came out in 1995, we obviously didn't talk about it at all in school.[7] Following the school syllabus of 1995, we were mostly busy making copies of past masters. I remember that at the time I made two copies, one for a school assignment and

---

7   Frances Stonor Saunders, "Modern Art Was CIA 'Weapon,'" *The Independent*, October 22, 1995, https://www.independent.co.uk/news/world/modern-art-was-cia-weapon-1578808.html.

the other for myself. If I remember correctly, I decided to paint the portrait of a boy with a hat by a French painter whose name I don't recall, and for myself Francis Bacon's 1973 self-portrait.

Considering that this is a topic that provokes debate and involves the CIA, it seems to me that it hasn't been sufficiently analyzed or discussed over the years. Provocatively, and comparing it to the situation of Albanian art after 1990, I'd say that this kind of issue isn't treated even in a historical perspective. The tendency of researchers who work for state institutions, the academics, is to ignore these questions. The people who direct the institutions don't want to analyze such fundamental aspects of the present; they invent the same pretexts used to avoid analyzing the year 1997. The excuses adopted by the artists who support the Socialist Party — we need time, we have to allow history to evolve, every judgment is premature, and we can't speculate based on only a few cases — are banal and should be tossed aside tout court.

But in what you ask there may be a different relation that concerns the same subject, which under very different circumstances surfaced elsewhere in the past, namely during the years 1950–1960. I find it very interesting to analyze the whys of yesterday and the whys of today. The whys behind the selection of certain musicians, jazz artists, writers, journalists, and painters who were supported by the CIA, in a promotional operation unlike anything seen before; and the whys behind the blacklisting of those who were put on trial in the United States. The exponents of abstract expressionism, Jackson Pollock, the masterful Mark Rothko, Robert Motherwell, Arshile Gorky, etc., were promoted in a secret operation by pontiffs in incognito, along with philanthropists, in order to win an intellectual war against the Soviet Union and China. First of all, it was necessary to win the war of communication by humiliating the ideology represented by socialist realism and showing to the whole world a different, free art produced through unbridled intellectual freedom, chiefly also by authors ideologically on the left. The operation was geopolitical. Art itself, and culture, as in the case of Action Painting, but also that of literature, took on an important role in the program of power expansion. The operation also included Europe and left-wing European intellectuals, framing itself as a way to contrast the European traditionalism of the distant past, which was surpassed thanks to the great freedom of expression in the art we're talking about.

Big shows were organized. The artists were backed and encouraged to carry on with their ideas, which had become the main vehicle for the American government's propaganda. And when you have such total support you forget to ask yourself questions, you go on riding the wave. The operation was so sophisticated that it wound up being an international market success, and still is. The "freedom" these artists believed in is just what you said, it is camouflaged slavery that sucks you in, which in a certain sense has determined today's market.... The real slaves of the propaganda were perhaps (and still are) the Americans more or less drugged by that optimistic politics, more than the socialist realist painters/revolutionaries.

There can be no true freedom in a painting if you only consider the way it is painted, and you can't speak about freedom if this freedom is always confined within a conceptual framework that has already enclosed and imprisoned the sign. You have to go beyond the work. The artists mentioned above never thought of their work as a way to promote social and political change; rather, they thought of it as a path to success and the creation of their own myth. It was for just this reason that they were the best suited to carry out a strategy of this kind. To find a link between abstractionism and politics we need to look back and reread Kazimir Malevich and study, for example, the African American painters whose abstract and expressive works confront colonialism and racism....

At the 2015 Venice Biennale I also exhibited a copy of a painting by Spiro Kristo,[8] a marvelous Albanian socialist real-

---

8   Spiro Kristo (1936–2011) was an important Albanian painter, especially well-known during the socialist realist period. His works were part of the international show *documenta* 14 in 2017.

ist painter. I chose Kristo because I had written *Recapitulation*[9] with his painting in mind. The idea behind our pavilion's display was to make it move in time, in the sense of creating a pavilion from the seventies, the first Albanian pavilion to ever be presented in Venice, in order to speak about the future and the absence of freedom in our day. The entire apparatus came from those years, and my works had their starting points during that period too, the intention being to offer alternative instruments for interpreting our global future. The installation focused on issues of economic exchange, inequality, terrorism, government propaganda, legislation and surveillance, financial speculation, sovereignty, nationality, etc.

After the demise of the great ideologies Kristo wasn't successful at riding the (new) wave. When I was doing research for the pavilion I saw all the works he had done after 1990. They were very weak and constrained. Like many great Albanian artists of the socialist realist period, he too was lost and unable to control his own work, which was no longer based on an ideology. He tried to go beyond representation, his strongpoint. He tried to become abstract, to set himself "free," as it were, and to produce something that had nothing to do with any political concept. His new work, more constricted than open, controlled him rather than freeing him. There were others affected by this ideological effect, other great painters of the Albanian socialist past who tried to become abstract, and almost all of them failed. Analyzing the political, economic and social context of those years, we can understand now why these painters suddenly changed their style, why they became imitators of expressionist and abstract artists. There's no doubt that this has to be understood as a political act, even if it was destined to fail.

Aesthetics and politics again. Albanian art in this millennium has been seen as an art of rupture and has created enormous interest. I'd like you to consider the problem of Albanian aes-

---

9   See Track 01, p. 40, n. 8.

thetics. Let's take an example: Dammi i colori (Give Me the Colors) *by Anri Sala.*[10] *A video that virtually everyone in the art world has seen. A very famous video that owes much of its fame not only to its subject (the very boring painted buildings) but also to a well-defined aesthetics. The framing that almost always works, the low resolution, the hand-held camera, the unrefined but "contemporary" photography… in short, a video that works visually. That works aesthetically. A video that has won over many people thanks to its aesthetic choices, like the idea of the painted buildings. But what is actually behind this almost romantic vision of the Albanian art of the first years of this millennium? What is Edi Rama really trying to do? What has he continued doing? How has Albanian art been exported in international festivals and shows?*

The fall of the regime, the year 1997, and the Balkan wars have offered starting points for producing the current narrative, a false narrative of contemporary art in the country, which needs to be revisited.

As we all know, contemporary art, or better, the presence of Albania on the contemporary art scene, is marked by a fatal joke that occurred in 2001, sensationally realized on the occasion of the first Tirana Biennial.[11] It produced a worldwide scandal, and its echo reverberated for years. Afterward it led to many fakes, besides the artists themselves, but then it was buried so deeply that virtually no one talks about it anymore in Albania. It was

---

10 Anri Sala (b. 1974), is an Albanian artist who mainly works with video and musical installations. He has made sculptures, photographs, and drawings. He is a close friend and collaborator of Prime Minister Edi Rama. His video installation *Dammi i colori* (2003) shows the development of Tirana at the turn of the 21st century.

11 On the occasion of the 2001 *Tirana Biennal,* a fake Oliviero Toscani (in reality, as it turned out, the artist Marco Lavagetto) managed to get himself accredited as a curator and presented four fictitious artists, pulled out of thin air, bringing works attributed to them along with a critical essay that was published in the magazine *Flash Art* and in the show's catalogue. The joke was discovered only when the real Toscani reported the incident and sued the organizers.

buried so deeply that the new generations think the first Tirana Biennial was held in 2003, when the socialists had the buildings painted in gaudy colors. As early as 2003 this operation was understood to be a lie by the members of DebatikCenter. In a project that was a satellite of that Biennial, we performed an intervention that analyzed the economic system of microcredit. Other topics treated were immigration, political corruption, the practice of biennials disseminated all over the world, and the painted buildings that could in no way change what was inside: they couldn't penetrate or change the mentality of the population, but only interfere temporarily in the way the reality created was perceived externally. To us this seemed to be a manipulation. The real joke was that this operation wanted to give life to a narrative that was stillborn. It was the exact opposite of what had happened in 2001, because then the project was meant as a joke and could only survive if the joke was discovered. I think that the case of this second, real, joke is very significant. It should be studied carefully because in a certain sense it opened a curtain on the future, the artistic and political present of our day.

The art world and the majority of artists pray for a war, a natural cataclysm, an earthquake, in order to have the system's reflectors pointed at them. Then the figurines create themselves, and the ingenuity and banality of what is narrated afterward become the rule for referring to a nation. Dissidents who were never dissidents surface, pioneers who never understood what it means to be a pioneer, and all sorts of other things. Then an image is created that shares the features the mother image revealed after the catastrophe, capable of insinuating itself into other narratives, planting roots like a virus, and remaining in the archives of history in a stable, protected position. An image you are not allowed to recover is produced. An image kept at a distance, incapable of evolving on its own. Just like when the power of a state or the system has launched a satellite or a spaceship into space (after the one launched in 2001). "They" can follow it while it is rotating in orbit and gathering information, but they don't want to let it return to earth. Because they would never want to retrieve the data that hasn't been transmitted, which has been accumulating all the time and can only be found on the satellite. If the spaceship can't return, someone else has to go up there, take what has been lost, what is still hidden, and then come back to the earth, assuming that s/he'll have the strength to return and send another picture capable of evolving on its own.

I don't believe that any form, whether abstract or pop, has the power to make everything produced after World War II, or during a year like 1997, go up in air. I am actually fascinated by colors and by pop culture and it is not my intention here to criticize its enormous diffusion, its success on a planetary scale, its aesthetic dimension, more precisely the component that implies a sort of deliberate intellectual indolence, but instead to point out the (re)production of a mindset that tries to avoid any kind of profound thought. That's why, though Pop Art is important, as soon as you try to lie to Pop by adding to Pop, Pop has the potential to show you up. The socialist buildings in Tirana, painted in semi-abstract shapes and vivid colors, work perfectly in this globalized world, but they still represent only weak signs for today's world. The political operation behind the colored buildings was announced from the start as a winner, but in reality it formed the basis of a political movement that couldn't survive over time, since it was the matrix of a corrupt system that couldn't bring about any concrete change. It is a political project that never really wanted to make a revolution of colors, but proved to be an authentic *Fake Case.*

The purpose of the operation as it was perceived by the majority of people was not in the least what had been hoped for, because the project wasn't done — and didn't develop — in relation to the utopian goals of the avant-garde or the Suprematists. As a matter of fact, it was more closely related to the conceptual constraints of relational aesthetics, at a time when what was urgently needed was a revolution like the one attempted by Joseph Beuys, though not for it to be used like political propaganda understood as a perverse form of political performance.

The Prime Minister ceased to imagine at the very moment he had the buildings painted and ceased to create at the moment his naked photo appeared in the media.[12] That's why, in a recent show in Budapest dedicated to contemporary Albanian and Kosovar artists, I sent all the participants a work titled *La rivoluzione siamo noi* (*We Are the Revolution*): T-shirts printed with the photo of the naked Prime Minister, accompanied by a signed document in which I asked all the artists to wear the T-shirt if they thought he was still an artist, or else to frame it if they thought he was just another corrupt politician. I don't know exactly what they did in the end, but the fact is that I didn't see anyone wearing that T-shirt. The end! The people supported Rama because initially they believed in his actions. I think the year 2006 was when everything should have ended. That was the right time for him to withdraw permanently from politics, but he didn't. He went on digging in the subsoil of an idea of

---

12   In 2016, ten years after the image first appeared in the media, during his television broadcast *6 ditë pa Ermalin* (*Six Days without Ermal*), the Albanian comedian and host Ermal Mamaqi showed a photo of Edi Rama naked, in the presence of Rama himself, who invited him not to censor it. "I saw the picture for the first time during the municipal elections of 2006. I happened to be in Tirana for work on a video in the Sharrë landfill, which at the time was at the center of a corruption scandal, and Edi Rama was Mayor. I remember that the Mayor was always appearing on TV planting trees everywhere and, paradoxically, behaving like Joseph Beuys. The photo always appeared in newspapers and on television with a purple/pink circle covering the genitals. Exploiting the well-known taboos of Albanian society, the Democratic Party was using the photo to destroy its electoral opponent, but as it turned out this plan was a total failure. This photo is particularly emblematic. First of all, since it was an act used as a sign of rebellion (breaking a taboo) it came to embody the proof of the naked truth of the corruption of this government (or of the emperor's new clothes), but also because the color of the circle used by the media to cover his genitals in 2006 is now the color the Socialist Party (Rilindja) uses for its propaganda. I borrowed the title of Beuys's *We Are the Revolution* (1971) so that people could understand the enormous difference that exists between real art and corrupt politics." Armando Lulaj, artist's statement for the *Teatri i Gjelbërimit* exhibition, curated by Vincent W.J. van Gerven Oei, Stefano Romano, and Ardian Isufi, Tirana, FAB, 2016.

politics he'd borrowed and studied for one purpose only: to put an aesthetic mask over the corruption that is now out of control.

Today the Albanian Fake Case is clear to see for everyone who looks at it critically and independently — all the artists, intellectuals, academics, and journalists who aren't connected to political structures or institutions supported by the state. All this reflection makes me think back to the beginning, to 2001, to the buried past that has become the future, and the filter everyone has to pass through to become part of this narrative. From the start I chose to stay out. Partly because my works dealt with political issues, politicians, and social situations, and partly because of my way of seeing things, since I didn't support any political party, much less "their" party, the one currently in government. In a certain sense, from the very start I didn't belong to their narrative.

What do you think of subtitles in videos? Videos from non-English-speaking countries are always subtitled in English to be able to participate in foreign shows and festivals. Who controls these translations? How reliable are they? Is there censorship in the process of translation?

I've always liked subtitles for their visual impact, and the more incomprehensible they are the better. They are signs made over another sign. I love seeing the subtitles of Indian or Thai films, less and less English ones. Even if I don't know the languages, I like seeing those incomprehensible signs over the image.

There's a discriminating factor, in my opinion, as regards the translation of non-English-language materials. It's often done by the artists themselves, with mistakes made deliberately, though not always. The deliberate mistakes fascinate me because in them we can also find something that has to do with writing and rewriting the narrative, which interests me a lot. I've seen many Albanian films, and video art as well, where the subtitles have been intentionally smoothed over by the directors themselves so as to offer the foreign public a different narrative, one the directors feel flows better and is more perfect and authentic, so not with the idea of confusing the spectators on purpose. But if a director wants to hide something in the translation and is doing this intentionally, with a precise idea in mind, s/he won't be able to hide this from everyone. That's really something worrying, and it says more about the artist than the work of art. Depending a lot on the material we're dealing with it should also be said that for an artist the problem is different, since artists aren't fixed entities. They're continually in movement, and often feel the urge to edit their own truth infinitely. Artists can change their own words in translation, as well as the words of others; they can translate them in another way, using a version different from the original, a poetic version I would say…, just as they can cut up and edit the image. Artists are in constant movement, they aren't immobile like directors, they're always searching for a meaning, a personal sound, as it were. Video artists are more artists of the image than of the spoken language, which they often don't "respect." In that case they are censoring a truth, but no one can say they aren't producing an alternative truth in their creative naivety. The artist puts everything on the same plane, characters, narrated text, even documents. One thing is certain: it's always possible to understand when a truth has purposely been manipulated, especially if it's been done to hide it. The director, the figure I feel closest to, knows very well what it means to manipulate (or "to translate") the reality of filmed material, especially if it's a documentary.

Translation is a very complicated art. Changing a comma changes the whole phrase, the whole meaning of the phrase. These days I am very careful when I have my works translated, I don't show them if they aren't perfectly correct, though I can't deny that I myself have made that mistake in my past video works, especially when in 2007 we tried to translate a text of political economics, Karl Marx's *Capital*. That translation is a catastrophe, done by a person who didn't know English well enough. But then again, what the character in the video is reading is also a catastrophe: washing a book in the blood of animals being butchered, he chooses passages from *Capital* — phrases, words taken from here and there, in the end producing speech that is almost impossible to follow, often senseless. I called this work Passion (2007) and I've never retouched it, in the sense that I never edited it again. I let the mistake become a tool for reading this work.

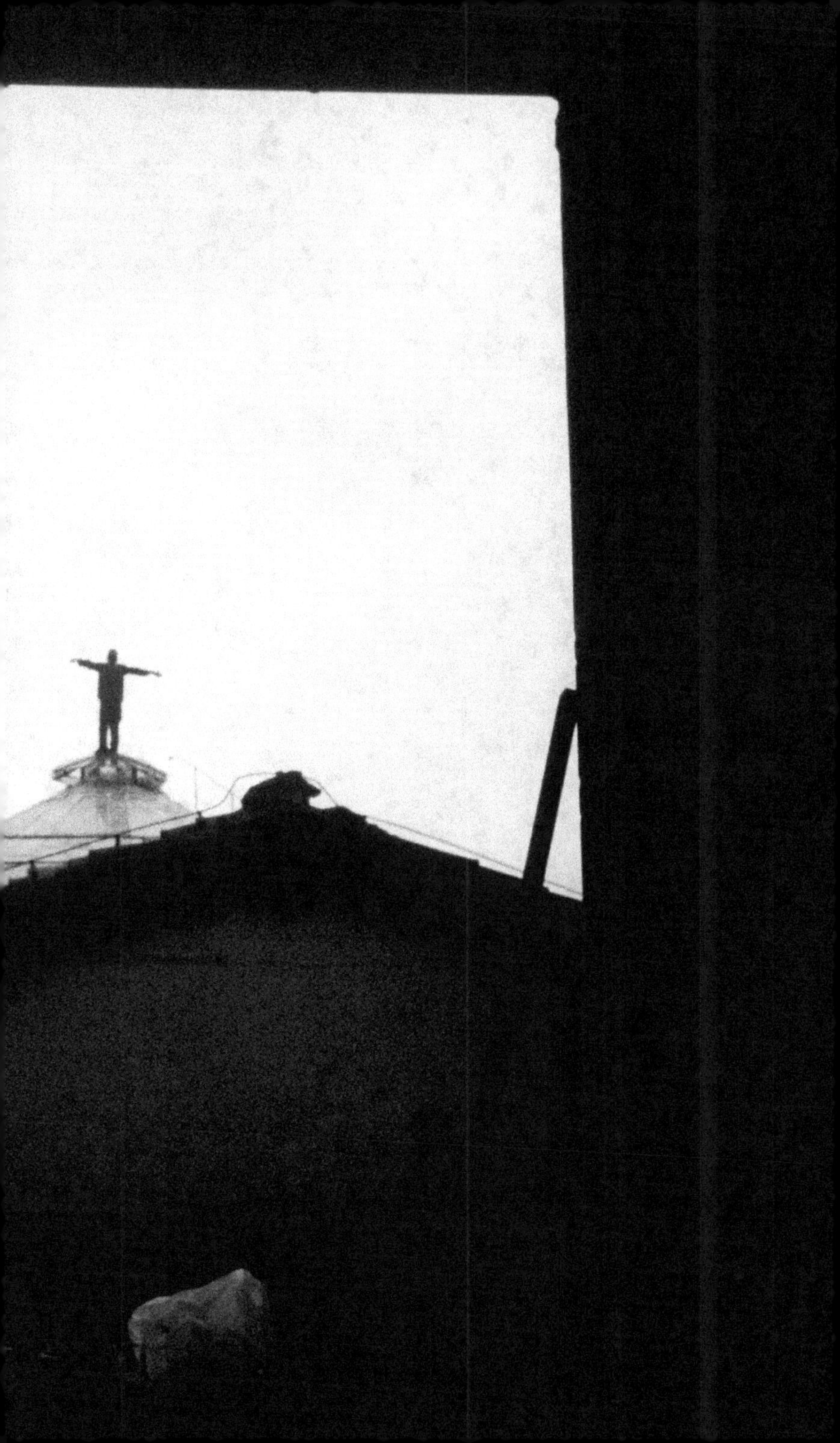

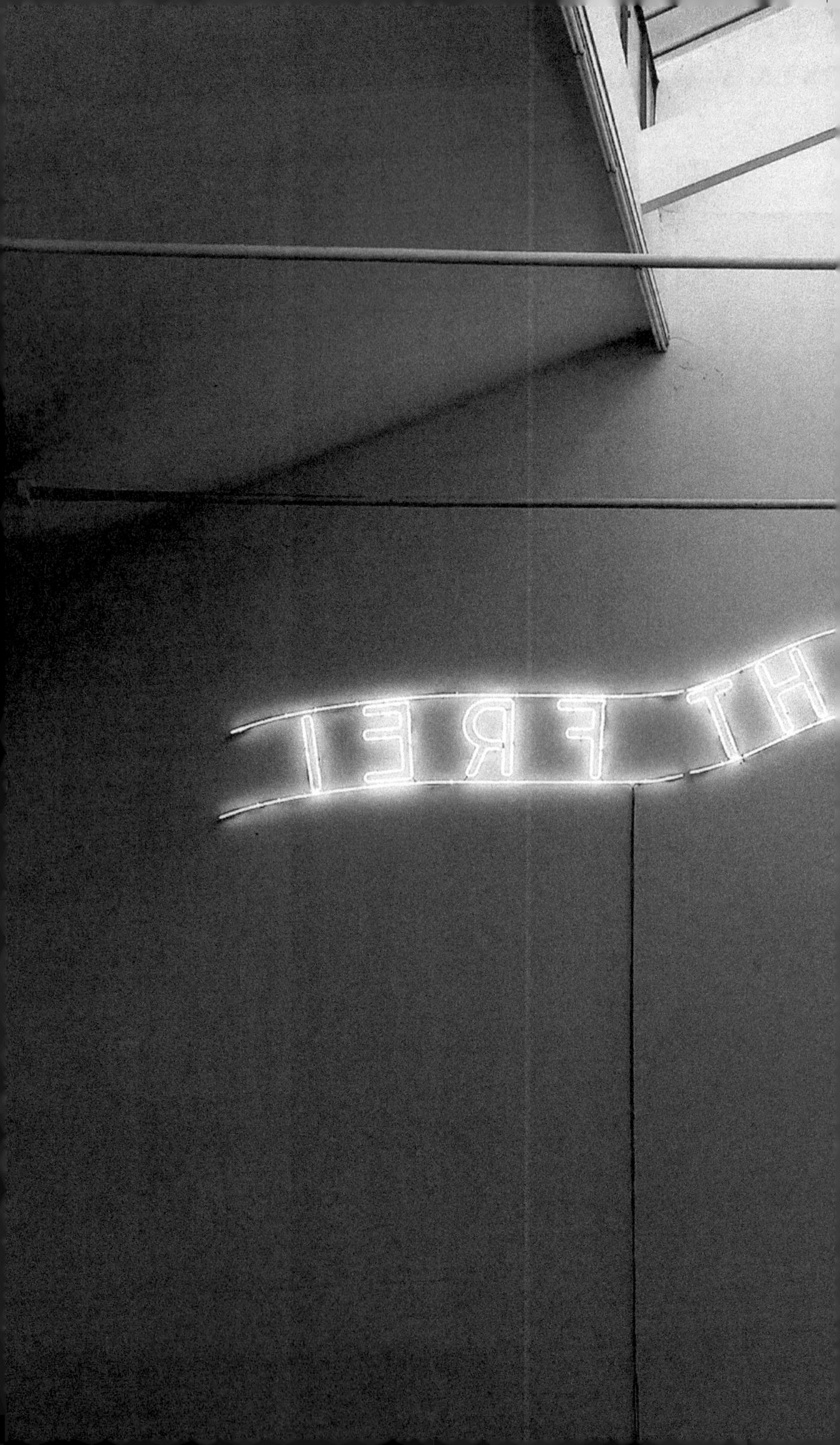

ARBEIT M

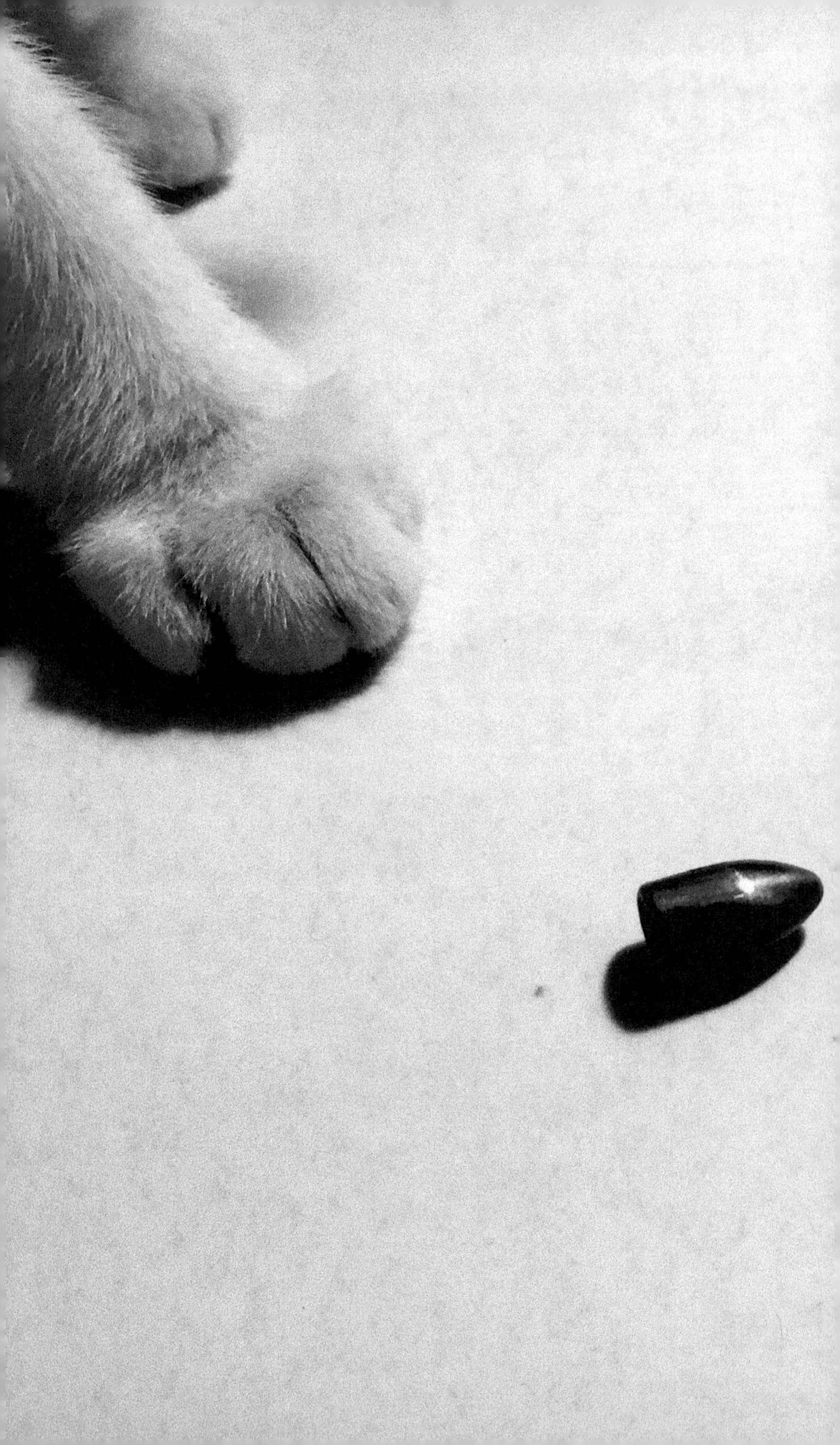

"BULLET IN ENVELOPE"
ARMANDO LULAJ

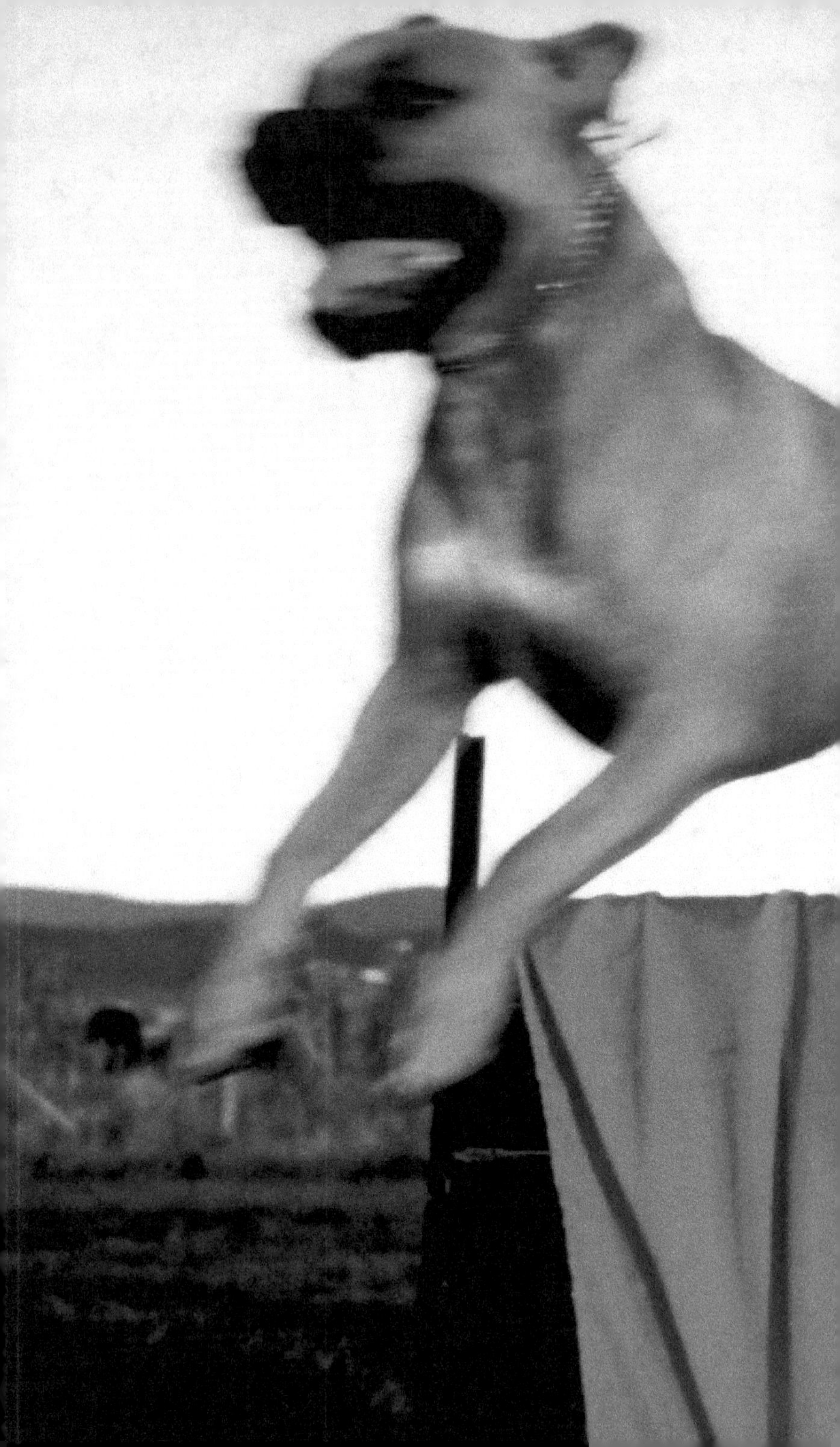

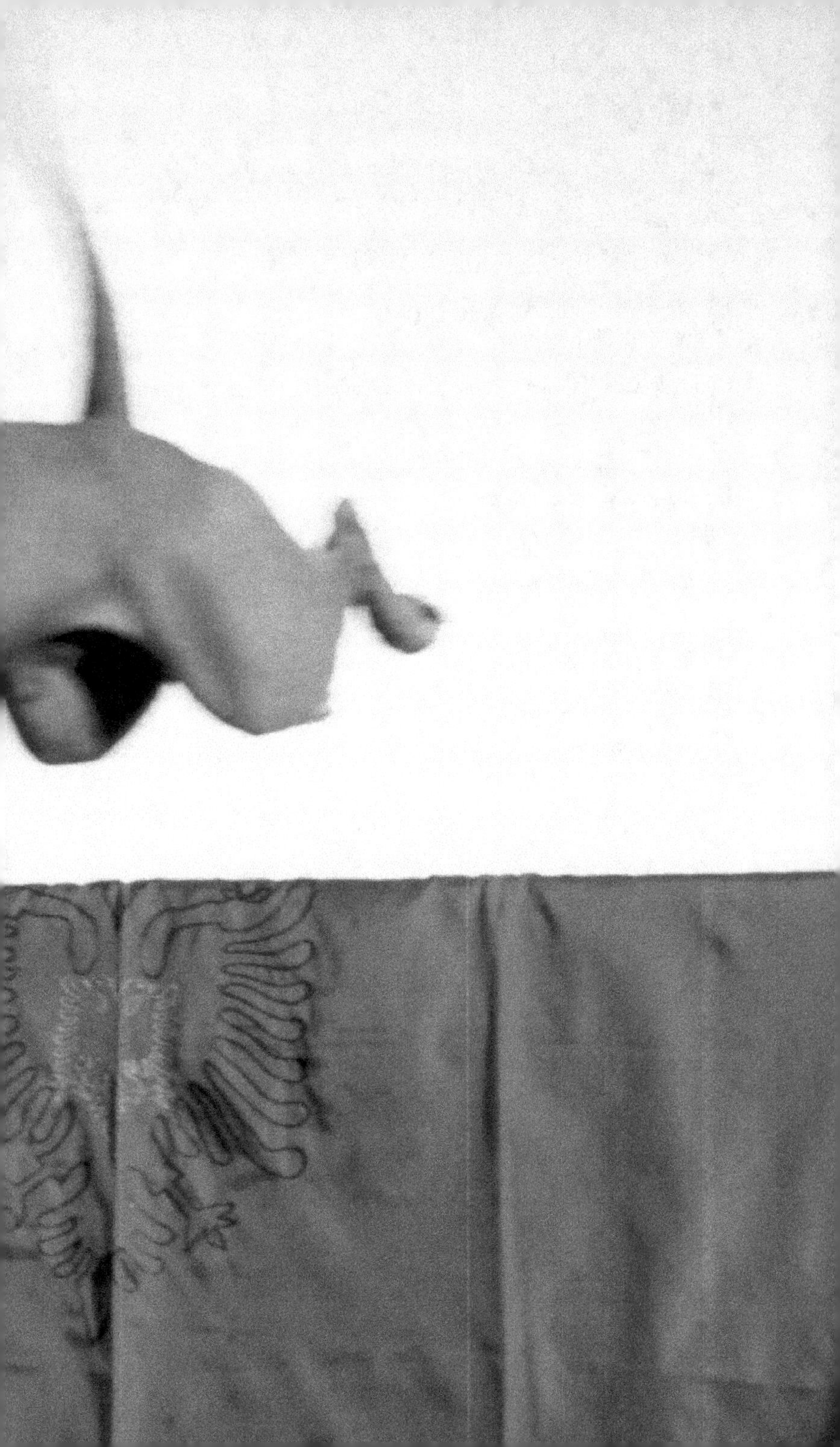

Fig. 17. Walking Free in Harmony by Armando Lulaj, 2001.
Documentation of the performance above the Gallery of Academy
Museum's roofs. Florence January 23, 2001.
Photo by Salvator Qitaj. Armando Lulaj's personal archive.

Fig. 18. UNTITLED, by Armando Lulaj, 2010.
White neon. Installation at Artra Gallery, Milan, during the solo show
NO MERCY, 2011.
Courtesy ARTRA Gallery, Paolo Maria Deanesi Gallery. AGI Verona
Collection.

Fig. 19. Bullet in an Envelope, by Armando Lulaj, 2018.
Installation. Work in Progress. Courtesy DebatikCenter of Contem-
porary Art.
Production photo by Pleurad Xhafa.
Courtesy of DebatikCenter of Contemporary Art.

Fig. 20. POWERSHIFT CIA, by Armando Lulaj, 2001.
Documentation of performance at the Amerigo Vespucci Airport
(Florence).
Production photo by Salvator Qitaj.
Private Collection.

トラック04

君と検閲。 イタリアとアルバニアでは、 君はどのように検閲されたのか？ 露骨な検閲のエピソードはあったか？ この観点について敷衍（ふえん）してもらえるだろうか？ 君に何が起こったのか(最近の作品《Bullet in Envelope》でも…)？

様々なグループや個人が、 作品や表現の自由を制御するために、 アーティストを攻撃することは目新しいことではない。 今日、 検閲は依然として非常に広範囲に及ぶ現象であり、 明らかに何よりも、 批判傾向のある活動や、 権力を明るみに出す活動を対象としている。 政府の権力に始まり、 言うなれば、 グッゲンハイム・アブダビでの労働者達の待遇を告発するに到るまで、 あらゆる形態の力を露にする活動のことだ。 今日、 我々は制御不可能な状況に直面していると言わなければならない。 なぜなら、 権力はますます早い段階で検閲する傾向にあり、 批判が盛んに花開くことのできないように、 芽を摘みにかかっているのだ。 ここ数年、 僕の経験において、 この現象を例示できる様々な状況があった。 しかし 外国に関しては相違点がある。 と言うのも、 僕の出身地が重要な役割を果たしたと僕は信じているからだ。 僕の母国に比べて、外国の構造は遥かに複雑で、階層化されており、複数のレベルがある。非常に少数の例、本来ならば、それらが規範となるべきなのだが、それらの例を除き、僕の考えでは、アルバニアの芸術の構造だけでなく調査報道の構造も、政府によって独占的に統制されている。アーティストが、統治方法に関する事案、例えば政府の腐敗を扱うような場合、彼はあらゆる点で敵対者として分類され、彼らが「ブラックリスト」と呼ぶものに載せられてしまう。

　最近、政府の統制構造は－これらの現象の統制が、共産主義時代に始まる遥かに長い歴史を有しているとしても－大幅に改善された。以前は、本を焼却する、新聞社の社屋全体を延焼させるなどの残虐行為にまで身を落としていたとすれば、今日、我々を統治する専門家達は遥かに洗練されている。今日の状況は、1997年の出来事と我々が何ヶ月も体験した非常事態について、大いに考えさせる。今日の統治方法と1997年当時の方法に、共通する多くの側面がある。国家は司法府を完全に支配している。いわゆる司法の改革は、憲法裁判所の設立を長い間妨げてきた。行政府は明らかに、閣議法令または、寡頭政治の支配者達によって排他的に提案される特別法でのみ統治している。現在では慣例となっている、これらの常軌を逸した事態は全て検閲に関係があり、政府のメディア使用及び芸術の利用にも結び付いている。

　1997年終盤、国営テレビは芸術高等学校の学生達とテレビ番組を制作した。僕もそれに参加した。番組の目的は、社会の発展における芸術と芸術家の役割の分析を試みることだった。それは、被った衝撃を代償しようとした多くのテレビ番組の一つだった。その番組では、芸術家が果たすべきだった役割、改革されるべきだった制度の構造、そして芸術家達が受け継いだ役割について話し合った。それは、政治によって方向付けられ、強要された役割だった。政治は、創造性及び表現の自由の全レベルを明白に抑圧していた。翌日、番組が放映された際には、彼らは、僕達の挑発的な議論の大部分を削除してしまっていた。僕は非常に年若かったが、ざっくりと切り落とされたように感じた。高校の教師陣と他の同級生の大半が、僕達に対して取った立場も相俟って、僕は、ある種の疎外感を初めて感じた。この機会に、僕は初めて芸術機関の狭量を感じ取ったのだ。1年後の1998年、そのテレビ番組に出演した二人の友人とともに、僕達はフィレンツェに留学するために旅立った。僕はその地で、少なくとも今でもそうだと思っているのだが、あのテレビ番組で根付いた何かを進展させた。

アカデミアでは、《Walking Free in Harmony》(2001年)を実現する前に、別の二つの作品、《Guasto(故障)》(2000年)と《Acqua due volte al giorno(水遣りは1日2回)》(2000年)を実現した。それは極めて濃密な時期だった。何かが街中で胎動しており、新たなる気配がしていたからだ。議論はアカデミア美術学院内でも反響していたが、教員達には符合する所が一切なかった。教室は、絵画作品、廃れたデザイン、他の芸術家の模写で充満しており、それらは僕達が高校初期に既にやっていたことだった。そこは息苦しい環境だった。これが理由で、僕は《Guasto》を実現した。イーゼルを使った絵画授業の真っ最中、全員が粛々と沈黙の中で作業していた時、僕は教室の消火器を手に取り、安全弁を引き抜き、その環境を白い空間に変換した。真っ白な粉が床面に降り積もり、教室が間違いなく別の何か、 ある種の「White Cube(ホワイトキューブ)[1]」になった時、 僕は消火器の上に黒い字で「Guasto」という言葉を書いた。 これは作品の題名でもある。《Guasto》の後、 僕は教室にほとんど顔を出さなかった。 午前中はチラシ配達のアルバイトをし、 午後は国立図書館に行き、 当時、 心酔していたルートヴィヒ・ウィトゲンシュタインを読んでいた。 そのため、 あまりにも多くの欠席を蓄積し、 留年の可能性があったが、 僕は気に留めていなかった。 僕が作業していた教室の隅にあった僕のスツールの上に、 注意書きを添えて、 観葉植物のスパティフィラム(Spathiphyllum)、 英名「Peace Lily(ピース・リリー)」と呼ばれる植木を置いた。 フェルトペンで植物の名前と、 植物を長生きさせるための注意事項、 即ち、 水遣りは1日2回と書いた。 僕の考えでは、 植木に水を遣るのは教授達の義務であったが、 その任務を彼らが果たすことはなく、 植木は枯死した。

　フィレンツェのアカデミアは、 僕にとってはあまりにも問題を抱えていた。 伝統主義的であることに加え、 おおよそは、 ルネサンスを学びたいアメリカやヨーロッパの外国人学生向けに構成されていた。 学院内の事務局では、 国境警察からの圧力が感じられた。 非西洋の学生達、 いわゆる第三世界(当時、 アカデミアには、 第四あるいは第五世界の誰も在学していなかった)の学生達は、 真に酷い扱いを受けていた。 僕達を第三世界の者達だと見做していた学院の運営部に対しての、 義務付けられ、 制御・強制された服従は、 僕に吐き気を催させて

1　ホワイトキューブ(White Cube)は、 ジェイ・ジョプリング(Jay Jopling)が設立した、 現代アートギャラリーの中でも最重要とされるギャラリーの名称。 ロンドン(Berdmonsey Streetバーモンジー・ストリート並びにMason's Yardメイソンズ・ヤード)と香港に拠点がある。

いた。危機に晒されていたのは、アイデンティティそのものだった。これが、僕の作品を検閲するというよりも、彼らは僕のアイデンティティを検閲したと思う所以である。僕がこう言うのは、当時《Walking Free in Harmony》の行為が、芸術作品として、つゆほども認識されなかったからだ。僕に異議を唱えた全ての立論において、1990年代の移民上陸と1997年以降に固持されるようになった常套句に結び付いた、理不尽な、ほとんどファシスト的な推論で、僕の出自を「詰る」試みがなされた。僕が除籍になった数日後、アカデミアの同級生達が学院の中庭でコンサートを開催して、僕を送別してくれた。彼らの側からの実に高尚な行いであり、僕は非常に勇気付けられた。

フィレンツェの次に、ボローニャ（Bologna）に行った：余儀ない選択だった。僕が移住した当時、2002年は、ボローニャは非常に開かれた都市であり、議論の街、左翼の街であり、多くの自由を与えてくれていたが、徐々に状況は変わってしまった。

ボローニャで最初に見たものの一つは – 僕は長らくその衝撃におののき、今もなお震撼されているのだが – 聖ペトロニオ大聖堂のフレスコ画の一場面だった。正確には、地獄にいる裸体の預言者ムハンマドが描かれている、ジョヴァンニ・ダ・モデナ（Giovanni da Modena）作の15世紀のフレスコ画だった。そのイメージは非常に強烈で、僕が今まで見た中で最も強力な人物像の一つである。9月11日以降、何度かテロ襲撃未遂があったため、司教座大聖堂は常に監視されていた。僕がフレスコ画を見に行く度、じっくり観察しようとフレスコ画の正面に回り込むには配置が良くなかったので、警察が立ち会っていた。

2004年以降、僕は街の戦略的なポイントで作品を発表した。TPOに始まり、ヴェルディ広場、ガレリア・カヴールに到るまで。 TPO（Teatro Polivalente Occupato占拠下の多価値劇場）は名の知れたソーシャルセンターだったが、 後に、 界隈の「ジェントリフィケーション」施策と新居住圏建設のために、 当時の拠点は取り壊された。 ヴェルディ広場（piazza Verdi）はボローニャの政治史において、 非常に活動的で重要な空間である。 ガレリア・カヴール（galleria Cavour）は、 通廊アーケードのあるエリアで、 市内の最高級店が立ち並んでいる。 これら全ての場所は、 僕の手で、 都市の政治的及び文化的問題やその他のテーマを扱った問題提起のための舞台に変えられた。 2004年、 彼らはTPOから、 建物のファサードに設置されてあった僕のネオン・インスタレーション《L' Élégance du Temps(時の洗練)》を撤去した。 イタリア国旗の三色に設定されたその作品は、 ネオン管で綴られた文言「Hijack and Kamikaze Former Center(ハイジャックと自爆テロ犯養成センター)」開設を告げていた。 2007年、 僕は他のアーティスト達とともに、 ヴェルディ広場に別のネオン・インスタレーションを制作するよう招聘された。 僕は二つの文字表記を作成した。 白いネオンで《Piazza SSenza Valori(無-無価値広場)》、 さらに奥に、 赤いネオンで非常に楽観的なフレーズ《But Let Us Yet Put Forth Courageously》を作成した。 文言はトーマス・S・エリオットの詩「Departure and Arrival(出発と到着)[2]」から引用した。 白いネオンはアーケードが始まる箇所、 教会の壁

---

[2]　伊語訳： "Ma facciamoci avanti coraggiosamente".（だが、 それでもなお勇敢に前進しよう）詩作品「Departure and Arrival」は、 1922年の詩篇『荒地(The Waste Land)』で有名な、 1948年ノーベル文学賞受賞者、 トーマス・スターンズ・エリオット(Thomas Stearns Eliot,1888–1965)の初期作品の一つである。 ［訳注： 詩作品タイトルの和訳は伊語原文に基づいている。］

の近くの、広場を示す陶板の隣に設置され、その先に赤いネオンがアーケードの下に続いていた。そのインスタレーションは妨害された。最初に電源が遮断され、次にコードが切断された。この作品は、中道左派と中道右派の両方の組織から、教会だけでなく自治体からも攻撃された。この作品では、過去と未来について話す他に、広場で衝突を引き起こす「価値」の（極端な）過負荷を示したかったのだが、それらの存在しない広場も思い描きたかった。ハンス・ウルリッヒ・オブリスト[3]は、そのような広場の意味について語り、広場を構築することはできるのか、それが構築された場合には何を意味するのかについて話したことがある。偶然ではなく、僕が同意しない美学の極端な意向により、この広場はまさにティラナに、オブリストの思い入れが非常に強いと思われる街に構築された。スカンデルベグ広場は、記憶根絶の類い稀な例である。広場はピラミッド型に設計されており、まるで共同体・大衆を矮小化し、個人を高揚させる思想を与えんがためのようだ。その広場を設計した建築家達や政治家達によると、最上部に位置すべきは個人であり、大衆は絶対的にその下位に位置付けられるべきだと言う。

　2014年、僕の作品《UNTITLED》に関する無理解が、ユダヤ人コミュニティを困惑させた。僕はボローニャ芸術フェアに招待され、以前、ミュージアム空間用に設計した作品をガレリア・カヴールの柱廊下に展示することにした。そのインスタレーションは被収容者の手によって作られ、アウシュヴィッツ強制収容所入口に

3　1968年チューリッヒ生まれの美術評論家兼歴史学者の美術館キュレーターであるハンス・ウルリッヒ・オブリスト（Hans Ulrich Obrist）は、ロンドンのサーペンタイン・ギャラリー（Serpentine Galleries）の共同ディレクターである。

設置された「Arbeit Macht Frei(働けば自由になる)」という文言の鉄製看板の正確な複製である。複製はネオンで作成されているが、収容所の内側から読めたのと同じ様に、文言は鏡文字で表示されている。ボローニャのラビ(ユダヤ教律法学者)とユダヤ人コミュニティのメンバーが作品の面前、裕福さが弾けんばかりの中心街のこの空間に集結し、この作品を反ユダヤ主義だと見做したために破壊行為を辞さない構えだった。この作品は、メディア、自治体官僚の討論の的となり、芸術フェアのディレクターによっても、ユダヤ人コミュニティに対し作品の目的を文書で表明し、議論された。直面や言及を避けたものとは、作品の本来の目的、つまりミュージアム空間の意味と、移民に対する人種差別であった。この件では、また他のいかなる事案でも、僕の意図は決して騒ぎを起こすことではなく、もう少し掘り下げて、歴史と権力の交錯を衆目に曝すことだった。千の言葉を尽くすよりも、一つのイメージが、その複雑な絡み合いを上手く要約できるはずだ。

2012年以降、僕は再びティラナに居住している。アート界では多くのことが変わったように見えるが、限界の数々を突破しようとし、もう少し踏み込み、深く掘り下げようとすると、我々(彼ら/僕)は、まだ1997年のあのテレビ番組の中にいることに気付く。その目的は、分析に焦点を合わせることでは決してなく、問題の中核からますます遠ざかって行くことである。この国は非常に面白く、非常に複雑で、しばしば認識するのが困難で、ほとんどの者にとって解読不可能だ。真実は非常に厳しく、また同時にあまりにも無色透明なので、可視化することが大層困難な課題のままである。

僕の最近の作品では、物事の「完璧な」意味に到達し、資本主義システムによって開かれた傷口の上に、さらに深い傷を負わせるために、僕は（またしても）「危険な」要素を使用している。それらの構成要素は、慎重さ・冷静さ・客観性を持って分析されなければ、誤解されかねないものだ。正しい言葉がこれらなのかは分からないが、状況をさらに押し進めることで、別の反応を促すことができると思う。この成果を達成することは難しく、責任は非常に重大だと僕は認識している。なぜなら、アーティスト各人は、失敗するかもしれず、伝達したメッセージが誤解されるかもしれないと分かっているからだ：この場合、真っ先に全責任を負うべき張本人は、アーティスト自身のはずである。

《Bullet in Envelope》は、現在の国内の社会・政治的状況に関連して考案された、幾つかのディティールで構成された作品である。アルバニアの最も重要な芸術機関である、かつてのティラナ・ナショナル・ギャラリーこと、今日の国立美術博物館に宛てて制作された。ミュージアムが今日どうあるべきかという考え、そして世界に拡大中の、我々の元にも忍び寄っているフランチャイズの概念からミュージアムを守るという前提から始めて、僕は数々の限界の突破を試み、この[…]変革の試練の中で、この機関の本当の素顔を露呈させようとした。そこで働く人々はオープンな前衛派だったが、今では閉鎖信奉者である。彼らはお役人になってしまったのだ。この公的機関は公営でありながらも、不明瞭なある種の市場ルールで、民営機関のように運営されている。そういったわけで、異質な芸術世界のあらゆる観念に反対するのだ。

「この新ミュージアムは廉価の売春婦に他ならない」と吐き捨てながら、とある文化ジャーナリストが、憤懣遣る方なく記者会見を後にしたことがあった。《Bullet in Envelope》の主な構成要素は、不特定の場所で発射された弾丸の弾頭部と、肉眼では判読不可能で科学警察の顕微鏡下でしか読めない手紙である。

これらの二つの要素は、 飼猫デュシャンの協力を得て、 情報・住所・ユーモラスな言葉遊びがしたためられた、 白色の封筒に封じられた。 そして、 社会史や美術史から「も」拝借した要素を全て「嗅ぎ分け」可能な（否、 不可能かもしれない）機関に送付された。 ところが意に反して、 この作品は満場一致で – 僕は芸術機構及び博物館館長について言及しているのだが – 犯罪的な表現方法を用いていたがために、 暴力的で倫理に反する行為として国家警察に告発された。 芸術界の公的機関の評決では、 その表現方法を芸術と見做すことは不可能とされた。

　この作品を特徴付けるパラドックスと諸問題は、 僕を未だに非常に当惑させている。 犯罪警察の署長（全くの偶然だが、 芸術家として身を立てることができなかった故に警官になった元芸術家）だけでなく、 ティラナの検事正も、 証拠を慎重に調べ、 あらゆる優秀な警察犬-キュレーターの如く、 実に見事に「嗅ぎ分け」た後、 僕の作品は確かに芸術作品であり、 脅威では全くないという結論に達した。「芸術機関」側の解釈や申立とは異なり、 僕の作品には脅迫たり得る全ての要素が欠けていたのだ。 警察と検察によると、 脅迫を成立させる全ての必要条件が欠落していたため、 彼らはこの件を不起訴処分にすることを決定した。 この作品は、 芸術機関と政府について語っており、 その政府は国を現代性に向けて推進させることを堅く決意しているように思われる。 作品は、 その「現代の爆発的発展」と、 社会主義政府によって2013年に発表されたヴィジョンに、 まさに言及している。 しかしながら、 社会主義政府は、 いかなる復興・覚醒・爆発的発展も、 民主的制度の実際の開始も示したことはなかったし – 今後も示すことはできないだろう。 事実は、 全ての機関が冷酷に硬化して、 堅物になってしまったことにある。 政治と政府にますます結び付いた芸術機関は、 防壁の内に自らを遮蔽してしまった。ところが一方、真の爆発は既に発生しており、「Museo/Gal(l)er(i)a/Governoミュージアム/画(廊-牢)獄/政府」の壁の遥か彼方、路上で発生し続けているのだ。

《Bullet in Envelope》を僕が送付した1週間後、全ての学部で学生達の抗議運動が始まった。抗議が建築学部で口火を切り、法学部及び社会科学部を含む、他の全学部に拡大したことは非常に重要である。ナショナル・ギャラリーからの告発は、直観を証明したに過ぎなかった。彼らは学生達を脅し、細密に分断したものの、学生達は非常に重要な行いを成し遂げた。学生達は今度と言う今度は、政府のプロパガンダの強力な装置を破壊し、首相の、社会主義アーティストの化けの皮を剥がした。彼は、かつて労働者達からユートピア思想のブラジル大統領ルーラが評価されていたのと同じように、重んじられていた感が若干あった。学生達の全員一致の政治行為は、指導者もリーダーも擁立せず、政府と対話しないこと、特に首相と対話しないことだった。これは、徹底的に分析すべき兆候である。なぜなら、政府がどん底に達したということを再三に渡り示すことに加え、将来的に迅速な対処をしなくてはならない階層と複雑さをも我々に顕示しているからだ。

傲慢、統制、警察、脅迫、マフィア、懲役、強淫、麻薬密売、現代美術、デザイン、建築といった、この政府のルールは常に変わらないため、この世代のルールが変わった。

ナショナル・ギャラリーである団体は、共産主義の前も後も、国の芸術の変革に根本的な役割を果たしてきた公的機関である。だが最近は、政府の極端な傲慢さを我がものとした。政府は芸術機関にその統制を課しているのだ。彼らは、政治を支援する「再教育キャンプ」のシステムを設立し、政治のお墨付きのある芸術のみを世に出す。 芸術機関は、 厳重警備の刑務所の死刑囚監房まがいに成り下がりつつある。 このシステムは「新たな釘は古い釘を追い出す[訳注: 新たな心配ごとが生じると今までの心配は消えていく]」という有名な諺に従って働く。 全ての真実の破壊に傾倒する彼らは、 君に同じ懸案について何千もの偽情報メッセージを送り付け、 君を疲労困憊させようとし、 全ての事実の信憑性を失墜させ、 最終的には僕が最も危険視している検閲を実現しようとする。 その検閲とは先手を打つ行為に関わるもので、 即ち、 概念が成長するのを妨げ、 制作作業が始まるのを妨害し、 批判本が出版・配布されるのを阻止し、 調査映画に資金提供されるのを阻害することだ。 人々はますます話題にしている。 「奴ら」は、 真実を隠すことはできない、 証拠を隠滅し、 16歳のアルディット・ヂョクライ[4] にしたように君を殺害し、 ゴミの中に埋めることはできない。 だが、 奴らは別の真実を作り上げ、 金に物を言わせ、 世界の新聞の全ての頁にそれを然もありなんと掲載させることはできるのだ。 人々が話し始めた。 これを止めることは奴らにはできない。

　これが現在の概観、 あるいは《Bullet in Envelope》 の下地だ。 作品は、 当面は検察庁のコレクションに収蔵されている。

4　2016年8月7日、 ティラナの廃棄物の大部分を処分する目的で造成された、 真新しいシャアルゥ処分場(Sharrë)で、 夜勤労働者アルディット・ヂョクライ(Ardit Gjoklaj,当時16歳)の遺体がゴミに埋まっているのが発見された。 遺体には明らかな損傷が見られ、 事故の隠蔽をはかったものと思われる。 捜査の結果、 数ヶ月前の2015年11月25日、 業務上での事故の別の被害者、 4人の子供の母である48歳のミルヴェテ・ドゥーカ(Mirvete Duka)がいたことが判明したが、 当件でも沈黙のうちに揉み消そうとした。 この取り調べにより、 一連の行政上の不正行為と雇用・安全管理・事故防止における不履行が明るみに出た。

当然、将来の展覧会で、ティラナ・ナショナル・ギャラリー（国立美術博物館）に展示する際には、検事正宛に貸出許可を書面で願い出なくてはいけないのだが。

アルバニアとブラジル。ブラジルのアートシーンは昨今の選挙後に荒廃した、と多くの者が発言し、著述している。幾つかの点で、ブラジルは私にアルバニアを大いに思い起こさせる。それについて、君は何か述べたいことがあるか？　アルバニアには、どのような制限があるのか？　ブラジルの極右とアルバニアのシステムの間には、どのような類似点があるのか？

国の今日の左翼・右翼を分析すると、両者に大きな相違点はない。世界の他地域と比較した根本的な違いは、ヨーロッパの他地域のように、あるいはさらに遠方の、西方諸国やアジア諸国のようには、過激派の党や組織が（まだ）ないことだ。全てが未だに過去の体制や独裁政治、その極端な「マイナス面」とばかり比較されており、共産主義思想においてのように、共通の理想によってのみ生み出される「プラス面」は決して議論されていない。僕が大変気に入っているフレーズがあるのだが、それは、過去との違いについて、言わば大衆の考えを解説している：「From prison to poison is like from poison to prison.[5]」この立ち位置は、複雑すぎるだけでなく、負の側面での違いを我々に知らしめるだけに、ベルベットの手袋をはめて恭しく扱

5　刑務所から毒までは、毒から刑務所までのようなものだ2019年のヴィクトール・ストラト（Victor Strato）のビデオ作品名に言及している。参照：https://debatikcenter.net/strikes/from_prison_to_poison

わなければならない。 負の側面については、 人々は新自由主義に毒されるよりも刑務所を好むようだ。 そして、 ここで言う刑務所とは、 安全、 労働、 犯罪の減少を意味する。

　アルバニア社会は保守的で閉鎖的であり、 自由の概念は未だ理解されていない。 これは、 国が取り組まなくてはならない多くの重苦しい制限の一つである。 政治家達は我々の社会のこの特異性をよく理解している： それが、 彼らが自信満々にやりたい放題である理由だ。 社会党は、 これらの制限の解除を予測できるナレーションを、 提案することが可能だった。 国で最も不利な階級を援助すべきだった政党であるにもかかわらず、 結局この道に進むことはなく、 その層の住民をさらに犠牲にした。 前に述べたように、 政府の現首相の人物像は、 国の内外を問わず、 大いに支持されていた。 彼が提示したプログラム、 「国家再生」と「欧州（再）ルネサンス」のためだけではなく、 アーティストである現首相は、 右翼によって移植された退廃的システムを変革可能な改革者だと大衆から見做されていたことでも、 支援されていたのである。 現首相は、 ブラジルの労働組合員ルイス・イナシオ・ルーラ・ダ・シルヴァが想像されていたのと同じように、 大衆から見られていた。 自国民や世界中の人々に愛されていたルーラは、 長年に渡り政権を握ってきたが、 その政府は汚職の巣窟と成り果てた。 ルーラ政府とアルバニア現政府の間には、 分析すべき多くの類似点があり、 ルーラは現在刑務所に収監されているとしても、 この問題は我々の政府によって克服されたように見える。 なぜなら、 国際共同体の支援と共に、 体制側の統制が激化しているからだ。 国際共同体は、 たとえ信頼性を失いつつあり、 国民の歴史的な「敵」、 真の矛盾になろうとも、 この政府を支持し続けている。

　現政府は、 右翼政権のように、 ほとんどのメディア、 司法制度、 刑務所制度を支配している。 政府が批判される度にプロパガンダの謀略は、 2011年の抗議運動で4人の犠牲者を出した旧右翼政権と、 まだ誰も直接的には殺害していない彼ら自身とを比較対照することで反発する。 この擁護論は、 国の芸術家達やキュレーター達によっても共有されている。 社会主義政府は、 実際には民営化された政府であるが、 雇用不足や州の支援不足のために、 電気代の支払不能に陥った相当数の貧困層の人々を投獄した。 これらの人々の多くは自死に追い込まれ、 自殺者の数は増加の一途を辿っている。 この政府は、 さらに別の国家の悲劇にも責任がある。 その政策は、 アルバニア史の中で2番目に大規模な国外移住を引き起こした。 貧困は拡大し、 中流階級は姿を消しつつあり、 政府から恩恵を施されているのは富裕層だけだ。 それはおそらく犯罪、 現政府によって犯された殺人なのではないか?

　芸術に関しては、 文化の大発展について芸術家に為された全ての約束は、 雲散霧消に終わった。 この時代に唯一人顕現し、 市場を有する当国唯一の新進気鋭アーティストとして、 国際展覧会に出展可能な唯一人の芸術家は、 首相自身である。

　エディ・ムカ[6] が、 アルバニアの女性ジャーナリストに答えたインタビューでは、 通常であれば抗議されるのだがそれもないまま、 彼は今日のアーティストが関心を持つであろうテーマについて話した。 主に、 アルバニアの若手アーティスト達について言

6　スウェーデンに帰化したアルバニア人アーティスト兼キュレーターであるエディ・ムカ（Edi Muka）は、 美術アカデミーの元教授であり、 ティラナ・アート・ビエンナーレの共同創設者。 Röda Sten konsthallのキュレーターであり、 ヨーテボリ（Göteborg）国際現代美術ビエンナーレの共同芸術監督でもある。

及した。彼らは岐路に立っており、どうもそこから抜け出す術の見当が皆目付いていないようである。この政府を深く理解するために、ムカはアーティストが掘り下げるべき懸案を例として挙げた。それは、ブラジル、トルコ、トランプ政権下の米国などの右翼のシステムにまさしく関係している。それらの諸国では、独裁、検閲、人種差別が極めて激しいが、しかし、移住や地球温暖化などの他の問題もある。これらの世界規模の問題については、綿密な調査研究が展開された場合にのみ話題にすることが非常に重要であると思う。この国の緊急課題を隠蔽するためにではなく、それらの課題をより一層、可視化するためにこそ、世界規模の問題について話すことが肝要なのだ。したがって、この例は適切ではないようだ。グローバルな問題を反映したローカルの緊急性があり、これこそが、我々が話さなければならないものだ。

　ブラジルの問題と同一の、現代アーティスト達が真剣に取り組んだことのない問題があるとするならば、それは、かつて裁かれたことのない独裁政権の犯罪である。現代アーティスト達は、こういったことに専心することはない。アルバニアで公的支援を受けて活動するアーティストは、合法性、権力の使用と濫用、腐敗、政府による強淫の正当化、国立劇場解体のためのような特別法を気に掛けたりはしない。どうして、処分場で国の謀略によって殺された未成年アルディット・ヂョクライの殺人事件に関する全調査を、ナショナル・ギャラリーこと国立美術博物館に展示する準備万端の、勇気あるアーティスト達を招待することができないのだろうか？なぜ、過去に政府メンバー及び代議士達によって犯された、犯罪に関する捜査プロジェクトの展示を決して受け入れないのだろうか？我々は皆、多くの社会党議員が犯罪者、人身売買/密売の売人であり、性的暴力で有罪判決を受けていることを知っている。 なぜ、 国立美術博物館は、 国家自体による薬物の生産と、 このスキームへの政府と警察の関与についてのプロジェクトを展示しないのか? なぜ、 この国で最も有名なキュレーター達は、 首相の邸宅の建設、 資金援助、 その市場価格及び建築的価値に関する研究の展示に、 決して同意しないのだろうか? なぜ、 彼らは、 権力を象徴するあの邸宅の周辺での、 地震の小さな揺れを予測する計画を拒否するのだろうか? スルレル[7]（綴りもほぼシュール[Surreal]）で何ヶ月間も降雨が続き、 首相の住居を構成する4棟の建物の1棟に落雷する可能性があるという予測を展示することに反対するのは、 なぜだ? これらの懸案を避け、 他の諸問題に専念して、 グローバルなテーマと比較することは、 我々の現実の重大性を軽減するために、 あらゆる悪を別のより大きな悪と我々は比較すべきだと言う類いの、 意図的な狡猾さのように僕には思える。 なぜ、 2017年にブラジルでジュディス・バトラーが受けた手酷い接遇が、 社会党のエルヴィス・ロシィ市長によって犯された集団レイプよりも重要でなければならないのか? 現代芸術家である首相は、 その所業を若気の至りだったとして、その市長を何年にも渡り擁護した。 なぜ、 ロシィについて、 アーティストもキュレーターも男女問わず、 誰も話題にしないのだ? 何よりも、 これらの懸案のせいで、 この政府を批判する芸術はどこにも展示する場所が見付けられないのだ。

　今日、 巷に溢れる多くの展覧会、 ジャーナリズムの初回講義でのような幼稚なメッセージを伝播する展覧会の、 ポピュリズムの流れに足を掬われないように、 今日のアルバニア人アーティスト達

7　ティラナ近郊、 景観の町スルレル（Surrel）はダイティ山（Dajti）に向かう途上にある。 首都の住民（及び、 首相を含む要人達）が好む休暇スポットの一つである。

が取り組むべき懸案は、主に上記の問題だと僕は思う。僕の意見では、我々の、外国に対するある種の劣等感を考慮しながら、展覧会や芸術プロジェクトが行われていた時代は終わった。アルバニアは、我々が至る所で飽きるほど目にした作品を設置する場所ではなくなった。それどころか、今では海外に向けてローンチするための新たな提案、ニュー・ウェーブを展開でき、そうすべき場所になった。このことについてこそ、我々は話題にしなければならない。なぜなら、それに勝る緊急性は何もないのだ。前述したように、右翼と左翼の間では、結果に関して大差はなく、運用手法だけが（今のところ）異なる。両者のシステムはどちらも非常に効果的であるため「Fuck them both[8]」だ。

　アルバニアの右翼政党の方がより「誠実」に見え、国の左翼と比べると若干左寄りのようであり、その左翼は国の右翼政党と比べると右寄りであることを、認めなければならない僕自身に嫌気がさす。我々は、左翼とは名ばかりの右派によって支配されているのだ。

　右翼の検閲と左翼の検閲。こういった区別をするのは論理的であるか？　検閲とは、問答無用の検閲か？　これら二つのシステムにおいては、異なるタイプの検閲があるのか、それとも戦略は同じなのか？　共産主義時代に存在していた統制・検閲モデルはどのように変化し、現在の状況にどのように適応したのか？

8　どっちもくたばりやがれ。

アガンベンが主張するように、今日の政府というものは、洋の東西を問わず危機的状況を生み出し、危機は政府自身が生み出した戦略である。危機は、システムの違法性をますます表明し、権力が下した決定を是認し、合法としている。検閲は、このシステムの不可欠な部分である。統制ルールは常に同じなのではなく改良を重ね、絡み合っているものの、危機が多様変化するので、絶えず暴力的なままだ。政府のプロパガンダは、いかなる手段を用いてでも、制度的腐敗によって生じたスキャンダルと真実を隠そうとする。人々は政府の統制を恐れて、ますます自分自身の殻に閉じこもる。なぜなら、全てが彼らに対して向けられているからだ。2008年にグルデツで発生した旧弾薬庫の爆発のような、世界レベルでの不祥事である極めて深刻な事件の数々があった。グルデツでは、女性や未成年者が働いており、26人が死亡した。このビジネスには、当時の首相サリ・ベリシャ（Sali Berisha）の息子、政府そのもの、ペンタゴン、米国国務省も含まれていた。また、この政府を巻き込む他の状況もある。先述のように、存在すべきだった裁判所の欠如や寡頭政治家達のための特別法の恩恵などで、しばらく前から政府は民主主義的非常事態のパラメータの範囲内で行動している。領土内の至る所に大麻を植えることは、左翼政府の決定事項だった。マフィアは国家警察と共にプランテーションを管理し、政治家達は自分達の分け前をまんまと懐に入れ、今現在、我々が目にしているとおり、彼らは皆、その儲けを土木事業に注ぎ込んでいる。警察と内務省自体が麻薬事件に関与していた頃に、内務省前に建立された殉職警官の記念碑は、アメリカ人戦没者の記念碑の複製らしいが、幾つかの銀の星の代わりに大麻の葉形の銀色のシルエットを付すべきであろう。ティラナの処分場で不法就労していた16歳の少年の死は自治体の監督下でのことで、別の甚大なスキャンダルを生み出したが、国は、捜査を遂行するはずだった検事の親類に、請負契約を与えることで揉み消した。スカンデルベグ広場は腐敗の証しである。テレビがルポルタージュを完全に黙殺するとしても、これらの問題を深く掘り下げようとする何人かのジャーナリストがいる。彼らは組織的に検閲され、解雇あるいは脅迫さえされている。ある女性ジャーナリストの場合は自宅がマフィアの兇弾の標的になった。または、国の兇弾と言うべきだろうか？非政府組織、及び市民社会の表明は、存在しないように思われる。なぜなら、彼らは政府によって支援されており、ある意味では、彼らはその政府のために働いているからだ。多少の政治活動を行うアーティスト達は、開催される数少ない展覧会には入り込むことはできず、万一成功したとしても、調査ではなく、シンボル/ロゴやイメージ表現などの貧弱な手段のみを使用する。上述のジャンルの主題で作業する場合、誰よりも真っ先に、つまり国よりも先に、君を「糾弾する」のはアーティストとキュレーター自身である。彼らは、君が反対派の小集団に属していると咎め、さらに、ここ数年の間に創り上げられたナレーションをぶち壊していると君を非難する。即ち、現代美術は成功同然の結果を収め、世界で祖国の誉れとなった人物達を輩出した、そして、この過去を讃えつつ、この軌跡に続くべきだというナレーションだ。

　この国の洗練さはいつも曲解される。ミュージアムガラスの使用や、注文制作での完璧な額装を施すといった、空虚で知性に欠くやり方で、洗練さを表現することはできない。僕にとって、美とは隠された知性であり、それは現代美術教育の洗礼を受けた目では、もはや見ることができないものだ。検閲の一つの構成要素がある。全てのアーティスト・俳優・監督、及び、国の芸術システム（僕は所属していない）の他のメンバー全員において非常に明白なもの、自己検閲である。この手の検閲にさらに言及するのは、ありきたりだ。だが、それだけを扱うものではない。それは教育や育成、統合への欲求について扱うものだ。最近、舞台俳優達が、1930年代にファシストによって建てられた国立劇場の建物を解体するという、国の計画に対する抗議活動を派手に行った。その跡地に、権威ある建築事務所によって考案された新たな現代劇場を建設するための計画だ。その計画は、処分場での16歳の少年の死に関与する寡頭政治家によって出資されており、政府は特別法で、その者にプロジェクトを承認した。抗議理由は正当なものだ。街のアイデンティティ以上のものを保護することを論じている。俳優達の理解力と言葉遣いそのものは、彼らの抗議活動を始めた当時の非効果的な使用から、徐々に過激化している。当初、誰かが現実に近接し、その実情を、普段と異なる厳しい語法を用いて、どのように表現するかに肉薄した場合に、その者は話し方のルールを「銘記した」俳優達自身によって壁際に追い詰められていた。重要な役柄を演じるのを目にし、別の姿を想像していた俳優達が、台詞ではない自らの言葉を持たない様を見るのは、非常に興味深かった。ジェスチャーの威力を理解せず、舞台の場面の外の現実世界では身動きが取れない役者達を見るのは、痛ましかった。俳優達に身振り手振りが欠けているのを目の当たりにするのは、やるせなかった。

　国立劇場の現在の状況を注視し、高位高官の政治家達とマフィアの不法な資金流通が目的の、新建造物のスペースを作るために差し迫った解体計画を鑑みると、「教育された/礼儀正しい」言葉の使用は、それよりもさらに「教育された/躾の良い」議論、完全に実の無い、役立たずの議論をもたらすことに僕は気付

いた。 この「教育」とは、 文明、 統合、 民主主義の同義語として
定義されてきた。 僕にとって、 文明とは全くの別物である：僕は
（アーティスト像に関して言及すると）統合に反対であり、 このた
めに我々は戦わなければならない…最も悲しかったのは、 この
「教育」が慣例になってしまったようである（〜ようだった）ことだ
った。 もし、 アーティストが何かを教えねばならないのだとした
ら、 彼らは、 まず始めに彼ら自身の行動を変革すべきであり、
この役割を自分自身から引き剝がし、 火急の何かを世に知らしめ
るべきであろう：差し迫った状況での迅速な行動は、 緊急手段を
要するのだ。

　異なる反応を惹き起こすため、 僕は、 俳優達の抗議運動の
序盤に、 あるテクストを彼らに送付した。 それは、 彼らが抗議
していた広場、 その場所で演じるべきもので、 題名は「Il coro
(合唱)」、 長尺のオーガズムを中心に据えた、 洗練を極めた戯
曲である。 言葉のない演劇台本で、 ある特定の世代の舞台俳優
達、 1990年以前に活動していた者達のために、 そして、 彼らの
教え子達にもあてて、 僕が書いておいたものだ。 我々が目にし
ている、 抗議運動する者達こそ、 まさにその演劇研修生達であ
る。 1日1時間の集団的オーガズム。 この政治の屑と、 コンクリー
トで銭を洗う他の亡者ども全員が、 その公有地から撤退するその
時まで。

　絵画と政治。 アメリカでの「アクション・ペインティング」は、 ソ
ビエト連邦あるいは中国での政治的抑圧の芸術に反対して、
世界に輸出され「自由の芸術」と見做された、 芸術的な潮流で
あった。 しかし我々は、 「アクション・ペインティング」が茶番劇で

あり、「隷属」ロシアなどとは対照的に「自由な」アメリカという概念を伝播するために、支援された芸術であることをよく知っている。そのうえ、抽象芸術は、絵の視覚的内容に明確な政治的要素を有してはいない。抽象絵画において政治的なものは何があるか？　抽象絵画は、どのように政治的であることが可能か？

随分前から僕は、アルバニアにおけるアメリカ合衆国の存在についての、別のナレーションを書いているところだ。僕はそれを「The Third Love Affair」、第3のラブ・ストーリーと呼んでいる。

　フィレンツェの国立アカデミア美術学院から除籍された後、僕が最初に制作した作品の一つで、その後、このアーカイブに入れたのは、フィレンツェのアメリゴ・ヴェスプッチ（Amerigo Vespucci）空港近辺で行われたパフォーマンスの記録写真《Powershift CIA》(2001年)である。翌年、ティラナで作品を展示した際、アメリカ人外交官が僕の父に、作品のタイトルにあるCIAの3文字の意味についての情報を求めた。写真では、障害物を飛び越える1匹のアメリカン・ピットブル・テリアと、その障害物の上に二つに引き裂かれたアルバニアの赤い国旗が広がっているのを見ることができる。僕の父が何と答えたのかは分からないが、彼が僕に言ったこと、そして彼が長年続けてきたこととは、政治には決して関わるな、僕の作品で政治に一切言及するな、特に米国の政治には口を挟むなということだった。

　当時、僕が伝えたかったのは、僕が知覚していたこと、つまり、政策 – 特に国内で最も影響力のある存在だった米国の政策 – が、権力のコントロールと分配において決定的であった、ということだけだった。1990年代の政権交代計画だけでなく、 1997年の諸々の出来事も、 あまりにもよく構成されており効果的だったため、 組織体のみがそれらを実行できるように僕には思えた。 当時、 これらの推測は全て挑発的言動に過ぎず、 僕の手掛かりはしっかりとした根拠がなかった。

　芸術と文化に対する政治的関心は、 国内で活動していた − 現在も活動している − 全ての外国勢力にとって戦略的なものだった。 当初から芸術活動を支えてきた恒常的な存在は、 慈善家のジョージ・ソロスの財団である。 彼は、 自らの組織を通して、 非常に多くの美術展や、 多数のアーティスト及びミュージシャン、 相当数のフェスティバルなどに資金提供してきた。 事実、 キャリア(このような文脈で受け入れられる、 この用語を僕が使用してもよいのなら)を積んだアーティストや政治家の多くは、 この財団によって支援された者達で、 今もなおサポートされている。

　芸術分野において、 非常に興味深く、 非情に普及した、 この存在について、 僕は無意識のうちに《Performing Soros, A Friendship Cycling Tour》(1997–1999年)と題した、 最初のパフォーマンス活動を行った。

　1997年、 非常事態の最中に、 ソロス財団は「Journey of Hope - Friendship Cycling Tour」と言うプロジェクトを開始した。 僕の従兄が財団に勤めており、 このプロジェクトのマネージャーで、 僕と姉を招待したので、 僕はこのプロジェクトに参加することになった。 財団は全員(もしくは、 ほぼ全員)にビアンキ社のロードバイク自転車を贈呈した。 この自転車に乗り、 メキシコの他のサイクリスト達、 ホンジュラスのプロテスタント達、 アメリカの映画製作者達、 スペインからの他の人物達など、 このプロジェクト関係者全員が構成するグループ同伴で、 アルバニア・イタリア・ギリシャを走破しなければならなかった。 僕の記憶では、 彼らは他の参加者達全員に自転車を贈呈したが、僕にはくれなかったので、僕は自分のマウンテンバイクで道路を走ることにした。アルバニアでは、僕達は警察に護衛され、しばしば、多国籍軍のミッション部隊[9]の兵士達にも護衛された。1ヶ月に及ぶ旅の間に、財団は、この体験、リスクや転倒、グループ内での衝突、そして、道中で生まれた幾つかの恋物語についても語るドキュメンタリーも制作した。一言で言えば、団結のユートピア。この映画はその後、政治家達や外交官達が臨席した、ティラナの公会堂での盛大な夜会で上映されたことを覚えている。

この旅行に費やした期間中に、アルバニアで護衛してくれていたアルバニア人警察官達と僕は友達になり、バス移動を避けるため、彼らと一緒にパトカーで旅行した。その間、1年前に米国で入手した観光用のカメラで、僕は行程の写真を撮影していた。警官達、軍隊、サイクリスト・ウェアの参加者達、僕の従兄が携行していた札束で満杯のバッグ、そしてまた、混沌に包まれた国の道路でペダルを漕いでいたグループの姿、焼き尽くされたばかりの大地の上を流れ行く、場違いの川のように見えた、そのグループを撮っていた。大量の写真を撮影した。僕は、このプロジェクトが高度に政治的な企画で、何かについて語っていたということに直ぐには気付かなかった。その何かとは、僕が後になって理解

9　ピラミッド型金融スキーム崩壊後の深刻な危機に瀕したアルバニアには、各国が軍事介入。主に自国の在留住民を安全に避難させるために、米国軍によるシルバーウェイク（Silver Wake）作戦や、ドイツ軍によるリベレ（Libelle）作戦が実行されただけでなく、イタリアの主導で立ち上げられ、国際連合（ONU）と欧州安全保障協力機構（OSCE）によって承認された、多国籍防衛軍によるアルバ作戦（Alba mission）が実施された。

した数多くの影響によって作り出され、条件付けられたこの現実の、絶対的に不可欠な部分であった。僕達は「ダミー」だったのだ、政治操作の中で短い手綱に繋がれたマネキン人形だったのに、僕達はそれを分かっていなかった。これが動機となり、当時の無自覚に挑むために、僕は1999年に独りで再度旅程をやり直した。1997年と1999年の写真を使って、僕は初めてのスライド作品を実現した。

　さて、ここまでの前置きが長くなったのには、訳がある。僕の意見では、これまでの過去約30年間に渡り、ある特定のタイプの芸術が享受していた政治的支援の理由を、完全に理解する時が到来した。政権崩壊後にアルバニアで発展したこのタイプの芸術が、社会的認識と国内政治にどのような影響を及ぼしたかを解明する時が来たのだ。

　君の質問の行間から察することに関してだが、それは極めて挑発的なパラレリズムであり、僕が覚えているのは、1995年にフランシス・ストーナー・サンダース[10]の記事「Modern Art Was CIA 'Weapon'」が公開された時、教育現場では当然ながら一切話題に上らなかったことだ。1995年の教

10　フランシス・エレーヌ・ジャンヌ・ストーナー・サンダース（Franc-
　　es Hélène Jeanne Stonor Saunders, 1966〜）は、英国のジャー
　　ナリスト兼歴史家。アメリカの芸術家や批評家と米国諜報機関の
　　活動との間の繋がりに関心を寄せている。彼女は論考The Cul-
　　tural Cold War: The CIA and the World of Arts and Let-
　　ters, New York, The New Press, 1999(米国版)の著者。本文中で
　　言及された記事は、1995年10月22日付「The Independent」紙に
　　掲載された。2013年6月14日付になるが参考として：https://www.
　　independent.co.uk/news/world/modern-art-was-cia-weap-
　　on-1578808.html

育カリキュラムでは、主として過去の巨匠達の模写制作に僕達は専念していた。当時、僕は2点の模写を作成したことを覚えている。1点は学校の課題用で、もう1点は自分用だった。記憶違いでなければ、僕は、名前は忘れたがフランス人画家の、帽子を被った少年の肖像画と、そして、僕自身のために、1973年のフランシス・ベーコンの自画像を描くことにした。

　CIAを巻き込んだ議論の火種となるテーマであるため、何年のもの間、分析や討論の対象とされたのはごく稀だったと思う。挑発の意味も込めて、1990年以降のアルバニア芸術の状況とそれらのテーマを比較すると、その類いのテーマは歴史的な観点からですらも扱われていないと言える。国家機関で働く研究者達や学者達の傾向は、これらの問題に触れないことである。機関を運営する者達は、1997年を分析しないために使用したのと同じ口実を引っ張り出して、我々の現在のこれらの根本的様相を分析したがらない。時間を要する、歴史が発展するに任せなければいけない、いかなる判断も時期尚早だ、二つやそこらの事案から思索することはできない、といった社会党支持の芸術家達によって引用された弁解は、ありきたりであり、御託を許さずにぴしゃりと拒否されるべきものだ。

　だが、君が僕に尋ねていることにはおそらく、同じ主題に関係し、過去のどこかで非常に異なる状況で現れた別の結び付きがある。1950-1960年代。過日の理由と今日の理由、史上初のプロモーション作戦においてCIAの支援を受けることになった特定のミュージシャン・ジャズアーティスト・作家・ジャーナリスト・画家達の選出理由、米国で裁判にかけられ「ブラックリストに載せられた」その他の者達の理由、それらを分析することは大いに興味深いと思う。抽象表現主義の代表者達、ジャクソン・ポロック、巨匠マーク・

ロスコ、ロバート・マザーウェル、アーシル・ゴーキーなどは、秘密作戦において、正体不明の推進者達だけでなく慈善家達によっても、ソビエト連邦と中国に対抗する「知的」戦争を勝利に導くために後援された。なによりもまず、社会主義的リアリズムに代表されたイデオロギーを地に落とし、制限無用の「知的」自由をもってして、おおよそイデオロギー的には左寄りの作者達によって「も」生み出された、異なる自由な芸術を全世界に知らしめながら、コミュニケーション戦争に勝つ必要があった。作戦は地政学的だった。芸術そのもの、文化は、「アクション・ペインティング」の事例のように、また文学の事例でも、権力拡大のプログラムにおいて重要な役割を果たすことができた。その作戦には、ヨーロッパ、及び、欧州現地の左翼知識人達も含まれ、遥か昔の[…]ヨーロッパ伝統主義に「さえも」対抗する方法とされていた。それらの伝統主義は、僕達が話題にしている芸術においてと同様に、大いなる「表現の自由」に凌駕されたのだ。

　大規模な展覧会が複数開催された。アーティスト達は、アメリカ政府のプロパガンダの主要な源泉となったこの企画を押し進めるように、支援・鼓舞された。そして、このような全面的なサポートがある場合、人は疑問を抱くことを忘れ、波に乗り続ける。この作戦は非常に洗練されていたため、市場で国際的な成功を収め、現在も隆盛だ。あの連中が信じていた「自由」とは、まさしく君が言う通り、君の骨の髄までしゃぶる偽装された奴隷主義である。それが、ある意味では、今日の市場を確立した…プロパガンダの真の奴隷達はおそらく、社会主義的リアリズムの革命家-画家達よりもむしろ、あの楽観主義政治によってほぼ「陶酔状態にされた」アメリカ人達だった（今もなお、そうである）。

　絵画の制作方法だけを考慮に入れるのでは、絵画作品の内に真の自由はあり得ないし、既に記号を監禁・投獄した概念的枠組内に自由が常に囲われているのならば、自由について話すことなどできない。作品を超越しなくてはならないのだ。上記の芸術家達は、自らの作品を社会・政治的変革を促進するものとして考えたことは決してなく、むしろ、自身の伝説創造と成功の機会と捉えていたのであり、だからこそ、このような戦略を実行するのに最適だった。抽象主義と政治の間に繋がりがあるのだとすると、過去を振り返り、カジミール・マレーヴィチを再度読み直し、例えば、アフリカ系アメリカ人画家達を研究しなければならない。彼らは、抽象的で表現力豊かな絵画作品の中で、植民地主義や人種差別を扱っている…

　2015年のヴェネツィア・ビエンナーレでは、アルバニアの社会主義リアリズムの驚嘆すべき画家であるスピロ・クリスト[11] の絵画作品の複製も、僕は持ち込んだ。クリストを選んだのは、彼の絵を念頭に置いて《Recapitulation》[12] を書いたからでもあった。僕達のパビリオン展示の構想は、それを時空の中で移動させることだった。それは、'70年代のパビリオン、ヴェネツィアで発表された初のアルバニア館パビリオンを実現するという意味で、未来と今日の自由の欠如について語りかけるものにすることだった。全ての装置は当時のもので、僕の作品群はそれらの装置から始まり、我々のグローバルな未来を読み取るための様々な手段を提供することを目的としていた。インスタレーションは、まさしく、経済

---

11 スピロ・クリスト（Spiro Kristo, 1936–2011）はアルバニアの重要な画家であり、とりわけ社会主義リアリズムの時代にその名を馳せた。彼の作品は、2017年の国際美術展ドクメンタ14（サテライト会場：アテネ、ドイツ会場：カッセル）で展示された。

12 前述の脚注6を参照。

交流、 不平等、 テロリズム、 政府のプロパガンダ、 立法と監視状況、 金融投機、 主権、 国家などに的を絞っていた。

　壮大なイデオロギーの数々の終焉と共に、 クリストはもはや時流に乗ることができなかった。 僕がパビリオン設営のための調査を行っていた際に、 彼が1990年以降に制作した全作品に目を通した。 それらは貧弱で、 極めてこじつけがましいものだった。 社会主義リアリズム時代の多くの偉大なアルバニア人芸術家達のように、 彼も自らを喪失してしまった。 己の作品の制御不能に陥り、 作品はいかなるイデオロギーにも基づいていなかった。 彼は具象を超えようとしたが、 具象こそが彼の得意とするものであった。 彼は抽象的になることを目指し、 言わば「自由」を感じとろうとして、 政治的概念とは無縁の何かを生み出そうとした。 彼の新たな作品は、 開放的というよりも閉鎖的で、 彼を制御し解放することはなかった。 この「イデオロギー効果」は、 彼だけに関するものではなかった。 アルバニア社会主義時代の偉大な画家達は、 抽象的な作風になり、 ほぼ全員が失敗に終わった。 今、あの年代の政治・経済・社会的コンテクストを分析することで、これらの画家達が突如としてスタイルを変え、 模倣し、 表現主義者や抽象主義者になってしまった動機の容認が可能になる。 これは、 失敗に終わった政治的行為だとしても、 間違いなく政治的行為として見做されなければならない。

　引き続き、 美学と政治について。 2000年代のアルバニア芸術は、 断絶の芸術と見做され、 大きな関心を呼び起こした。 アルバニアの美学の問題について詳しく論じてほしい。 例を挙げてみよう。 アンリ・サラの《Dammi i colori(絵の具をくれたまえ)》[13]。アート界では、実際のところ、万人が見たビデオ作品だ。顕著に有名なビデオであり、その名声の多くは、扱われている主題(退屈極まりない塗装された建造物群)だけでなく、正確な美学にも負うところが大きかった。フレーミングは、ほぼ常に機能する。低解像度、アームカメラ、洗練されてはいないものの「現代的」な画…要するに、視覚的に機能するビデオ作品である。それは審美的に機能するのだ。塗装された建物群の発想と同様に、その美学で多くの人を感服させたビデオ。だが、2000年代初頭のアルバニア芸術の、このほぼロマン主義的なヴィジョンの背後には、実際には何があるのだ? エディ・ラマは、本当は何をしようとしていたのか? 何をし続けていたのか? アルバニア芸術は、どのように国際的フェスティバルや展覧会に輸出されてきたのか?

政権崩壊、1997年とバルカン諸国の戦争は、現在のナレーションの構築に必要なヒントを授けた。国内での現代美術の「虚構の」ナレーションであり、再検討されるべきものだ。

　周知の如く、現代美術、いやむしろ、現代のアートシーンでのアルバニアの存在というものは、2001年に発生した致命的な愚弄行為によって特徴付けられる。それは、第1回ティラナ・ビ

---

13 主に映画や音楽のインスタレーションに専念するアルバニアのアーティスト、アンリ・サラ(Anri Sala, 1974〜ティラナ出身)は、彫刻、写真、ドローイングを作成してきた。彼は首相エディ・ラマのパリ亡命時代の同士であった。ロンドンのテートモダンで展示された彼のビデオインスタレーション《Dammi i colori(絵の具をくれたまえ)》(2003年)は、20世紀から21世紀までのティラナの発展を反映している。

エンナーレ開催時に驚愕の方法で実行された[14]。 途轍もない、世界的なスキャンダルであり、 何年にも渡り反響を呼び続け、その後、 架空のアーティスト達そのものだけでなく、 多くの成り代わりの偽者を生み出した。 だが、 アルバニアでは、 もはや誰もそれについて語らないほど、 記憶の奥底に葬り去られた。 あまりに深く葬り去られたため、 初のティラナ・ビエンナーレは2003年開催、 即ち社会主義時代の建造物が派手な色で塗られた時だったと、 新世代の者達が考えるほどだった。 既に2003年の時点で、 デバティクセンターの当時のメンバーにとって、 この作戦は偽りの作戦に他ならなかった。 そのビエンナーレのサテライト・プロジェクトを通して、 僕達は、 マイクロクレジットの経済システムを分析する提言活動を実施したが、 さらに、 移民、 政治腐敗、 世界各地に普及しているビエンナーレの実践状況そのもの、 塗装された建造物群などのテーマも分析した。 それらの建物は上っ面を派手に塗り替えたところで、 内部/内面をいかなる手段でも変革することはできず、 即ち、 人民の精神に浸透し変革することはできなかった。 作り出された現実の外部知覚に、 ただ影響を与えることが一時的にできただけだった。 その現実は、 我々には小細工が弄されたように見えた。 それが真の愚弄行為であったのだ。 なぜなら、 死産で生まれ落ちたナレーションに、 命を吹き込もうとした

---

14 2001年ティラナ・ビエンナーレ開催時に、 偽のオリヴィエロ・トスカーニ（Oliviero Toscani: 実は全く別人のアーティストであるマルコ・ラヴァジェットMarco Lavagettoが扮していたと判明）がキュレーターとして承認されることにまんまと成功し、 根も葉もないでっち上げの架空のアーティスト4名を紹介した。 展覧会に、 彼らのものとされる作品と批評論考を送りつけ、 批評は雑誌「Flash Art」及び同展覧会のカタログ本書に掲載された。 本物のトスカーニが主催者を訴え、 事実を告発して初めて、 この愚弄行為の茶番劇が明らかになった。

からだ。2001年に起こったこととは全くの正反対だ。その時は、企みは悪ふざけであるがために生を受け、その悪戯が発覚した場合にのみ、生を謳歌することが可能だったのだから。この2番目の事案、真の愚弄行為は、僕の意見では、非常に重大であり、綿密に研究する必要がある。なぜなら、ある意味で、我々が経験している芸術及び政治の現在と未来を明らかにしたからだ。

　芸術の世界だけでなく、大多数のアーティスト達も、自身の頭上にシステムのスポットライトが灯るよう、戦争や天変地異のために祈りを捧げる。そして、ごっこ遊びが誰からともなく始まり、後に語られることの無邪気さと陳腐さが国家に言及するためのルールになる。反体制派だったことなどない反体制派や、先駆者とは何かを理解したこともない先駆者達、現象やらをでっち上げる。その次に、大惨事後に顕現する、イメージ母体の特性を備えたイメージを構築する。これは、他の複数のナラティヴ内部に楔のように押し入る能力を有し、ウィルスが根を張るが如く、そこに、歴史のアーカイブに、防護された固定位置に留まるためのイメージだ。君には回収が許可されないイメージが生成される。手の届かぬ所にあり、単体では発展できないイメージ。国力またはシステムの力が、（2001年にぶち放たれた事案の後に）衛星あるいは宇宙船を宇宙に打ち上げた、とする。「彼ら」は、宇宙船が軌道上を周回する間、情報収集する間には、船体を追跡することができるが、地上に帰還させることは望まない。なぜなら、彼らはデータの回収を決して望んでいないからだ。伝達されなかったそれらのデータは、その間ずっと集積され続け、衛星上にのみ存在する。宇宙船が帰還できないのならば、他の何者かが天空へ向かい、紛失されたもの、隠蔽されたままのものを回収し、 帰還する余力がある限りは地上に戻り、 単体でも発展可能な、 別のイメージを送信すべきである。

　抽象主義であれポップアートであれ、 いかなる形態も、 第二次世界大戦以降に生み出されたものや、 1997年のような1年の間に生み出されたものを全て蒸発させる力を持っているとは思わない。 色彩や「ポップカルチャー」に僕は魅了されているとしても: ここでは、 その大量拡散や惑星規模での成功、 その美的次元、 または、 特定の意図的な精神的怠慢に関する構成要素を批判したいのではなく、 厳密には、 あらゆる種類の深遠なる思考を回避しようとする(未だに)生み出された精神性について論評したい。 これゆえに、 ポップアートは重要なのだが、 ポップに付け足して、 ポップを欺こうとすると、 ポップは君に尻尾を出させる潜在能力がある。 ティラナの社会主義様式の建造物群は、 半抽象的な形状と鮮やかな色で彩られ、 このグローバル化された世界では完璧に機能するが、 今日の世界では「非力な」記号に過ぎない。 着色された建物の政治的企ては、 当初から勝利作戦として発表されたのだが、 実際は、 ある政治運動の基盤だった。 だが、 その運動は時代を生き残ることができなかった。 なぜなら、 具体的な提案を一つも歯切れよく論述できなかった腐敗したシステムの母体だったからだ。 この政治プロジェクトは、 色彩革命を起こすことを決して望んでいなかったが、 本当の「フェイク・ケース(Fake Case)」であることが証明された。

　大衆が(その内と外で)知覚した作戦の狙いは、 望まれていたものでは全くなかった。 なぜなら、 そのプロジェクトは、 前衛派あるいはシュプレマティズム実践者達の理想郷的概念に関連させた上での、 位置付け – 展開 – がなされなかったからだ。 それはむしろ、 ヨーゼフ・ボイスが訴えた類いの改革が急務とされ、 政治的パフォーマンスの倒錯手法での政治的プロパガンダとして利用されない改革がより火急とされていたその時に、 関係性の美学の概念的制約に一層結び付いたものだった。 首相は、 建造物に彩色した瞬間に想像するのをやめ、 自らのヌード写真がメディアに登場した瞬間に制作するのをやめた[15]。 これらの理由から、 アルバニア人及びコソボ人現代アーティスト達に捧げられた、 ブダペストでの最近の展覧会で、 僕は参加者全員に一つの作品を送った。 それは《La Rivoluzione siamo Noi(我々が革命だ)》と

---

15 2016年、 アルバニアのコメディアン俳優・司会者のエルマル・ママチ (Ermal Mamaqi)が、 テレビ番組「6 Dite Pa Ermalin(エルマルのいない6日間)」の放送中に、 エディ・ラマの裸の写真を当の本人の前で見せて、 検閲しないように懇願した。「2006年自治体選挙で初めてこの画像を目にした。 僕は、 たまたまティラナにいて、 当時、 汚職スキャンダルの中心であったシャアルゥ処分場でビデオを制作していた。 当時のティラナ市長だったラマは至る所に木を植え – 逆説的に – ヨーゼフ・ボイス(Joseph Beuys)のように振る舞いながら、 常にテレビに出演していた。 その写真は、 彼の性器を隠すための紫色/ピンク色の円形が施された状態で、 新聞やテレビに常時、 掲載・表示されていた。 アルバニア社会の有名なタブーを利用して、 民主党は選挙で敵を打破するためにその写真を使用していたが、 この目論見は完全に失敗に終わった。 この写真は格別に象徴的だ。 なぜなら第一に、 反乱(タブーを破る)の印として用いられた行為が、 この政府の腐敗(あるいは裸の王様)についての赤裸々な真実の証拠を具現化するようになったからである。 さらに、 2006年に彼の性器を隠すためにメディアによって使用されていた円形の色が、 今ではアルバニア社会党(Rilindja)がプロパガンダ目的で利用する色だからでもある。 真の芸術と腐敗政治との間に存在する大きな相違を人々が理解できるように、 僕はボイスの《La Rivoluzione siamo Noi (Die Revolution sind wir)》(1971年)からタイトルを拝借した。」アルマンド・ルラーイ(2016年)。

いう題名で、裸の首相の写真が印刷されたTシャツだった。もし、彼が今でも芸術家だと思っていたらTシャツを着用するように、あるいは、彼が「別人の」汚職政治家だと思ったらTシャツを額装するようにアーティスト全員に依頼した、僕の署名入りの文書を添えた。僕は、彼らが何をしたのか正確には知らないが、要するに、そのTシャツを着ている者は誰もいなかった。ストップ！大衆がラマを支持していたのは、当初これらの行いを信用していたためだ。僕にとって、2006年は全てが終結すべき時だった。それはまた、彼が政治から永久に引退するに相応しい時だったが、彼はそうしなかった。自らが着手し、練り上げた、その政治的アイディアの下層を、彼は掘り下げ続けた。それは、たった一つの目的のため：今や、彼の手に負えず制御不能となった腐敗を美化することだ。

　今日、アルバニアの「フェイク・ケース」は、それを自主的に分析する全ての人々、芸術家・知識人・学者・ジャーナリスト達によって精査されている。彼らは、政治構造にも国家に支援される機関にも縛られていない。この推論は全て、言うまでもなく、その始まりを、2001年を、葬り去られたあの過去を考えるようにと僕を誘導する。その過去は未来となり、フィルターをも形成した。そのフィルターを、このナレーションの一部となるためには、誰もが通過しなければならない。当初からずっと、僕の作品が、政治課題や政界人達、社会状勢を扱っていたこともあり、また、僕は、いかなる政党も、当然「彼らの」政党、現在の与党も支持していなかったという意味での僕の見地からも、部外者であることを選んだ。ある意味では始めから、僕は彼らのナラティヴから逸脱していたのだ。

ビデオ作品の字幕をどう思うか？ 英語圏以外の国のビデオは全て、外国の展覧会やフェスティバルに参加するために、常に英語で字幕が付けられている。 これらの翻訳を管理するのは誰なのか？ それらはどのくらい信頼性があるのか？ 翻訳プロセスにおいて検閲はあるか？

視覚的インパクトという意味において、僕はこれまでずっと字幕が好きだった。 字幕は分かりにくければ分かりにくいほど好ましい。 それらは別の表象の上に重なる記号である。 僕はインドやタイ映画の字幕を見るのが非常に好きで、英語の字幕はあまり見ない。 それらの言語を知らなくても、映像の上にこれらの不可解な記号を見るのが好きなのだ。

　僕の意見では、素材の英語への翻訳に関しては、アーティスト本人によって行われることが多く、必ずしもではないが、意図的に誤訳するという識別要素がある。 故意によるミスは僕を魅了してやまない。 なぜなら、ここにはナレーションを書いたり書き直したりする要素もあり、僕は非常に興味を持っている。 監督自身が字幕を意図的に推敲した、アルバニア映画やビデオアート作品を多く観てきた。 その監督達によれば、外国人の視聴者に、多くの場合、より流暢かつ完璧で真正な、別のナレーションを提供するためであり、観客を故意に混乱させるためではない。 もし仮に監督が隠蔽するために翻訳するとして、彼がそれを実行に移す時には、特定の目的を念頭に置いて意図的にそうするのであり、これは万人に隠すことができないものである。 これは実に憂慮すべき側面であり、作品ではなくむしろアーティストについて語ることである。 我々が扱っている素材に大きく左右されるのだとしても、アーティストにとっての問題は、別の形で生じることも言っておかなけ

れ ば な ら な い 。 アー ティ ス ト は 固 定 さ れ た 実 体 で は な く 、 柔 軟 で 可 動 で あ り 、 往 々 に し て 、 自 ら の 真 実 を 無 限 に 編 集 し た い 思 い に 駆 ら れ る か ら だ 。 彼 は 自 ら が 発 し た 言 葉 、 ま た 他 者 の 言 葉 を も 翻 訳 で 変 更 で き る 。 実 際 の も の と は 異 な る バー ジョ ン 、 言 う な れ ば 詩 的 な バー ジョ ン を 用 い て[...]、 映 像 を 切 り 取 り 編 集 す る の と 同 じ 方 法 で 、 別 の 形 に 翻 訳 す る こ と が 可 能 だ 。 アー ティ ス ト は 常 に 動 き 続 け 、 監 督 の よ う に 不 動 で は な く 、 常 に 何 ら か の 意 味 や 個 人 的 な 音 を 見 出 そ う と し て い る 。 ビ デ オ アー ティ ス ト は イ メー ジ 言 語 の 学 者 で あ り 、 度 々 、 話 し 言 葉 を「尊 重」し な い 。 そ う す る こ と で 彼 は 真 実 を 検 閲 す る が 、 彼 の 創 造 的 な 純 真 さ に お い て は 、 彼 が 別 の 真 実 を 作 り 出 し て い な い と は 誰 も 言 え な い だ ろ う 。 アー ティ ス ト は 全 て を 同 じ レ ベ ル に 据 え る 。 登 場 人 物 、 読 み 上 げ ら れ た テ ク ス ト 、 ド キュ メ ン ト さ え も 。 一 つ 確 か な こ と が あ る： 彼 が わ ざ と 真 実 を 操 作 す る 時 、 特 に 真 実 を 隠 す た め に 手 を 加 え る 時 に は 、 い つ で も 分 かっ て し ま う の だ 。 僕 が ひ と き わ 愛 着 を 持 つ 人 物 像 、 監 督 は 、 特 に ド キュ メ ン タ リー の 場 合 、 映 画 素 材 の 現 実 を 操 作(ま た は「翻 訳」)す る こ と の 意 味 を よ く 知っ て い る 。

　翻 訳 は 非 常 に 複 雑 な 芸 術 で あ る 。 コ ン マ 一 つ を 変 更 す る と 、 文 全 体 、 文 の 全 て の 意 味 が 変 更 さ れ る 。 僕 の 作 品 を 翻 訳 し て も ら う 際 に は 、 僕 は 非 常 に 慎 重 に な る 。 そ れ ら が 完 璧 で 正 確 で な い 場 合 は 発 表 し な い 。 僕 も 古 い ビ デ オ 作 品 で 、 そ の よ う な「過 ち」を 犯 し た と 言 わ な け れ ば な ら な い の だ が 。 と り わ け2007 年 に 、 政 治 経 済 学 の テ ク ス ト 、 カー ル ・マ ル ク ス の『資 本 論』を 僕 達 が 翻 訳 し よ う と 試 み た 時 の こ と だ 。 そ の 翻 訳 は 、 英 語 の 知 識 が 十 分 に な い 者 に よっ て 訳 さ れ 、 惨 憺 た る も の だ 。 だ が し か し ビ デ オ の 出 演 者 が 読 み 上 げ る 内 容 も 負 け ず 劣 ら ず 大 惨 事 だ 。 そ の 登 場 人 物 は 、 屠 殺 さ れ て い る 動 物 の 血 で 本 を 洗 い な が ら 、

『資本論』のそこかしこから拾った文や単語、 一節を選び出す。 最終的には、 筋を追うのが非常に困難な、 しばしば無意味なスピーチを生み出している。 この作品を《Passion》（2007年）と名付けたが、 もう二度と編集しなかったという意味で、 その作品に触れることはなかった。 この作品を読み解くための仕掛けともなるように、 僕は間違いを残しておいた。

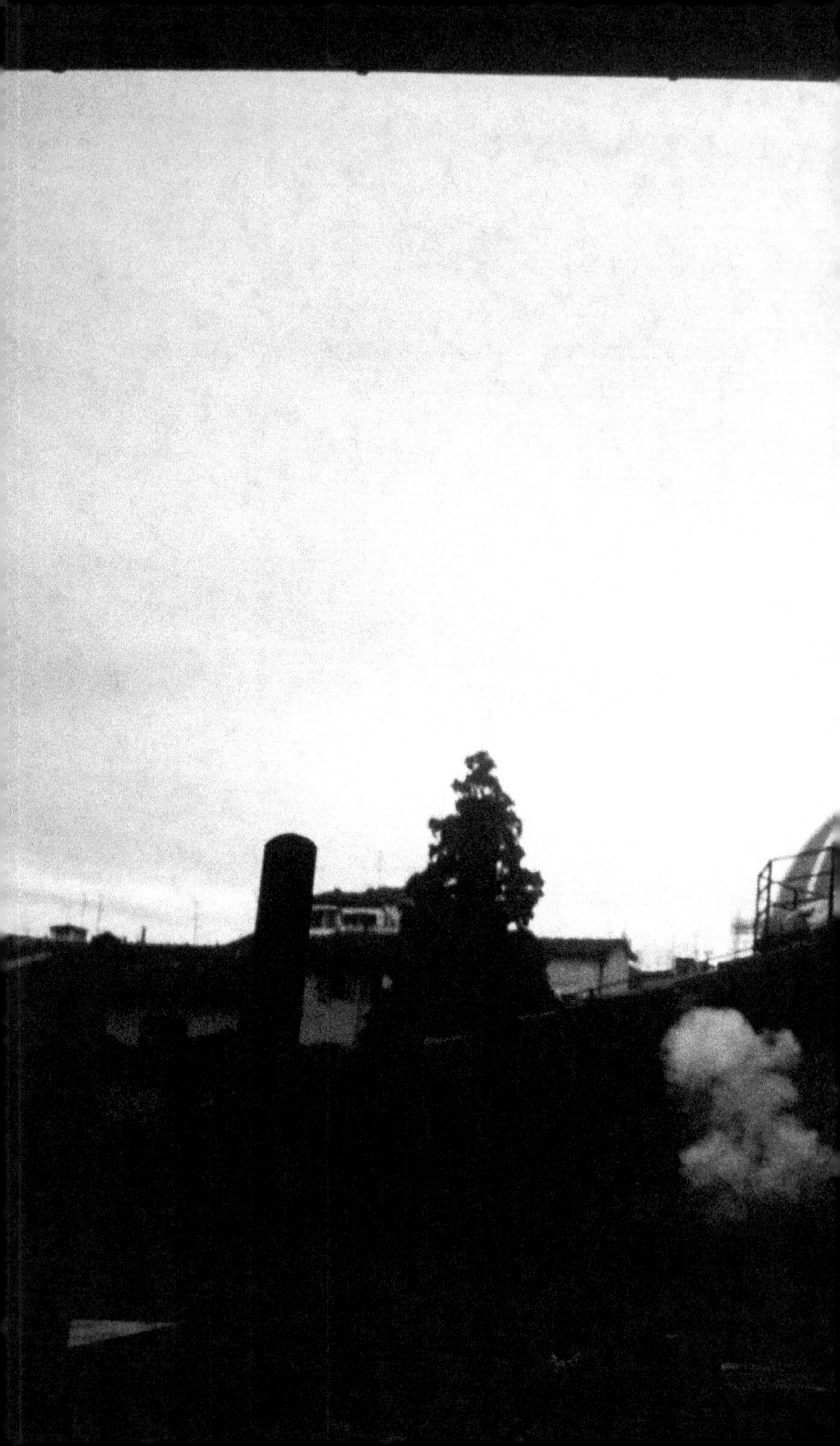

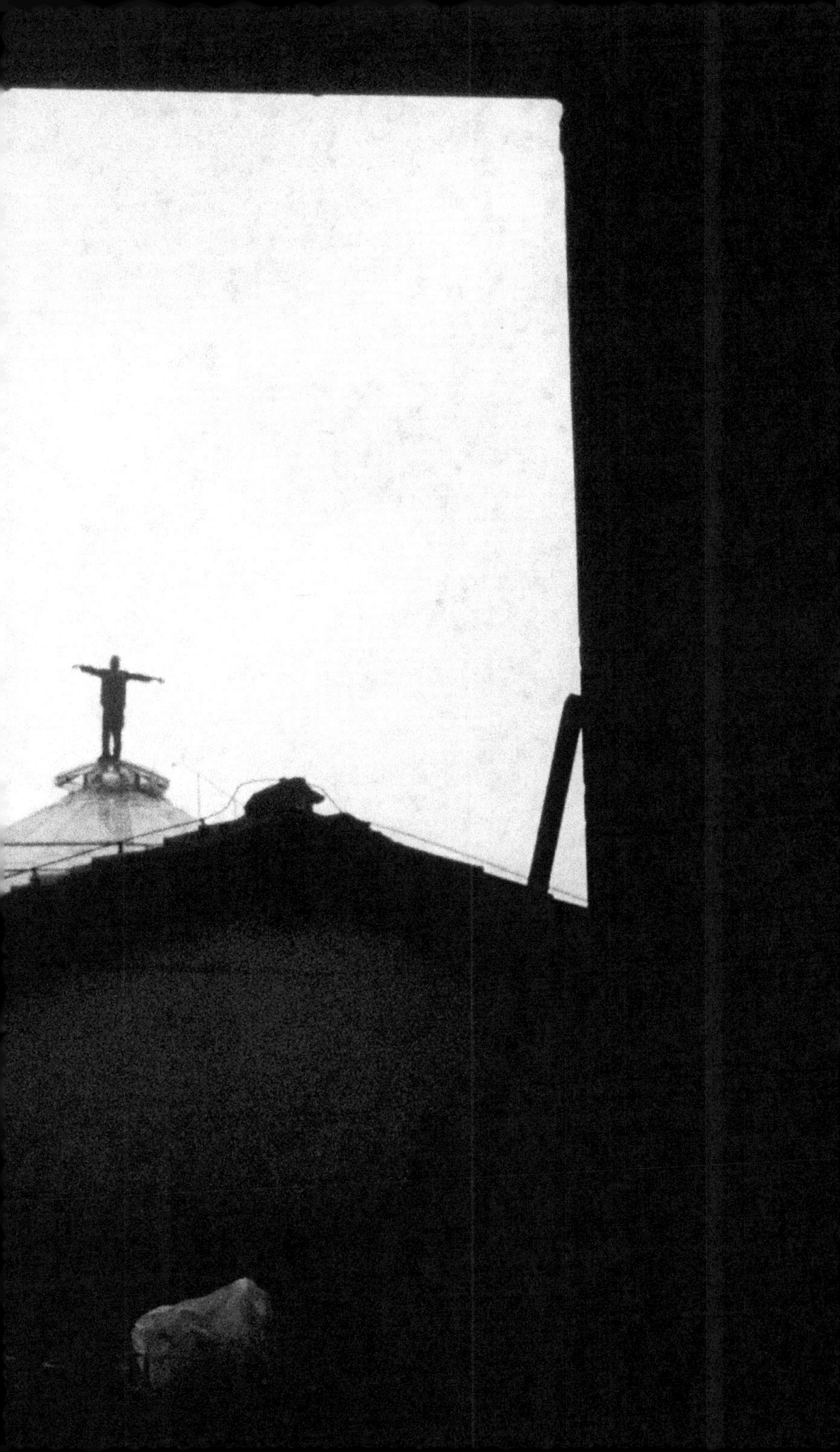

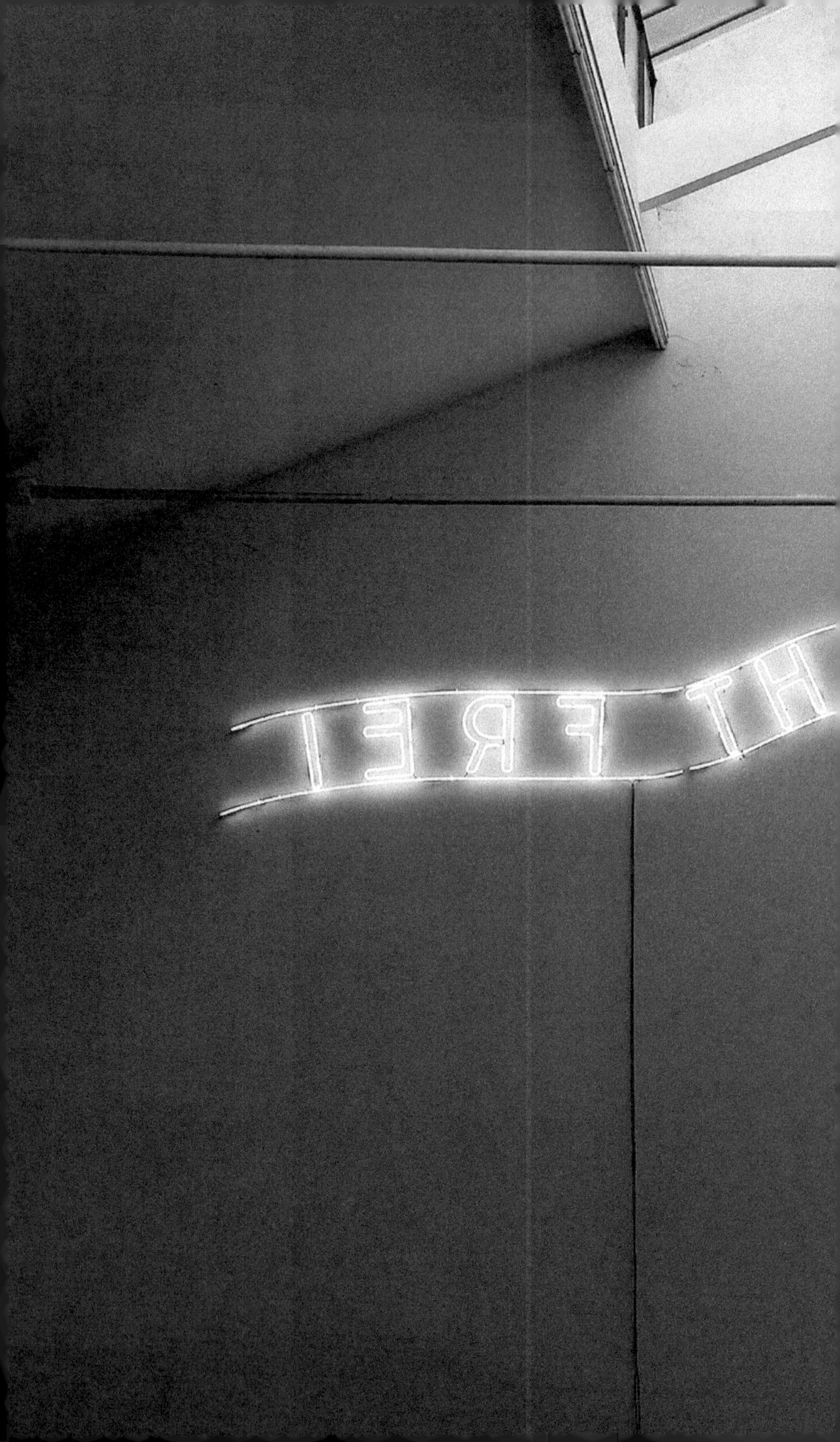

ARBEIT M

BULLE

AR

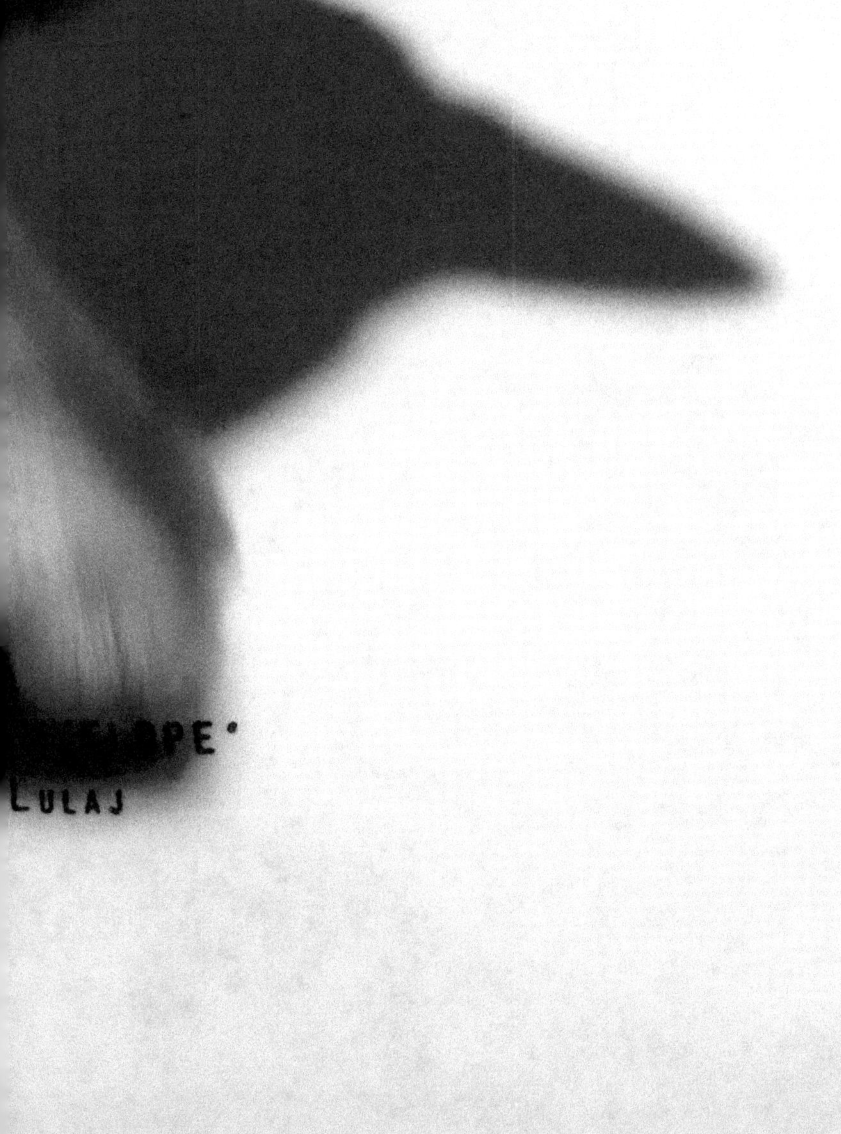
PE'
LULAJ

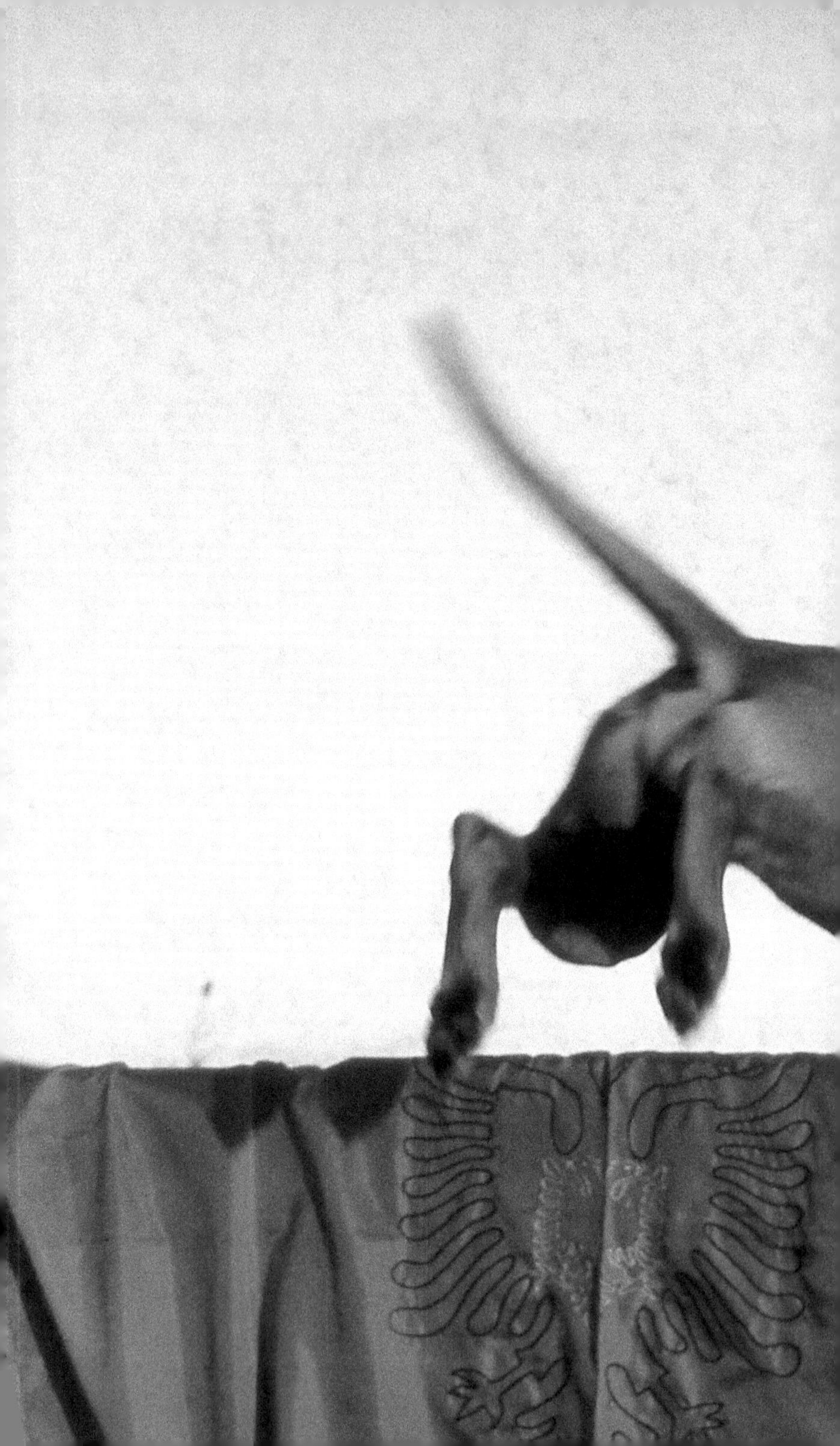

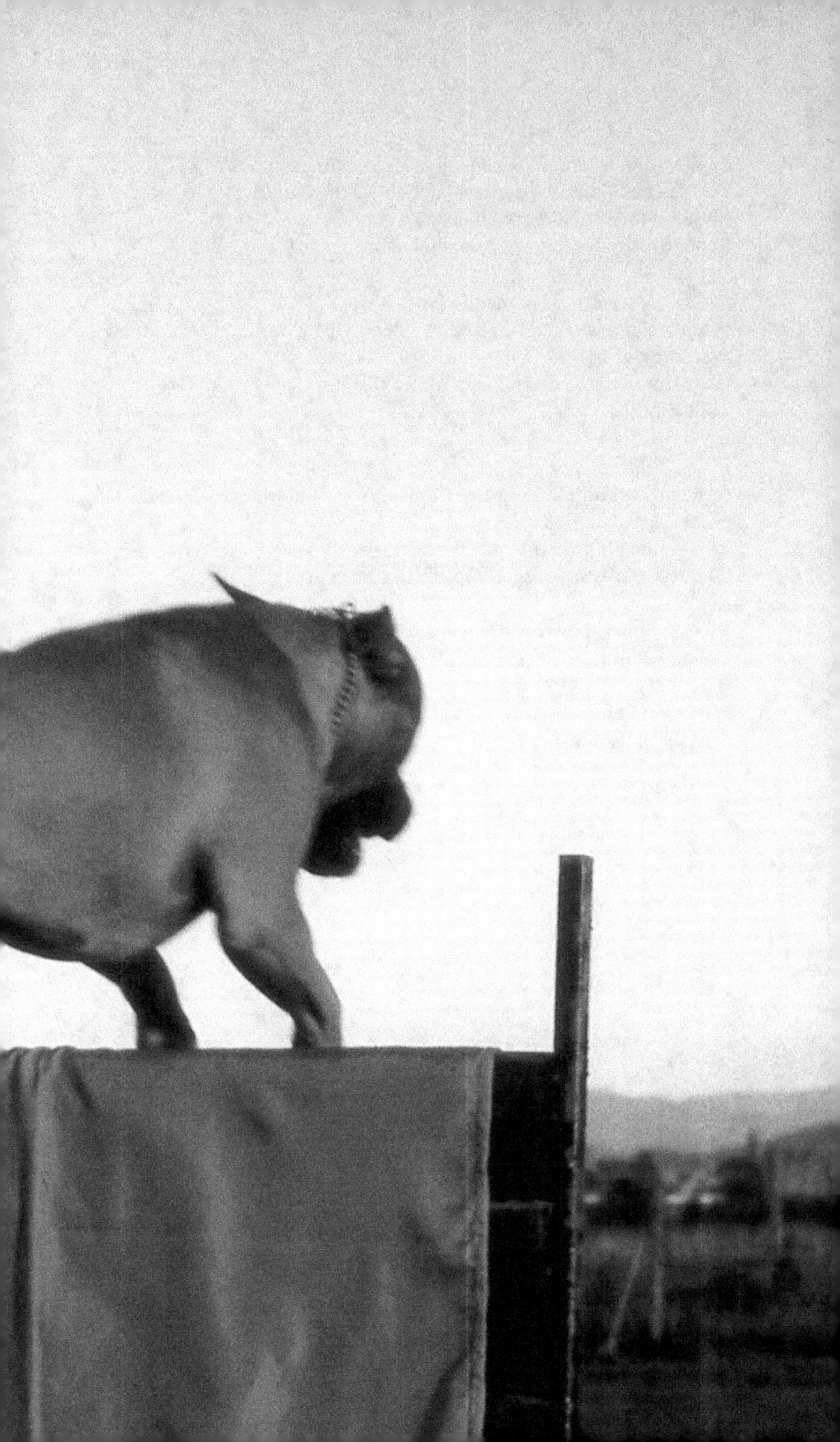

Fig. 21. Walking Free in Harmony by Armando Lulaj, 2001.
Documentation of the performance above the Gallery of Academy
Museum's roofs. Florence January 23, 2001.
Photo by Salvator Qitaj. Armando Lulaj's personal archive.

Fig. 22. UNTITLED, by Armando Lulaj, 2010.
White neon. Installation at Artra Gallery, Milan, during the solo show
NO MERCY, 2011.
Courtesy ARTRA Gallery, Paolo Maria Deanesi Gallery. AGI Verona
Collection.

Fig. 23. Bullet in an Envelope, by Armando Lulaj, 2018.
Installation. Work in Progress. Courtesy DebatikCenter of Contem-
porary Art.
Production photo by Pleurad Xhafa.
Courtesy of DebatikCenter of Contemporary Art.

Fig. 24. POWERSHIFT CIA, by Armando Lulaj, 2001.
Documentation of performance at the Amerigo Vespucci Airport
(Florence).
Production photo by Salvator Qitaj.
Private Collection.

TRACK 05

CONTROL.[1] *In February of 2019 I came to Tirana to photograph one of your works. It was a part of* CONTROL. *I was especially struck by the almost theatrical impact of the scene, alongside the powerful visual component. I found a certain lyricism in the work, as if the representation of death and decapitation was shown through a dramatic filter, where there was not only the physical death of the five figures decapitated and hung on the coffin, but also the complete death of metaphysics. It made me think of Rodin while I was taking the pictures. Or rather, of a "reversed" Rodin, expressed "the other way round," in the opposite way. While I was taking the photos I tried to shoot the scene as though I was once again shooting the sculptures of Rodin that I photographed many years ago in Paris, in 2000.* CONTROL *is a work intimately connected to landscape, meaning that it seems to speak about something that's in the air, something surrounding us in the landscape. What are the signs of "control"—media, psychological, political, religious, sexual, etc.—present on Albanian territory and in the landscape? What can be understood when we try to interpret the Albanian landscape? What can be felt about "control" and "domination" by reading the landscape, "inside" the landscape?*

---

1   Armando Lulaj, CONTROL (2018), *DebatikCenter,* https://debatikcenter.net/strikes/control; David Kampi, CONTROL (2019), *DebatikCenter,* https://debatikcenter.net/strikes/control2.

CONTROL is a work made up of two parts. The first part is a digital video lasting 35 minutes and the second part is composed of sixty photos taken in 6×7 medium format. In both parts of the work the framing, the camera, and the video camera are in steady-stare surveillance, meaning in fixed position. In the first part the walk-ons pass in front of a giant advertising billboard very similar to a movie screen. The milk-white screen is next to one of the most congested highways in Albania. But it's not the only one: there are hundreds of empty billboards along this highway, and the same goes for every other main road in the country. It's almost like the project of an artist who'd imagined them just so as to leave them empty. While the rest of the landscape seems to have been tainted by reality, these surfaces, taken together, create spatial extensions that offer the possibility to look beyond it. They are like black holes frozen in time. While doing background research for this work, for the conceptual heart of the project, we were always looking for invisible images present in the landscape. Data from information black holes, from the dark net, extracts of documents taken from Wikileaks, images that had escaped the monitoring of the Facebook offices in Manila, but also information about the secret government and army maps of unknown territories.

This sort of information is always hard to dig up. It is part of a vast archive that is increasingly difficult to access, which is rather like the holy grail for anyone interested in archives, the ultimate prize in a never-ending treasure hunt. Traces of these images, made up of data hidden to the naked eye, are always present in the landscape, in the landscape that is watching us, and to dig them out you have to adopt the same technological tools and systems used by the power structure.

For *CONTROL* the means at our disposal were the most basic imaginable, really primitive if we compare them to the instruments referred to above. Starting out from what we had on hand, in the end we produced something very different from what we'd imagined, even if the aim of deciphering the landscape was and is still present. While we were working on writing the subtext we were thinking of John Nada's glasses,[2] but the only subliminal message that emerged from that screen-billboard were the stupendous images of Fabio Mauri's *The End*, which are also a departure point for something different. So for the second part of the project we produced an image using a violent picture, a topical, very medieval image that had crept in from a recent story I couldn't get out of my mind — in fact, it had been hanging in my bedroom for over a year.

Before starting to shoot the first part of CONTROL we carried out some inspections. The billboard is located in the vicinity of a small town called Vorë, which is approximately ten kilometers outside of Tirana. The screen is placed to the northwest and covers — or better hides — the part of the landscape leading to the village of Gërdec, which is about two kilometers from the screen as the crow flies. As was mentioned before, in 2008 there was an explosion at a weapons and munitions depot there, which resulted in twenty-six fatalities. Afterward, a considerable portion of the weapons that were still in good condition were sold in global conflict zones by various Albanian and American contractors. The main explosion in Gërdec involved over 400 tons of propellant that were being stored in containers, and it destroyed hundreds of houses within a radius of several kilometers, as well as breaking the windows of cars passing on the highway where we are now. This is just some of the information offered by the landscape, enclosed in the trap that forms the scene. We didn't approach the scene with the intention of analyzing the crime, either the one already committed in the past or the one we had committed during the research we did in the days before filming. Instead, we wanted to restage another, parallel crime — to be honest not only one but more than one, and more than once. In fact, the concomitant duration of the

---

2   John Nada, played by the actor Roddy Piper, is the protagonist of *They Live*, a 1988 cult science fiction thriller directed by John Carpenter, which is about an unemployed factory worker in Los Angeles who by chance comes into possession of a pair of black glasses, thanks to which he discovers that many human beings are in reality extra-terrestrials trying to control earthlings through subliminal messages.

scene makes a definitive narrative impossible, producing more than one.

In the first part of the work, the camera stands by the roadside and faces the screen, i.e., the billboard, diagonally. (The screen-billboard is also visible in the series of photographs we realized for the second part of CONTROL, albeit from a distance.) The space between the camera and the screen is divided by the highway, where vehicles are driving by at top speed in both directions. The control exercised by the camera and the act of snapping my fingers, which I do every time a walk-on passes in front of the camera or the screen, is control aimed at the uncontrollable aspect of reality. In a certain sense, the resulting video is a chain reaction produced by the screen for the screen, and not by me and my camera. It's as though the flow of reality produced by the screen also controls the direction of the walk-ons and then also controls my reflex reaction in its attempt to immortalize an invisible and empty historical moment, thus penetrating this dying political landscape.

The second part of CONTROL is very different because it is an unveiled scene, a break, a violent intrusion, but also a failed act. After analyzing all the components of the scene, David Kampi[3] and I decided to add yet another force to the forces that control the landscape. We wanted to identify the invisible, the truthfulness of the invisible, in order to amplify the significance of this political landscape and then disappear, hiding our traces and leaving everything to go on as before.

At times I feel like an intruder in the scene and my aim is to hide this intrusion as much as possible. I'd like to amplify the click of the camera shutter of the photographer who enters the scene, magnify it as much as possible, while pretending to hide all traces of the act.

Like all social and political life in this country, I think that the landscape itself is situated halfway between the society of discipline and the society of control. This halfway position has enabled the emergence of some of the interesting phenomena

---

3   David Kampi is a ficticious Albanian artist.

that my work is generally based on. This is a landscape in constant transformation, more and more so thanks to — mainly but not only — the corrupt plans and projects of those in power, which are in continual evolution (meaning involution). What I want to say is that in this land, in a geographical area that isn't enormous after all, the landscape can be perceived in the most varied ways imaginable, often as a landscape that has been brutally violated, occupied, controlled, privatized, fenced in and constrained, concealed, falsified again and again, deserted and abandoned. Yet, and this is the most interesting thing, in the end it is still possible to see a "free landscape."

To return to your question, the corrupt architecture and urbanization resulting from the individual proposals of the so-call oligarchs form an important pilaster for the future of the country. These obscene proposals get the green light directly from the parallel state of the Prime Minister and his government. If you examine these proposals you realize that they don't take people into account anymore. The architecture produced in this overall context, and I'm referring here to the legislation and architecture produced by the state, by the power structure, doesn't need the collective or the idea of a project for an inclusive society. On the contrary, it is only interested in how to neutralize the collective.

Collectiveness has become *Collectivemess.*

In this landscape, or better in the midst of these landscapes, it is still possible to encounter a certain resistance however, chiefly in the form of wasted energy combined with fragments of power always trying to go further. I'm referring here to the informal constructions erected immediately after the fall of the communist regime. This sort of building reveals another aspect of capital in its continual evolution parallel to the state over the last thirty or so years. The buildings I'm talking about embody something very different. In the totality that contains this form of potential resistance, of creative resistance, there is the primitivism, the radicalism, the surrealism, and the idea of revolution that everyone en masse wants to uproot. These buildings have not been designed by architects, but by the inhabitants themselves, who come from the country's outlying areas. This is how things generally went: first the land was occupied or bought, then (often) the paperwork was falsified, the land was resold and rebought, then it was registered with the authorities and then, *if* legalized, it was (also) legalized illegally. Within this absurd platform of power these almost free structures have sprouted: surreal, unfinished dwellings that are undergoing a never-ending process of construction and transformation. Inside these buildings, the doors open onto the void and the windows look onto walls; they cannot be used to illuminate or ventilate the building — not the existing one anyway but perhaps a structure we have yet to see, one that will come later; they have staircases that look wrong because because they lead nowhere, are often upside-down, possibly because of a mistake in the construction... that makes them seem built for a species that walks head-down. There are over ninety-thousand such buildings all over the country, which have the marks of future plans but so far only show their shadow. What interests me more than their form or construction details is to follow the phantasmagoric outlines of buildings that — for the time being — we can only imagine.

Again, the control and realism of the image. When we photographed CONTROL *we discussed the frame at length, and it seemed to me that you wanted to create a very fine balance between forms and landscape. It seemed to be a "final" and "terminal" image, like the last frame of a historical or epic film. It wasn't an easy image to create, even if it was very direct. I know that this work started out from a real image, namely from bodies really decapitated, which you then reworked with David Kampi in the second part. Who did the decapitated bodies in the photo belong to? Why did you choose that photo?*

My collaborators know my way of producing, let's say, an image, but they in turn interpret it in their own characteristic ways, which I know well and want to add to the work. I describe the scene, my ideas about how I think it should be in the end, and what I really want to capture. I never provide support for getting there or how to get there, because I often don't know myself. Only a few fixed codes, overall harmony, and a lot of suggestions. Just as my work is influenced by the power structure or by something ineffable — in this case, nature, the landscape, and reality itself, which I can't control because it is unpredictable, in the same way I try to work with my collaborators to create these traps. What happens in some cases, for very few seconds, is often unimaginable: it is the uncontrollable reality, both hidden and revealed, that can only be seen by paying careful attention. While it's still true that I'm interested in seeing things in different ways, seeing things from two or more points of view simultaneously, to control the uncontrollable is the purpose, the intent, and ultimately the goal of my work.

I clearly remember my first time watching a horror film. This was in the mid-eighties, when every weekend one of the main Yugoslav TV channels would broadcast a vampire film. At the time we lived on the first floor of a socialist-style prefab. I remember that I was sitting in a wine-red armchair with gold decorations in the living room of our flat. The television was in front of me on a very tall, modern piece of furniture made of black wood and glass. To my right was the hallway leading to the bathroom, the bedroom, and then to the front door. My parents were sitting with me in the room, too. I don't remember the title of that film and I've never found it since, but I can clearly remember that while I was watching the bloodcurdling images on the screen my thoughts were always focused on the front door, because it was the only way out of the flat. But I couldn't get up because I was afraid that some invisible external force might come in through that door. I found myself frozen in the middle, in the main room, between the bloody images of the film and those unknown powers. The greater terror was obviously that of the powers that could come in through the front door, so I kept on watching the film, even if I shut my eyes to the most gruesome images.

The reaction to terrifying images has always interested me, and the horror films of the past can still set off this reaction. I think a film like *Nosferatu* is a work of genius. In it, Friedrich Wilhelm Murnau performed an exceptional experiment, showing a naked image. To achieve the maximum effect, in one scene of the film he used the negative of the frame instead of the positive. And, as the saying goes, *the bigger the lie the more they believe.* Other auteurs, like Pier Paolo Pasolini and Michael Haneke, have succeeded intelligently in this difficult undertaking, producing images that make the public react, activate them, nail them to their seats and force them to focus on the image, the screen. This is just what interests me, since I'm not interested in the powerless spectator — on the contrary.

Today we're surrounded by the violence of images, products of what is called necro-capitalism. We're surrounded by raw images like the decapitations of Daesh, the "poetic" and theatrical productions of Mexican criminal gangs like the Los Zetas syndicate, which forcefully remind us of Goya and Géricault, as well as of Francis Bacon. Rapes and mass murders infiltrate our computers or are freely broadcast on air (at times integrally on television networks) along with other images produced by capitalism, which we observe without analyzing or rejecting, and which are also violent because they tacitly influence our minds and so in a certain sense format us.

For some time now I've been working on creating an archive. This vast research project has been growing over the years. It is comprised of very powerful images, but it has a purpose: to find the *perfect* image, comparable only to the image of the body of the lifeless poet. The image (or images) I'm talking about isn't a sublime icon from the past. Instead, it is an image of the present, at once simpler and more complicated, and it contains the flaws of modernity. It may be that this image doesn't yet exist, and that's why I try to *create* it, and why a lot of the space in my hard drive is occupied by these raw, increasingly heightened images that come from all over the world and are like pieces of a totality that has not taken shape yet. It remains a missing image, which can't be created like Brook's burnt butterfly.[4] Nor would it accept being created only as a false image, like the one made by the photographer in the famous scene from Jean Genet's *The Balcony*.[5] It has to be a composition achieved by emptying out the whole of all these different forces.

The image used for the second part of CONTROL was shot in 2013 in the town of Jizan in southwest Saudi Arabia. As seen in the stingy information provided by the press, the bodies pictured are of five Yemenites tried for theft and murder, crimes punishable by death according to Sharia Law. Their heads were cut off with a sword, stuffed into plastic bags along with their bodies, then tied by a rope to a beam supported by two cranes in the square in front of Jizan University while the students were taking an exam. The photos of the scene were published by the Saudi Press Agency and retweeted by a lot of people on Twitter, so that those photos, many in low resolution but still very powerful, travelled all around the world. I could discover nothing else about the trial of those five people.

Even though the work is finished, the questions I ask myself are the same. What needs are satisfied by this picture that I kept in my bedroom for over a year? Can this picture reflect and demonstrate the deplorable state of our civilization? Why has this picture become a trap and why did I want to put this form inside another form like the cinema? If images are produced by our reality, why do we have to censor them from the general public, and why was this image shared, why did it escape control while others didn't and don't? Can this image be the final product of power, of religion, of politics? Is it the final monologue of the strength of power, or maybe just a self-portrait? Why do those suspended bodies remind me of the body of a poet?

---

4   Director Peter Brook (b. 1925), at the end of US, a theater piece on the Vietnam War written with Denis Cannan and staged in London in 1966, had the actors burn a butterfly, which was in fact fake but which the public was meant to think was real.

5   *The Balcony* is a two-act play written by Jean Genet in 1956 and performed in 1960. It reveals the perversions of those in power. Among the characters there are three photographers, called Blood, Sweat, and Sperm.

> *What is your reaction to and your position about the "political"
> use of punishment, from prison to the death penalty? Another
> thing — I'd like you to propose an interpretation of the "politi-
> cal" use of homicide. Is it possible to think of a relationship
> between the progressive changes in the languages of contempo-
> rary art — not only in Albania — and the use of capital punish-
> ment as a "political strategy"? Is there a relationship, and if so
> what, between the museum and the gallows?*

Here in the waiting room of Tirana's Penitentiary 313, while I'm
trying to answer this question, I can hear the soundtrack improvised by Miles Davis for the film *Ascenseur pour l'échafaud*
in the café next door. The title of the film suggests a very powerful image for me. The trap… the empty gallows… the difficult
upward motion… no descent… blocked… blocked inside the
suffocating mechanical elevator of justice… the state… political
power… the act accomplished…

Da capo. The repetition… no escape route inside the narrative…

In this elevator of history, what comes to mind is one of the
cruelest images of those years — the image, which chills my
blood even now. I could call it the image of one of the most bru-
tal stories of racist murder ever committed, a case that has been
reopened, an image I can't bear to look at for long. It is the open
coffin of Emmett Till.[6] The coffin of Emmett Till in the Museum.

Some time ago, a member of an association active against
the death penalty spoke to me about a video game circulating among law students, mainly in the United States but also
in impenetrable countries like China and some Middle Eastern
states. In this game, emblematic historical cases that ended with
a death sentence were re-opened. From what I understood, it
was a very complicated educational game that gave the possibil-

---

6   Emmett Louis Till (1941–1955), an African American teenager native
to Chicago, was assassinated for reasons of racial hatred in the town of
Money, Mississippi. His mother demanded that his funeral be held with an
open coffin, to show the state in which the assassins had reduced her son.

ity to try out new strategies based on the penal codes of countries that have the death penalty. The aim was to put the thread of justice and the right to life into an invisible needle, and so to "save" the life of a victim who had been tried and executed by clicking on computer keys. In this very difficult legal trial the adversary was this program, which was almost impossible to beat: you were caught in a sort of vicious circle against the right hand of God, against a sentence already pronounced.

The spectacle of the death penalty is cruel, with various dramatic and theatrical techniques that have changed over time. Today we have lethal injections administered in the chamber of the end. The invisible plexiglas filter is a screen separating the death chamber from the spectator who is a witness to the act, but also a witness to himself as representative of the state, to cite Jacques Derrida. Even though in our day there are still people who support these verdicts, the number of executions is far lower than in the past. Kumi Naidoo comments as follows on the statistics on the death penalty for the year 2018, "The dramatic global fall in executions proves that even the most unlikely countries are starting to change their ways and realize the death penalty is not the answer."[7] As for me, I am against it and think that a life sentence should be the maximum penalty imposed for any crime.

The question of capital punishment is very complicated and to get a clear idea of it you have to keep in mind history and all its atrocities. I grew up under a dictatorship where the death penalty was part of the legal system. My grandfather was a judge in those years. The communist show trials, better known as "people's trials" or "special trials," were the most important though not the only legal proceedings that resulted in the death penalty in the majority of cases. The charges in these political trials were by and large trumped up by the state and the accused had no defense to speak of. The state evidence and the confessions

---

7   Kumi Naidoo (b. 1965) is a South African activist, formerly Executive Director of Greenpeace, and currently Secretary General of Amnesty International.

of the victims (already below ground while still alive) were extorted under torture and by threats. The most interesting thing is that those trials were often held in movie theaters. It was a performance carried out right against the white cinema screen, in which everyone involved became part of a movie with a foregone conclusion that was known to all. The public was witness and jury at the same time and the entire state apparatus inside the movie theater made a very special, very Kafkaesque gallows.

Another important aspect of the past regarding the political use of those executions is that the persons responsible have never been tried themselves. The crimes of the past are condemned only as historical phenomena, but the people who took part in these trials are still alive (and I'm talking about ministers, public prosecutors, judges, and members of the secret police) and have never had to face a real trial. In a certain sense, history has been betrayed. A criminal pact among political forces in the nineties sanctioned this, and in a certain sense even amnestied the guilty parties, leaving all responsibility for the executions and atrocities to the distant past, to the ideological ghosts of the past, to the dead. Entire sectors of today's administration, up to and including important state officials and even judges, are filled with people who used to be part of the old system. This phenomenon has permanently damaged the credibility of the state and the people's faith in justice. As in most formerly socialist countries, the past has become readymade history. The museums recently opened by the government, dedicated to the crimes and atrocities of communism, are grand installations conceived by superficial artists. Inside there are only the names of the victims, but not the names of the persecutors, which are actually known to everyone. In this way the past is shoved even further back into the distance. These museums are merely oases of oblivion for Albanian society, or spaces for the occasional tourist. The very people who put the poets and dissidents of the past below ground are those who represent culture and the state today. The memory of these dissidents is nurtured as mere political propaganda. It's not found in school textbooks, on the contrary. In many elementary schools controlled by the executive, traces of this past that has not yet been properly examined are recalled by children who are thus being exploited both by the government and the educational system. In our day when everyone has lost faith in the state, nostalgia for the ideology of the past, for the force of law, for security and jobs, leaving all the atrocities of the regime and of its ideology hidden, is used by political forces merely as a way to gain more votes. The pact made in the early nineties, with international endorsement, has justified the executions of the past, and the dignity of the Albanian people has been buried with the trials that never took place. I've already mentioned my work *Powershift CIA* from 2001, which also talks about this, this change in the game, even if it has often been seen as being only about the wave of Albanians who migrated to Italy in the early nineties. It was exactly in those years that a large part of the archives of the Ministry of Internal Affairs and the secret police, which housed classified information about higher-ups in the state apparatus, were destroyed.

The dossiers that are being opened now, containing information about citizens and public figures of the past, are still being used to blackmail these people, as well as artists from those days who are still active and are critical of the government, those who express their dissent from the state's corrupt, destructive programs. The past is still under the domination of the authorities.

Because of the lack of independent art institutions, the figure of the artist is still represented through old(er) models. The artist must be an obedient individual, respectful of politics and politicians, beloved by foreigners and even resembling a foreigner, a supporter and member (understood as a condom on the phallus) of the party. If your art and your expression use other forms, like disobedience and rebellion, you are immediately labeled as a hooligan, a person to avoid. I've been called that more than once by an influential elderly artist whom "they" consider important for the(ir) country's contemporary image…. In my eyes this artist is, in fact, a false dissident who has made use of the same techniques of fabrication (of his life as a dissident) used by many "victims" of political persecution by the past regime that have falsified their stories. These individuals try to overshadow real dissidents like the poet Havzi Nela,[8] executed by the state in 1988. His death penalty was a political murder perpetrated by the state apparatus of the entire Albanian Labor Party, barring no one. The order was also signed by an important artist who was a supporter of the regime, Kristaq Rama, the father of today's Prime Minister. The body of the poet was buried vertically, feet down, to keep him from ever finding peace, in a hole made by removing a very tall electricity pole.

None of these problems from the past that are still very much part of our present are dealt with critically either by contemporary artists or by "responsible" curators. The paradox is that these protectors of the false dissidents condemn, for example, a work like *Bullet in Envelope,* while they haven't got the courage to face our past honestly.

I said before that we stole and copied our future and that elements of this future, which in a certain sense are not desired, are impossible to eliminate from the package. I think the strategy of political murder will take on very different valences in the future, but for now, when the state is collaborating with organized crime, which is becoming a decisive factor in the way the nation is changing, it remains exactly the same as ever.

By contrast, the political use of punishment is spreading. Dissidents and investigative journalists above all, the people who get in the way, are targets of intimidation and threats by this mix of *criminalpoliticalrenaissance.* Compared to the oppressive culture of the past, it's much easier today for the state to intimidate and suppress you by finding your weak points, incarcerating you and pushing you aside. The majority of the voices that should be critical, the so-called intellectuals, don't speak out or perform any sublime act; on the contrary, they sell themselves to the state. They cost less than a hunk of bread. In a climate like this, suicide and desertion are the only serious political acts to face up to the country's socio-political set-up. In this panorama,

---

8   Havzi Nela (1934–1988) was a dissident Albanian poet born in the village of Kollovoz in the district of Kukës and sentenced to death by the communist regime.

the armed ideological organizations I spoke about before don't yet exist, but their presence and development are like an ever-more visible specter.

For the *Moving Billboard* project, which we finished in 2018, we would have liked to invite Masao Adachi, too. What interests me personally in this historical-political figure is exactly this shadow I'm talking about, a shadow that is increasingly clear and that covers ideology, art, religion, politics, struggle — in a word, the traces of all of those things threatened with elimination in the social and political life of this small country of ours. I think it would have been interesting to have him here, first of all as an artist in the current panorama, but not only. We also wanted him because of his militancy as a historical member of the Japanese Red Army. We weren't able to have him here because the only possible agreement between us had to be based on collaboration free of other interests, but the aim was to start exploring the missing ground that I think has disappeared from the Albanian artistic landscape, and to throw light on other important presences in the land.

There is a group of Uighurs living in Albania who are former Guantánamo Bay prisoners. Having been captured by the Americans as suspected terrorists in the aftermath of the 9/11 attacks, they were detained for several years but had to be released eventually due to lack of evidence. Since they are considered terrorists by China, they can't ever return home, which is how they ended up being deported to Albania. In an inaccessible camp near Tirana, live a considerable and constantly growing number Mojahedin-e Khalq[9] members, a group that was classified as a terrorist organization until 2004 but no longer is, and so now they are protected persons under the Fourth Geneva Convention. However, for Iran and Iraq the MEK still constitutes a terrorist group. I feel that their presence in the country is very important for our artistic life. Recently, some members of the

---

9   Mojahedin-e Khalq is an Iranian political party founded in the 1960s, in determined opposition to the theocratic regime that has governed in Iran since 1979.

Mojahedin-e Khalq left the camp and are now considered terrorist deserters by the organization itself. They live and work in Albania under the surveillance of the Albanian and American secret services. Other examples of traces of the violence that is in the air are the Albanians who have gone to fight in Syria, or still others who are part of terrorist organizations like ISIS. The future museum is also being made up of these stories, which are generally ignored.

Each time I go into a museum I try to find something that proves me wrong, or that proves me right by proving me wrong. This mechanism is perfectly activated inside the structure, in the display inside the exhibition space, when you stand in front of a work. I'm not interested in speculating about the connections between the gallows and the museum. I'm more interested in finding different ways to excogitate strategies inherent to the logic of the system itself: to the oil refinery as museum even; to privatization; to the workings of the market; to surveillance in that space; to private security; to the workers who hang the artworks and those who do the cleaning; to the spectators, etc.; and, finally, in discovering how to empty it all out all and find ways to escape the constraints of that space.

The economy is the gallows of contemporary art. The system of art has stopped relating to life and now relates mainly to the economy, and the trade show is the space where all the system's currents flow together. I've done various projects concerning this subject, but I've also written up projects I've never done, often because they were impossible. One of them, which I included in *100 SPAMS* (2017–2018), consists of an army device that makes an incursion into an art fair, a robot like the ones used to remove bombs. The robot is to be guided so as to record, in a certain sense to control, the works in the booths, in the gallows of the market, the economy and politics, and it is also meant to serve as a filter through which to see the works on show.

Going back to the creation of the image I spoke about before, I can say that one example of the creation of this image, which is also potentially the most significant for contemporary art in this country, is the frozen but continually evolving image of the object on the façade of the Prime Minister's Office in Albania. Following the latest wave of protests in the country, the Société Spectrale is preparing to become a surveillance force in the background of the protest, to search for ghosts in these demonstrations, which are organized like marine earthquakes caused by weapons that shoot electromagnetic waves. The scene is set just as it should be. The police spread grease on the lamp poles where they've placed surveillance cameras and loud speakers that amplify the voice of state control. It's not possible to climb up and deactivate this voice, because you slide back down. Removing them to leave a hole as deep as a man is tall, right there in the middle of the Bulevardi "Dëshmorët e Kombit" (Martyrs of the Nation Boulevard) might be easier. The crowd takes aim at the Prime Minister's Office. One of the demonstrators picks up a shaft and hits the armored door of the palace of power. A safari in the Boulevard. A work of art has been targeted together with the building. By destroying it, they've brought it to life. Bits of it, ruins, remains of teargas bombs, cartridges, fragments of smoke bombs, and the plastic gloves of the scientific police are by now part of the archives of the Société Spectrale.

The other work of art I feel personally very involved in because of what it represented and still represents, is found on the façade of the building, above its massive front door. It's been packaged, protected, and armored by the state.[10] Packed as if it were in a container, it seems ready for an imminent journey to an art fair. A surveillance camera has been placed on the corner of the Prime Minister's Office to monitor the armored work, guarding it second by second. The reflection produced by this image is no longer opaque as it used to be, on the contrary. The object tells about the art market, the stock market, the militarization of museums, populism, and shoddy politics and ideologies. I think that the ghost produced by these protests is a clear image of the future of contemporary art that is being pro-

---

10 This is *Marquee Tirana*, 2015, by Philippe Parreno, installed by the Prime Minister on the façade of the Palace of Government to mark the entrance into the exhibition space on the ground floor of the building.

duced in real time. Exhibited like this, wrapped in a straitjacket on the façade of the palace of power, it looks completely naked. Attacked by the masses, it reveals its hidden truth. I see it as the single most potent image of contemporary art made in the last thirty years, the only real image this country has been able to produce. In my opinion, it represents a step forward in the development of contemporary art: a totally new image, present, but at the same time a final image. Powerful, armored, produced during the process of a show of force, it is an *Armored Breath,*[11] a readymade object, a witness. The armored breath of Tirana in May, 2019. The sultry breath of my fellow citizens.

---

11 Armando Lulaj, *Armored Breath,* 2019, available at *DebatikCenter,* https:// debatikcenter.net/strikes/armored_breath.

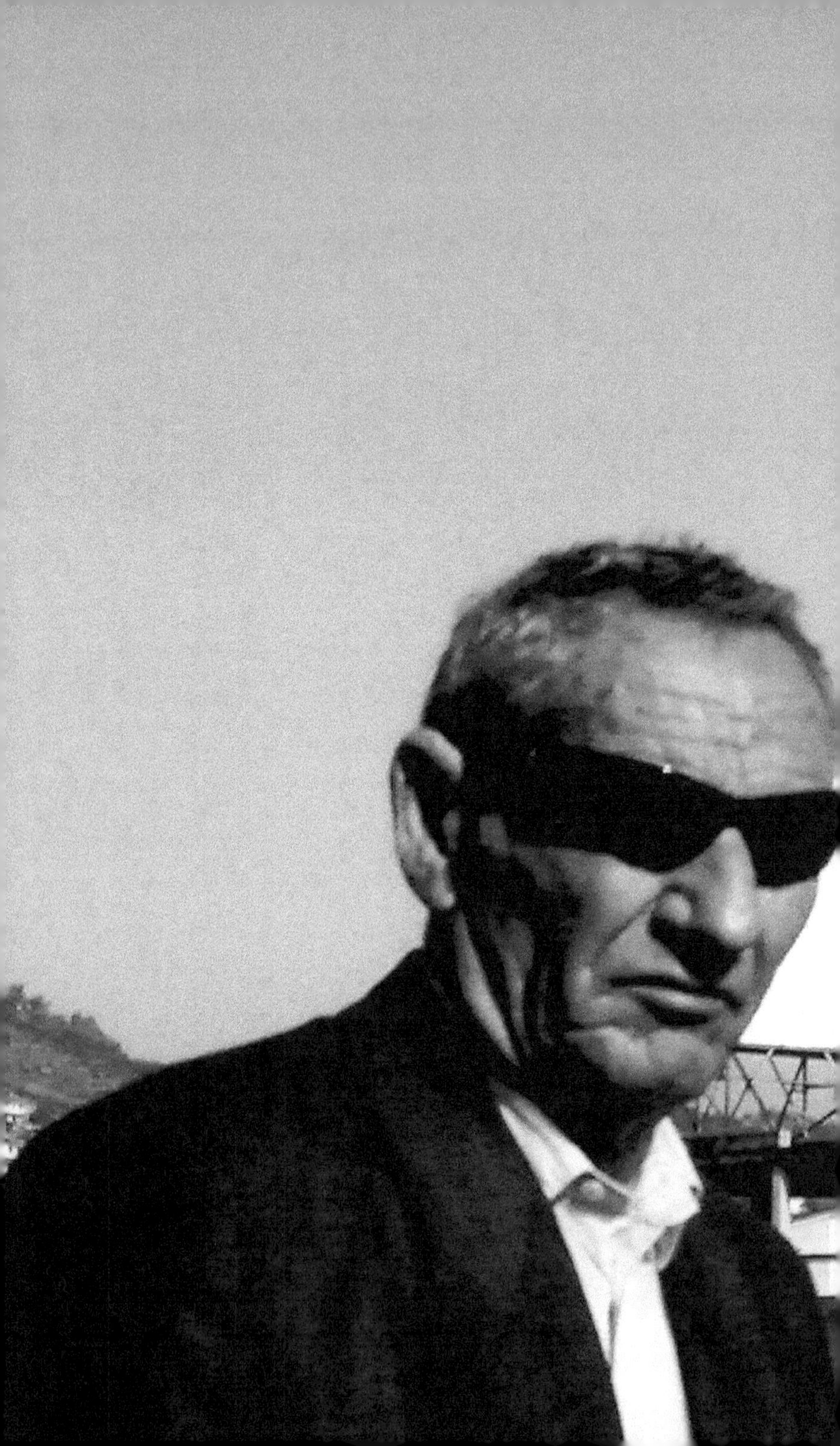

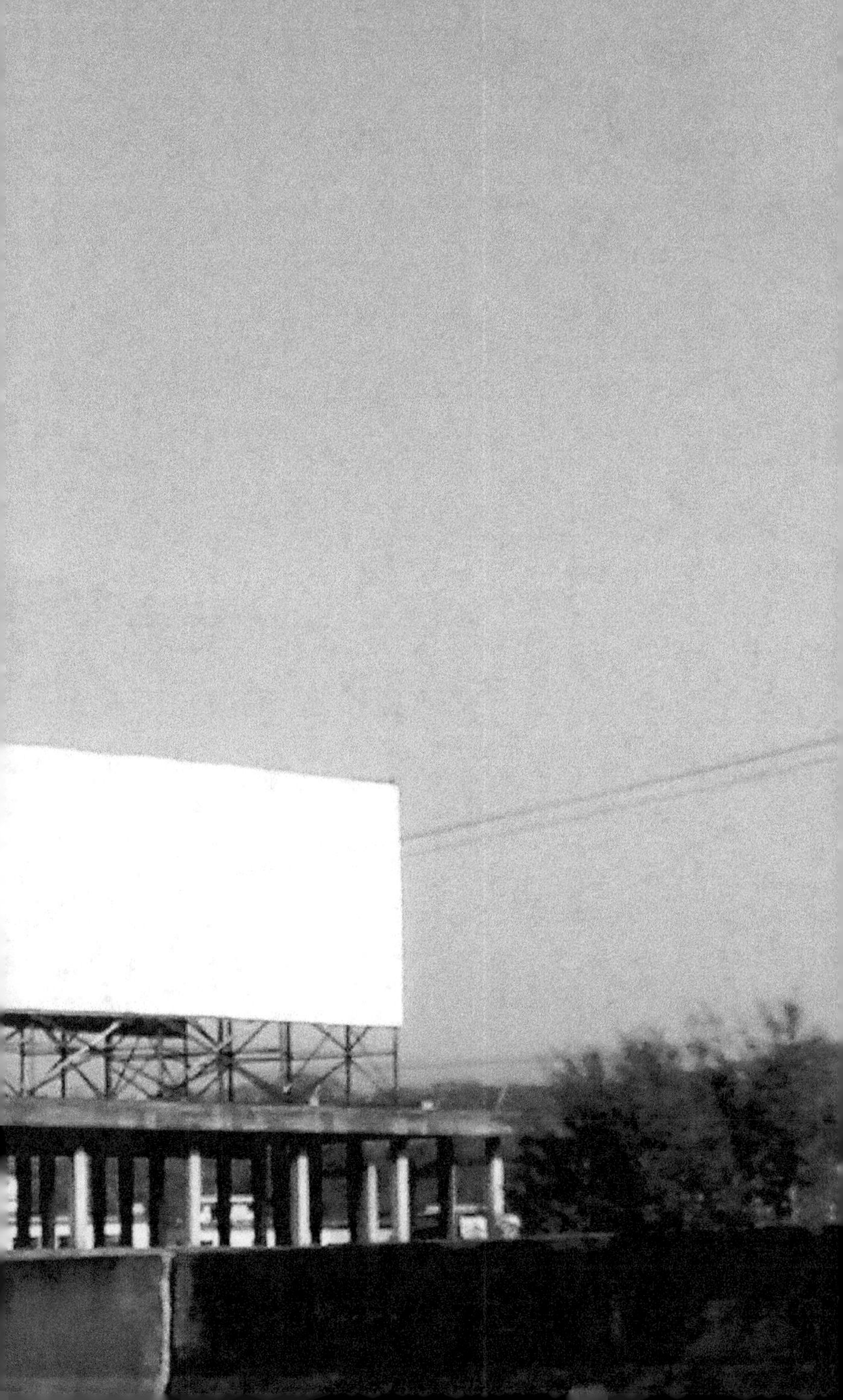

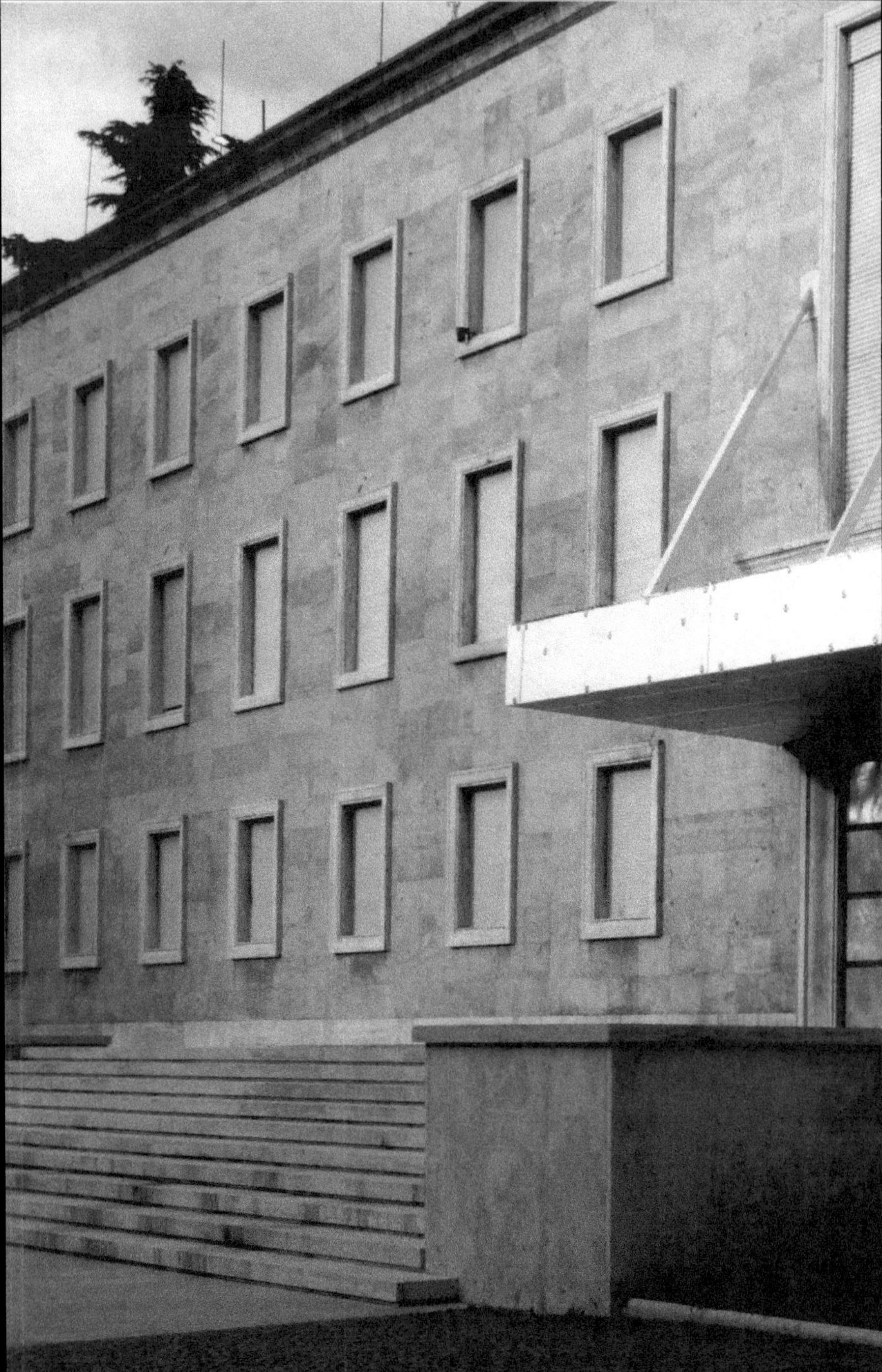

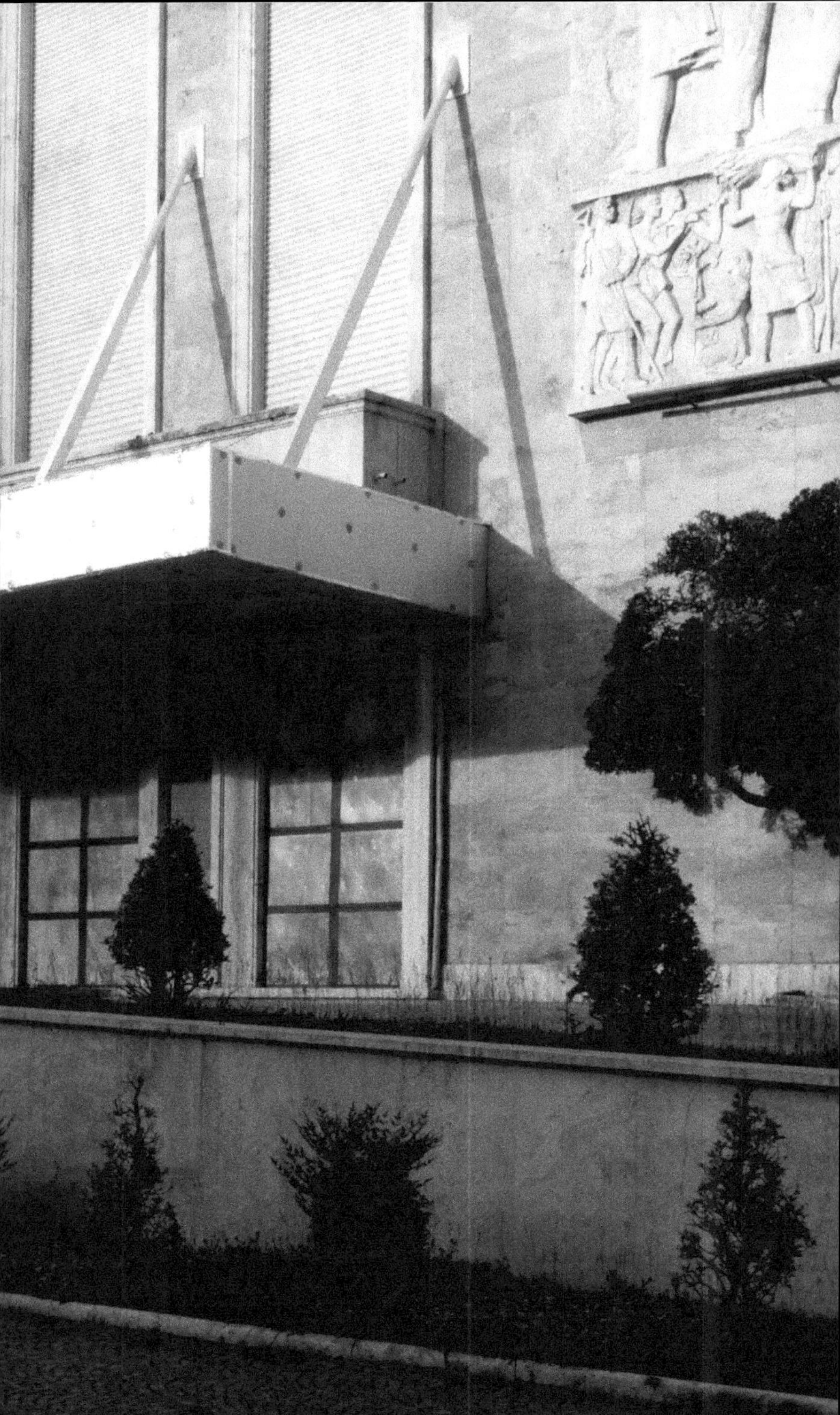

Fig. 25. CONTROL by Armando Lulaj, 2018. Film. Color. Sound. 35'.
Courtesy of DebatikCenter of Contemporary Art.

Fig. 26. ARMORED, by Armando Lulaj, 2019.
Site-specific installation. Armored structure signed by Armand Lulaj
in the upper part, on the left, on the very edge, 2019.
Production photo by Victor Strato.
Courtesy of DebatikCenter of Contemporary Art.

トラック05

《CONTROL》[1] について。2019年2月、私は君の作品を撮影するためにティラナにやって来た。《CONTROL》の一部分を扱うものだった。強力な視覚的構成要素だけでなく、その光景のあたかも芝居がかったかのようなインパクトに、私は非常に感銘を受けた。この作品に、死と斬首の描写が演劇的なフィルターを通して示されたかのような、ある種の叙情性をも私は見出した。そこには、水平な軸に吊り下げられた、5人の斬首された人物達の物理的な死だけでなく、まさに形而上学での完全な死があった。写真撮影している間、ロダン(Rodin)についてよく考えさせられた。言うなれば、「正反対の」方法で「真逆に」表現された「逆さまの」ロダンについて。私自身も写真を撮りながら、パリで何年も前に、2000年に撮影したロダンの彫刻を再び撮影しているかのように、その光景を撮影しようと試みた。《CONTROL》は、風景と密接に結びついた作品である。即ち、風景の中の、我々の周りにある何か、宙空

---

1 参照：https://debatikcenter.net/strikes/control；第二部《Control II》（2019年）は、デヴィッド・カンピ（David Kampi）の名で署名されている：https://debatikcenter.net/strikes/control2

にある何かを語ろうとしているように思われる。アルバニアの領土と風景に存在する－メディア、心理的、政治的、宗教的、性的といった－「統制/制御(controllo)」の兆候とは、どのようなものがあるか？アルバニアの風景を読み取ると何を感知するのか？「制御」と「支配」について、風景を読み取ることにより、風景の「内側」で何を感じるのだ？

《CONTROL》は二部構成の作品である。作品の第一部は35分のデジタルビデオで、第二部は6×7フィルムで撮影された60枚の写真である。作品の両方の部分での画面構成と、写真機及びビデオカメラの位置は「安定した監視(steady-stare surveillance)」によるもの、つまり定点監視である。第一部では、エキストラが映画スクリーンに酷似した巨大な広告看板の前を通過する。この乳白色のスクリーンは、アルバニアで最も交通量の多い高速道路の脇にある。だが、それは唯一無二ではない。高速道路のルート上には、領土全体の他の幹線道路と同様に、何百もの空白のビルボード(billboards看板)がある。アーティストがそれらを空白にしておくように考案したプロジェクトのようにすら見える。一方、その他全ては現実によって塗り潰されているように見えるが、これらのスクリーンの表層は、一纏めにすることで空間の広がりを形成し、その先を見据える可能性を君に与える。まるで時間の内に凍結されたブラックホールのようだ。この作品のための調査の間、プロジェクトの概念的な中核に関して、僕達は風景の中に存在する不可視のイメージを常に探していた。情報のブラックホール、ダークネット(darknet)からのデータや、ウィキリークスから抽出されたドキュメントの抜粋、マニラのFacebookオフィスでの監視を逃れた画像だけでなく、政府や軍の未知領域の機密地図の情報など。

　後者の機密地図情報は抽出が常に困難である。それらは非常に厖大なアーカイブの一部を成しており、侵入はさらに難攻不落で、アーカイブに興味を抱く誰にとっても、終わりなき狩りの標的、ある種の最終目標だ。このような隠されたデータで構成され、肉眼では見ることが不可能な、これらのイメージの痕跡は、風景のその中、我々を観察する風景の中に常に存在し、それらを抽出するには、権力の技術システムとツールを用いる必要がある。

　《CONTROL》において、僕達が利用可能だった手段は、上記のツールと比較した場合、可能な限りに基礎的な手段、原始的な道具だった。手元にあったものから始めて、僕達が制作したものは、想像とは遥かに異なったものだった。風景の解読についての目標はそのままで、常に現存しているにしても。［訳注：作品本編の下敷きとなる］サブテクストの草稿に取り組んでいる間、僕達はジョン・ナダのサングラス[2] について考えたが、その看板/スクリーンから溢れ出ていたサブリミナルな唯一のメッセージは、ファビオ・マウリの驚嘆すべき《The End》[3] だった。

2　ジョン・ナダ（またはネイダJohn Nada：俳優ロディ・パイパーが演じた）は、ジョン・カーペンター（John Carpenter）作、SFスリラーのカルト映画『ゼイリブ（They Live）』（1988年）の主人公。ナダはロサンゼルスの失業中の労働者で、偶然に黒いサングラスを手に入れる。それをかけると、多くの人間が実際にはエイリアンであり、サブリミナル・メッセージを介して地球人を支配しようとしていることを発見する。

3　ファビオ・マウリ（Fabio Mauri, 1926–2009）は、イタリア芸術の前衛派の立役者の一人。多面的な作家である彼は、インスタレーション、パフォーマンス、彫刻、オブジェを制作した。これらの中でも《Schermi(スそして、それらの「The End」はまた何か別のものの始まりでもある。そんなわけで、プロジェクトの第二部では、最近の史実から忍び込んだ暴力的表象を使用してイメージが作成された。これは、僕の頭から離れず、1年以上前に寝室の壁に貼り付けられた画像で、とても中世じみた、当節のとある画像である。

　《CONTROL》の第一部を撮影する前に、何度かロケーション・ハンティングで下見を行った。ビルボードのある場所は、ティラナから約10キロメートル離れたヴォウル市（Vorë）周辺である。北西に位置するスクリーンは、そこから最短距離で約2km離れたグルデツ村（Gërdec）に向かう風景の一部を覆って – というよりむしろ、隠して – いる。グルデツ村では、2008年に武器及び弾薬の旧保管庫が爆発し、前述のように、26名の死亡事故を引き起こした。良好な状態のかなりの数の武器が、アルバニア及びアメリカの様々な「請負業者/契約者（contractors）」によって世界中の紛争地域で販売された。グルデツの主たる爆発は、容器に入っていた400トン以上の推進剤に引火し、半径数キロメートル以内の数百軒の家屋を破壊し、僕達が位置していた高速道路上を通過中だった車両の車窓をも、爆風で破損するほどだった。これらは、シーンを形成する「トラップ」の中に封じ込められた風景によって提供される情報の一部に過ぎない。僕達は、過去に既に犯された犯罪を分析する意図ではなく、撮影前の数日間の調査中、それより前に犯された犯罪でもなく、むしろ、また別の並行する犯罪を再現するために、実際には、一つではなく複数の犯罪を複数回再現するために現場に迫った。したがって、シーンに

　クリーン）》は際立っており、1950年代終盤に制作された最初のモノクローム作品群で、それらには映画への言及、そしてイメージの現代文明への言及がすでに含まれている。

付随する継続時間は、 このようにして、 あらゆる決定的なナレーションを排除し、 複数のナレーションを生み出す。

　作品の第一部では、 道路脇に設置されたテレビカメラ正面に、 斜め横位置のスクリーン、 即ちビルボードが見える。 ビデオ制作中に写真撮影されたカットでも作品［としてのビルボード：訳注］は遠方に見える：テレビカメラは、 エキストラである近隣の住民達が必ず通過する位置に設置されている。 テレビカメラとスクリーンの間の空間は高速道路で区切られ、 車両が高速で双方向に走行している。 エキストラが、 カメラ前あるいはスクリーン前を通過するたびに、 僕は指を鳴らす。 テレビカメラと指を鳴らす行為によって課せられた制御は、 現実の制御不能な要素に対する制御である。 ある意味では、 結果として得られるビデオは、 僕とカメラによってではなく、 スクリーンのためにスクリーンによって生成された、 反射された帰結だ。 それはまるで、 スクリーンによって生み出された現実の流れが、 エキストラの進行方向をも制御しているかのようだ。 その流れは僕の「反射」行動をも、 瀕死のこの政治的風景を看破することによって不可視で空白の歴史的瞬間を不滅化しようとする行動でさえも制御しようとするかのようだ。

　《CONTROL》の第二部は、 非常に異なるものである。 なぜなら、 それは暴かれた光景であり、 分離、 暴力的な侵入、 及び実現しなかった試みでもあるからだ。 シーンの全ての構成要素を分析した後、 デヴィッド・カンピ[4] と僕は、 風景を制御する様々な力の中に、 別の力を導入することにした。 それは、 不可視のもの、 不可視の真実性を検出できる力である。 その力は、 この政治的風景の意味を増幅することができ、 その後、 消失し、 痕跡を隠し、 全てが以前のように過ぎて行くようにできた。

4　前述の脚注27を参照。

　時に、僕はシーンへの侵入者であるように感じ、この侵入を可能な限り目立たなくすることが僕の目標である。僕は、後に痕跡を隠すという要求のもと、シーンに介入する写真家がシャッターを切る瞬間の密度を最大にすることで拡張したい、現実を引き伸ばしたいと望んでいる。

　国の全ての社会・政治的生活と同様に、僕は、風景自体が規律社会と統制社会との間に位置し、この中間地点にあることが、非常に興味深い複数の現象の発生を助長したと思う。概して、僕の仕事はこれらの現象に基づいている。この風景は絶え間なく変化しており、主として権力者の汚職まみれの計画やプロジェクトに拍車をかけられ、ますます変貌し続けている。これらの計画やプロジェクトは、発展/進化（と書いて衰退/退行と読む）の途上にあるが、それだけではない。領土内、つまり広大無辺ではない地理的空間内で、より様々な想像可能な方法で、この風景を知覚できる。しばしば、凌辱され、占領され、制御され、民営化され、囲の内に強制され、覆い隠され、幾度となく改竄され、放棄されて見捨てられた風景として知覚できる。しかし、ひときわ興味深いのは「自由な風景」をまだ認識できることである。

　君の質問に戻ると、俗に言う寡頭政治家達の個々の提案から生じる腐敗した都市化と建築は、国の将来にとって重要な礎を形成する。彼らの悪趣味な提案は、首相と彼の政府のパラレルステート（Parallel state）から直接ゴー・サインを受け取る。これらの提案を分析してみると、人間はもう考慮されなくなっていることに気付く。この総体において生み出された建築、僕はここで、国家及び権力によって生み出された法律と建築について言及しているのだが、その建築はもはや集団性や、万人のための社会プロジェクトの案を必要とせず、この集団を無力化する方法にのみ興味がある。

「CollectivenessはCollectivemess[5] になってしまった。」

しかしながら、この風景には、ある種の抵抗がまだ見出され、まさしく、この一連の風景の真ん中にある。その抵抗は、常に先へ先へと進もうとする権力の断片と組み合わさった、浪費されたエネルギーの形で、即ち、政権崩壊直後に建設された「違法な」構造物として顕現する。この建設形態は、資本の別の側面を明らかにし、過去（ほぼ）30年に渡り、国家と並行して発展し続けてきた。僕が話している構造物には、非常に異なるものが組み込まれている。抵抗のこの潜在的な形態、創造的な抵抗のそれを含む総体には、原始主義、急進主義、シュールレアリスム、皆が「一丸となって(en masse)」根絶したいと願う革命の概念がある。これらの建物は建築家によって建造されたのではなく、国内の郊外出身の住民達自身の手によって建てられた。一般的には次のような流れだった：まず手始めに土地が占領あるいは購入され、次に（往々にして）書類原本が偽造され、転売されて、再び購入後、国に対して文書化されたものが、その後「もし」公的証明されたのなら、それは違法に公的化（も）されたのだ。権力のこの不条理なプラットフォーム内で、こういった「ほぼ」自由な構造物、これらのシュールな住居が芽吹き、未だ完成していないものの、常に絶え間なく構築と変容を遂げている。これらの構造物には、虚空で終わる扉、外を見られない窓、建物の換気や採光のために使用不可能な窓があるのだが、おそ

5　伊語には翻訳不可能な言葉遊び：逐語伊訳では"La collettiv-
　　ità è diventata caos, casino collettivo".(集団性は混沌、集団での
　　大混乱になった)

らく我々がまだ見ぬ構造物、次に来たる構造物のためのものなのだろう。どちらの方向にも向かわないがゆえに間違っているように見える階段、しばしば上下逆さで、多分、建築ミスによるものだろうが[...]、頭（こうべ）を真下にして歩ける種族のために作られたような階段を有している。領土全体で9万を超える、未だに違法なこれらの構造物には、未来のプロジェクトの徴候が含まれているが、現時点ではそのものの影しか明らかにしていない。それらの形状や建造上の特殊性を超越して、僕が一層興味を抱いているのは、– 今のところ – 我々が想像することしかできないこれらの構造物の亡霊のような手がかりを追うことである。

引き続き、制御/統制とイメージのリアリズムについて。我々が《CONTROL》［訳注：第二部、写真作品］を撮影した際、フレーミングについて多くのことを議論したが、フォルムと風景の間の非常に緻密なバランスを構築したいと君は思っていた、と私には見えた。歴史的あるいは叙事詩的な映画の最終ショットのような、「最終」で「終着」のイメージのように見えた。非常に直接的でありながらも、構築するのが単純なイメージではなかった。この作品は実物のイメージ、即ち実際に斬首された身体から着想されたことを私は知っている。その後、君は第二部でデヴィッド・カンピ[6]とともにそのイメージを再構築した。君が見た写真の斬首された遺骸は誰のものだったのか？なぜ、その写真を君は選んだのか？

6　デヴィッド・カンピ（David Kampi）は架空のアルバニア人アーティスト。

僕の共同制作者達は、僕の制作方法、例えば、僕のイメージの作り方を分かってはいるが、彼らの方でもそのイメージを自分達の特性で解釈することができる。僕は彼らの特徴を熟知しており、作品に付け加えたいと思っている。場面を描写し、その実現に関する全ての僕のアイディアを説明するが、本当に「捕捉」したいと思っていることについては、決して言い表すことはしない。そこに到達するための取っ掛かりや、どのように到達するのかを示すことはない。なぜなら、僕自身、それを分かっていないことも多いからだ。僅かな決まり事、全体的な調和、そして数多くのヒント。僕の作品が、権力や定義不可能な何か – この場合、自然、風景、そして、予測不可能であるが故に制御できない現実そのもの – に影響されているのと同じように、僕は彼らと、これらの「トラップ」の構築において協働しようと努めている。場合によっては数秒の間、何が起こるかは想像もできないことが多い。それは制御不可能なものであり、潜在したり顕在したりして、細心の注意を払った場合にのみ目撃されることが可能になる。僕は、物事を様々な方法で見ることに興味があり、二つ以上の視点から同時に物事を見ることに関心があるとしても、制御不能なものを制御することが狙いで意図であり、目的でもある。

初めてのホラー映画を観た時をよく覚えている。毎週末、旧ユーゴスラビアの主要テレビチャンネルの1局が、吸血鬼映画を放送していた。当時、1980年代半ば、僕らは社会主義様式のプレハブの1階に住んでいた。家のメインルームで、金色の飾りの付いた、ボルドー色の肘掛け椅子に座っていたことを覚えている。僕の前には、木材とガラスでできた、非常に背の高い、黒いモダンな家具の上に置かれたテレビがあった。僕の右側には、バスルーム、寝室、そして玄関へと続く廊下があった。僕の両親も、僕と一緒にその部屋で腰掛けていた。僕は、その映画のタイトルを覚えておらず、二度と見付けることは叶わなかった。だが、テレビ画面上の身の毛もよだつ画像を見ている間ずっと、僕の思考は玄関扉に向いていたことをよく覚えている。なぜなら、そこがアパートからの唯一の脱出経路であったからだ。だが、不可視の外なる力がその扉から入り込めるのではと恐れて、僕は立ち上がることができなかった。僕はメインルームの真ん中、その場所に、映画の血腥い光景と、それとは別の未知なる力との間で身じろぎ一つもできなくなっていた。無論、僕がより恐怖を感じていたのは、正面玄関から忍び寄る得体の知れない力に対してだった。それゆえ、残酷極まりない光景を前に目をつぶってもなお、僕は映画を観続けた。

　慄然とさせるイメージに対する反応に、僕は常々関心を寄せており、昔のホラー映画は今でも僕の中でこの反応を解き放ち得る。『吸血鬼ノスフェラトゥ(Nosferatu - Eine Symphonie des Grauens)』のような作品は、僕にとって天才的な映画であり続ける。その作品中でフリードリヒ・ヴィルヘルム・ムルナウは、剥き出しのイメージを見せて異例の実験を行った。映画のある場面で、最大限の効果を得るために、彼はポジの代わりにネガ・フィルムをモンタージュしたのだ。そして、かの名言［訳注：ヨーゼフ・ゲッベルスJoseph Goebbelsの発言にまつわる］から慮るに「嘘吐きが大法螺吹きなほど、真実もまた重大なのである」。ピエル・パオロ・パゾリーニのような他の監督達、ミヒャエル・ハネケもだが、彼らはこの困難な企てに知性を発揮することに成功し、観客に反応させて活気づけ、座席に釘付けにするイメージの創出を成し遂げた。それらのイメージは、スクリーン正面でその画像を目にした観客に、強制的に何らかの立場を取らせる。僕はこの側面に非常に興味がある。無気力な観客には僕は興味がないので、むしろ逆である。

　今日、我々は、彼らがネクロ キャピタリズムと呼ぶものによって生成されるイメージの暴力に取り囲まれている。ダーイシュ（DAISH）の斬首刑の数々や、麻薬シンジケートのロス・セタスのようなメキシコの犯罪組織による「詩的」で劇的なスペクタクルといった、生々しく残酷なイメージに我々は取り囲まれているのだ。それらはゴヤやジェリコー、はたまたフランシス・ベーコンをも甚だしく連想させる。レイプ、あるいは大量虐殺。それらは、我々のコンピュータに忍び込んだり、鮮明に放送されたりもする（時には、テレビ・ネットワークで完全に放送されることもある）。さらに、資本主義によって生成される他のイメージにも包囲されている。我々はそれらを分析せず、拒否することなく知覚している。それらのイメージも暴力的だ。なぜなら、ある意味で我々をフォーマットするために、我々の記憶に暗黙のうちに刻み込まれるからだ。

　僕はしばらく前から、アーカイブの構築に取り組んでいる。これは長年に渡る広範かつ徹底した調査研究であり、極めて冷酷非情な画像を含むが、一つの目的があってのことだ：それは「完全無欠な」イメージを見つけること、それが匹敵しうるのは絶命した詩人の遺骸の画像のみだ。僕が話している（単数あるいは複数の）イメージは、過去に遡る崇高な図像ではなく、現代性の欠陥の数々を包含する、現在のよりシンプルであると同時にもっと複雑な画像である。おそらく、このイメージはまだ存在していない。それゆえに、僕はそれを「構築」しようとしている。これが、僕のストレージ・デバイスの容量の大部分が、これらの残酷なイメージで占められている理由である。これらのイメージは常に激化し、世界のありとあらゆる場所から到来し、未だ構成されていない総体の細胞のようなものである。それは、未だに欠如しているイメージであり、ブルックによって焼かれた蝶[7] のように構築されるわけにはいかず、ジャン・ジュネの『バルコン』[8] の一場面で、写真家によって撮影された捏造写真のようにですら構築されることは「受容」しないだろう。それは、これら全ての様々な力の一式を取り除くことによって、実現された構図でなければならない。

　《CONTROL》の第二部に使用された画像は、2013年にサウジアラビア南西部のジザン市（Jizanジーザーン）で撮影された。報道からは、情報に出し惜しみがあるものの、写された遺体が窃盗及び殺人罪で裁かれた5人のイエメン人であることが分かる。シャリーア（sharī'ah）の戒めによると、これらの犯罪は死刑に処せられる。彼らの頭部は剣で切断された後、ロープで縛られたビニール袋に入れられ、胴体共々、2台のクレーン車で支えられた金属棒に吊り下げられた。遺体が公開されたのは、ジザン大学前の広場で、学生達が試験を実施している時だった。この光景の写真は、サウジ報道機関（Saudi Press Agency）から発表されたほか、何人かの人々によってツイッターからも公開された。それらの写真の多くは低解像度ではあるが強烈で、世界中を駆け巡っ

7　著名な監督ピーター・ブルック（Peter Brook, 1925〜）は、デニス・カナン（Denis Cannan）との共同脚本で1966年ロンドン上演の、ベトナム戦争についての演劇作品『US』のクライマックスで、俳優達に一羽の蝶を燃やさせる演出をしていた。実際には蝶は偽物であったが、観客は本物だと信じ込むべしとされた。

8　『Le Balcon』は、1956年にジャン・ジュネが書いた二幕演劇で、1960年上演。権力者達の倒錯を明らかにしており、登場人物には、血、涙、精子という三人の写真家が含まれる。

た。 僕は5人が提訴された裁判について、 それ以上、 究明することができなかった。

　作品を実現した後でも、 僕が自問する問いは相変わらず同じだ。 僕の寝室に1年以上保管しているこのイメージによって、どのようなニーズが満たされるのか？ このイメージは、 我々の文明の惨憺たる状態を反映し、 実証できるか？ なぜ、 このイメージが「トラップ」となり、 なぜ、 僕はこのフォルムを映画のような別のフォルムの内に挿入したいと思ったのか？ イメージがこの現実によって生成されるのならば、 なぜ、 一般の人々に対してそれらを検閲する必要があり、 どうして、 この画像が共有され、 統制から見逃されたのに、 他のイメージはそうではないのか？ このイメージは、 権力・宗教・政治の最終産物になり得るのだろうか？ それは権力の効力の最後の独白なのか、 それとも単なる自画像なのか？ なぜ、 それらの吊り下げられた死体が、 かの詩人の遺骸を思い起こさせるのか？

刑務所から死刑判決まで、 刑罰の「政治的な」使用に対する、 君の反応と君の立場はどのようなものであるか？ さらに、 殺人の「政治的」利用の解釈を提案してほしい。 – アルバニアにおいてだけではない – 現代美術の表現法の漸進的な変化と「政治戦略」としての死刑判決の利用との間に、 何らかの関連を考えることは可能か？ ミュージアムと絞首台の間に関係はあるか それはどのようなものか？

ティラナの313刑務所のこの待合室で、この質問に答えようとしている最中に、隣のバールから、映画『死刑台のエレベーター』[9] のためにマイルス・デイヴィスが即興で演奏したサウンド・トラックの音色が聞こえてくる。この映画タイトルは、僕にとって、極めて強烈なイメージである。罠…空っぽの死刑台…上昇するための難儀な動き…一切の下降なし…ブロックされた…正義の機械仕掛けのエレベーターの息苦しい内部にブロックされた…国家…政治権力…完遂された犯罪行為…

最初から。反復再開…ナレーション内部からの逃げ道はない…

歴史のこのエレベーターの中で、あの当時の最も惨たらしいイメージの一つが思い浮かぶ。それは今もなお、僕を凍り付かせる「画像」である。人種差別殺人の最も強烈な出来事のうちの一つと言える、再捜査が決定された事件の画像で、僕が未だ直視し続けることができないイメージ。エメット・ティルの開かれた棺[10]。博物館内に展示されたエメット・ティルの棺桶。

しばらく前、死刑に反対する団体のメンバーが、とあるビデオゲームについて僕に語った。そのゲームは、法学部の学生達の間で広まっており、主として米国内でだが、他の侵入不可能な国

---

9 『Ascenseur pour l'échafaud』(1958年)はルイ・マル監督(Louis Malle)のノワール映画の名作。ジャンヌ・モロー、モーリス・ロネ出演。マイルス・デイヴィス(Miles Davis)の有名なサウンド・トラックで知られる。

10 シカゴ出身のアフリカ系アメリカ人少年、エメット・ルイス・ティル(Emmett Louis Till, 1941–1955)は、ミシシッピ州マネーの町で人種差別的理由にて殺害された。彼の母親は、殺人者が息子を死に至らしめた凄惨な状態を世に示すため、棺を開いたまま葬儀が行われることを要求し、その意向が尊重された。この事件は2004年に再捜査が決定され、遺体発見当時、実施されなかった検死が行われた。

々、中国や中東の幾つかの国でも流通していると言う。このゲームでは、死刑判決で終結した裁判の、象徴的な、歴史上の事件が再審理されていた。僕が理解した限りでは、それは極めて複雑な訓練ゲームであり、正義と、生きる権利の糸を「目に見えない」針に通す目的で、死刑を執行する国々から借用した刑法典も用いて、新たな戦略を試す機会を与えていた。コンピュータを叩きのめし、当時、起訴され殺された犠牲者の命をそのようにして「セーブする/救う」。この至極困難な裁判では、訴訟相手はこのプログラムであり、打ち負かすことは、ほとんど不可能であった。既に出された判決に抗い、神の右の御手に歯向かうある種の悪循環に巻き込まれるのが落ちだった。

　死刑のショーは残虐な見世物であり、「最期」の部屋で行われる近年の致死薬投与にいたるまで、延々と継承されて来た幾つもの芝居がかった派手なテクニックを備えている。プレキシグラスの目に見えないフィルターは画面となり、行為の目撃者である観客、ジャック・デリダの言葉を借りるならば、国家としての自分自身の証人でもある観客から、部屋を分断する。これらの判決の多くは今日、大衆の中に支持者を見つけてはいるものの、処刑の数は、前年までよりも遥かに少ない。クミ・ナイドゥ[11] は、2018年の死刑統計について、このようにコメントしている：「死刑の大幅な減少が証明しているのは、あまり予測できない国々においてでさえもその姿勢を改め始めており、死刑は答えではないと理解し始めていることである」。僕に関して言えば、死刑には断固と

11　クミ・ナイドゥ（Kumi Naidoo, 1965〜ダーバン出身）は南アフリカ人活動家。グリーンピースの元エグゼクティブ・ディレクターであり、アムネスティ・インターナショナルの現事務総長である。［訳注：本文では伊語原文をもとに訳している。］

して反対で、 終身刑が規定されうる最大の量刑であると考えており、 僕はここにあらゆる種類の犯罪を含める。

　死刑問題は、 話題としては複雑すぎるままであり、 それについての明確な考えを持つためには、 歴史及びその残虐行為を頭に入れておく必要がある。 僕は、 死刑が法律の一部であった独裁国で育った。 僕の祖父はその当時、 裁判官だった。「共産主義裁判」は特別裁判としての方が知られており、 最重要ではあったが唯一のものではなく、 ほとんどの場合、 死刑判決を下していた。 これらの政治裁判は、 ほとんどが国によって仕組まれ、 弁護は存在しなかった。 国の手の内にある証拠、 （生きているのに既に死んだも同然な）犠牲者である被告人の自白は、 拷問と恐喝で強要されたものだ。 最も興味深いのは、 これらの裁判が映画館の空間内で執り行われたことである。 それはまさに映画館の白いスクリーンの下で行われたパフォーマンスであり、 そこでは誰もが、 既に結末が分かっていた映画作品の一部となった。 映画館の観衆は証人であり、 また陪審員でもあり、 映画館の空間内の国家機関全体は、 極めて特殊な、 実にカフカエスクな死刑台を形成していた。

　これらの死刑執行の政治的利用に関する、 過去のもう一つの重要な側面は、 責任ある者達に対して刑事裁判が行われることがなかったことである。 過去の犯罪は歴史的事象としてのみ断罪され、 これらの裁判に関与しており現在も存命中の者達、 ここで僕が言及しているのは、 大臣、 検察官、 裁判官、 秘密警察といった面々だが、 彼らは実際の裁判に直面したことが全くない。 歴史は、 ある意味で裏切られたのだ。 ’90年代の政治勢力間の犯罪協定はこれを可能にし、 ある意味で責任者達を「赦免」して、 死刑執行及び残虐行為に対する全ての責任を、 過去の「遥か遠い」時期に帰すものとし、過去のイデオロギーの亡霊に負わせ、死者になすり付けた。今日の行政当局や国会の諸部門、国の重要な官僚達、裁判官達は、かつて、これらの構造の一部であり、現在も活動を続けている。この現象は、国家の信頼性と司法への信用を永劫に損なった。過去は、ほとんどの旧社会主義国のように、歴史的な「レディメイド」になった。政府が最近開館した、共産主義の犯罪と残虐行為に捧げられたミュージアム群は、見せかけだけの芸術家達によって考案された巨大なインスタレーションである。そこには被害者達の名があるだけで、我々全員が苗字も名前も知っている迫害者達の名はない。このようにして過去はさらに遠ざけられ、これらのミュージアムはアルバニア社会の忘却のオアシスでしかなく、たまたま通りがかった観光客達のためのぱっとしない空間でしかない。過去の詩人達や反体制派の人々を闇に葬った輩は、今日の国家と文化を代表する者どもでもある。反体制派の記憶は政治的プロパガンダとしてのみ供給されており、教科書には含まれていない：正反対の扱いだ。行政府に管理されている多くの小学校では、未分析の過去の痕跡が子供達によって呼び覚まされており、その子らは政府や教育機関によって都合良く利用されている有様だ。誰もが国家への信頼を失ったこれらの時代には、過去のイデオロギーや法の力への郷愁、安全や仕事といったものに対する慕情は、政体及びイデオロギー自体のあらゆる残虐性を伏せた上で、より多くの票を得るためだけに政治によって利用される。'90年代初頭に締結された密約は、国際的な承認を得て、刑罰の執行を正当化し、アルバニア人の尊厳は実現しなかった裁判とともに葬りさられた。既に言及した、僕の作品《Powershift CIA》(2001年)は、このこと、このゲームの変化についても語っている。しばしば、この作品は、'90年代前半のイタリアに大挙して押し寄せたアルバニア人移民のみに関すると考えられていたとしてもだ。まさにその当時、国家機関の重要人物達に関する機密データを保持していた、内務省と秘密警察のアーカイブの大部分が破壊された。

　現在公開され始めている文書は、市民や過去の公人達に関する情報を含み、これらの人物達を脅迫するために未だに使用されている。当時及び現在も活動中の、政府を批判する芸術家達に対しても使われている。彼らは、国の破壊的で腐敗にまみれた諸計画への不一致を表明している。過去は、未だ当局の支配下にあるのだ。

　独立した芸術構造の欠如により、アーティストの姿は過去の追憶で描かれたままである。アーティストとは、政治と政治家を尊重する従順な個人でなければならない。外国人達に愛され、自らも外国人のようであり、政党の支持者で（ファルスの避妊具として解釈された）メンバー/性器［membro: 訳注］のように見える者でなくてはならない。君の芸術や表現方法が、不従順や反乱といった他の形式を使用している場合、即刻、ならず者、つまはじきにすべき者というレッテルが貼られる。僕自身が、年長の有力芸術家から、何度もそういう風に呼ばれた。「彼ら」は、その芸術家を、国の（彼らの）同時代性にとって重要だと考えている［…］が、僕にはむしろ、彼の姿は「偽の反体制派」のように見える。自らの歴史を偽造した者達、共産主義旧政権の数多の「政治体制の犠牲者達」によって用いられたのと同じ、（自身の反体制派らしき人生を）製造するテクニックを駆使した者の姿に似つかわしく見える。この者どもは、1988年に国家によって殺害された詩人ハヴズィ・ネラ[12] のような真の反体制派を、 日の当たらない所へ、影へと追いやろうとする。 彼の死刑は、 全党員挙げてのアルバニア労働党の国家組織によって犯された、 政治的殺人であった。それは、 重鎮の芸術家で旧政権の代表者であったクリスタチ・ラマ (Kristaq Rama)、 今日の首相の父によっても署名された命令によるものだった。 詩人の遺骸は、 安らかな眠りに就くことが決してないよう、 高架電柱の撤去後に残った穴の中に直立不動のまま埋葬された。

　この現在の現実と混じり合う、 過去のこれらの問題全ては、 現代アーティスト達や、 いわゆる責任者のキュレーター達によっても、 分析的に扱われていない。 矛盾をはらんだ事態なのは、 これらの偽の反体制派の後ろ盾となる者達が、 例えば《Bullet in Envelope》のような作品を糾弾するものの、 実際のところは過去に立ち向かう勇気がないということである。

　先程、 我々の未来は我々が盗用し複製したものであり、 ある意味では望まれ「なかった」この未来の構成要素は一纏まりの中から削除することは不可能だと述べた。 政治的殺人の戦略は、将来的には非常に異なる価値を帯びると信じているが、 組織犯罪と国家が手を組んでいる現在、 国の変化の決定的要因になりつつある今現在に関する限りは、 その戦略がそっくりそのまま残っている。

　他方では、 罰の政治的使用が普及してきている。 反体制派、 真っ先に調査ジャーナリスト達や、 不都合な者達は、 この「Criminalitypoliticalrenaissance(ハンザイセイジテキフッコ

---

12 ハヴズィ・ネラ (Havzi Nela, 1934/2/20–1988/8/10) はアルバニアの反体制派詩人、 クカス地方 (Kukës) のコロヴェツ村 (Kollovoz) 出身。 共産主義政権によって死刑判決に処された。

ウ)」の交雑の側からの威嚇と脅迫の標的になっている。過去の抑圧的な文化と比べると、今日では、国家が君の弱点を衝き、君を投獄し追い遣ることで脅し、君を八方塞がりにするのは遥かに容易である。批判的な声の大多数、いわゆる知識人達は、発言したり崇高な行いをしたりすることはなく、それどころか国家に身売りする始末だ。彼らの売値は、一切れのパンも買えないような端た金だ。このような状況では、自殺と脱走が、国の政治社会的展望に関しての唯一の真剣な政治行為である。この風景には、僕が前述したイデオロギー的武装グループはまだ現存しないが、彼らの存在、その形成は、ますます可視化しつつある亡霊のようだ。

　2018年に完了した《Moving Billboard》プロジェクトでは、足立正生氏も招待したいと僕達は考えていた。この歴史・政治的人物について、僕が個人的に興味を持っているのは、まさに僕が話しているこの影であり、ますます明るみに出始めている。この影には、イデオロギー、芸術、宗教、政治、闘争が含まれる。一言で言うならば、それらは、排除せんとされる数々の徴候であり、この我が小国の風景や社会・政治的生活の中に存在し認知される。僕にとっては、何よりもまずアーティストとしての彼の存在を、この眺望に組み入れるのが興味深いことだったのだが、それだけではなかった。日本赤軍の歴史的メンバーとしての彼の積極的活動によっても、僕達は彼の参加を望んでいた。彼の参加は、我々の間での – その他の利害のない共同制作以外の – いかなる他の条件も可能ではなかったため、実現されなかった。彼の参加の狙いは、アルバニアの芸術のパノラマの内に消失したと言える、失われた領域を踏査し始めること、そして地域の他の重要な存在に光を当てることにあった。

　アルバニアの領土には、グアンタナモ収容所の元収監者であるウイグル人のグループが居住している。彼らは、9.11の後にテロリストとしてアメリカ人達に逮捕され、その後、証拠不十分で、アルバニアに強制追放された。彼らは中国から来たテロリストと見做されており、かの地には決して帰還することができない。ティラナ近郊のアクセス不可のキャンプには、モジャヘディネ・ハルグ(Mojahedin-e Khalq,略称MEK)[13] の相当数のメンバーが居住しており、その数は増加の一途を辿っている。2004年までテロリストと見做されていた組織だが、そのように判断されることはなくなり、現在ではジュネーブ第4条約に基づき「保護された人々(protected persons)」である。しかし、イランとイラクの両国にとっては、彼らは未だにテロリスト集団である。領地内のこれらの存在は、僕にとって芸術生活上、非常に重要である。MEK所属の大規模なグループが最近キャンプから分離し、同組織のテロリスト離脱者になった。彼らはアルバニアに住んで働いており、アルバニアとアメリカの秘密情報機関によって監視されている。きな臭い気配を醸し出し始めているこの暴力の徴候の他の例は、シリアでの戦闘に赴いたアルバニア人達、あるいはISISのようなテロ組織の一味である同国人達である。「近頃の」ミュージアムも、これらの避けて通りたい物語で形成されてきている。

　ミュージアムの空間に立ち入る度に、僕の言い分を間違っているとする何か、換言すれば、僕の言い分を認めないことで僕の正当さを示す何かを常に探してしまう。このメカニズムは施設内で

---

13 1965年にイラン政府の打倒を志向して設立された反体制武装組織。メンバーの高齢化及び支持基盤の弱体化によって、大規模テロを実行する能力をほぼ失ったとされる。MKO(Mojahedin-e Khalq Organization)の略称が使われることもある。

作品の前に身を置いた時、展示空間のディスプレイの内で、完璧に発動する。僕は、絞首台とミュージアムの間の繋がりについて、熟考することに興味があるわけではない。僕は、システム自体の論理、ミュージアムとしての石油精製所、制限/限界、民営化、市場の影響の仕方、その空間内の監視、民間警備、作品を壁に掛ける作業員、清掃員、観客などに付随するシステムをひねり出すための、別の方法を探すことの方に一層興味があるのだ。そして最終的には、これら全てを空にするにはどうしたらよいか、空間に課せられた制約の中での脱出システムを見付けることに、さらなる関心を寄せている。

　経済が現代美術の絞首台である。アートシステムは、主として経済と連動するために、生活と関連することを止め、フェアはシステムの全ての流れが交錯するのにぴったりの空間だ。このテーマに関して、僕は様々なプロジェクトを実現したが、往往にして不可能だったため実施に到らなかったプロジェクトも書き留めていた。そのうちの一つは、《One Hundred Days of SPAMS》(2017–2018年)に含めたもので、爆弾処理に使用されるロボットのような軍事装置のアート・フェア突撃によって表現されていた。ロボットは、様々なスタンド内、市場・経済の絞首台で、また政治の死刑台でも、作品を記録し、ある意味で「統制する」ように操縦されることになっており、展示作品を鑑賞する際にふるい分けるフィルターを提供するはずだった。

　少し前に僕が言及していた、イメージの構築の話題に戻ろう。この国の現代美術に関して、最も意義深いイメージともなる潜在力を持った、このイメージの構築の一例とは、凍結されているが絶え間ない進化を続けるイメージであると言える。

それは、 アルバニア政府庁舎のファサードにあるオブジェの心象だ。 国内の最新の抗議行動に続いて、 Société Spectraleは抗議活動の地盤深部で監視団体の如く行動し、 電磁波を発する武器に誘発される海底地震振動のように組織されるこれらのデモ集会で亡霊を追跡している。 場面設定は上手い具合に組み立てられている。 警察は、 街路灯の支柱にグリースを塗りたくる。 支柱には、 監視カメラ及び制御音声を増幅する国の拡声器が取り付けられている。 よじ上り、 制御音声を消すことはできない。 滑り落ちてしまう。 デシュモレットゥ・エ・コンビット大通り（Boulevard Dëshmorët e Kombit「国家の殉難者達」大通り）の真ん中に、 人の背丈と同じ深さの穴を開けるため、 それら支柱を撤去することの方が、 おそらく、 より容易いのだ。 大衆は政府庁舎を攻撃の的にする。 抗議者の一人が棒を手に、 政府の装甲された扉を殴打する。 並木道の大通りでのサファリ。 庁舎とともに、 敷地内の芝生に設置されていたある芸術作品が標的にされた。 それを破壊することにより、 彼らは作品に命を吹き込んだ。 その作品の断片、 証拠物件、 催涙弾の残骸、 爆発物のカートリッジ、 発煙筒の破片、 科学警察のプラスチック製手袋といったものは、 現在、 ソシエテ・スペクトラール・アーカイブの一部を成す。

　別の芸術作品は庁舎のファサードに設置されており、 大きな扉の上に庇として据え付けられている。 かつてその作品が象徴していたもの、 そして今現在、 象徴しているものに、 僕は個人的に、 非常に関与していると感じている。 その作品は梱包・保護され、 国によって装甲された[14]。 このように梱包されていると、

---

14 フィリップ・パレーノ作品《Marquee Tirana》（2015年）のことである。 建物の1階にある展示スペースへの入り口を示すため、 首相により

コンテナ内に積載され、何処かのアート・フェアに向かう旅の出発間際、出立の準備万端に見える。装甲された作品を秒刻みで見張り、モニター監視するために、政府庁舎の角に監視カメラが設置された。この画像から生成される投影された姿は、以前のようにおぼろげではなく正反対だ。このオブジェは、市場、証券取引での株式、ミュージアムの軍隊化、ポピュリズム、劣悪な政治やイデオロギーについて語っている。これらの抗議活動によって生成された亡霊は、リアルタイムで生み出された、現代美術の未来の鮮明なイメージだと思う。このように衆目に晒され、権力の宮殿のファサードで拘束衣に包み込まれて、その作品は一系纏わぬ裸身であるかに見えるのだ。大衆から力任せに攻撃されて、己の隠された真実を剥き出しにする。僕にとって、それは、ここ30年の間の現代美術の、唯一の強烈なイメージである。この国が生成し得た唯一の真のイメージは、僕にとっては、現代美術の発展における一歩前進を象徴している。完全に新たなイメージは、今現在であると同時に、最終のイメージである。強烈で、遮蔽防備され、力と力の激突のスペクタクルでのプロセス中に生み出された、それは《Armored Breath》[15]、一つの「レディメイド」であり、証人なのだ。2019年5月の、ティラナの装甲された息吹。我が同胞の蒸し暑き息遣い。

　政府庁舎正面に設置された。

15　言及しているのは、2019年にアルマンド・ルラーイが制作した別の短篇ビデオ作品（5分32秒）のタイトルである。同作品はデバティクセンターのウェブサイトにて公開中。政府庁舎の厳重警備が敷かれたファサード前に配備された警官隊が映し出されている。(https://debatikcenter.net/strikes/armored_breath)

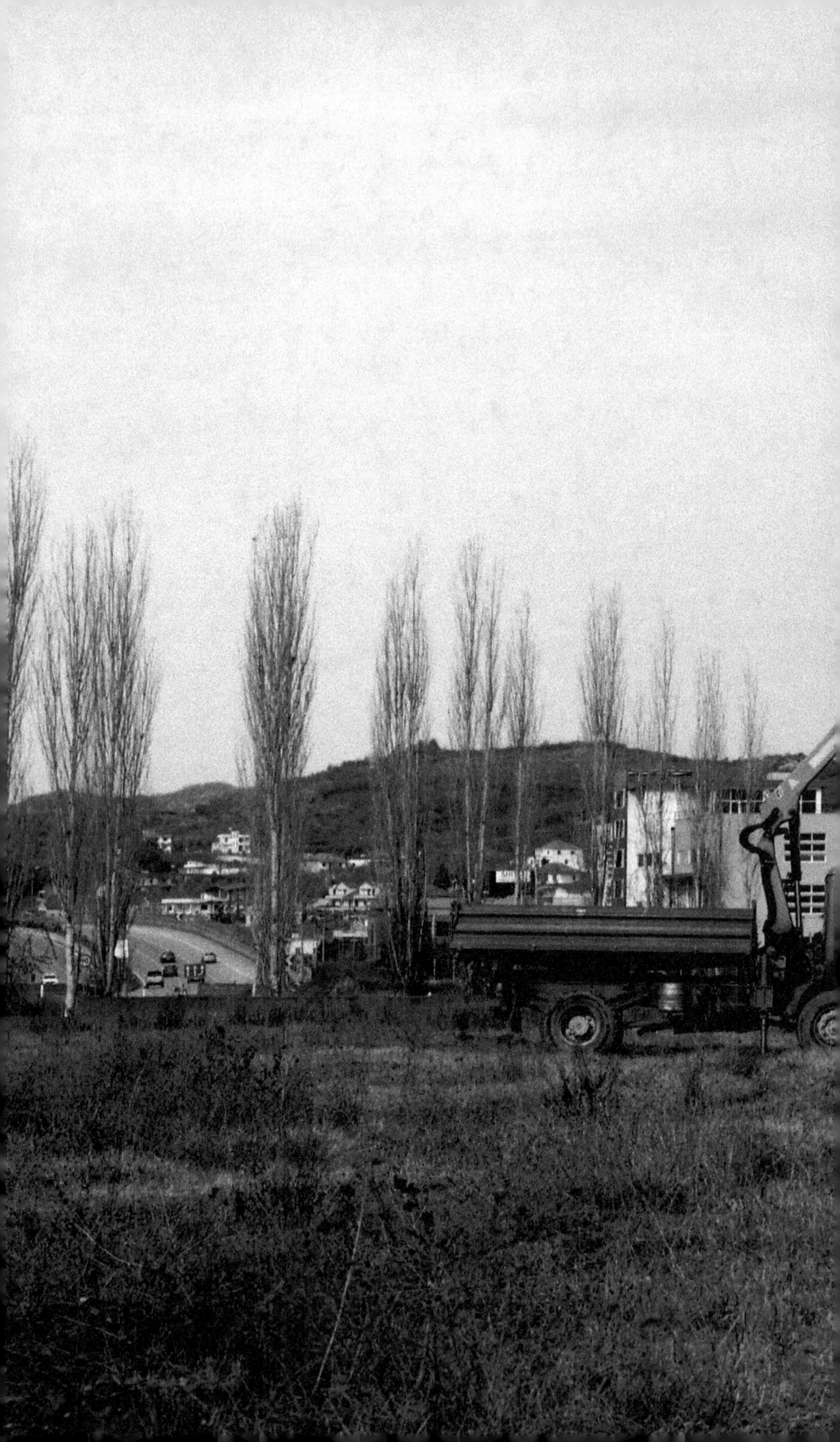

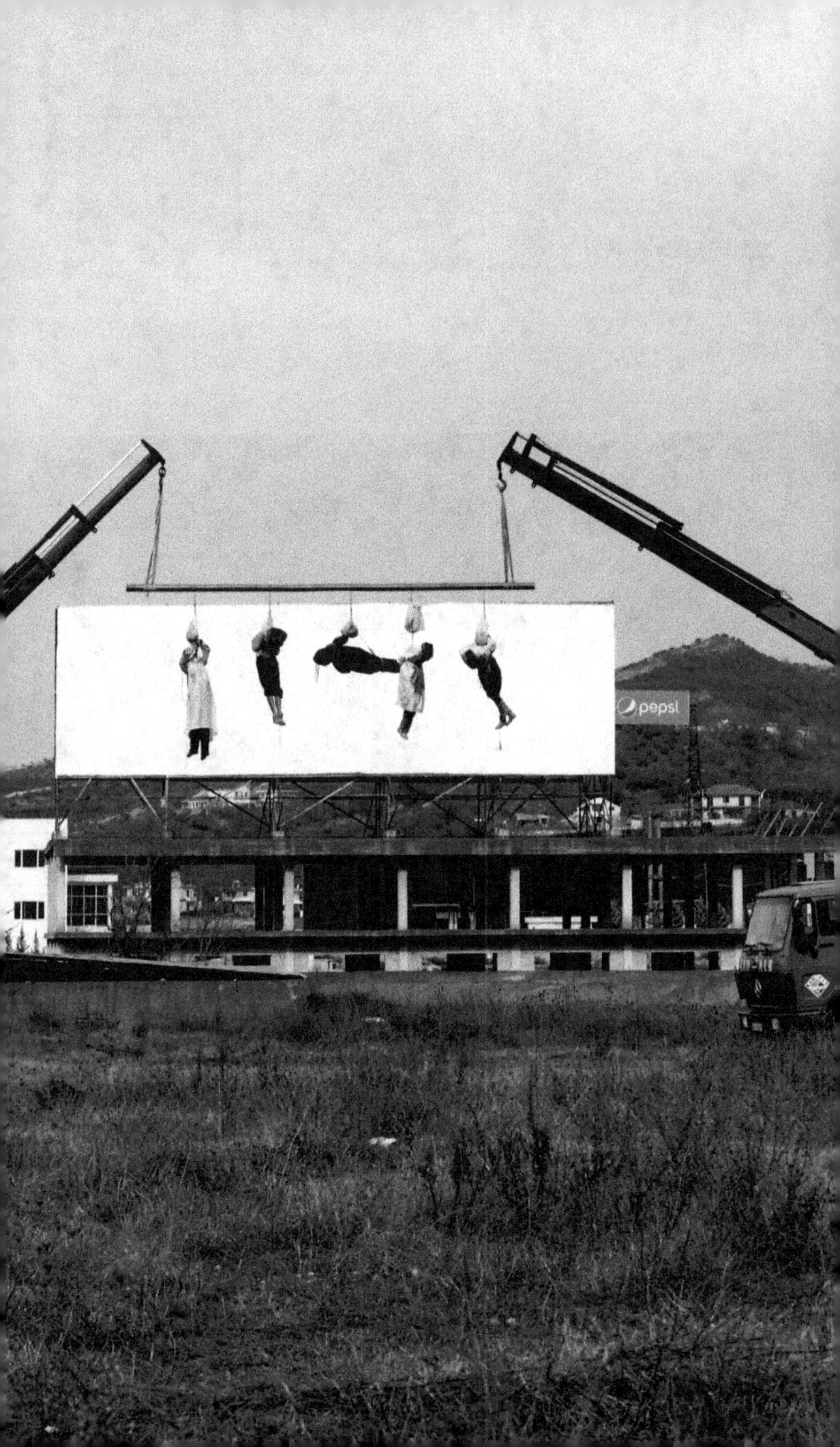

pepsi

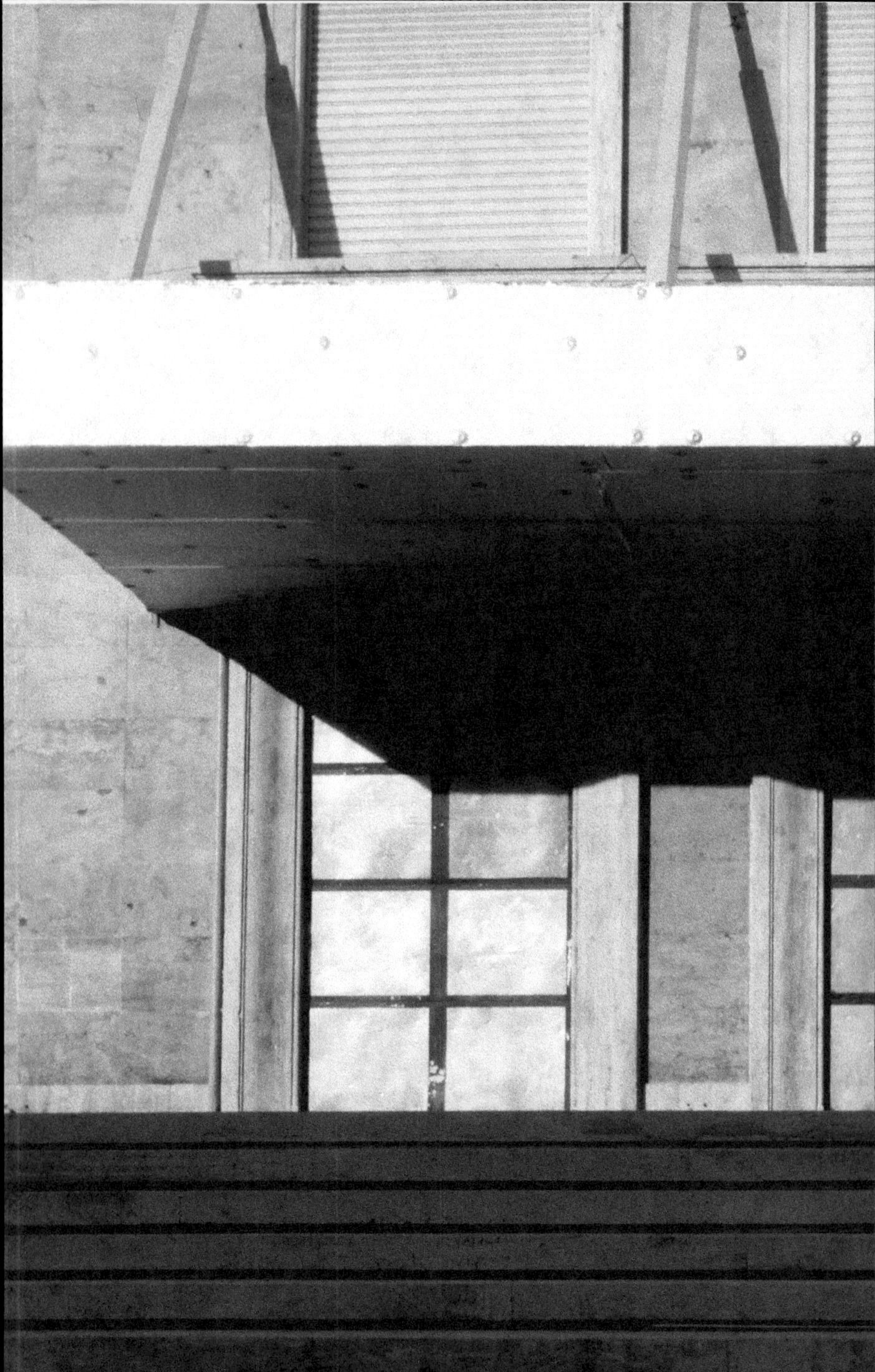

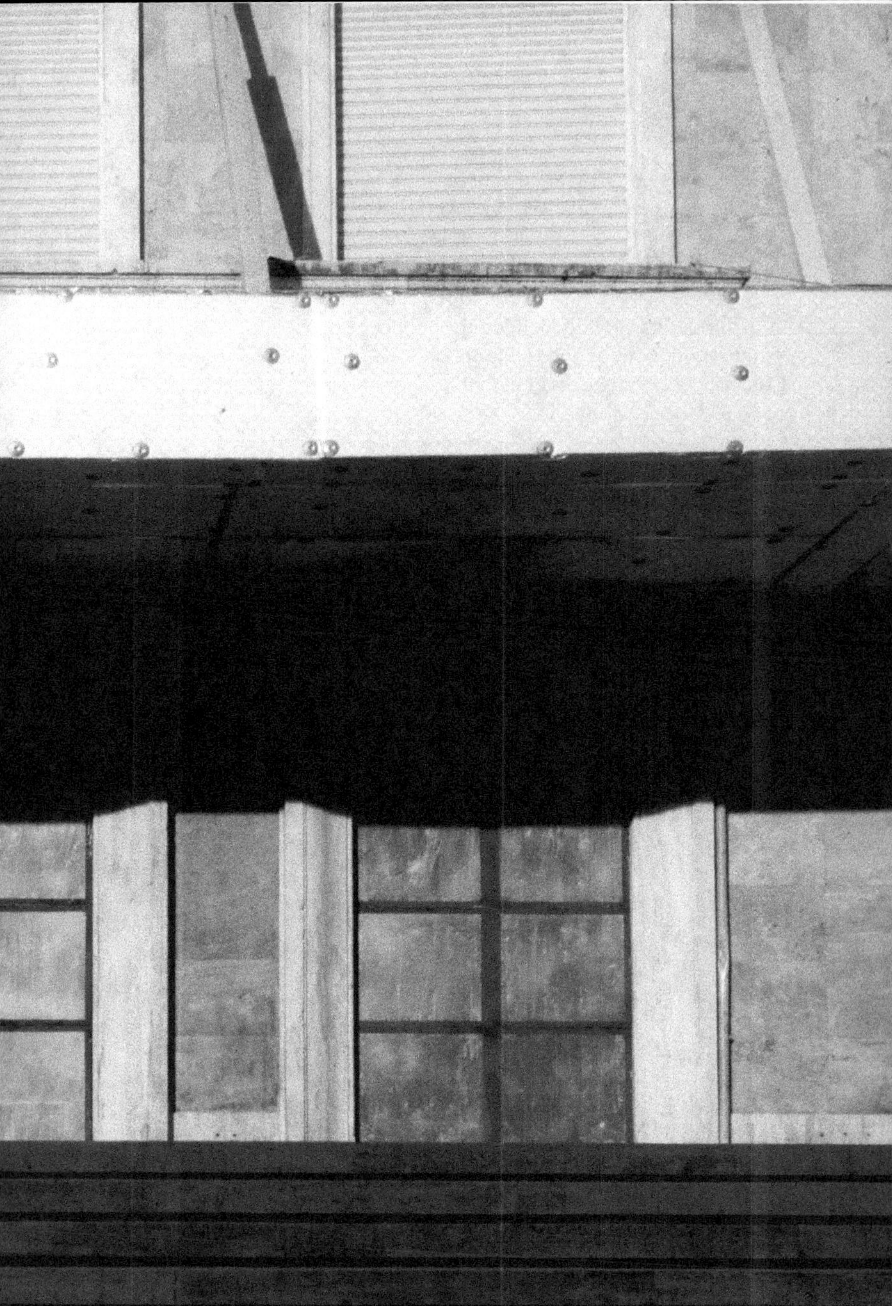

Fig. 27. CONTROL II by David Kampi, 2018.
Happening. Excerpt of a series of 60 photos.

Fig. 28. ARMORED, by Armando Lulaj, 2019.
Site-specific installation. Armored structure signed by Armando Lulaj
in the upper part, on the left, on the very edge, 2019.
Production photo by Victor Strato.
Courtesy of DebatikCenter of Contemporary Art.